Douglas Lockhart was born in Scotland. He trained as personal assistant to Dr Maxwell Cade in the Biofeedback Department of the Franklin School of Contemporary Studies during the 1970s, while writing short stories and books. Since moving to Australia in 1979 he has also written radio scripts and his first play. He is the author of *The Paradise Complex* and *Sabazius: The Teachings of a Greek Magus*.

by the same author

The Paradise Complex
Sabazius
Skirmish

JESUS

THE HERETIC

*Freedom and Bondage
in a Religious World*

Douglas Lockhart

ELEMENT

Shaftesbury, Dorset • Rockport, Massachusetts • Melbourne, Victoria

© Element Books Limited 1997
Text © Douglas Lockhart 1997

First published in Great Britain in 1997 by
Element Books Limited
Shaftesbury, Dorset SP7 8BP

Published in the USA in 1997 by
Element Books, Inc.
PO Box 830, Rockport, MA 01966

Published in Australia in 1997 by
Element Books
and distributed by Penguin Australia Ltd,
487 Maroondah Highway,
Ringwood, Victoria 3134

Cover design by Mark Slader
Page design by Roger Lightfoot
Typeset by Footnote Graphics, Warminster
Printed and bound in Great Britain by Creative Print & Design, Wales

British Library Cataloguing in Publication
data available

Library of Congress Cataloging in Publication Data
Lockhart, Douglas.
Jesus the heretic : Freedom and bondage in a religious world /
Douglas Lockhart.
p.   cm.
Includes bibliographical references and index.
ISBN 1-86204-001-X (alk. paper)
1. Jesus Christ—Rationalistic interpretations.   2. Christianity—
Controversial literature.   I. Title.
BT304.95.L63   1997
232—dc21   97–25235
                                                            CIP

ISBN 1-86204-001-X

CONTENTS

and the world at large, and the problem of Paul's archetypal theology deteriorating into a pagan literalism.

5   PAUL'S TWIST OF PERCEPTION
    The historical background to Paul's thinking, the humour apparent in Jesus' upper room appearance to the disciples, and the utilitarian nature of Jesus' visionary appearances to Paul, and others.

6   THE ARABIAN CONUNDRUM
    The book of Acts as a patchwork quilt of fabrication, fact and fancy, the probable doctrinal discoveries of Paul while in Arabia, and the necessity of breaking the taboo against suspecting that Jesus planned and physically survived his crucifixion.

7   PRIMORDIAL CHRISTIANITY
    The existence of an Arabian Christianity centuries before Jesus, the problem of the New Testament Jesus being partly composed of a previous Jesus-type figure, and the fact that Jesus did not consider himself co-equal with God.

PART TWO: THE BOUNDARY OF BEING

ACKNOWLEDGEMENTS

First, I must acknowledge my continuing indebtedness to my partner Robin Mosley for her indefatigable editorial efforts on my behalf, and for her cheery disposition in times of stress and pressure. And, similarly, thanks to John Baldock, consulting editor for Element Books, whose suggestions helped strengthen the book's structure. Thanks also to the late Dr Hugh Schonfield for his personal inspiration, and for the texts he so skilfully and honestly created – the debate is ongoing because of his courage, and the courage of others like him. And thanks too to the many, many scholars upon whose work I have long lingered and without whom the writing of this text would have been an impossibility. Anything of a scholarly nature achieved in this volume is due to their previous efforts; the mistakes which must necessarily exist are due to my own inadequacies as a researcher and thinker.

But this I confess unto thee, that after the way
which they call heresy, so worship I the God of
my fathers . . .

St Paul – ACTS 24:14

For I have received of the Lord that which also I
delivered unto you.

St Paul – 1 CORINTHIANS 11:23

PROLOGUE

The collapse of the Soviet Union came suddenly and unexpectedly; it simply fell apart before everyone's eyes. Down came the Wall; up came the problems. If Christianity came apart in the near future, if it finally collapsed under the strain of new documents surfacing, of new insights putting paid to 2,000 years of speculation masquerading as untouchable truth, then Western society would be faced with an even greater crisis than is now evident. For, as can be seen all around, Christianity has lost its grip on the human imagination; it is simply no longer respected. Its humanitarian acts are gratefully received, but its intellectual credibility is perhaps at the lowest it has ever been.

Over the last 50 years this loss of respect has intensified and helped create, in conjunction with many other forces, a spiritual vacuum: an almost barbaric secularization of daily life which reflects, on the whole, not a healthy scepticism but a sour cynicism born from inner defeat. The inner life of countless individuals is surfacing dry and brittle, devoid of feeling, and in real danger of destruction. Why? Because in their heart of hearts they know they have been let down, abandoned, duped by doctrines which have neither basis in reality nor the psychic energy left in them to keep the religious charade on the move. Either the Catholic Church (and her Protestant neighbours) faces up to this fact, wakes up and courageously accepts – as the Australian novelist Morris West has so eloquently stated – its 'spiritual responsibilities', or it goes down to dust and rubble just as surely as did the Soviet system. The Church may have lasted much longer than Communism, contributed more by way of positive values over the centuries, but there has also been an unscrupulous cashing in on the energies of the human psyche by way of symbol manipulation, and the result of this has been a blinding of individuals to their inner capacities.

In saying this I am not upholding the view that human beings can somehow pull themselves up by their own psychic bootstraps. I am asking for recognition of the fact that 'belief systems', whether religious or secular, are simply not enough in themselves when it comes to changing the human heart – indeed, that such a path is actually tantamount to the mind playing games with itself. Emotional and intellectual attachment to this or that form of Christianity, to this or that political system, has certainly helped with crowd control down the centuries, but neither has delivered that intrinsic transformation of the individual which both have striven for with all their might. Utopian politics has turned into raw pragmatism, and the Gospel story has failed to significantly inspire the Western mind and become no more than a series of culturally hallowed fairytales. And so we are at a crossroads where energyless systems of religious and political belief are being dropped in favour of more intolerant points of view – points of view fast becoming visions for the future which, if ever fully developed, will probably pull our societies, indeed our very civilization, asunder. This is to say that we are again in deep, deep trouble, and that it is time to wake up.

Ralph Martin, the well-known speaker and leader of the Catholic charismatic renewal movement in America, and writer of *A Crisis of Truth*, agrees with me to the extent that he too recognizes that the Roman Catholic Church is in crisis, and that her Protestant neighbours are in a similar state. But from there on in our ideas are just about as far apart as it is possible to get. Yet there are occasional points of contact, such as his rejection of secular humanism's claim that religious answers to life's great questions are without foundation. To my way of thinking, belief in humanity's ability or capacity to perfect itself and properly solve the world's problems without a spiritual perspective is not just unlikely, it is a sad dream. But this should not be interpreted to mean that the spiritual perspective must necessarily be Christian, or simply a revival of 'old-fashioned' Christianity. John-Paul II may be of the opinion that 'ethical causes' have so won the hearts of modern Catholics that they 'get the better of the central message to be transmitted',[1] but for me this begs the question of what that central message either is or ought to be. It is one thing to talk on and on about Truth; it is quite another to spell out how that singular truth might be shaped. To push this particular line is merely to say that what is already being taught ought to be taught more forcefully, not that its meanings or relevance should be re-examined in the light of authentic spiritual experience. The answer to our dilemma, surely, is not simply to polish up the old, old story and head for the street corner, but find out why that story is no longer being taken seriously.

Way back in 1956 Harry Blamires published *The Secularist Heresy*, and in the introduction to a new American edition (1981) says that there is 'much to suggest that we may now have reached a turning-point in Christian thinking'.[2] Tackling the issue of a secularized and politicized Church by questioning the move towards 'doctrinal liberalism' and the Christian acceptance of 'perverted idealisms', Blamires builds a case for a return to 'the supernatural reality at the heart of all Christian dogma, practise and thought'. He then asks for a rejection of a premise that tries to 'convert Christianity into a naturalistic religion by whittling away the reality and comprehensiveness of the supernatural basis'.[3] This is an interestingly written book which, like Ralph Martin's *A Crisis of Truth*, highlights the inherent inadequacy of a humanist tradition devoid of a spiritual dimension. But when all is said and done, both writers fall short of delivering a vision with the potential to resuscitate the flagging human spirit, producing merely an injunction to somehow stay within the confines of a Christian tradition which advocates 'worship' and 'sacrament' in relation to Jesus the Nazarene. Such a stance, apparently, is all we need for a meaningful spiritual life.

I do not agree.

Martin's basic premise is that in Jesus 'all that is required for man's salvation is provided';[4] Blamires praises the attitude of the Middle Ages because the 'Christian message remained uncorrupted'.[5] Martin tells us that 'The power that Satan and his infernal legions exercise over the human race must be broken';[6] Blamires seems to back this point of view by saying 'The Middle Ages handed on to us a body of doctrine scrutinized, analysed, and illuminated so profoundly that all succeeding ages have cause to be grateful for the legacy.'[7] Here then is the tenor of that which is supposed to interest the intelligent mind, satisfy the heart and offset the plight of the Church. Because Christians are 'swamped by . . . a humanistic philosophy of life',[8] they should again seek out the 'supernatural basis' of Christianity and rest there without question. Now one can understand and sympathize with a Church under constant attack, but to believe that this root inadequacy in humanist perception should be replaced with a kind of wonder-filled acceptance of dry doctrine and a return to supernaturalisms is farcical nonsense.

N T Wright agrees. In his capacity as Dean of Lichfield and a member of the Church of England's Doctrinal Commission, Wright pens the following statement in his book *Who was Jesus?*

> There have been many Christians over the years, and there are many today, for whom the point of Christianity is basically that it is supernatural. It isn't so much that they believe in Jesus, and then find that their world view needs stretching to take in things that they hadn't bargained for within their prevailing culture. It is more that their basic commitment is to the idea of a supernatural dimension to life, and they find this conveniently confirmed by Jesus. This supernaturalism has been under attack for the last two hundred years. Frankly, it deserved it. It needs to be said as clearly as possible that the 'supernatural' is not the same thing as the 'Christian'.[9]

But old habits die hard, and not least of them the view that Jesus was somehow an agent of the supernatural let loose in the first century.

We are each and every one of us going to die some day, and we will do it alone – death simply cannot be shared with the living. How much better then to face our death knowing that we bring to it a mind shorn of superstition and vain hope, a mind within which something of reality has not only been allowed to register, but also allowed to take root. Christianity may claim that death has been conquered through Jesus' sacrifice on the Cross – that all one has to do is 'believe' that this is so and everything is fixed up for all eternity – but such a view is no longer tenable for thinking men and women. The notion that a 'belief' held by the limited ego complex could so influence the Supreme Being as to make personal effort ultimately meaningless is not only to be under sway of a delusion, it is to make a mockery of human suffering and the very existence of the cosmos. Yet this, basically, is what many congregations are still being asked to believe, and what many Christian apologists wish to reinforce in the Christian imagination. All you need is Jesus, for in some incomprehensible manner Jesus was/is God, and unless this is believed your spiritual life hasn't even started.

I am not a biblical scholar; neither am I versed in Semitic languages. I am not a historian, and neither am I a philosopher or psychologist. I am just deeply interested in life, death and meaning, and find myself driven to reply to those who think they have the right to dictate the form my spiritual life ought to take. Like every other thinking person born within Christendom, I have a spiritual investment in knowing something of the truth, and if not the truth, then at least the nature and seriousness of the lies. As a writer of fiction, and a sometimes journalist, what I bring to this subject is not great knowledge or expertise, it is simply an editor's eye, a novelist's sensibilities and a researcher's curiosity – the rest is a matter of hard work, diligence, basic intelligence and integrity. Spiritually, my position is that of Robert Graves and Joshua Podro when they published *The Nazarene Gospel Restored* in 1953:

> [We] acknowledge no spiritual authority, except the still, small, nagging voice of conscience – a survival from our early Scriptural education – which urges us to tell the truth as we know it. We are, in fact, amateurs or irregulars, well aware . . . of the deep mistrust which our book will arouse among those whose livelihood depends on a careful observance of theological etiquette.[10]

But I have to say that I have not come to this subject ill-prepared or totally unschooled in New Testament thought; the subject has been of interest to me for well over 30 years. I even considered entering the ministry before my early studies began to reveal what I had no wish to know - that the New Testament was riddled with problems. Within a few years I gave up any hope of ever being able to reconcile the Jesus of history with the Christ of faith, and went off and did other things. These 'other things' have revealed much of life, and made me intrinsically aware of death. And so my approach to the subject of Jesus, his intentions, hopes and aspirations, is not one of idle curiosity; and neither is it laced with some unconscious resentment or anger. If I am angry at all – and I cannot deny that some anger exists in me at the conscious level – it is not with Jesus or the early Church Fathers, or with Christians in general, it is with the many modern Christian apologists, ministers and priests and bishops who wilfully ignore what is going on in the halls of higher learning because they have a fixed belief system which is either too fragile, too delicate, or simply too rigid to bear the extra weight of insight and discovery.

Christians at all levels of intelligence and capacity are being denied access to vital information concerning their religion, and this curtailment of information helps breed either an attitude of ill-founded complacency, or one of smug self-certainty. Living in a kind of metaphysical dream, the custodians of 'old-fashioned' Christianity stumble from one futile explanation of New

Testament events to another. Jesus was sinless; Jesus was sexless; Jesus was all-knowing; Jesus is the Saviour of the *whole* World; Jesus *is* God. Such sentiments slip easily from the lips when the mind has been overtaken by spiritual vertigo due to intellectual undernourishment.

So is it any wonder when documentaries questioning the efficacy of the Christian faith turn up on television around Easter, that the reaction of the Church is sometimes quite hysterical. Metaphorically, doors are bolted and windows barred to save the 'faithful' from contamination. At the end of one particular BBC programme many years ago, there was a telephone number given which Christians could ring for guidance, a 'helpline' to deal with their *expected* doubts and fears. That intrigued me. What had happened to the spirit that had once animated Christians and made them invite the jaws of beasts to devour them? Where was the unshakable certainty, the jutting jaw of immovable faith? What had happened to so reduce Christian certainty that it could be so easily threatened? The only conclusion I could come to was that many Christians had realized deep down that the Good News was fatally flawed.

That this breakdown in certainty was partly due to the 'secularising spirit of the age' cannot be denied, but to blame it wholly on that is to overlook the fact that there is real unease among Christian leaders concerning past doctrinal indulgences – indeed, a sense of shame for the persecution of minority groups during the Church's long and violent history. And in an age where foreign peoples can no longer be treated as inferior because they are bereft of Jesus, the definition of 'missionary' has had to be put through the interpretive wringer. Things are no longer clear and easy, no longer watertight and unquestionable. In fact, Christian certainty is leaking like a sieve. The *ifs* and *buts* and *maybes* punctuating doctrinal statements have never been so prolific, and the attempt to appear intelligent yet at the same time argue for ever more complicated metaphors concerning Jesus' relationship to God, history and humankind, has reached an impasse.

By way of emotional reaction some Christians have swung over to an unfounded certainty and sounded a clarion call to the faithful. The ship of faith and belief must not be allowed to sink, even if in the end it means taking it out of the water altogether. I mean by this that many Christians are going to find themselves intellectually high-and-dry if they are not careful, for if they do not take a stand on behalf of sensible scholarship and spiritual discrimination, they are going to find themselves caught up in a Church willing to sacrifice 'growth' and 'discovery' in the mistaken and arrogant belief that nothing can, or should, be added to the Christian corpus. This is to make of Christianity a dead religion, a stagnant pool within which life cannot continue to exist. Carl Jung put it best when he said: 'The advocates of Christianity squander their energies in the mere preservation of what has come down to them, with no thought of building on to the house and making it roomier. Stagnation in these matters is threatened in the long run with a lethal end.'[11]

Sensible scholarship will be denied to me for having the temerity to suggest that Jesus survived the Cross, so making his Resurrection a 'resuscitation' by necessity. 'Oh not that old, tired theory again,' I can hear Churchmen say. 'Don't they ever learn?' Learn what? That Jesus was *physically* alive after his crucifixion? The Church has been teaching that for 2,000 years. It's just that some of us don't swallow the idea that his 'aliveness' was due to divine intervention. And why should we when we not only have corroboration from perfectly respectable Christian sources that God does not deal in supernaturalisms, but also endless indications in the gospels and in history that Jesus was a man and no more than a man? Why then interpret the Resurrection as a supernatural event? And because I cannot think of an alternative explanation that allows God to intervene without his intervention being some kind of miracle, some kind of supernatural tinkering with reality, I have to come down on the side of the resuscitation theory. Jesus' own words, I soon came to realize, were all the proof I required. 'Behold my hands and my feet, that it is I myself: handle me, and see; for a spirit hath not flesh and bones, as ye see me have.'[12] That is about as explicit as you can possibly get. And by implication it leads not to some grand Ascension but to an eventual descent into the grave like everyone else. I therefore accept the theologian Rudolf Bultmann's statement that Jesus' bones lie rotting somewhere in Palestine as self-evident.

To break the taboo on divine intervention with regard to the Resurrection is the first step not only in an enlightening process, it is also the first step towards a renewal of Christianity in the twentieth century. Why? Because it will allow many Christians to apprehend the *alien otherness* of their God, and appreciate that such a Mystery should never have been put into such an absurd theological straitjacket.

Muslim writers call Jesus 'Prophet' and 'Teacher', and round off their description of Israel's rejected Messiah with the term *Insan Kamil*, 'Complete Man'. This title, it seems to me, is the correct one. For as Burton L Mack shows in *The Lost Gospel: The Book of Q and Christian Origins* (hereafter referred to as *The Book of Q*), Jesus has gone through a series of cultural shifts, each shift allowing him a different status. So it is nice to think that he has now come full circle and can again appear as he really was – not as God or King or Emperor or Cosmic Christ, but simply as 'man perfected': that is, man fully conscious, aware and awake – redeemed. Now N T Wright and many another will probably find this kind of thinking 'heretical', but the point I'm making should not be confused with 'New Age' aspirations: it should be understood strictly in the context of a perfecting or *ensouling* of the human psyche, not personality-based techniques applied to mind alone. In relation to ego, 'mind' is a mere blip on the huge radar screen of consciousness.

Burton L Mack is Professor of New Testament at Claremont School of Theology, and he states flatly in his book that Jesus' first followers neither believed him to be the son of God nor imagined that he rose from the dead. Spelling out this bold premise, he quite literally explodes the Christian myth, and with a series of tight scholastic observations tells us that the 'early Christians imagined their myth as history.'[13] You can't get more direct language than that. The idea of 'a brand new pattern' in the gospels is set aside because everything and everyone has a past – *newish*, perhaps, but not brand new. Agreements were made, symbols were settled on, a mythic time-frame was projected towards the future, and the rest became . . . theology. Producing a 'powerful superhero to right the world's wrongs',[14] Roman Catholic Christianity eventually endowed Jesus with superlative wisdom and divinity, and out of this mythic move fell to imagining that it too had superlative wisdom. Alas, history does not agree. The persecution of those designated 'heretics' is a sad tale not often enough told.

Oddly enough, Jesus too was a heretic. The Apostle Paul inadvertently makes him so when in Acts he says, 'But this I confess unto you, that after the way which they call heresy, so worship I the God of my fathers' (Acts 24:14). Because he also

claims to have received what he teaches from Jesus' own lips
(1 Cor 11:23), Jesus is by definition a heretic. And this is not to do
Jesus an injustice, for in the light of his non-conformist teachings
and behaviour, he was without doubt a heretical figure in Jewish
eyes. And if he returned today, he would, likewise, be a heretic in
the eyes of the Christian Church.

The Jewish scholar Dr Hugh Schonfield referred to throughout
this book was also considered heretical by some Christians, and I
too am a heretic by classical definition. But I also claim to be a
'natural' heretic, and mean by this that I've always had a tendency
to question things, whatever their origin or supposed status. I do
not consider this tendency pathological. And neither do I consider
my taking a stand against Christianity's claims for Jesus a
spiritual impertinence. In fact, I feel the opposite. I feel, deeply,
that Jesus the Nazarene has been done a great disservice by many
of those claiming to hold him in high esteem. All I see is a sad-
eyed prisoner of the Christian imagination locked inside a
paradigm he did not, and would not now, condone.

In two books which shall ever remain on my bookshelves, and
to which I am grateful for the earlier quote from Bultmann, Dr
Peter Cameron explains what a heretic is, and in the process poses
some interesting arguments against literalist definitions and
interpretations of scripture. And he knows what he is talking
about, for he was himself gifted the title of 'heretic' by these
selfsame literalists in 1993 (the literalists I'm referring to
constituted the then Sydney Presbytery of the Presbyterian
Church of Australia), and found himself the centre of an
extraordinary amount of media attention. Accused of having
challenged the authority and infallibility of the Bible, and of
supporting the ordination of women, he underwent a trial before
the Presbytery, and on the basis of statements considered
inconsistent with Chapter 1 of the Westminster Confession,
emerged guilty. Of what? Of having had the audacity to question
the authority of those who claimed an absolute authority based
on a particular interpretation of New Testament happenings.
That, really, was the charge. It was not at all a confrontation with
some great unchanging Truth, either in the Bible or in the
Westminster Confession, it was just a head-on collision with a
group of short-sighted individuals who claimed incomprehensible
access to such an imagined Truth. All in all an exercise in futility,
the repercussions of which we have not yet heard the last, and

certainly a worrying indication of how far some Christians are prepared to go in the exhibition of dangerously literal beliefs.

Much could be said about the basic mentality involved in such a case, but that is not the direction in which I want to go. The direction which attracts me is that of confronting intelligent, well-informed Christians with the fact that they bear direct responsibility for their less well-informed brethren. To sit back and let such nonsenses take place is to abrogate Christian responsibility and allow an overt form of religious bullying to take root and grow into what unchecked bullying always becomes: violence. To sit back and do nothing, say nothing, is to collude in the activities of religiously-blinkered Christians. Christianity may not be a democracy at heart, but it need not turn into an actual dictatorship. And that, as Peter Cameron and other thinking Christians know only too well, is exactly what is happening on a wide front. When blinkered religious mentalities gain either political power or control of the media, the possibility of *sanctioned* hysteria and prejudice are just around the corner. Splice such hysteria into madcap conspiracy theory (as is being done in America) and you have the basic formula for widespread psychical disaster. Scaremongering? Not at all. The fuel for such a bleak scenario is already all around us, and *in* us. When epidemic strikes, even the strong-minded are susceptible.

Peter Cameron speaks of a God *beyond* that of the God many Christians worship. He speaks of an 'unexpected God, who challenges all kinds of preconceptions', and he speaks of an 'oppressive God' with its back to the wall who has to be unmasked as more interested in 'exposing the faults of its devotees than in making any attempt to offer itself to outsiders'.[15] To this Christian's way of thinking, salvation is 'the discovery . . . of an overall significance.[16] Ecclesiastical theologians might feel, or even believe, that they possess God, that God's freedom is somehow 'circumscribed by their proprietary rights', but nothing could be further from the truth. To Peter Cameron, God is not part of a closed-shop mentality. In fact, he tells us 'that if this God were ever to be reached, it would have to be in spite of the Church'.[17] Professor Jacob Needleman captures the subtle nature of this dilemma in his book *Real Philosophy*. Speaking of academic philosophy, he inadvertently throws light on Peter Cameron's 'in spite of the Church' statement with an interesting metaphor. He says, 'These formulations are like the tracks in the forest left by a living creature, while the creature itself, the real question, is still alive and moving somewhere else'.[18] Dr Cameron agrees. In the final chapter of his book he suggests that the real God is 'elsewhere altogether'.[19]

What Christians believe and do not believe is going to progressively affect my life in the closing years of this century, and I have no wish to find myself behind a barricade. What we're dealing with here is not 'religious theory'; it is the underlying quality of our individual and collective sanity. To believe and attempt to force others to believe that Jesus walked on water, that he rose from the dead, that his mother was a perpetual virgin and that he was somehow actually God, knew it, and propagated such a notion, is to put far too great a strain on the intelligence and patience of most thinking human beings. And not only that, it is also to put too great a strain on the New Testament. It is time for Christians to wake up to this fact. The discovery of an overall significance to life is not to be found in limited sets of ideas, in beliefs about anything, but on touching, and being touched by, the *presence* of one's own reality. Meaning what? Meaning that to be awake and aware and attentive and not perpetually subsumed by thought and deed and emotion is to be properly alive.

There is a mystery here, and this book attempts to explore the heart of that mystery. Through an examination of early Christianity, and the powerful influences which helped shape it, it is the author's hope that Jesus the Nazarene might be glimpsed for who and what he really was. There is a *lost* Christianity. There is a lost core of meaning at the heart of Christianity, a lost experience beyond emotion and intellect, and we have to find it again before it is too late. We may not like what we find, but on having found it we should at least consider it carefully before rejection sets in. For it may just be that what is there, hidden and obscure and difficult at first to understand, carries within it the unexpected seed of our spiritual freedom, our liberation.

The canonical gospels are virtually empty of what Jesus had to tell us about ourselves – they have been made into conduits for orthodoxy's late belief that Jesus' message was that Jesus was the message. That, to my way of thinking, is the main stumbling-block. We have lost the message and elevated the messenger because we rightly sense that the message he carried was very important, and that he himself was highly unusual. Yes, he was the Messiah of Israel, but was he perhaps more than that? Finding a category to fit Jesus into seems to have posed a problem for those who knew him, and even more of a problem for those who came to believe in him as a result of Paul's curiously-worded Christology.

The question is, if Jesus himself was not the message, then what exactly *was* the message? Is it possible to identify what it may have been? Are there still traces of it around? As a sentiment 'love one another' may appear to be an important ingredient of the message, but as each of us knows only too well, love, like hate, cannot be conjured out of thin air – it has to spring up inside of us due to a profound connection between 'self' and 'other'. We seldom hate for the same reason that we seldom love – lack of a profound connection.

I think Jesus understood the dynamics of 'connectedness', the meaning of love, and hate, but that what he had to tell us has been changed into an exercise in self-propaganda, a narcissism which we have each taken up in our own way. The injunction to love God before any other, if pursued, may well deliver up the capacity to love others as we so wish; but if we think loving God can only be accomplished through carrying in our finite minds a fixed set of beliefs *about* Jesus, then that is perhaps the reason why the Western world is in its present state. Something is missing. Something, as they say, has been lost in translation. Let's see if we can find out what that something might be.

PART ONE

THE MYTH OF SALVATION

ONE

DR JEKYLL & MR HYDE

The Church's fear of the historical Jesus, the forgotten humanity of Jesus remembered, and the crumbling Christ of Chalcedonian orthodoxy identified.

When I met the Jewish scholar Dr Hugh Schonfield in London in 1983, he was already beyond his ninetieth year, frail, but still mentally alert. His wife had died and he was living alone. He came to dinner, and we talked about ancient history, and about the furore a recently published book on the life of Jesus had caused among Christians. He did not agree with the book's central theme (that Jesus had married and had children), and as the evening progressed, delved deeply into his reasons for rejecting that premise. As I listened, I began to realize that the man before me was just about as careful a thinker as I had ever encountered. The book in question was *The Holy Blood and The Holy Grail* by Michael Baigent, Richard Leigh and Henry Lincoln. Richard Leigh had shared with me every breath of their researches over a period of some five years. As a result of the extraordinary publicity the book generated, Jonathan Cape set up a debate on the issues involved at the Edinburgh Festival, and Dr Schonfield was the Biblical scholar chosen to test the authors' mettle. When the debate was over and everyone had gone home and we were having dinner in a crowded restaurant, the authors and Dr Schonfield were still vigorously debating the book's central thesis.

This is not to say that Dr Schonfield entirely disagreed with the authors' historical findings. In fact he later congratulated them, in print, on their having drawn to his attention an alchemical work in the possession of Nicolas Flamel, Grand Master of the Priory of Zion in the fourteenth century, and admitted to being enabled to amplify vital European research in relation to both the Templars and the Essene Brotherhood as a result.[1] As I sat listening in the privacy of my own home to what this remarkably well-informed man had to say, it was at the back of my mind that he himself had authored two books which had caused a similar storm in Christendom some years before.

In 1965, after 40 years of study and research, much of it into the life and times of Jesus Christ, he had published his best-selling book *The Passover Plot*. To say that the book was an instant success is to gloss over the fact that many found what Schonfield had to say about Jesus and his mission just as repellent and unconvincing as anything suggested by Richard Leigh and his companions. In fact, a reviewer for *The Observer* described the book as 'an unscrupulous manipulation of men and women which neither Law nor Prophet would approve'. And this in spite of the fact that ten years earlier the same man had been greeted with enthusiasm for his translation of the New Testament. Described by the *Times Educational Supplement* as 'an excellent translation fully entitled to a place alongside those of Goodspeed, Moffatt and Knox', Schonfield's *The Authentic New Testament* was praised for its 'imaginative insight into the minds of the New Testament writers'. And it was noted that this publishing event represented the first English translation of the New Testament ever made by a Jewish scholar. Readers were informed that Dr Schonfield was fully conversant with the Semitic background of the New Testament, and that he had spent many years in preparatory researches involving considerable travel and study of ancient materials. This reflected a statement made by the Dean of Exeter in 1939 when Schonfield had published *Jesus: A Biography*. In a review for the *Sunday Times*, Dr Carpenter observed: 'He may be said to have studied his material with intense care and to have pondered long over its significance . . . Where he excels is in painting fresh pictures . . .' *John o' London's Weekly* agreed: 'A scholarly and moving piece of work that should shock nobody and enlighten not a few.' So what went wrong? What did this Jewish scholar of high repute do wrong in 1965?

To answer this question fully would require a book in its own right. Suffice to say that Dr Schonfield directly challenged the Christian establishment with a series of explosive observations concerning Jesus and his 'secret intentions'. Scholarly churchmen reeled from the blow, then rode out the storm as best they could, relying on stock answers endlessly repeated until interested listeners succumbed to mental numbness. Throughout Part One of this book, and with the assistance of many other thinkers, I will attempt to highlight some of Schonfield's past challenges because I think it vital that this man's profound contribution to the subject of Jesus the Nazarene not be lost amidst the jungle of new theories now surfacing. If there was ever a sane note in what has become a veritable cacophony of speculation, it is Dr Hugh Schonfield who sounded it loud and clear.

THEOLOGICAL OVERLAY

In the introduction to *The Passover Plot*, Schonfield quotes a well-known hymn which runs, 'Tell me more about Jesus', and observes ironically that many are afraid that the telling will destroy an illusion, that the man behind the myth will prove 'less alluring, less consoling and less inspiring.' Schonfield's problem with the New Testament story, as seen through Christian eyes, was that the Jesus of Faith had virtually eclipsed the Jesus of History. The flesh and blood individual called Jesus, the realistic and approachable 'man of the people', had disappeared beneath a theological overlay of awesome proportions. Embroidered and embellished and mercilessly projected upon, the idealized Jesus had become baffling in relation to everyday reality.[2] And so Schonfield was able to say that it is 'not practicable to invest the theological Jesus with convincing historicity'. The Jesus of history, the Jesus who 'wept' and 'thirsted', the Jesus who 'listened' and 'forgave' had been transmuted into a figure of power and judgement, a being whose every word had to be treated as a divine utterance.

But the story of this scholar's attempt to rescue the historical Jesus from the miasma of theological speculation based primarily on Paul's theological creations does not end in 1965. In 1968 he again rocked the ecclesiastical boat with *Those Incredible Christians*. Picking up at the point where *The Passover Plot* left off, he proceeded to reconstruct the first 150 years of the Church's existence and revealed a wholly Jewish and Messianic movement struggling to exist in a pagan environment. In *The Passover Plot* he had rejected the traditional portrayal of Jesus and revealed him to be a Jew who believed himself to be the Messiah. No more and no less. Jesus was an ordinary man. Without doubt a highly intelligent man, a man of faith and conviction and insight – but just a man, not a deity.

Those Incredible Christians again pursues the theme of Jesus as Jewish Messiah and ordinary man. In his introduction to this book, Schonfield clearly states his case against Jesus' being identified with God. 'What is not readily perceived,' he says, 'is the root cause why Christian thinking, instinctively as it would seem, shapes itself to a pattern involving the apprehension of God through the personality of a man.[3] He goes on to say that it is our fear of the incomprehensible *otherness* of God which causes us to do this – the 'otherness' described by Frances Young as 'the contrast between the Creator and his creation'.[4] With the help of a human figure, a 'created' figure, we sublimate our fear of the alien otherness of God and remain 'related under the skin to the devotees of Adonis and Osiris, Dionysus and Mithras'.[5] Tackling the same problem, Don Cupitt remarks that the doctrine of the incarnation has 'created a cult of the divine Christ which let Deity itself fade into the background, and when God the Father was reaffirmed, he was envisaged as an old man'.[6] The road back to paganism had been unwittingly reopened.

Christian scholars bridled at Schonfield's statements and fought back. Christians in general vigorously attacked this Jewish scholar, and in extreme cases resorted to anti-Semitic sentiments. His being a Jew was sufficient proof for some that he was 'writing polemically in a conspiratorial attempt to discredit Christianity'.[7] No mention of meticulous scholarship and the painting of 'fresh pictures' here. No mention of materials studied with intense care. No mention of his translation of the New Testament, or the fact that he had been selected to work on the Dead Sea Scrolls. No mention of the fact that these controversial books were only two out of dozens of published studies which had earned Schonfield a solid and unassailable worldwide reputation as scholar and humanitarian. And, in particular, no mention of his being nominated for the Nobel Peace Prize in 1959 for his services towards international harmony. Just a knee-jerk reaction from those who wished to illegitimately fix for all time the story of Jesus Christ in the form the Church deemed safe and acceptable.

Theologians may tells us that faith does not require the dismantling of reason, but the evidence is otherwise. The Catholic Church in particular daily flouts reason and intelligence with imposed standards of behaviour and thought for which it claims a transcendent authority, and the Protestant Churches are not far behind with their own brand of spiritual authority derived, one can only presume, from the same invisible source. But larger and larger numbers of people are rejecting this claim to spiritual authority, and some of the dissenters are among the clergy. An article rescued from my morning paper tells me that thousands of Belgians packed cathedrals across the country in solidarity with the sacked French Bishop Jacques Gaillot of Evreux. Sacked? For what? For saying straight out what many Catholics already believe: that the use of condoms to prevent the spread of AIDS should be allowed; that priests ought to be allowed to marry; that a more tolerant attitude towards homosexuality should be taken by the Church.[8] In the name of the Holy Spirit Churches of all persuasions claim an authority greater than our courts of law, and with an arrogance sometimes verging on the monumental make claims in public which under any other circumstance would be enough to debar them from the company of reasonable human beings.

When I first met Dr Schonfield in 1983, he had just completed a new book, *The Essene Odyssey*, but had been unable to find a publisher. No one seemed interested in his most recent researches into the Essene Teacher of Righteousness. Too dry. Too dusty and academic. Not written with the purpose of attracting the popular reader. In other words a book identical in seriousness and purpose to everything he had written throughout his long and vital life. And this is not to say that *The Passover Plot* and *Those Incredible Christians* somehow lacked in scholarship because of their more popular style; nothing could have been further from the truth. For it was his very meticulousness in paring away the Christ of faith overlay from the figure of the historical Jesus that had revealed the disturbing and controversial image of the Jewish Messiah, the ordinary man of flesh and blood which early Christianity had so successfully borrowed and eventually reconstituted as God incarnate. On the basis that what it taught was divinely revealed, the Church had 'achieved a mastery over human reason' and had been able to 'bring within the area of its own rulings matters which in fact were the fruits of its own very human speculations and contrivances'.[9] We discussed some of these human speculations and contrivances over dinner, and I suggested that he let me talk to Michael Mann of Element Books about his unpublished manuscript. To this proposal he agreed. On being contacted, Michael suggested that I read the manuscript and send him a written evaluation. This I was delighted to do, and as a result *The Essene Odyssey* reached the public in 1984.

DOCTRINAL BAGGAGE

According to this Jewish thinker, the modern dilemma of Christianity stemmed from a creed which demanded that we see God and Jesus Christ in one frame of reference. This theme, insisted upon down the centuries, had so distorted perception that we were now in danger of being unable to conceive of God's existence without Jesus.[10] This is an accurate observation and should not be pushed aside. Christians find it extremely difficult to think of God except through the idea of Jesus as God revealed in the flesh. So the danger for them is that anything which undermines the deity of Jesus also undermines their faith in God, and perhaps even their very capacity to relate to the presence of God as *otherness*.

Don Cupitt says straight out that the doctrine of the incarnation has had some harmful effects not only upon our understanding of Jesus' message but also on our comprehension of his relationship to God, and on the way Christians now relate to God.[11] Here is the same message from two sides of the fence: Jesus is carrying too heavy a load of doctrinal baggage to be properly understood. If seen, or for that matter even glimpsed, by the general public in his proper historical context, in his flesh and blood reality, in his day-to-day role as wandering Jewish teacher and philosopher, then a dangerous shift in perception could take place which would in turn undermine the Church's doctrinal credibility and authority.

This is perhaps why the Church always reacts so strongly to any attack on Jesus, even to the merest suggestion that he is not quite as the Christology of Paul seems to have him. It is sensed that the Christian faith might well disintegrate once bereft of its central archetypal image. For that is what Jesus the Jewish Messiah has turned into: an archetype, a psychically charged idea which has overtaken and annulled historical reality. Hence the rather odd manifestations of faith in Jesus which produce such things as stigmata and individual and collective visions of his now equally divine mother. Everything fits and is of a piece. The nail holes are always in the palms of the hands, not in the wrists (where they ought to be), and the Virgin Mary as *Theotokos* (Mother of God) supports the Church's interpretation of things by her very turning up, and by what she is said to intimate during moments of astronomical and meteorological anomaly. All in all a self-supporting and self-validating system with which it is virtually impossible to argue.

Don Cupitt remarks that the concept of *Theotokos* is a *prima facie* blasphemy which the orthodox have actively promoted perhaps because of its very provocativeness.[12] Burton L Mack, reminds us that myths, mentalities and cultures go together. 'Myths,' he tells us in his eye-opener of a book on Christian origins (*The Book of Q*), 'are celebrated publicly in story and song, mentalities are nurtured just beneath the surface of social conventions by means of unexpressed agreements. Myths, mentalities, and cultural agreements function at a level of acceptance that might be called sanctioned and therefore restricted from critical thought. Myths are difficult to criticize because mentalities turn them into truths held to be self-evident, and the analysis of such cultural assumptions is seldom heard as good news.'[13]

And then there is the unwillingness of Christian scholars, and of Christians in general, to accept as a normal part of their thinking that Jesus was a member of the Jewish race, that he belonged to a *definite* culture in a *definite* period of time. First and foremost, the Jesus revealed in the writings of Dr Schonfield is a Jew. Now some might consider this a rather obvious discovery, a banal observation hardly worth mentioning, but it is in fact a highly pertinent and important fact which most Christians either overlook or ignore or admit to without fully realizing its implications. N T Wright considers Jesus' Jewishness to be now thoroughly understood, accepted and integrated into Christian thinking, but I think he has overlooked rank-and-file attitudes. Unconcerned with the historical pressures on Jesus as he went about his messianic business in the gospels, most Christians tend to avoid the dynamics of the historical period and attend only to the 'myth' and 'marvel' superimposed on daily events by the New Testament writers. As Schonfield points out, many Christian clerics are still not prepared to admit that the Jesus of history is radically different from the Jesus of theology. The scholarly may come halfway to meet such a submission, but for obvious reasons cannot go beyond a certain point.[14] Or simply cannot afford to be seen to agree for fear of being classed heretical by less well-informed colleagues. Some clerics and theologians do of course cross the line and admit that all is not as it seems, but they are few and far between and are massively outnumbered by the 'careful' and the 'convinced'.

In his book *Jesus, Son of Man*, Rudolf Augstein blasts the general run of theologians with the following observation: 'The Churches still draw no conclusions from the discoveries of their theologians, who themselves prefer to keep their gods in the storehouse instead of distributing them among the people. The true meaning is often found in the footnotes, set out in fine print as on the back of an insurance policy.' Augstein goes on to quote the Quaker theologian and Harvard professor Henry Joel Cadbury's belief that 'today as at all times theology tends to obscure the approach to the historical face of Jesus.'[15]

And so when some scholarly outsider attempts to put the historical record straight, to cut through centuries of theological overlay and help release Jesus from the shadow of Christological construction, there is an uproar in the Christian camp. But as Richard Leigh succinctly states in *The Messianic Legacy*, 'Each contribution in the field of biblical research is like a footprint in sand. Each is covered almost immediately and, so far as the general public is concerned, left virtually without trace. Each must constantly be made anew, only to be covered again.[16] Why is this the case? The answer lies in Rudolf Augstein's previous statement about theologians: they 'prefer to keep their gods in the storehouse instead of distributing them among the people'. Leigh is of the same opinion:

> Anyone in the ministry, anyone training for the ministry, is, as a matter of course, confronted with the latest developments in biblical research. Any seminarian today will learn at least something of the Dead Sea Scrolls, of the Nag Hammadi Scrolls, of the history and evolution of New Testament studies. *Yet this knowledge has not been passed on to the laity*. In consequence, a gulf has opened between ecclesiastics and their congregations. Among themselves, ecclesiastics have become eminently sophisticated and erudite.[17]

The latter part of this statement is, to say the least, damning. And it is repeated by no less a figure than John Shelby Spong, Episcopal Bishop of Newark in his highly controversial book *Resurrection, Myth or Reality?* With reference to believers' being protected by the clergy from the ravages of higher biblical criticism, Bishop Spong tells us that clergy are introduced to these new methods of analysis and interpretation during theological training, but are not encouraged to use this new knowledge when preaching from the pulpit. It is far better, they are told, to just keep on telling the old, old story with an occasional modern accent.[18]

But there is also another angle to all of this, and it is a worrying one, for it reveals subterfuge and straight-down-the-line intellectual dishonesty on the part of some would-be clerics in theological training programs. I'm referring to what Dr Peter Cameron has revealed about seminary training in his book *Heretic*. A man blessed with the ability to doubt, Dr Cameron notes that many of his fellow candidates for the ministry entered theological training believing that the Bible was 'authoritative, inspired and infallible', and that after the initial shock of having their presuppositions challenged, 'recoiled in anger and indignation and avoided any further unpleasantness by surrounding themselves with a sort of protective cocoon'.[19] Within this cocoon they held their notion of an inspired and infallible Scripture intact, ignored the higher learning being offered to them, and when the time came to sit exams and take their degree, paid no more than lip-service to what they had been taught.

So here we have the other side of the coin – the side which reveals not a paternal withholding of ideas and discoveries from congregations considered too vulnerable to know the truth, but prejudice and preconceived notions of a most limited type overruling what ought to be an on-going exercise in discrimination and judgement.

ECCE HOMO

And then there is the problem of Jesus' humanity, of his existence in time and space as a flesh-and-blood human being – flesh and blood and bone and sweat and everything else that goes along with being human. Can Christians really fathom this fact? Do ministers and priests, as they stand in their pulpits talking about their double-natured Lord, ever sense the human being that walked on earth? Do they ever sit down and really *think* about Jesus' humanity? For instance, did he ever twist his ankle or break a leg? Did he sneeze all over his disciples when he had a cold? Did he smell badly after a particularly spicy meal? What about headaches, and irritability, and that bad temper of his when roused? What about sore feet and cuts and bruises and sore stomachs and the bites of insects? And what about picking up on things the wrong way on a particularly dense day? And what about women? Did he at any time ever consider them sexually in his life? Or did he perhaps before he came to the conclusion that he was Israel's Messiah and dedicated himself to that unenviable task? What did he think about as he wandered along those dusty roads flanked with disciples who often did not understand what he was saying to them? And when he prayed to God, to whom did he think he was speaking?

The German theologian Rudolf Bultmann had something quite enlightening to say about the physical and mental life of Jesus. According to this highly respected and often quoted Christian thinker, Jesus as a flesh-and-blood individual 'does not concern us; what went on in the heart of Jesus I neither know nor want to know'.[20]

In his quite excellent book *The Life of Jesus*, the Italian writer Marcello Craveri has this to say about the humanity of Jesus:

> If we can separate the 'Christ of faith', who is the creation of the fanaticism of his believers, from the 'Jesus of history', who is obvious to us in the accounts of the Synoptic gospels, the personality of Jesus emerges quite clearly: ultra-human, even in his sudden changes of mood, at one moment gentle and tender, almost feminine in his lassitude, at another sharp and vehement, quick to anger and scorn; often locked in deep sorrow, and above all moved by constant unrest, which is not a sign of madness – at least in my opinion – but the mark of a great soul, aware of an almost impossible mission that has become the idea of his whole existence.[21]

What we have to remember is that the gospels were written with hindsight, after the destruction of the Temple by the Romans, and are therefore tailored documents made to fit Jesus like a suit of clothing, a suit carefully designed by the writer-compiler-editors to reconstruct his messiahship, wanderings and statements as symbolic of his divinity in what they thought to be the Pauline mould. So at some point we have to ask ourselves the all-important question, the question Bultmann did not care to consider: How did Jesus perceive himself? Did he think of himself as the son of Joseph and Mary? Did he early on sense himself as having a destiny, a future related to the spiritual needs of his people? Or did his mission only come into focus with maturity – with his baptism, perhaps? Is it possible, as many seem to believe, that he knew himself to be a direct expression of God, a sort of hived-off emanation of God experiencing his creation from the inside? Or if, for historical reasons, the word 'emanation' is unacceptable, then could he possibly have experienced himself as simultaneously wholly human and wholly divine, as Athanasius seems to have believed but was never really able to explain?

The great Anglican Churchman Charles Gore (1853–1932) did not really agree with Athanasius, and neither did he agree with his Tractarian predecessor H P Lidden's acceptance that Jesus' nature had somehow simultaneously straddled both the human and divine without contradiction. Don Cupitt has written an interesting essay on this relationship entitled 'The Christ of Christendom', and reveals now Gore almost single-handedly modified the Anglican approach to this question of Jesus' earthly life. Gore was apparently more in sympathy with the ideas of Sir John Seeley, particularly as expressed in his essay 'Ecce Homo' published in 1865; and that in spite of its sentimental and, as Cupitt points out 'by scholarly standards fictitious life of Jesus'.[22] Gore thought Seeley's ideas historically relevant for one particular reason: they pointed to the reality of Jesus' human life, which he felt the Church had 'obscured'.

Don Cupitt explores this issue in fresh and vital language, and carefully builds a picture of the transition point in Church of England theology where the humanity of Jesus began to take on serious implications for the Christ of faith. Charles Gore was not a radical thinker, but he did think: he was 'old bourgeois England, an Anglo-Catholic, and a socialist, albeit of a very pale pink colour'.[23] His knowledge of Rabbinic Judaism was nil, his biblical criticism conservative, his belief in the incarnation orthodox. Yet he changed how the Church viewed the incarnation by highlighting one factor: Jesus' humanity. Seeley's anonymously published essay, 'Ecce Homo' (Behold the Man), had stirred up something in Gore's breast, and he began to explore a 'full imaginative realization of what it was for the divine Word to have actually lived a *fully* human life'.[24]

H P Lidden, Anglican theologian, arch-conservative advocate of the principles of the Oxford Movement and author of *The Divinity of our Lord and Saviour Jesus Christ* (1865), was quite at odds with Gore's infatuation with Seeley's divine-yet-fully-human Jesus. And this in spite of the fact that Gore had not broken with orthodoxy, merely focused on Jesus' humanity while at the same time accepting Jesus as the divine Word made flesh.

But even to fractionally shift the emphasis from the divine Word to that of the flesh and blood man was enough to initiate a raising of ecclesiastical eyebrows, and an eventual change in the climate of opinion concerning the incarnation. For Gore, as Don Cupitt reminds us, was an 'insider', not an 'outsider'.[25]

Lidden believed that there was no difference between the historical Jesus and the Jesus of theology. Gore avoided the idea that there might be a conflict between those two figures, but allowed for a real distinction, a certain tension between them. It was this which caused the gradual refocusing of attention on Jesus the man.[26] His main argument, Don Cupitt tells us, was that the doctrine of the incarnation did not explain the incarnation, it merely acted as a 'boundary' around it. But this idea only worked as long as the orthodox dogma was seen as coherent; if it was once seen as incoherent (as not making internal sense) it could no longer function as a boundary for the Christian mind. To Gore, the integrity of Jesus' humanity was put under threat when he was viewed through Lidden's eyes, when the two spheres of Jesus' existence and personality were magically welded together without impairment. Lidden's incarnate Lord was simultaneously 'all-knowing and ignorant'; Gore's incarnate Lord was governed by a human psychology, by divine attributes 'dimmed' and 'veiled' because of the burden of human flesh. This is to say that Gore had gently laid aside the doctrine of the two natures in its historic form and had, almost against his will, psychologized Jesus because it was the only way he could get his Lord's suffering back into a real spiritual context, a context which showed Jesus truly sharing the sorrow and suffering of mankind. Frances Young neatly sums up Gore's problem when she says: 'If the Logos is inherently perfect and incapable of change, progress or suffering, he is no more able to mediate than the transcendent God himself.'[27] For Gore the notion of the Logos suffering without suffering (*apathos epathen*) was just too much to take on board.

Gore did not believe that the old Tractarian message – the message that the Church through its sacraments was the sole divinely appointed channel of the grace of Christ – could be repeated without reformulation. Lidden was of the opposite opinion. Gore believed that the time had come to correlate Christian theology with scientific and historical knowledge and to translate it into social action. Lidden's conviction was that Christian unity had to take first preference – that is, the boat should not be rocked. In his Bampton lecture of 1891 entitled 'The Incarnation of the Son of God', Gore gave offence by what is termed his 'kenotic' interpretation of Jesus' human knowledge. This is to say that Gore had finally come to believe that Christ had laid aside his divinity on his incarnation. Unwavering in his adherence to the historic creeds and his insistence on their use as a test of clerical orthodoxy, he nevertheless fell foul of traditional orthodoxy for what was considered 'idealistic assumptions'.[28] But the cat was out of the bag – a flesh and blood Jesus was taking his first tottering steps into the nineteenth century.

This then raised the problem of Jesus in the role of authoritarian monarch. Don Cupitt describes Gore's Jesus as 'that somewhat old-fashioned figure, a privileged person with an earnest social conscience'; whereas Lidden's Jesus was literally 'a universe away' in rank and scale.[29] And it is between Gore's and Lidden's views of Jesus that the fourth-century Christ, the Christ of Chalcedonian orthodoxy, began to crumble from within – the sinless autocrat of the gospels speaking with authority and increasing self-assertion was under question. And rightly so. Don Cupitt's analysis of the framing of the classical doctrine of Christ reveals an extensive paganization of faith, worship and social organization within the Church. A pagan iconography of Christ was developing under the pressure of political needs, and the Hellenistic philosophy of kingship was at the bottom of it all.

As God was to the cosmos, and the king was to the state, so the divine Logos indwelt the king and in turn became a king by association. The king, acting in a Godlike manner, and as a shepherd to his people, was seen as a kind of incarnate God, a link between heaven and earth, and the divine Logos as incarnate God was promoted to universal cosmic Emperor who, understandably enough, validated his almost divine deputy's every action. A neat little package which quickly bestowed dignity and privilege, dress and insignia upon the Church's chief ministers, and in turn allowed the king to parade himself as God's earthly representative. Borrowing extensively from court ritual, these chief ministers of the New Christian Order successfully buried Jesus the Jew for a second time.

Don Cupitt catches the pathos of the situation when he says, 'Almost the only remaining trace of Jesus is his dark Semitic face, peering out with understandable sadness from his incongruous new setting.'[30] And in *A Short History of Western Liturgy*,

Theodore Klauser augments this setting by pointing out that those associated with Jesus were similarly exalted: 'Mary became the Mother and Empress, the apostles were turned into a senate, the angels now constituted the household of a heavenly court, and the saints were represented as guests seeking audience and bringing their offerings.'[31]

This is to say that the Jesus of flesh, blood, bone and historical reality had finally disappeared among a welter of projections fashioned into an orthodoxy, an orthodoxy which at base was composed of an avalanche of unsound and historically untenable opinions. A *heresy*, in other words. A series of half-baked truths and imaginings about Jesus' life and times made culturally respectable through a process of theological sleight-of-hand and numbing repetition. As the theologian Michael Goulder says concerning his own past belief in Jesus as the Son of God: 'Trembling beliefs . . . are reinforced daily by the repetition of the liturgy.'[32]

But although hidden, and ignored, and endlessly conjured out of existence by ecclesiastics defending the religious status quo, the Jesus of flesh and blood and historical reality began at last to surface. And as this figure emerged into the daylight of reasonable discourse and proper historical analysis, a hysterical fear set in among less well-informed ecclesiastics – a fear that erupted again and again and caused much mental anguish to those daring to tease the real Jesus out into the light of the twentieth century. Mercilessly attacked and scoffed at by theologians and members of the clergy for attempting to uncover and present the historical Jesus to the general public, scholars like Dr Schonfield were made a laughing-stock by those who ought to have known better. In his introduction to *The Passover Plot* Schonfield set the standard of the debate with the following words:

> The only way in which we can hope to know the real Jesus is by first becoming conscious of him as a man of his own time, country and people, which necessitates an intimate acquaintance with all three. We have resolutely to refuse to detach him from his setting, and let the influences which played upon him play upon us. We have to mark the traits in him which were personal, individual, whether pleasing or unpleasing, which convey to us the attributes and idiosyncrasies of a creature of flesh and blood. Only when this Galilean Jew has made an impact upon us in the cruder aspects of his mortality are we entitled to begin to cultivate him and estimate his worth, allowing him to

communicate to us the imaginations of his mind and the motivations of his action.[33]

As Frances Young admits in the face of modern knowledge of genetics: 'Jesus must have been part of world history and the inheritor of the normal genetic links in human descent.'[34] This is to say clearly that Jesus was not somehow God squeezed into a human frame; he was a man of God with a distinct and unique vision of what it means to be human attempting to liberate the mind and sensibilities of his age.

TWO

THE PAGANIZING OF CHRISTIANITY

The Church sets up a cosmic personality cult, indulges in hindsight interpretations of the Gospels, and unwittingly changes Jesus into a pathologically abnormal being.

Dr Schonfield seriously suggests that Christians are still related under the skin to the devotees of Adonis and Osiris, Dionysus and Mithras, and that in spite of the fact that Christianity considers itself to be the spiritual point of view which did away with paganism. Conquered by Christianity, paganism retreated into its dark corner. C S Lewis imaginatively captures this retreat in one of his novels by having the great magician Merlin locked up inside a block of ice. Christ is on the throne; the Devil and all his works are, more or less, under control.

That's the theory – and as a theory it has worked well down the ages. But what if this is not the case? What if paganism, instead of being banished, has been absorbed? For if any religion ever developed the capacity to absorb what it could not fully overcome, it is Christianity. The history of the Christian faith is punctuated with this porous ability to absorb cultic and cultural anomalies. Now this in itself could be argued as simply a necessary formula to help wean people away from unsound ideas deeply rooted in their psyches – within time the pagan connections would fade and the following generations would not even be aware of what had happened. Fair enough. But what Schonfield is referring to goes much, much deeper than that. Schonfield is pointing at the fact that the very thing Christianity has invested so much energy in historically – the stamping out of pagan ideas – is the very thing it is blatantly guilty of in the setting up of a cosmic personality cult with Jesus the Jewish Messiah as its unwitting centrefold.

Before going into this, we have to digress for a moment and again look at the idea of Messiahship, for it is at exactly this point that Christianity shows itself capable of epistemological sleight of hand.

THE JEWISH MESSIAH

Rudolf Bultmann, a theologian who more than anyone else has assisted with the process of demythologizing the New Testament, pronounced many years ago that Jesus did not consider himself to be the Messiah of Israel. With one deft sweep of his theological eraser, this Christian thinker single-handedly removed the picture so carefully wrought by the evangelists of what Jesus believed himself to be. Since then Churchmen of all types have taken to agreeing with Bultmann (much in the same way as the Catholic Church seems to be only too willing to agree with the scientific finding that the Turin Shroud is a medieval forgery), and a survey of Christian literature seems to suggest that Bultmann is right and the evangelists quite mistaken. So what is going on? Why did it become necessary to deny Jesus' Messiahship? What is it about 'Messiahship' that makes the Church feel so uncomfortable?

The answer to this question lies in the fact that too close a scrutiny of Jesus in the role of Jewish Messiah unravels the Church's compulsory Christ of faith – the Christ of faith argued into existence by Bultmann as an alternative to the elusive Jesus of history. Bultmann's New Testament researches not only erased Jesus' Messiahship, they also erased just about everything about Jesus. Virtually nothing in the New Testament, he concluded, was reliable – present-day scholars are no longer satisfied with this approach. In spite of this, however, we had still to assume 'some personal nucleus that makes comprehensible the tremendous momentum of the early Christian movement, even though we admit that it would have been unthinkable without Paul and perhaps owes its success to him alone'.[1]

And yet, as the German writer Rudolf Augstein shows in his excellent book *Jesus, Son of Man*, Bultmann had an almost tragic reverence for the fourth gospel because in it Jesus 'as the revealer of God reveals nothing except that he is the revealer'.[2] This is a telling statement, for it unmasks Bultmann's weakness for Jesus as the God-man who had foreknowledge of everything. The historical Jesus was as nothing in comparison with the God-man; in fact it was necessary to utterly demolish the historical Jesus so that the God-man could surface without contradiction. And because the concept of Jesus as the Messiah too closely linked Jesus with the ordinary world of Jewish life and politics, he was the first to go.

But scholarly opinion has now come full circle. J H Charlesworth, general editor of *Jesus and the Dead Sea Scrolls*, has this to say about Jesus' Messiahship: 'Jesus' messianic self-awareness, which once seemed unlikely to many scholars, is now being acknowledged by a wide spectrum of them.'[3] Charlesworth even allows for the possibility of Jesus' having being influenced by Essene messianology, and this observation, backed as it now is by a mass of evidence from the Scrolls that Jesus was perfectly aware of the Qumran Essenes, and the Qumran Essenes perfectly aware of him, allows for a more realistic assessment of Jesus and his intentions.

Augstein points out that it is the fourth gospel, John's gospel, which more plausibly lays out the reasons for Jesus' death on the Cross. John's account, in spite of all the gnostic theology, is nearer to the reality of Jesus' public life. Unlike a mere chronicler, the writer of John's gospel seemed to know what was really going on. Jesus was far too popular and unpredictable and alarming to the Temple aristocracy to be left alone. The priesthood were in paroxysms over Jesus – he was the leader of a Messianic movement of some proportions. And then comes the telling statement picked up on by Augstein: the High Priest Caiaphas' summing up of the situation. 'It is better for you that one man should die for the people than that the whole people should be destroyed.'[4] This is obviously a reference to the fact that Jesus' Messianic movement was getting out of control, that it was strong enough to attract the attention of the Romans, and that such attention could only lead to one result – the obliteration of the Jewish people. To Bultmann's liking, the fourth gospel then comes up with a quite superfluous statement to keep Jesus in the mould of God-man. Apparently Caiaphas was not making a political statement, he was simply prophesying that Jesus should die not only for the Jewish nation, but for *everyone*. The cards had been neatly reshuffled.[5]

This piece of lurching propaganda for a heaven-appointed human sacrifice would be amusing if it were not that so much distortion has been built on it. The writers of the gospels knew exactly what they were doing. Once allow Jesus to be fully identified as the Jewish Messiah and the image of him as divinely appointed saviour of the world would not only seem unlikely but downright ludicrous. And so the 'sacrificial element' in Jesus' fulfilment of the Messianic Plan found in the Old Testament and in the mental perambulations of the Essenes is amplified into a paganized version of what had been a purely Jewish vision of profound religiosity. Jesus is no longer Jewish, no longer the Galilean of roughish speech surrounded by followers and highly suspect contacts. He is the glistening, transformed Christ of Pauline imagination, the God-man which his original Nazarene disciples will soon flatly reject as a Jesus they do not recognize.

Once in place, this paganizing of the Jewish Messiah was later pushed into reverse and made out to be God's preordained model for a spirituality designed to replace paganism – a clever manipulation of events the audacity of which almost takes one's breath away. Enter Paul in all his out-of-season glory. But the original Nazarene disciples of Jesus will not listen to him. He is treated as an outcast, as a fly-by-nighter who wants to present a Jesus to the people that is not at all to Nazarene liking. But this Jew, this Hebrew of the Hebrews with Roman citizenship is tenacious to the point of obsession. He classifies the original disciples of Jesus as 'false brethren'[6] and sets up a series of Churches in the name of his version of Jesus – a Jesus now magnified beyond all credibility – at least, that's how it seems. As Bultmann confesses, this early Christian movement would be 'unthinkable without Paul and perhaps owes its success to him alone'.[7]

Don Cupitt's assessment of this paganized Jesus brings us back to the doctrine of the incarnation, the doctrine which, in its varying versions, allows for a fullness of God in Christ which is permanent. As such, Christ can be worshipped as God without fear of error. Praying directly to Christ – as distinct from praying to God through Christ – originated in the fourth century and was made part of the liturgy. Opposed by many, Christocentric worship slowly spread and became the accepted norm. However well-intentioned, the focus had been shifted from God to man, and this shift would eventually legitimize a cult of humanity, a reverence for the human individual which would quickly deteriorate into the almost idolatrous belief that the 'human' was all that mattered, that the 'spiritual' could be approached only through the figure of the deified God-man. Deity would slowly fade into the background, the *otherness* of God would be translated into an old *man* in the sky who sometimes stretched a disembodied hand out of a cloud.[8]

THE GOSPEL WRITERS

Christians unfamiliar with the history of how the gospels came to be written, and when they were written, and of the critical studies made of them, will probably find the idea of the gospel writers' tampering with the image of Jesus unacceptable. But what they may not realize is that it is highly unlikely that the writers of the gospels ever knew Jesus – the writer/compilers themselves are utterly unknown. In *Jesus, the Evidence*, Ian Wilson informs us that the canonical gospels bearing the names Matthew, Mark, Luke and John were not necessarily written by those particular writers but given these names by way of mere attribution. The earliest writers to mention the gospels fail to mention the authors' names because they were designed for quite separate communities and only later came together in the form now known. He also notes that the earliest texts lacked the easy identification features they now possess. For instance, everything was written in capital letters; there were no headings or chapter divisions or even verse divisions – these identification features did not appear until the Middle Ages. And there was practically no punctuation or even spaces between words. Wilson remarks: 'it does not take anyone with a PhD in theology to recognize that the Christian gospels can scarcely be the infallible works fundamentalists would have us believe.'[9]

The gospels attributed to Mark and Matthew were apparently first named by Bishop Papias of Phrygia around 150 CE, the gospels of Luke and John (the beloved disciple) by Bishop Irenaeus of Lyons in about 180 CE. Giving these books the names of apostles enhanced their credibility for some centuries, but the advent of German biblical scholarship in the mid-nineteenth century eventually produced dates for each gospel which showed the earliest of them to have been composed *at least* a generation after the events they contain. Ian Wilson describes an earlier attempt at critical analysis by H. S. Reimarus, Hamburg Professor of Oriental Languages, as a 'faltering start', and says revealingly that Reimarus published his findings (that Jesus was a failed revolutionary) posthumously for fear of recriminations.

Not so cautious was David F. Strauss, the Tübingen University tutor who published a two-volume critical study of the life of Jesus – and was dismissed from his post for his efforts.[10] With the German school well established, there then appeared Wilhelm

Wrede and Albert Schweitzer's penetrating studies of the New Testament. Wrede's interestingly-titled book *The Secret of the Messiahship* (1901) revealed that Jesus had deliberately made a secret of his Messiahship, and noted that most of his disciples had failed to recognize him as the Messiah until after his death.[11] In *The Quest for the Historical Jesus* (1905), Schweitzer came to the conclusion that Jesus had never existed at all, and stated that the image had not been destroyed from without but had fallen to pieces from within due to unsurmountable historical problems associated with the gospels. Over the ensuing years highly critical studies of the New Testament were produced in Germany by Baur, Lachmann, Weisse, Wilke, Holtzmann, Bultmann and Barth, to mention but a few. Bultmann's contribution was 'form criticism' (*Formgeschichte*), and so was born the scientific approach to critical analysis.

The New Testament contains 27 books. These books grew in number over the years, and for a long period of time it was not known by the early Church whether the canon of the New Testament was closed or not. It is now known that these books first appeared separately, in different localities and at various intervals of time, and that for many years the canon was not limited to 27 books. Other books – such as the *Shepherd of Hermas* and the *Epistles of St Clement* – were held in equal regard, and only later considered unsuitable, or apocryphal. Church thinking is that the 'apocryphal' books, when examined and contrasted with the 27 books being seriously considered, revealed themselves to be lacking in dignity and 'inspired uniformity'. Between 200 and 400 CE some 16 catalogues of the New Testament books were published in Palestine, Cyprus, Asia Minor, Alexandria, North Africa and Italy in either Greek or Latin. There was much variety and independence between these catalogues, and Churchmen struggled hard over which to accept and which to reject. Not every catalogue included the Apocalypse (Revelation), and we know that Origen rejected the books attributed to Jesus' brothers, James and Jude. So, in effect, the New Testament came together gradually over a period of 400 years, and took its final form as a result of a Church Council, not, as some seem to think, as a result of divine intervention.

Bishop Athanasius of Alexandria finally compiled a list of works to be included in the New Testament in 367 CE, and the Church Council of Hippo ratified this list in 393 and again in

397. The New Testament which we know today was agreed upon by those Councils, and many books with just as much historical validity and holy purpose were rejected. This carefully vetted list is what underlies the now sacrosanct and untouchable New Testament in its variously translated editions, and it is a nice touch to have conveniently built in at the end of the book of Revelation a dire threat to the effect that if anyone adds to or takes away from that strange prophetic vision, then they shall be 'removed from the book of life'. This curse, although it applies only to the Apocalypse itself, is unconsciously felt to apply to the whole of the New Testament. The door of necessary change or modification or discovery is therefore firmly closed. A kind of magical taboo has been placed on the New Testament corpus, changing its highly challengeable contents into Holy Writ.

But the New Testament is in fact no such thing. It is a series of historical documents written, compiled, arranged and edited like any other similar collection – those that were rejected, for instance. Each and every book, all 27 of them, have undergone multiple additions and deletions, and the corpus contains material which often points to early sources of information about Jesus and his Mission which do not properly gel with what the compilers, as opposed to the original writers, wished to say, or the Church Fathers wished to know. The early Church, with a stroke of its magisterial pen, had consolidated its doctrinal position and initiated the process of scholarly reification which would more and more stunt Christian intelligence concerning New Testament make-up and composition. Necessary it may have been for the sake of continuity and coherence, for the sake of social control and the eradication of ideas already deemed heretical by the ruling elite – but it would eventually lead to a massive distortion of historical and spiritual reality.

The writings were carefully selected and arranged not, as many might think, for the purpose of conserving the earliest records of Christian beginnings, but for the express purpose of collating several differing avenues of Christian persuasion into one fully sanctioned text, so making the differences evaporate. Four gospels there might have been, but as from that moment they were no longer four gospels offering four versions of Jesus' life and teachings, but four *aspects* of one Jesus skilfully amalgamated into a single image.[12] So it was not a matter of Athanasius and his council scratching their heads and eventually coming up with a mutually agreed corpus of texts. It was a matter of recognizing that that corpus of texts was already significantly in use by the Churches, and of use to the Church by dint of its structural shape and content. The four gospels plus the letters and journeyings of Paul were simply too good to pass up. There was nothing else quite like them. The early merging of what is believed to be source material with the narrative story borrowed from Mark, and the fact that each writer seemed to have been either a first-hand witness to Jesus' travels, trial and final tribulation, or favoured with a 'Damascus' experience such as Paul's, marked this collection of documents out as special, as carrying undeniable apostolic sanction and authority. And so the style was set: the New Testament corpus must only contain materials written by apostles.

A recent evaluation of the gospels made by Professor Burton L Mack helps bring everything into focus. Mack has it that the narrative gospels began to appear during the latter part of the first century. Mark is said to have been written during the 70s, Matthew during the 80s, John during the 90s, and Luke sometime early in the second century. Following a plot worked out by Mark which shows his gospel to have been written *after the destruction of the Temple*, the other gospel writers produced their own stylized versions. Setting the gospels side by side for comparison, scholars noticed that the story-line in Matthew and Luke agreed only when it followed the gospel of Mark. This meant that Mark was the earliest narrative gospel and the original template used by these writers. But there was also a large quantity of 'sayings of Jesus' not found in Mark, much of it identical in Matthew and Luke. This suggested that these writers had had access to a second document. Scholars gave the name 'Q' to this document, from the German word *Quelle*, meaning 'source'. What was eventually realized, however, was that this 'sayings of Jesus' document was not merely another source document in the same vein as Mark's, but that it constituted the original source material upon which, and around which, *all* of the gospels had eventually been constructed. And this source document had not been a gospel complete with story-line: it had been no more than a collection of sayings, a veritable grocery list of observations and pronouncements made by someone called Jesus.

Referring to the earliest followers of Jesus as 'the people of Q', or 'the Jesus people', Mack tells us that:

They did not take his teachings as an indictment of Judaism. They did
not regard his death as a divine, tragic, or saving event. And they
did not imagine that he had been raised from the dead to rule over a
transformed world. Instead, they thought of him as a teacher whose
teachings made it possible to live with verve in troubled times. Thus
they did not gather to worship in his name, honour him as a god, or
cultivate his memory through hymns, prayers, and rituals. They did
not form a cult of the Christ such as the one that emerged among the
Christian communities familiar to the readers of the letters of Paul.
The people of Q were Jesus people, not Christians.[13]

This is quite a statement. It suggests a process of elaboration and
embroidering going on at the very inception of Christianity – a
process of story telling and creation with a definite purpose. And
it reveals a number of levels, a sequence of Q levels, each a fuller
and more historically involved level of story telling within which
a new Jesus, a Jesus with a different or evolving point of view,
speaks and acts – a point of view created for him by the writer-
compilers of the gospels after his death, and by some of his
followers during his life.

This is to say that Jesus' sayings were *appropriately added to* by
his early followers, and eventually made to fit a historical pattern
by later followers and devotees convinced of his divinity as a
result of Paul's teachings. And the gospels themselves reveal
different groups with different interpretative slants on Jesus'
teachings – groups which were probably quite separate from one
another but which were eventually made to coalesce through the
simple positioning together of the gospels. Seen as one story told
from four points of view, four quite distinct stories were united
into a synoptic vision with the help of Mark's basic story-line.
Toying with the same notion, Rudolf Augstein says:

> Given the spareness of the evidence, we may well ask whether the whole
> conception of Jesus is not a creation resulting from the syncretistic
> blending of several figures and ideas, built up in the imagination of
> the Hellenistically educated Jews as a personification of the expectation
> of redemption by the Jewish people.[14]

From my reading of Mack's fascinating and highly informative
book on Christian origins, I can only conclude that the Jesus
of the gospels is not the real Jesus. He is a creation. But he is
a creation based on a real personality and placed within a
mythological landscape of miracles and curious happenings
which reflect – but do not necessarily accurately describe – actual

historical events. There is real history here, and a real Jesus. But what cements these two things together seems to be a series of inventions or contrivances which point to a generic Jesus who had real followers and who had pertinent things to say, sayings that were later interpreted as having a meaning quite different from the original meaning because Jesus had been elevated from a man to something like the Supreme Deity. Statements and actions of a purely ordinary nature were taken to mean more than they were ever intended to mean, and with a little help from the writer-compilers such statements and actions were eventually backed by bold assertions written into the gospel texts.

Burton L Mack's formulation of things is vastly helpful and insightful, but it may not be the whole story. It may be that what he and his fellow scholars think of as isolated sayings of Jesus in a cynic-sage mould signify more than a wandering teacher's pithy observations of life. To assume that Jesus was not in some way plugged into the religious and political climate of his day, that he was somehow free-floating and independent, that his teachings were no more than clever aphorisms scattered to the wind, is to go further than I think it is legitimate to go. There are too many factors involved to utterly divorce Jesus from his time and his people, from the difficulties of Roman occupation and the fears of the religious establishment concerning nationalist aspirations. There are too many hints in the New Testament that something else is going on just beneath the surface to totally abandon the scenario of Jesus as Nazarene leader and Jewish Messiah – and that in spite of Q.

True as it is that the differing levels of Q reveal subtle layers of thought, interpretation and historical event invisibly mended into a highly complex tapestry, I think it can still be argued that there is a real Jesus in the gospels and that he was up to something, or up to his neck in something which eventually demanded a brutal, ritualistic penalty. The trick, I think, is not to abandon him altogether, to see him as no more than a phantom, but to attempt to see him as a flesh-and-blood man struggling with a religious climate sadly lacking in common sense, and a political climate dangerously fused with religious expectations. We have to keep reminding ourselves that he was not a god, that he was not *God* peering through human eyes. That's what bedevils us and stops us from seeing the real man, the ignored man of flesh and blood complete with his own agenda. He was not God. He was a clever, witty, sharp-eyed and sometimes sharp-tongued religious teacher-cum-philosopher who quite probably took on the role of Jewish Messiah and tried to steer Israel away from military suicide. He failed in this; but he did not fail to impress his many followers with his dignity, intelligence, and iron will. To move him entirely outside of the Gospel narrative is to perhaps violate some other level of the text not yet fully understood, a level containing a more realistic and acceptable formulation of his life and mission.

The Jesus of the New Testament is a myth, a construction, a layered series of imaginings brought teetering to the edge of reality – physical reality. Yet he is at the same time real in the most real sense of 'real', for in spite of the mythological and almost magical overlay it is still likely that he did function in history as a human being and a messianic figure. The problem is in disentangling him from this overlay, from the miracles and self-promotions, from the perceptibly evolving notion of him as some kind of divine being set down in, or sent down into, history. Mack would have it that we also have to disentangle him from history – the history as presented in the gospels – but this may not be necessary, not entirely. It may be that he is not totally a phantom with borrowed words on his lips, words cleverly aligned with historical events and either stretched or directly augmented to prove a point. He may just as easily be a real human being pulled out of historical context and existential shape by the very mythology scholars acknowledge to exist.

In his book *Jesus*, A N Wilson reacts similarly to the suggestion that Jesus never existed. With a deep knowledge of the background of the New Testament he says:

> The realistic details are too many, and too old, for me to be able to accept that they were all invented by some unsung novelistic genius of the first century of our era; though they are so heavily outweighed by improbable stories, and so soaked in 'teaching' that I fully sympathise with any reader who has hitherto supposed that it was impossible to find a 'real' Jesus amid so much religion and folklore.[15]

Those who push for Jesus' intending to found a Church, and for his first followers' being quite obviously the first Christians, are almost certainly mistaken. He probably had a 'community' of some sort in mind, but not the 'Church' which eventually appeared through a distortion of his teachings. Jesus' disciples were not Christians, and neither were the members of the

Nazarene Party to which he belonged. He was a Nazarene leader, and it is in this organization that we find the rudimentary man of the gospels, the leader of a *named* sectarian community which was part of a larger movement of sectaries. Jesus did not materialize out of thin air – he stepped into the limelight as a sectarian leader with a private agenda at variance not only with Judaism but also with those of his closest sectarian neighbours *and* with the Nazarene sub-movement to which he belonged.

Dr Schonfield was of the opinion that Jesus' kin formed a family succession similar in type to that of the dynastic caliphates among the later Islamic community, and Jesus' brother James certainly seems to have had more authority than the other disciples after the Crucifixion. Peter's supposed elevation to leader of the group by Jesus does not ring true as an event within the overall framework of the gospels. The other gospels do not mention any such investiture, and this omission, especially in the gospel of Mark (it is venerable tradition that Mark's gospel reproduces all of Peter's teaching) is, as Marcello Craveri states, 'inexplicable as an historical fact'.[16] The role of the Nazarene movement, and of Jesus' family in relation to that movement, has been virtually ignored by Christian scholars in spite of important indications in both the gospels and the book of Acts that the Nazarenes had an agenda with which Jesus eventually disagreed. So it is only when we see the Nazarenes in proper perspective, when we highlight their strange past history, that the role played by Jesus in the gospels can take on historical substance and cease being no more than a conduit for *present-day* interpretations of Pauline theology. The gospels, as A N Wilson points out, contain not only 'mythological' truth, but also 'facts'.[17]

THE ECCLESIASTICAL CHRIST

Dr Schonfield reports that many of the Christians he spoke with were not even aware that the term 'Christ' or *Christos* was simply a Greek translation of the Hebrew title *Messiah* (the Anointed One), and thought somehow that it referred to the Second Person of the Trinity. So connected had the word 'Christ' become with the idea of Jesus as God incarnate that the title 'Messiah' was treated as something curiously Jewish and not associated. Don Cupitt notes that Rudolf Bultmann expels Jesus the Jew from Christianity as an irrelevance and holds up for veneration the ecclesiastically created 'Christ', then goes on to say that the ecclesiastical Christ is nowhere to be found in a 'critical' reading of the gospels. He adds insightfully that the theological task of the modern period is that of 'shifting Christianity from the dogmatic faith of the Christendom period to the critical faith which is to succeed it'.[18]

Richard Leigh comments that the designation 'Jesus the Christ' was distorted into a proper name, Jesus Christ, and ceased to be a purely functional title.[19] The term 'Christ', to many Christians, signifies everything that the Church teaches about Jesus, and has nothing whatsoever to do with the anointed one of Israel, the Messiah. It is almost as if the Messiah had hidden the fact that he was the Christ, and that Peter's stumbling reply to Jesus' question 'Whom say ye that I am?' was some kind of blinding revelation which proved Jesus to be divine. But Peter's reply 'You are the Christ,' meant no such thing: it was merely one man's recognition of Jesus as God's anointed, and therefore 'appointed', servant – the Messiah who would lead Israel into and through the great tribulation of the Last Days. The Bishop of Lichfield agrees:

> One of the most persistent mistakes throughout the literature on Jesus in the last hundred years is to use the word 'Christ', which simply means 'Messiah', as though it was a 'divine' title.[20]

An 'Anointed One' also referred to a king, and so in the Old Testament King David became a 'Messiah' or 'Christ', and every subsequent Jewish king of the house of David was similarly known – an interesting point in view of the fact that Jesus' lineage is said to have been of the house of David, and he is officially designated King of the Jews by Pilate. Don Cupitt reminds us that the idea of 'incarnation' is, in its full and proper sense, nowhere present in the gospels.[21] The incarnation of Jesus as God in the flesh is a construction built on patches of evidence from the gospels which are themselves interpretations belonging to each writer – writers who wrote *long after* the events in question, but who had at the back of their minds Paul's highly developed Christology as they rewrote and edited early Christian documents. All is not quite as it seems. The four gospels have some strange and quite noticeable additions, but actually stop short of fully asserting the idea of Jesus as God. It is only later, in hindsight, that innocent situations in the gospels are interpreted as directly carrying this very un-Jewish point of view. This point of view will eventually be made to apply to everything in the gospels, and the transmutation of Jesus from Jewish Messiah into what is thought of as the Pauline Christ will be complete. John's gospel does of course throw all of this into reverse with Jesus' explicit statements concerning his own divinity. Marcello Craveri lists these statements – 'I am the light of the world'; 'The Father himself, which hath sent me, hath borne witness of me'; 'I proceeded forth and came from God'; etc. – and adds that if we accepted these statements attributed to Jesus in John's gospel, 'we should be likely to look on Jesus as pathologically abnormal.'[22]

An excellent example of 'hindsight' interpretation is to be found in Luke's story of Jesus and his disciples' infringement of the Sabbath ruling on the harvesting and milling of grain. While walking through a field of wheat, Jesus and his disciples break off a few stalks and eat the grains after rubbing them in their hands. Witnessed by some Pharisees, they are reprimanded for breaking the Sabbath. Engaging these upholders of the Law in debate, Jesus reminds them that King David had also broken the religious law when he entered the temple in Nob and shared out the shewbread on the altar with his companions. Jesus' opinion was that David's offence (an offence condemned by no one) was perfectly justified because of the factor of hunger, because he was 'in need of food'. And so it followed that he and his disciples were also innocent of any offence, for they too had been *hungry* and *in need*. But he does not stop there; he goes on to say: 'But if ye had known what this meaneth, I will have mercy, and not sacrifice, ye would not have condemned the guiltless.' And then he gets right to the point: 'The Sabbath was made for man, and not man for the Sabbath. Therefore the Son of man is Lord also of the Sabbath.'

Commenting on this passage, Craveri stresses that the words 'Son of man' are to be read simply as 'a man'. If they are, then Jesus' thinking is absolutely clear. The Sabbath as a day of rest should be put to man's use, to

> refresh him after the six working days, not to impose penances and hardships on him. But traditional exegesis, prejudiced by the conviction that 'the Son of man' should mean a declaration of his own divinity by Jesus, explains these words in a very different way, nullifying the very human and unselfish concern of Jesus with those who labour and are burdened: 'I, the Son of man, am Lord of the Sabbath,' and hence: 'The Holy day should be dedicated to me alone' – not for rest but for worship![23]

In Leslie Houlden's view, the specialness of Jesus was described in a variety of ways by the ancient writers. Some spoke of him as an eschatological prophet, as the Son of man, as the Messiah. Some saw him as the embodiment of the pre-existent wisdom of God. Others described him as the Logos (word of reason) of God. This way of talking sometimes became personal, intimate, and he became God's pre-existent Son come down to earth – a verbal re-minting of ideas which, although imprecise and perhaps even incoherent, accurately reflected the state of mind of those who sensed a refreshing and radical departure from energyless credal notions. Houlden puts this change in language into a living context and reminds us that through the teachings of Jesus the people's sense of God had been reshaped and revitalized.[24]

In Jesus as the Messiah of Israel, a stage of theological creativity had erupted which signalled a breaking away from ossified religious ideas. But no Jew in his right mind believed that Jesus was God incarnate, that he was somehow God roaming around in a human body. Such a notion, if voiced, would have earned a stoning. The Jews believed that the Kingdom of God was at hand, and that everyone, Jew and Gentile, would be affected. Israel, if she remained holy in the Last Days, if she could muster a grand and collective obedience to the will of God, would help usher in an age of collective understanding, an age of peace and prosperity for the whole world through the auspices of an 'Anointed One', a Messiah. History was about to come to a juddering halt, and Jesus, much to his disciples' growing dismay, was carrying the Messiah's mantle.

Christianity has got around the problem of the double nature of Christ by ignoring the 'Messiah' and theologically working the 'Christ' up into what has been described as the *Christos Pantocrator*. Jesus as the 'Messiah' is the human being; Jesus as the 'Christ' is something entirely different. Don Cupitt succinctly captures the problem of Jesus' double nature by saying that 'it is as if Jesus were at one moment Clark Kent and at the next Superman.'[25] The incarnation doctrine has it that the Two Natures were so intrinsically fused that Jesus was simultaneously *all* human and *all* divine – an utterly impossible combination of opposites quite beyond anyone's capacity to understand or explain. And yet this incomprehensible notion continues to be voiced from pulpits, and congregations and men of the cloth take it for granted. Well, some do; but certainly not all. Some simply dismiss it as a verbal ritual, a kind of poetry which has become part and parcel of the Christian edifice – a way of talking which elevates through hyperbole the fact that Jesus had introduced a new note into the religious thinking of his day. To carry such an idea as the Two Natures as a literalism is for many thinking Christians quite impossible. To accept the idea of Jesus having Two Natures, a Virgin Birth, a Resurrection and an Ascension, not to mention a dazzling Return and a Day of Judgement, is for a rapidly growing number the equivalent of being asked to believe that Jonah swallowed the whale, and not the whale Jonah.

Offering a sober, cautious note on the issue of Jesus' sonship to God, J H Charlesworth says:

> We would be wise not to venture further with speculations about the precise meaning of sonship in the mind of Jesus. Certainly we must avoid jumping into the use of Greek concepts and vocabulary, as did the Greek fathers, and attempt to equate the substance of God with son.[26]

He adds immediately that a more reliable method of comprehending Jesus' perception of sonship is to consult Jewish reflections on the matter. I agree wholeheartedly.

THREE

THE ESSENE CONTRIBUTION

*The Church's attempt to dissociate Jesus from his time and culture,
the direct and undeniable influence of that culture on Jesus, and the
attempt by Jesus to ritualistically inaugurate the Kingdom of God
on Earth.*

Prior to the discovery of the Dead Sea Scrolls, it was believed by
Christian scholars that the Old Testament was the principal
influence on Jesus' idea of Messiahship. But with the translation
of the Scrolls it quickly became evident that Jesus and his contemporaries must have been directly influenced by the writings
and teachings of the Essene Brotherhood. Some researchers (W H
Brownlee in particular) claim that Jesus' cousin John (the Baptist)
had most probably been a member of the Essene community,[1] and
Marcello Craveri notes that John's preaching was not unlike that
of the Essenes.[2] It should also be remembered that Jesus seems to
have inherited John the Baptist's disciples, and some scholars
believe him to have initially led a similar Baptist movement.[3] Otto
Betz observes that John's baptism for the forgiveness of sins did
not have to be backed by sacrifices in the Temple, but by 'fruit
that befits repentance'. He suggests that this 'fruit' can be
compared with the 'works of the Law' offered at Qumran. In that
this clearly separates John's teaching from the Temple cult and
links him with Essene attitudes,[4] Jesus' taking over from John is
highly significant. The promise to build a 'temple not made with
hands' is to virtually cite Qumran scripture.[5]

Back in 1967 Craveri was able to say that the belief that Jesus
was a member of some Essene group was gaining ground. Modern
researchers, on the whole, do not go this far, but they have swung
round to the belief that the Essenes directly influenced Jesus, and
that he was very much aware of their existence. And the fact that
the Essene *Rule of the Community* contains the words 'In the
wilderness prepare the way of Yahweh' rather suggests that John

the Baptist either was influenced by Essene doctrine or was a mouthpiece for that Brotherhood.[6] Unlike the Pharisees and Sadducees, Jesus and the Essenes believed that the End Time had arrived, and his attitude to the Temple was remarkably similar to theirs. In the Sermon on the Mount Jesus blesses 'the poor in spirit', and in Luke 6:20 he blesses 'the poor' and promises them the kingdom. Both of these terms were employed by the Qumran Essenes as 'technical self-designations'.[7] It is the poor who will finally conquer. So how to explain two messianic movements with overlapping doctrinal points of view who were either not aware of one another, or not in contact?

The first to suggest an Essene influence was Karl F Bahrdt (1741–92), who was considered a dreamer. Offering more supporting evidence, the Jewish scholar Joseph Klausner (1874–1958) repeated the theory. But it is only with the latest archaeological discoveries that we have confirmation of their hypothesis.[8] Dr Shonfield was certainly of the opinion that Jesus had been directly influenced by Essene thinking, and felt that it did not take much intelligence to discover links between the Essenes and primitive Christianity. Many similarities between Essenism and early Christianity have been detected (the Eucharistic meal of bread and wine for one), but the most striking similarity is that the sacred writings of the Essenes speak of a great teacher, a *Teacher of Righteousness* who is yet to come. However, some texts speak of this figure as already come, and add the rider that he suffered martyrdom and reappeared to his followers.[9]

How odd that both the Essenes and the group led by Jesus should have been 'shaped by the galvanizing force of one prophetic and charismatic person: specifically Jesus and the Righteous Teacher'.[10] So, thinks J Charlesworth, hidden within the Dead Sea Scrolls are numerous terms and phrases and concepts once believed to be unique to Jesus. This fact alone shows him to have been a man of his time, a man whose mentality was shaped and influenced by his culture. In an essay entitled 'Recovering Jesus' Formative Background', Paolo Sacchi discusses the place of Jesus within the ideological movements of his time, and suggests that 'This might be a first step in overcoming the rigidity with which Jesus' uniqueness has been assessed.'[11]

The inner mental territory of the Essenes only became available to scholars in the middle of the twentieth century as a result of the Qumran manuscripts. Following the translation of these astonishing documents the well-guarded secrets of Essene thought and speculation began to surface – albeit at a snail's pace. But everything was not quite as straightforward as the scholars working on the scrolls at first assumed, for to guard their secrets the Essenes had employed not only cryptic language but also various codes and ciphers. Charlesworth informs us that the Qumran Essenes wrote in codes so as to hide their message from the uninitiated, and also used mirror images of texts and different alphabets and symbols.[12] One such cipher was discovered in the Old Testament book of Jeremiah by Dr Schonfield. This was a simple cipher which exchanged the first eleven letters of the Hebrew alphabet for the last eleven in reverse order. This cipher was named *Atbash*, being derived from the play of letters. When applied by Schonfield to some of the unintelligible and apparently meaningless words in the Scrolls, this simple cipher immediately delivered up sensible text.

A prime example of this is the unscrambling of the name Taxo from the key sectarian book the *Assumption* or *Testament of Moses*. Because it was an unintelligible name, Schonfield applied the Atbash cipher and came up with the Hebrew personal name *Asaph*. This too was not all it seemed. Asaph was reputed to have had a hand in the building of Solomon's Temple, and it was known that his descendants had become choristers in the Temple. A legendary figure in both Jewish and Muslim literature, and a master of secret arts and medical skills, Asaph began to align as a possible historical shadow for the central figure in Essene thought, the True Teacher, or Teacher of Righteousness. This figure – mysterious, enlightened and nameless – flitted ghost-like throughout Essene teaching and seemed to anticipate the idea of the Messiah through suffering and rejection. A figure of extraordinary power and presence, the True Teacher had guided the Essene community towards a fulfilment of God's will and the conditions necessary to initiate the Last Times. Writing of his discovery, Schonfield admits to at first not sufficiently appreciating the importance of the Asaph material, and this in spite of the fact that aspects of it cropped up from time to time in the specialist literature. The penny did eventually drop, however, and he turned with great interest to the medieval document *The Sacred Book of Abraham the Jew*, and to writings from the East which told of a teacher by the name of Jo-asaph or

Yuz-Asaf. Carefully tracking the Asaph story, our intrepid
scholar then tackled the Jo-asaph aspect, and turned to the
biblical account of Jacob's favourite son, Joseph, whose *supposed*
death was the central theme of the story.

In Joseph, the Essenes had seen an anticipation of their True
Teacher, and there soon emerged the figure of a 'Son of Joseph'
Messiah, and a 'Son of David' Messiah. For Schonfield, the
pieces of the puzzle were beginning to fall into place. There
was a long and complicated history lying behind the idea of
Messiahship, and Jesus could not possibly have entertained the
idea of his being the Messiah of Israel without a direct awareness
of that history, and contact with those who were propagating it
during those difficult years of Roman occupation. The term
'Messiah', as everyone then realized, meant an 'anointed king',
and an anointed king in the popular mind referred to a 'liberator',
a figure of unquestionable political intention.

A Messianic mythology was attached to the True Teacher
of the Essenes, and this mythology was linked to Joseph, son of
Jacob, feared dead by his father, but actually alive and very much
in control as the ancient story showed. Apparently slaughtered,
Joseph had survived, and the children of Israel were instructed
henceforth to make atonement for themselves once a year.
Schonfield asks if there is perhaps more to this simple story than
meets the eye. Why is the death of Joseph linked with the Day of
Atonement, since Joseph did not die? And in another of the
sectarian books, the *Testament of Benjamin*, what was meant by
Joseph's younger brother's statement: 'In thee [Joseph] shall be
fulfilled the prophecy of Heaven, which says that the blameless
one shall be defiled for lawless men, and the sinless one shall die
for godless men.' Schonfield knew this text could not possibly
apply to the biblical Joseph; it did not make any sense. And
neither did the reference to the Day of Atonement make sense
when applied to Joseph – Joseph had not died, he had merely
appeared to die.

In Essene terminology, 'Messiah ben Joseph' (the Anointed Son
of Joseph) designated the Man who would undergo suffering and
perform the perfect will of God. This Man, this very special
human being, was linked esoterically with the Man Celestial, the
Son of Man, or Sky Man, in whose image Adam had been
formed. Behind all of this lay the Essene Teacher of
Righteousness, the True Teacher conceived by the Essenes as 'the

Man, the archetypal man who reflected the divine qualities to be found in the creation'.[13] Known only to the initiates of the Essene Brotherhood, this Teacher's identity is still being debated. But that he was instrumental in bringing the Essene movement into existence is certain, for it was he who drew up the code of behaviour that they followed, and it was certainly he who initiated the study and distribution of the oracles concerning the Messiah.

The Essenes, it seems, had developed a two-pronged philosophy of the Messianic – the spiritual and the political – and believed that you could not have the one without the other. This meant that a would-be Messiah had to satisfy on two levels: the priestly and the regal. Such a dualistic interpretation eventually led to the development of a doctrine which postulated two Messiahs, one of priestly stock, the other of regal stock. In Israel both the high priests and the kings were 'anointed ones'. These 'sons of oil' were thought of as 'Messiahs', which is to say 'Christs', and their offices were of eternal duration according to God's covenant with Levi and Judah.[14] Schonfield points out that at the beginning of the Christian era the followers of John the Baptist identified him with the former, and Jesus with the latter – John was the son of the priest Zechariah, Jesus the son of Joseph, who was of the line of David.[15]

Jewish speculation also allowed for two messiahs: Messiah ben Joseph and Messiah ben David. The outcome of the idea of a True Teacher and of two messiahs are later seen in the New Testament where both roles, that of priest and king, sufferer and ruler, are assigned to Jesus. So it seems that John the Baptist and Jesus responded to the idea of two messiahs and perhaps played out the roles ascribed to these figures by the Essenes – roles which the gospels dutifully record along with certain misunderstandings or camouflagings.[16] What has to be fully appreciated is the undeniable impact the ideas of the Essene Brotherhood had, not only on the thinking of John the Baptist and Jesus but on the whole religious and political climate of the times. And because John the Baptist was to die early on, and Jesus was a blood relation, it was entirely legitimate for Jesus to take on the double role of priestly and regal Messiah if indeed John was the other Messiah.

The eventual home of the Essene Brotherhood was at Qumran, close to the Dead Sea, and although overrun by the Romans in

67–70 CE, Essenism survived in both Syria and Egypt, where the Brotherhood were known as Therapeuts (also sometimes referred to as Gnostics). Schonfield is at pains to make clear that these offshoots continued for centuries. Qumran was without doubt an inhospitable place. The Roman historian Pliny described it thus:

> On the west coast of Lake Asphaltis [the Dead Sea] are settled the Essenes, at some distance from the noisome odours that are experienced on the shore itself. They are a lonely people, the most extraordinary in the world, who live without women, without love, without money, with palm trees for their only companions.[17]

In *The Messianic Legacy* Richard Leigh observes that the Essenes belonged to the third major sub-division of Judaism, and that in both life-style and teaching they were more rigorous and austere than either the Sadducees or the Pharisees. This is an important point. The Essenes were not some tiny sub-group, some insignificant sprinkling of half-crazed desert dwellers out of sight and out of mind. They were the third major sub-division of Judaism, and as such had as high a religious profile as either the Sadducees or the Pharisees. They were, it seems, mystically inclined, and probably subscribed to some form of reincarnation theory. They were skilled in the therapeutic use of herbs, enamoured with astrology, numerology and other esoteric studies, but were always careful to apply such knowledge in a strictly Judaic context. Leigh also records that the Essenes were 'looser and more diffuse in their organisation, less centralised and less uniform than the Sadducees and the Pharisees'.[18] Not all Essenes, we discover, subscribed to precisely the same things: what they had in common was a belief in a direct, experiential knowledge of God. But the most important of Leigh's descriptions of this sect is that four major misconceptions still cling to them: that they lived in exclusively isolated monastic desert communities; that they were few in number; and that they were wholly celibate and wholly non-violent. All of these ideas are now known to be erroneous.[19]

That the Essenes were to be found not only in the desert but also in the urban centres is not generally realized. In fact there seems to have been a network of houses belonging to the Essenes which were used by themselves and other wandering brothers. J H Charlesworth refers to such an arrangement in the Foreword to *Jesus and the Dead Sea Scrolls*,[20] and Leigh and his co-authors reveal that this network of houses was community-based and self-supporting: craftwork, commerce and trade were pursued to cover upkeep. It is also noted that not all Essenes were celibate, and that neither the Dead Sea Scrolls nor any other known Essene document mentions celibacy. Josephus is the source of this widely-held notion, but admits that there were Essenes who married. The Scrolls themselves flatly contradict the notion of enforced celibacy by supplying rules specifically designed to cover married sect members with children. As for the idea that the Essenes were non-violent, Essene documents found at the fortress of Masada in the 1960s rather suggest the opposite. Masada held out for two years against experienced Roman commanders and well-disciplined troops, and some of the defenders were unmistakably Essene in religious orientation.[21]

The popular conception of the Essenes as a small, insignificant religious group buried out in the desert, and therefore out of contact with everything and everyone, is quite wrong. Professor Robert Eisenman has blasted this myth to pieces by tracing the various names by which members of the Essene community referred to themselves. The list is long and informative, and includes the Sons of Light, the Sons of Truth, the Sons of Zadok, the Men of Melchizedek, the Ebionim, the Hassidim, and the Nozrim or Nazarenes.[22] These groups constituted a 'movement', and this movement was at base an Essene conglomerate – the *Essean-Essene*, the 'Holy Ones'. Of particular interest is the fact that Eisenman includes the fanatical Zealots in this grouping. The Zealots, founded by Judas of Galilee at the dawn of the Christian era, are described as 'zealous for the Law', and in this piece of shorthand lies a clue by which members of the same movement can be identified. Leigh draws our attention to the fact that in the Acts of the Apostles (21:20) the Nazarenes, as part of the general Essene movement, are described as being 'zealous for the law'. This description carries Zealot overtones. Eisenman does not differentiate between Zealots and Nazarenes, and even suggests that the families of Jesus and John the Baptist may well have been related to Judas of Galilee, leader of the Zealots.[23]

THE ROUGH GALILEANS

Jesus' home was the semi-heathen and despised Galilee, his mother-tongue Galilean Aramaic – the uncouth dialect which identifies Peter as a Galilean when he supposedly denies Jesus in Jerusalem. Conquered by Aristobulus I in 104–103 BCE, Galilee was forcibly converted to Judaism, even to the extent of its population's having to undergo compulsory circumcision. Marked out as a place lacking in orthodoxy, a place of political rebellion, unrest and resistance, the term 'Galilean' was often used to describe those of the Zealot Party. In the forefront of the resistance movement against the Romans and the Jewish authorities subservient to them, the Galileans were considered hot potatoes wherever they turned up. Dr Schonfield points out that the Pharisees had an 'uphill struggle to contend with the Galilean way of life'.[24] Affected by feelings of bitterness and distrust, the Galileans and Judeans stood apart in just about everything. The idea of the Messiah's coming out of Galilee, was, to most Judeans, almost unthinkable. Jesus' Galilean disciples are shown to be unhappy with his desire to go to Judea, and remind him that the Judeans tried to stone him. It must also have been at the back of their minds that the Judeans had called Jesus a demon-possessed Samaritan. Schonfield remarks, 'We are so familiar with the application of the term "Jew" to all persons of Jewish faith that we may not realise that in the New Testament the name is sometimes used in the narrower sense to mean Judeans, the inhabitants of Judea, compared with Galileans or Samaritans.'[25]

Galilee was also the centre for sectarian activities. The Rechabites and Kenites, both with ancient tribal histories, flourished there near to the Sea of Galilee. And the early 'Penitents of Israel', composed of the purist Sadducees from the Temple in Jerusalem, left Judea and made their headquarters in the land of Damascus. Many sectaries founded settlements in the northern districts, and these 'Elect of Israel' of the latter days interacted with like-minded spirits among the groups devoted to the old Nazarite way of life. And it is here, in Galilee, that the Aramaic term 'Essean-Essene' is coined to describe these loosely related groups, each bearing a different name but united in vision. Schonfield reveals that in that region in the time of Jesus an ancient Israelite religion was evident, and that it persisted in spite of efforts by the Judeans to wipe it out.[26] That Jesus' Galilean disciples must have felt out of place in the cosmopolitan atmosphere of Judea and Jerusalem is certain – their rough speech would have caused comment, and Jesus himself would have faced similar difficulties. 'Who would heed a prophet,' says Schonfield, 'who spoke the outlandish tongue of the north?'[27]

In his book *Jesus the Jew*, Geza Vermes describes the northern-most district of Palestine as 'a little island in the midst of unfriendly seas'.[28] To the west Galilee was bordered by Ptolemais; to the north by Syro-Phoenician Tyre and Sidon; to the east by Gualanitis, Hippos and Gadara; and to the south it was separated from Judea by the Hellenistic territory of Scythopolis and *hostile* Samaria. During the New Testament period Galilee was thus an autonomous and self-contained politico-ethnic unit with an administrative machine distinct from that of Judea. Throughout the life of Jesus Galilee was administered not by the Romans but by the Herodian tetrarch, Antipas. The Romans only assumed control of Galilee (but not the region of the Lake of Tiberias) from 44 to 66 CE. The Herodians were the native aristocracy and administered all of the 204 cities and villages of Upper and Lower Galilee. Due to its extraordinary fertility of soil, and its devotion to agriculture, Galilee was economically self-supporting and relatively wealthy. Vermes suggests that Galilean self-sufficiency, side by side with its historical legacy and unsophisticated simplicity of life was 'likely to have nourished the pride and independence of its inhabitants'.[29] This 'independence' was in fact a fierce nationalism from which stemmed, according to Simon Dubnov, 'all the revolutionary movements which so disturbed the Romans'.[30]

It is in fact a possibility that all Zealot agitation against the Romans sprang from one Galilean family, that of Judas of Galilee, son of the chief brigand, Ezekias. Spoken of as 'an object of terror to all men', Judas the Galilean became co-founder of the politico-religious Zealot movement along with a Pharisee by the name of Zadok. The Jewish historian Josephus describes these staunch Galilean nationalists as lovers of freedom who 'always resisted any hostile invasion' and were 'from infancy inured to war'.[31] So it is with interest that one considers the question put to Jesus by his disciples (Acts 1:6): 'Lord, will you at this time restore again the kingdom to Israel?' Are we to assume that the kingdom of Israel and the often-mentioned 'Kingdom of God' were one and the same? Jesus was without doubt considered politically and religiously suspect by the rulers of Jerusalem simply because he was a Galilean with a Galilean following: such a following automatically qualified him as a potential rebel. And his words and deeds throughout the New Testament seem to support the concept of his being a rebellious spirit, a religious teacher with highly unorthodox views and, it would seem, something to hide.

THE ZEALOTS

Members of the Zealot movement, or Party, came from among the sectaries. At the time of Jesus, Zealot agitation against the Roman Empire was already under way, and becoming dangerous. Acting as envoys (apostles), the Zealots sought support among the Jews of Judea for what they believed would be the final defeat of the Roman scourge. Richard Leigh describes Zealot activity as 'perhaps the most important backdrop against which Jesus' drama enacted itself'.[32] Hopes for a future free of Roman domination were running high as Jesus and his followers almost dizzily went from town to town. Amidst mounting excitement and fervour Jesus delivered his heavily veiled messianic message – too direct a statement at any moment would have resulted in his immediate arrest. The atmosphere was electric. Warned by the pious that the grand Climax of the Ages was about to strike, the Jewish people steeled themselves for the appearance of their Messiah, their promised war leader who would initiate the Last Days and lead them to a glorious victory over the hated Romans.

Rome was the arch-enemy in Palestinian eyes. Jews who supported the Roman rule were scorned and despised – particularly those of the priesthood whose Graeco-Roman sympathies were seen to directly undermine Israel's holy standing before God. The battle with the Romans and their Jewish sympathizers had been going on for many years. Between 65 and 37 BCE, there had been a series of long, sanguinary wars. Too many to enumerate, these wars systematically destroyed parts of the nation and helped divide it against itself. The heady days of Maccabaean military success were over. Prior to the Maccabaean backlash against the Romans, Judea had been an insignificant district, a mere extension of Syrian Palestine. Herodotus, painstaking by any definition, never mentions Judea, but he does refer to the 'Syrians of Palestine'. Through the Maccabeans, the borders of Judea were enlarged and 'Philistia' became the land of Israel. John Hyrcanus conquered Samaria, Edom, parts of Moab and probably Lower Galilee; Judas Aristobulus conquered and Judaized Upper Galilee; and Alexander Jannaeus conquered Gadara, Amathus, Pella, Dium, Hippos, Gerasa, Gaullana, Seleucia, the fortified city of Gamala across Jordan, and the towns of Philistia which had been completely Hellenized. From that moment Philistia (Palestine) ceased to exist, and took on the name of Judea – the land of Israel.

By the end of the reign of Alexander Jannaeus, the enlarged Judean boundaries were almost identical with those of David and Solomon. The defeated cities were compulsorily Judaized and/or repopulated by Jews; those who refused to accept Judaism were destroyed. The irony of this is that the Jews themselves had already undergone, and would again undergo, identical forms of persecution. The Maccabaean backlash was the result of such persecutions, its victories and its enforced subjugation of peoples a replay of its own earlier anguish and bitterness. And so, from being a tiny principality virtually unknown to the Romans, Judea swallowed her neighbours, established through conquest and conversion what it believed to be its ancestral home, and in turn attracted the attention of the ever vigilant Roman Empire.

But even at the height of its success, all was not well. The sons of Alexander Jannaeus, Hyrcanus II and Aristobulus II, soon became rivals for the throne. Deterioration set in quickly. Enter the father of Herod the Great (Antipater the Edomite) to stir up trouble over the high priesthood, and Aretas, King of Arabia, to murky the waters of dispute. Civil war resulted, and the beginning of the destruction of the land of Israel with the intervention of Pompey's legate Scaurus. For the next 30 years Israel would be methodically stripped of all her territorial gains, the final insult being the enforced enthronement of the Roman puppet Herod the Great. Combined with Herod's tyranny, and followed by the Romans' assuming absolute power in Judea, these wars eventually destroyed the Jewish nation's fighting edge, undermined it as a state, and ended by stirring into this mix of deterioration and despair the hope of a political Messiah and the idea of a priestly Messiah who would enact a miraculous two-pronged rescue of the nation when the time was right. Such hopes, harboured in the heart and contradicted daily by total subjection to Roman authority, bred confusion in the popular mind, and without doubt deeply affected Jesus in the early days of his ministry.

In a potted history of rebellious events, Dr Schonfield reminds us that when Herod the Great was dying, pious youths hacked to pieces the golden eagle which the king had set up over the great gate of the Temple. And we learn of outbreaks of violence following his death; of the exploits of Judas the Zealot leader of Galilee; of a bloody battle with the Romans in the Temple courts; of the later opposition to the imposition of Roman tribute when Judea was incorporated in the province of Syria; and of the massive demonstration against Pontius Pilate when as governor he sent troops with their effigy-adorned ensigns into the holy city. 'These and many other incidents,' says Schonfield, 'testify to the acute spiritual sensitivity of the Jewish people at a period when they believed the hour of Divine Destiny was about to strike, and which engendered a mood of extreme self-criticism joined with a reckless disregard of personal safety.'[33] When all of this is taken into consideration, the sheer placidity of the gospels is difficult to comprehend. The Romans and the Zealots are there, in the distance, but everything has been carefully dampened down and smoothed out, made palatable to Roman sensibilities at the time of compilation.

There is no mention of the Zealots in the gospels, and this omission may not wholly be the result of the gospel writers' trying to avoid annoying their Roman readers – it is more probable that they were simply avoiding the possibility of an inadvertent link being set up between Jesus and this band of mad-hatter terrorists. And so Jesus' Galilean profile is lessened by drawing attention away from the Zealots to the Pharisees and Sadducees, no difference being made between those of Hellenistic persuasion and those who were ever faithful to the religion of Israel. For the truth of the matter, whether Christians like it or not, is that Jesus was crucified as a Zealot, and that the people he was crucified with were described as *lestai*, the term used by the Romans to identify Zealot fanatics. Jesus may not have been a Zealot himself, but as Leigh reminds us, there are some very awkward passages in the gospels which rather suggest that he had a side to his nature not generally broadcast.

The absence of the Zealots in the gospels is as mysterious as the absence of the Essenes – although this double mystery may not be as mysterious as it first appears. If Jesus, as Nazarene leader and Israel's awaited Messiah, was calculating Israel's spiritual future in alignment with Old Testament prophecies, then he himself was the central pivot of the general sectarian thrust towards the Last Days, and would have rigorously avoided being recognized as such until the time was ripe. The question is, ripe for exactly what? Armed rebellion against the Romans on a massive scale? Or something utterly incomprehensible to the modern-day mind, a perhaps parallel accomplishment of ritual death and resurrection designed to literally propel Israel into the near future as a Holy Kingdom, a bastion of peace and righteousness on earth which all nations would willingly acknowledge as divinely appointed?

THE MESSIANIC TIMETABLE

The basic premise and main thrust of *The Passover Plot* is that Jesus engineered his own crucifixion and apparent resurrection in order to demonstrate and confirm that he was the promised Messiah. To do this, he embarked on a course of action calculated to fulfil the prophecies concerning the Messiah. Believing himself to be involved in a task of supreme spiritual significance, he steeled himself against the horrors of crucifixion and methodically controlled events so that he might be betrayed and condemned, flogged and pierced. In the last few hours, as everything collapsed towards the point of no return, the sense of crisis in the gospels reveals carefully wrought plans coming to fruition. Events are moving fast. With intense messianic faith and an iron will, Jesus undergoes examination and interrogation, a beating and a crowning. Lucid with intent, he consciously directs the unfolding drama and approaches the dread moment.

Preposterous? Not at all. The recognition that Jesus was working to a timetable of events related to Old Testament pro-phecies is not denied by the Church. Even the gospels state that a fulfilment of prophecy was taking place – but perhaps not quite in the manner suggested. It was not so much that events were somehow mysteriously following an Old Testament blueprint, a blueprint superimposed on reality by a higher power, but rather that Jesus (with not a little help from others) was literally stage-managing the entire drama to convince his disciples and the people of Israel that a messianic mystery was being played out. And this should not be construed as cheating, as somehow underhand or dishonest; it was anything but. He was simply following through on what he believed to be the will of God, the plan of God for the Last Days which had to be orchestrated in exactly the right manner, and in doing so was putting his life on the line. If things went wrong he would be a dead Messiah, and a dead Messiah would not be of much use to Israel. He expected to survive, and his expectation of survival was based on the same kind of planning and timing observed in the events leading up to his crucifixion. But most important of all, his belief that he would survive was bound up with his own extraordinary courage, with his unshakable belief in himself as the chosen Messiah. And this was no parochial notion, no small-time hope allied to some hazy set of religious ideas. His survival would be an event of spiritual significance which would reverberate far beyond the confines of Israel.

That Jesus planned his crucifixion and his resurrection is not only conceivable, it is highly probable. When the prophetic texts, or 'oracles' as Schonfield calls them, are considered in their entirety, and not in isolation, a clear picture of what Jesus must have expected, and therefore diligently worked towards, is evident. It is simply not acceptable that this highly intelligent man went blindly along with events; he was fully conscious of his Mission and had to bring his will to bear on the situation to ensure that the oracles were fulfilled to the letter. The texts which acted as a spur to Jesus' actions, to his arranging of events, to his sense of timing, clearly stated that he would survive the ordeal of being pierced. The oracles spoke of a conspiracy to destroy him, but went on to speak of God's mercy sparing him complete extinction of life. The words both familiar and heartening to Jesus were: 'For thou wilt not leave my soul in the grave; neither wilt thou suffer thy holy one to see corruption. Thou wilt show me the path of life.' And, similarly: 'After two days will he revive us: and on the third day he will raise us up, and we shall live in his sight.' Revive? The oracles spoke of his being 'revived', 'saved', 'delivered' and 'redeemed' from the grave. Every possible way of saying the same thing was found by the ancient writers: he would survive. 'To this end,' says Schonfield, 'it was essential that the duration of his sufferings should be reduced to a minimum.'[34] Joseph would metaphorically appear again miraculously alive in spite of the bloody evidence supplied to his father Jacob.

For most Christians there is no difference between the Jesus of the gospels and the Christ of dogma. The Christ of dogma and theology and the Jewish boy who roamed Palestine are one and the same. And so they will find the idea of Jesus planning his crucifixion and resurrection an affront to the idealized picture they have of him. 'Why would he have to?' they will ask. Why should the Son of God, indeed God incarnate in the flesh, have to plan anything? A look from the heavens, or some such act, and everything would be accomplished. No problem for God to raise Jesus from the dead, none at all. And anyway, he had to die so that our sins could be forgiven, so that he could become our intermediary, our redemptive sacrifice. It is at exactly this point that the Jesus of theology, the Jesus of faith, the Jesus legislated into existence by Constantine as *wholly God*, obscures the Jesus of history, the Jesus of flesh and blood, the Jesus who lived an ordinary everyday life in spite of his being the Messiah of Israel. This is the Jesus who offered himself up as a human sacrifice, a sacrifice which would help initiate the awaited Kingdom of God.

So did Jesus survive his crucifixion? Dr Schonfield thinks not. The spear wound, he conjectures, killed Jesus and thwarted his plan of survival. End of story? Obviously not. Richard Leigh and his co-authors argued cogently against Schonfield's interpretation back in 1982. And the gospels themselves specifically state that Jesus survived, that he was alive after the ordeal of crucifixion and burial. At this point, however, it is necessary to read the gospels not only with great care but with present-day common sense, for the compilers have quite obviously elevated Jesus' physical survival into a miraculous event to accommodate and consolidate Paul's fully developed Christological myth. In the context of the gospels, the word 'resurrection' is equated not with survival of death in the normal sense but with the idea of divine intervention. This is to say that Jesus survived as a result of being *brought back to life by God* after he had died, rather than of his being saved from death through natural processes of resuscitation. If one wears Pauline spectacles, divine intervention is the name of the game. If, however, one is of a modern cast of mind and reasonably well-informed about how the Pauline Christological process developed, and from what it developed, then acceptance of the doctrine of divine intervention is an intellectual impossibility. To gain insight into how Paul developed his extraordinary ideas about Jesus, we have to travel back in time by way of the Nazarenes.

FOUR

THE NAZARENE PARTY

The Church's unwillingness to properly relate Israel's religious development to Jesus' idea of Messiahship, the sectarian dream of initiating the redemption of Israel and the world at large, and the problem of Paul's archetypal theology deteriorating into a pagan literalism.

The early followers of Jesus were eventually known as Nazarenes, and Jesus himself was called 'the Nazarene'. The name refers to a community whose members thought of themselves as 'preservers of the true faith of Israel'. The Nazarenes were still in existence in northern Palestine in the late fourth century. As northerners, the Nazarenes were opposed to the Judean, or southern, traditions which, they believed, had falsified the Law of Moses. Present-day Nazarenes of the Lower Euphrates are also known as 'Mandeans', and are formerly from northern Palestine. Simone Pétrement links the Mandeans to Jewish Christianity (Nazarenes) and Christian Gnosticism, but admits to being puzzled by the fact that the Mandean-Nazarenes later viewed Christianity as an 'enemy' in spite of having saviour figures and a system of mortality analogous to Christian morality. She is also puzzled by the fact that they put themselves under the patronage of John the Baptist.[1] According to Dr Schonfield, however, the Mandean-Nazarenes 'are a baptising sect holding John the Baptist in special honour, and before they moved to Mesopotamia they could well have had a relationship with Essene and other groups who practised ritual ablution'. Schonfield also mentions that he has found a direct link between the Mandeans' *Sidra d'Yaha* (Book of John the Baptist) and the Aramaic *Genesis Apocryphon* discovered among the Dead Sea Scrolls.[2]

Extending from the second century BCE through the period covered by the gospels and the Acts of the Apostles, the Temple priesthood had prostituted itself to the Herodian kings, accommodated itself to Roman administrations and become deeply influenced by Greek secularism. An alternative priesthood was therefore formed from the purist breakaway Sadducee group (Essenes, Zadokites or Zaddikim), and this group, upholding the principle of the expected Davidic Messiah, psychologically harassed its Temple counterpart by its very existence. Schonfield, quoting from the *Clementine Recognitions*, refers to this break-away group as the 'first Schism',[3] and confirms that these Sadducees are Zadokites, members of the *same* Essene sect as those at Qumran. These 'Sons of Zadok' deliberately separated themselves from the Temple priesthood so that they could properly uphold the Law and avoid pollution. The Talmud says that Israel did not go into captivity until 24 varieties of sectarians had come into existence.[4]

THE OLD ISRAELITE RELIGION

The Israelite religion of northern Palestine so dear to the Nazarenes seems to have absorbed much of the worship of the Syrians and Phoenicians. This older faith carried folklore and ideas and usages foreign to its southern neighbour, and the pre-Christian Nazarenes of the north are shown by Epiphanius to have had an affinity with the gnostically inclined Samaritans, and the Samaritans with the Essenes. There is also thought to have been a connection with the Rechabites, who led a bedouin-type existence and are suspected of having become as much a sect as a clan while living in the wilderness. Through northern Arabia, the wilderness linked Syria with Mesopotamia, and the sect-clans which lived there were known as the 'Holy ones of God' (Essean-Essene), a description corresponding to the northern Aramaic word *chasya* meaning 'saint'. Jesus the Nazarene was leader of a community of the 'Way', and this was much like the 'Way of the Wilderness' followed by the disparate Essene groups as listed by Eisenman in his 1983 study *Maccabees, Zadokites, Christians and Qumran*.

Schonfield draws our attention to the curious fact that Saul of Tarsus (later to become Paul) travels to Damascus to arrest Nazarene followers of the already crucified Jesus. After Saul's 'blinding' revelation en route, someone by the name of Ananias of Damascus appears, and Saul's sight is secretly restored – or if you prefer, he has his eyes opened *with a few explanations*. From there on Saul/Paul preaches in the name of Jesus. Ananias is described as 'a devout man of the Law, having a good report of all the Jews which dwelt there'. He informs Saul/Paul that he has been chosen to 'see' and 'hear' the Just One, and like any typical Essene urges him to wash away his sins by baptism. Dr Schonfield homes in at this point on the fact that after his conversion, Paul returns to Damascus, probably to stay with a Nazarene community, suggesting that Ananias was himself a Nazarene. This would account, he suggests, for 'several features of the Pauline doctrine (the Heavenly Messiah and the Second Adam) which are still reflected in the literature of the Mandean-Nazarenes, and the passages in the Pauline Epistles reminiscent of the Dead Sea Scrolls.' He adds for good measure: 'The Just One of whom Ananias speaks recalls the revered Teacher of Righteousness of the Qumran Essenes.'[5] Ever careful, Schonfield slowly elaborates, and we learn that the Just One had been the leader of the Penitents of Israel, and that we are meant to assume that Jesus the Nazarene was the expected Just One.

And yet Jesus did not function in quite the expected manner. Teacher he certainly was, but his behaviour did not belong to the wilderness traditions. His idea of Messiahship was at odds with those of his family (dynastic leaders of the Nazarene movement), and he kept company with the wrong people. His idea of Sabbath observance was to act as if many of the laws and customs did not exist, and he was of the opinion that one could eat anything without being defiled. But most damaging of all was the fact that he wanted the 'secret' teachings of the saints, the Holy Ones, shouted from the rooftops. So was Jesus an apostate? Was he a false Messiah? As Messiah ben Joseph, Jesus had taken on the role of Suffering Servant, and in doing so had embodied a mystery, the mystery of a Just One carrying the characteristics of the old Syrian cult of Adonis-Tammuz, the old northern Palestinian fertility cult in whose liturgies the Suffering Servant is addressed as 'Shepherd'. When Jesus said 'I am the good Shepherd', he was speaking, however distantly, as the dying god Adonis-Tammuz; yet at the same time he was in strict accordance with messianic thinking.

In *The Messianic Legacy*, Richard Leigh names Paul as the originator of a new religion around Jesus' life and teachings which eventually becomes an adversary of Judaism. Paul's message, he says, 'is fused with Greco-Roman thought, with pagan traditions, with elements from a number of mystery schools.'[6] Schonfield too is of the opinion that foreign elements belonging to the old Syrian religion have been grafted onto the main stem of northern Palestinian messianic tradition – there is an echo, however indistinct, of the dying god Tammuz being offered for the sake of the land, and the people. And the question has to be asked concerning Isaiah's Suffering Servant in the Old Testament: Why was he suffering? What is this image of a man being so maltreated all about? Is it possible that the Suffering Servant of antiquity, the man so brutally treated that he is virtually unrecognizable, was being ritually sacrificed? Some readers will lift up their hands in horror at such a suggestion, but the history of Israel, like the life of Jesus, is full of surprises. And it is now known that the Essene sectaries embodied a theme of salvation allied in some way to suffering.

The Jewish nation did not always worship Yahweh with complete fidelity. The prophets of Israel seem to spend an inordinate amount of time trying to convince the children of Israel that they had gone astray from the living God of their ancestors. And there are indications throughout the Old Testament of a rival form of worship, of two priesthoods, of two perceptions of religious duty. There is even mention in the book of Ezekiel (8:7–14) of a secret room in the Temple itself where what appears to be a rival Sanhedrin of 70 members practises abominations. This room, described by Ezekiel, is said to have been decorated with animals, and to be dedicated to a goddess – probably Astarte. In the same chapter we learn that at the north gate of the temple there are women lamenting the death of Tammuz. So things were not always as neat and straightforward in Jewish religious affairs as many would like to think.

The Nazarenes, under James the Just (Jesus' brother), had a set of beliefs tantalizingly close to what Paul eventually advocated, and it only took a little twist in perception to see things Paul's way and change the whole direction of sectarian messianic thought – well, a portion of it at least. Later, after the destruction of Jerusalem, the death of James and the scattering of his flock, many Jews would experience that tiny twist of perception and come out on Paul's side. And as the Gentiles were already only too familiar with the idea of gods who died special deaths for the sake of the land, and therefore the people, then Paul's hyperbolized Messiah would eventually be widely accepted.

In his precise and highly detailed study of Jesus' life, Marcello Craveri clearly spells out what was going on with regard to Paul:

The idea of a Messiah who must suffer and die in order to accomplish the redemption of the people of Israel was totally alien to the Jews. Even if traditional theology likes to pretend that the notion already existed in the lifetime of Jesus, everyone knows that it was instead the most startling of innovations introduced into Christianity by Paul.[7]

This is all quite true, but as already stated, the Essenes did have a conception of redemption at the heart of their teachings, and the Essenes were not strictly Jews (Judeans) – they were northern sectaries holding quite different doctrinal points of view from those of the Pharisees.

Richard Leigh's summation of Paul's new religion is also worth looking at. In alignment with Craveri he tells us that it is possible to trace specific elements to the traditions surrounding Tammuz, Osiris, Attis, Adonis, Dionysus and Zoroaster. Most of these figures had had a god for a father and a virgin for a mother. Mithraism in particular had exerted an enormous influence on the coming together of Christian traditions. This religion, highly influential among the soldiers of Rome, 'postulated an apocalypse, a day of judgement, a resurrection of the flesh and a second coming of Mithras'. On his return, Mithras was expected to defeat evil. And as if this were not enough, Mithras was held to have been born in a cave or grotto and attended by shepherds. The shepherds even brought gifts! But the most astonishing part of this story is a passage from the Mithraic communion where Mithras says: 'He who shall not eat of my body nor drink of my blood so that he may be one with me and I wish him, shall not be saved.'[8] So was it particularly this kind of influence, and challenge, which made Paul push the concept of the Jewish Messiah further than it was supposed to go, or had there always been – as Dr Schonfield suggests – a pagan element deeply buried in the conception of the Suffering Servant?

Living as Christians do in the world of Pauline Christology, in the perfectly formed, comfortable, and wholly encompassing revelation of Jesus as divine being sent to earth for the redemption of all human beings, they have felt no need to seriously contemplate the possibility of pagan influences on either the prophecies or their outcome. Everything is simple and straightforward. Jesus died on the Cross for our sins and that is the end of it. God did it all. There is simply nothing further to talk about. But this does not change the historical reality; it merely causes the one who thinks this way to step further into the shadows of improperly formed thought and conclusion. And because all sidestepped realities have a nasty habit of breaking into view when we least expect them or desire them, it is surely better that we attend to such realities than wait to be overtaken by them. Yes, the arguments for pagan influences on Jesus and Paul and the later Roman Catholic Church have been done to death by many a writer on this subject, but such influences did exist, and scholarly unwillingness on the part of Christians to properly integrate such knowledge into their mental picture of Jesus is a real failing. And recent discoveries in relation to the Essenes demand that we re-evaluate what was going on way back then.

The story of Jesus and the Christian faith is not simple and straightforward; neither is it devoid of political pressure and cultic influence. Christianity, as we have seen, has been carefully cut loose from its Nazarene/Essene beginnings, but it so intrinsically embodies these influences that the truth of its origins cannot for much longer be held at bay. Christian scholars are slowly waking up out of their comfortable dream of everlasting salvation through Jesus and having to face the fact that their interpretation of things past may be somewhat lacking, indeed comically top-heavy with interpretations resting on suspect premises. Maybe it isn't all as simple as it looks. Maybe Jesus' supposed death on the Cross held another significance, another meaning which got lost in the furore of a nation under brutal attack. Maybe by ignoring the Jewish background of the gospels, and indeed of Jesus himself, we have grossly distorted Jesus' life and created a being suspended between fact and fancy, a hybrid, a sexual and ethical paragon whose effect on the world has been to confuse, distract and anger.

THE MELCHIZEDEK LEGACY

It cannot be doubted that seasonal changes have powerfully impressed and influenced the human mind down through the ages, and it is certain that some kind of attempt was made to control these grand climatic processes. Winter was a dark and deadly calamity; spring a great joy; summer virtually a paradisiacal experience. At some point human beings imagined possible control over the seasons, and invented rites and spells and ceremonies to ensure the return of rain, sun, animals and fruits. In the course of time this magical conception slowly gave way to the more advanced notion that there were powers or forces behind the seasons. These powers waxed and waned in strength, and were eventually interpreted as great beings susceptible to birth and death. As this process developed, highly imaginative stories were invented to capture and embody the intricacies of the mysterious patterns encountered. And as the human mind itself began to evolve its own highly complex patterns of behaviour and interaction, these myths of creation and seasonal change began to take on a sophistication and depth which further stretched human mental capacity. Magical theory had been replaced by religious theory, but much that was magical in conception continued to circulate within the confines of religious sensibility. It was imagined, for instance, that the failing energies of the life principle, the god who ruled spring and summer, could be induced to return, and that these energies only did return because of the ceremonies performed. Religious theory was now thoroughly blended with magical practice, and the one could not be separated from the other without a rupturing of the anthropomorphic vision underlying both.

The most striking of the climatic changes was of course to vegetation. The influence of the seasons on animals was certainly noticeable, but not as dramatic as that which happened to plants and trees, flowers and grasses. However, as the bond between animals and plants was believed to be even closer than it actually is, and the seasonal reviving of plants was equated with the union of the sexes, then both animals and human beings were seen as indivisibly connected to the world of vegetation. Under the names of Osiris, Tammuz, Adonis, and Attis, the peoples of Egypt and Western Asia personified the yearly decay of life, particularly vegetable life, by a god who annually died and rose again from the dead.[9]

For the Semitic peoples of Babylonia and Syria, the god worshipped was addressed as Adonis, Adonis being the Semitic *Adon*, 'lord', the title of honour given by the Semites to Tammuz, the vegetation god. In the Old Testament the title 'Adonai' is often applied to Jehovah. It is interesting to note that the Greeks, through a misunderstanding, changed this title of honour to a proper name, just as the title 'Jesus the Christ' has been shortened to the proper name Jesus Christ. It is thought that the old priestly kings of Jerusalem regularly played the part of Adonis/Tammuz in special ceremonies, and the names of the old Canaanite kings seem to confirm this. For instance, 'Adoni-zedek' is reckoned to be a divine name rather than a human title – it is thought to mean 'lord of righteousness', the equivalent of 'Melchizedek', the name of the famous Jebusite king to which the kings of Israel are considered to be directly connected. So it is not really surprising that we later find Ezekiel complaining that the women of Jerusalem are lamenting the death of Tammuz at the north gate of the Temple: they were simply continuing a custom observed by the early Canaanites before the Hebrew invasion.[10]

According to J G Frazer, Jerusalem had once been the seat of a 'dynasty of spiritual potentates or Grand Lamas, who held the keys of heaven and were revered far and wide as kings and gods in one'.[11] King David, a warrior with an eye for the main chance, obviously chose Jerusalem as his new capital for this very reason, not just because it was a natural fortress. For on taking Jerusalem, David made himself heir to the ancient kings of the city and plugged into the repute of a dynasty of kings considered to be gods, thereby taking on a royal crown *and* a god's nimbus.[12]

Melchizedek is a figure of mystery and importance in biblical tradition because he is believed to have been both a king and a priest, connected with Jerusalem, and revered by Abraham, who is said to have paid a tithe to him. He appears in person only once in the book of Genesis, and gives bread and wine to Abraham on his return from battle (Genesis 14:18–20). That Abraham should recognize the authority of a Canaanite priest-king is startling – there is nothing like it anywhere else in biblical literature. So highly respected must this priest-king have been that even Abraham felt the need to acknowledge the other priesthood's authenticity and authority. Melchizedek's priesthood is considered special in both the Old and the New Testaments – and this in spite of the fact that his god was El Elyon, considered to have been the chief god of the Canaanite pantheon. El Elyon was venerated in Jerusalem prior to David's conquest, and only later assimilated by Israel and used as an appellation for Yahweh.

Kamal Salibi, Professor of History at the American University of Beirut, doubts the existence of Melchizedek, but confirms

Frazer's comments concerning the equating of the Jebusite god El Elyon with Yahweh. He notes that 'Elyon' is cited in the name of the God of Israel in more than 20 passages of biblical text, where it is interestingly translated as 'Most High'.[13] There is little doubt that David consciously cultivated the connection with the Canaanite priesthood because, like Abraham, he was in awe of it – the Melchizedek story is believed to have reached its final formulation during the early Davidic monarchy. Psalm 110 describes the occupant of Judah's throne as possessing forever by God's own oath a priesthood *of the kind that Melchizedek held*, so strengthening not only the idea that that priesthood was held in high regard, but of there being an intrinsic connection between the two priesthoods which allowed them to so easily coalesce. And in Acts 2:34, the figure of Melchizedek is applied as a foreshadowing of Christ's role as 'true king of righteousness and peace' – a play on the meaning of this supposed Canaanite king's name. This is another way of saying that the priesthood of Christ was superior to that of the Levitical priesthood, for as Abraham (the ancestor of Levi) had paid a tithe to Melchizedek, so Christ as a type of Melchizedek should be seen as greater than the priesthood which eventually condemned him, and this in spite of the fact that Melchizedek probably had no historical existence.

THE DIVINE KING

The early history of the Hebrew kings suggests that they were in a sense thought of as divine, as somehow representing, and to some extent embodying, Yahweh on earth. The king's throne was called the throne of Yahweh, and the anointing of the king's head with oil was believed to impart to him a portion of the divine spirit – a ritual linked with the fat of sacrificial victims. The Hebrew kings were also held responsible for drought and famine, and it was believed that they could heal the sick. Referring to this theory of sanctity, perhaps even of divinity, afforded the Hebrew kings, J G Frazer notes that in spite of there being few traces to this effect found in the Bible, any objection is weakened by the fact that these books assumed their final edited shape during the religious reforms of King Hezekiah many centuries later. Any reference to kings' being invested with the attributes of deity would have been immediately erased.[14] All incidents suggestive of pagan influence on Hebrew kings or prophets would have been smoothed away by the censors' deft touch.

The 'dying god' image behind the idea of Messiahship lies hidden in Israel's distant past; the idea of Messiahship itself lies in the Hebrews' inspired reading of the riddle of creation and the destiny of humankind. Dr Schonfield says:

> Though some of its features did not originate with the Hebrews, they absorbed them and brought them into relationship with a great vision of the ultimate Brotherhood of Man under the rule of the One God and Father of all men. The vision was not simply a cherished ideal: it was associated with a plan for its realization. According to this plan God had chosen and set apart one nation among the nations of the world . . . to be the recipient of his laws, and by observing them to offer a universal example. The Theocracy of Israel would be the persuasive illustration of a World Theocracy: it would be a 'kingdom of priests and a holy nation' witnessing to all nations. Manifestly, according to this view, the redemption of humanity waited upon the attainment by Israel of a state of perfect obedience to the will of God. By so much as Israel failed to meet the Divine requirements, by so much was the peace and well-being of mankind retarded.[15]

THE ELECT

Israel's punishment for failing to meet God's requirements constitutes the history of the Hebrews. Conquest and oppression, pestilence and famine and exile was Israel's reward for disobedience. Everyone was involved. From highest to lowest, Israel's rulers, priests and citizens carried the responsibility of humankind's ultimate redemption. When failure was apparent, God's holy prophets appeared. After centuries of minimal success, it was thought improbable that the whole nation could be brought to a suitable pitch of consecrated holiness, and so hopes were pinned on the Elect, the faithful penitents, the Essean-Essene, by whose obedience the redemption of humankind would be speeded up. But if the time of the End was prolonged, if it was pushed further and further into the future, then the pious themselves would fail to endure, so it was necessary to be aware of the signs which set the length of the term of endurance. This final stage of the messianic hope would see God intervene directly through his Anointed Ones. When the End came, these special beings would appear to announce the End Time and usher in the Kingdom of God.

This idea of Anointed Ones, of Messiahs, or of a single Messiah embodying both the regal and the priestly roles, came slowly into focus from the second century BCE onwards, based on predictions hundreds of years old and distantly shaped by pagan conceptions long since absorbed and forgotten about. The move from the 'collective' to the 'individual' was under way – the move from the individual glorified as an expression of God on earth (a legitimate and non-literal conception already developed in Judaism) would soon turn into that individual's being directly equated with God in full pagan fashion: Christianity was just around the corner.

REDEMPTION OF THE WHOLE WORLD

The Nazarenes, in conjunction with many other sectaries, expected their Messiah (Jesus) to initiate the redemption of Israel and the rest of the world through the ritual of the Cross, through the suffering of God's Anointed One. The predominantly Gentile Roman Catholic Christian faith which evolved *after Paul's death* saw Jesus not only as the redemptive sacrifice but also as having personally accomplished the deed because he was somehow God incarnate – a literalization of ancient Jewish messianic texts. To many modern Christian scholars Jesus was without doubt the awaited Messiah of Israel; he fulfilled the messianic prophecies and clearly identified himself as such in the gospels. But as Schonfield observes, 'the Messiahship of Jesus is asserted, and then side-stepped in order to disclose him in a light more congenial to Hellenic rather than Jewish concepts.'[16] The gulf between Jewish Christians and Gentile Christians was in place, and that gulf would quickly grow into a chasm, a veritable abyss which would one day almost swallow the whole Jewish nation as Christianity's inflated pagan saviour finally collapsed in on itself and produced a spiritual vacuum, a personal emptiness and almost manic individuality backed by an exponentially growing loss of faith in God. Plugging directly into the religious impulse of the German nation, Adolf Hitler would become Christ's black counterpart, Christ's shadow – Christ reversed, projected and worshipped. An archetype had run out of control.

In Christian eyes, Jesus was the awaited Jewish Messiah, but not the Messiah the Jews had hoped for. Christian reasoning went something like this. As a Messiah of love and forgiveness, a universal Messiah and Redeemer, Jesus did not fit Jewish expectations of a warrior king who would rid them of the Roman yoke. And so he was rejected, spurned, denied and eventually murdered. But this is in fact a total misconception of the Jewish Messiah. Schonfield puts things right by pointing out that such a Messiah was certainly hoped for by the peasantry of Palestine, the oppressed and ill-used masses to whom the 'niceties of prophecy mattered little',[17] but that the real expectation of the Messiah was in a righteous king who would put his trust not in men and weapons but in 'truth'. The violent ones (Zealots) were denounced by the Pharisees as not obeying the will of God. So what of Jesus' rather surprising statement that he had come to bring not peace but a sword (Luke 22:36)? What of his instruction to his disciples to purchase a sword even if it meant selling their garments? Commenting on these very passages, Richard Leigh says 'It is difficult to reconcile such references with the tradition of a mild, pacifist saviour.'[18]

True. But there is perhaps a way round this problem. As a Nazarene, Jesus was part of a multi-pronged sectarian movement which ended up with a double agenda because of a split in its ranks – a split inaugurated by Jesus himself because he was more interested in 'truth' than in 'war'. The main agenda had been to confront the Romans militarily, but Jesus broke with this view, caused a powerful splinter group to form, and then *consciously enacted the ritual of the Suffering Servant* to fulfil Old Testament prophecy and hasten the appearance of the Kingdom of God. This is to suggest that Jesus was one of two pivotal characters in the general sectarian push against Rome, the other being the Teacher of Righteousness (identified by some as John the Baptist), and that he had the sense to see that a national tussle with Rome could only end in the destruction of the Jewish nation, not its liberations. For Jesus and the Nazarenes, Imperial Rome, in spite of its splendour and military prowess, would be overcome not by force of arms, or ultimately even by the sectaries' living blameless lives on behalf of the Jewish nation, but by the power of God released through the obedience of Israel's Messiah to God's sacrificial plan. Hypnotized by a truly remarkable set of religious ideas, the Nazarenes believed that Rome would be brought to its knees not by military might but by one man's drinking 'the cup of affliction', by staging the almost magical ritual of the Suffering Servant. Another order of reality was at work, and Jesus the Galilean Messiah was the specially prepared bait.

This mystery, this extraordinary conception of divine justice and mercy held by Jesus, is what Saul-turned-Paul would eventually transpose, like a piece of music, into the doctrine of Jesus as *reflection* of God on earth. In conjunction with what he discovered about Jesus after his conversion, Paul would inadvertently release the pagan echo in the old messianic texts, and the juggernaut of Gentile Christianity would be fuelled and ready to roll. No matter that it was mixed with delicately-framed Jewish ideas about the Messiah's archetypal relationship to God – such delicacies of thought were quickly lost as pagan minds wrestled Paul's doctrine of the Mystic Christ into an interpretive framework they could understand and pass on. But for the Nazarenes, for Jesus' kith and kin, Paul's vision would be interpreted as blasphemy. Yes, Jesus had certainly been a special being, an Anointed One, a Messiah – but that was as far as it went. Ultimately he was just a man of flesh and blood born of ordinary parents. This was certainly his brother James' opinion, and James – chosen by the Nazarene Party as Jesus' natural successor, his successor by way of dynastic leadership – would eventually take on Paul and put him in his place.

THE SPLINTER GROUP

The idea of Jesus as leader of a splinter group is not as foreign as some might think. Dr Craveri notes that Jesus was a follower of John, to whom he was related, rather than the converse, and that Christianity was born as a splinter from the sect of John which survived John's death and which was later called Mandean.[19] So it seems that there had been a very close connection between John the Baptist and Jesus prior to the split. Craveri adds that the Mandeans were also known as Nazarenes, as Dr Schonfield and Simone Pétrement attest, and the fact that this Jewish scholar has also discovered a direct connection between the Mandean book of John the Baptist and the Aramaic *Genesis Apocryphon* discovered among the Dead Sea Scrolls, suggests what Eisenman has already stated: that the main sectarian groups were all part of one general movement (Essean-Essene).

Further confirmation comes from Dr Barbara Thiering in her book *Jesus the Man*, where she tells us that there is a strong *prima facie* case for believing that John the Baptist was in fact the Essene Teacher of Righteousness, and Jesus the 'wicked priest' who separated from him.[20] Suddenly the jigsaw burgeons with a picture – but it is a picture that will again and again change as new information displaces old, and different scholars bring their interpretative imaginations to bear on the often disjointed fragments of Qumran history.

With the destruction of Jerusalem and the Temple, the wholesale slaughter of the populace and the fall of Masada some years later, the fact of Jesus' basic humanity and mistaken identity should have become only too obvious to even the most starry-eyed of the sectaries. For the truth of the matter was that Jesus' Messiahship had, to say the least, failed, and failed miserably. The Romans were still in power and the Jewish nation, along with just about everyone else, was still subject to their might and arrogance. Those sectaries and Jews who had held the hope that Jesus was truly God's Anointed One now believed that they had been mistaken. Jesus had been an apostate Messiah – a fake. The mainstream Pharisees and Sadducees had not believed in him, and had said so. And not all the sectaries had been behind him – he had led a sizeable splinter group astray with his pacifism and depleted sectarian forces. So, best forgotten – and that in spite of the pathetic efforts of the Nazarenes led by his brother James to save face, to rescue a small something out of such a monumental disaster. They were still trying to say that Jesus was the Messiah, that he was God's Anointed One, and had even trumped up the story that he had survived the Cross and was still alive, and active.

FIVE

PAUL'S TWIST OF PERCEPTION

The historical background to Paul's thinking, the humour apparent in Jesus' upper room appearance to the disciples, and the utilitarian nature of Jesus' visionary appearances to Paul, and others.

The theological twist applied by Paul to Nazarene thinking eventually changed the whole trajectory of Jewish sectarian intentions and later furnished the defunct messianic vehicle with an almost demonic energy. Sectarian hopes and aspirations had been dashed, but Paul's Gentile Christians had received not the standard but the revised version of Jesus' Messiahship, and were more able to handle the fact that God's superlative 'kingdom' had not yet materialized. And there was a certain truth in what Paul had reported about Jesus' enriched Messiahship: after the Resurrection he had acted with the authority expected of such an august messianic figure. A powerful personality, self-assured and without any doubt concerning his Mission, Jesus must have had an almost hypnotic influence on those he encountered. This can be sensed throughout the gospels and the Pauline epistles, and is part of his mystery, part of his strange fascination. There is no doubt that he fully expected to be around after his crucifixion, and did in fact survive that event according to the gospel reports. Resurrection it may have been called, under the influence of Paul's expert theological guidance, but 'resuscitation' would have been a better and more truthful description.

Dr Schonfield sets the scene prior to the crucifixion when he tells us that Jesus expected to be 'revealed in all the majesty of his more comprehensive and immortal sovereignty'.[1] He then adds:

> The sceptics may regard his conviction as a mental aberration, or as a fantasy induced by the prevailing Messianic emotional atmosphere. But for Jesus his faith was of the order which could remove mountains, and therefore he could plan so far as this was humanly possible for his triumph over death, for his availability in the land of the living for

that transformation which would signal God's exaltation of him to the throne of a world to be newly born to the accompaniment of the thunders and lightnings of heavenly judgement.[2]

These are telling words. They carry us into Jesus' mentality and reveal the deep-seated fantasy which probably held him entranced.

Nazarene thinking, Jewish tradition and multi-pronged Essean-Essene speculation already held many of the secret ingredients which Paul would later enlarge upon and build up into his grandiose vision of the 'Christ'. And it should be realized that Jesus too used this same rich heritage when speaking of himself. There was, for instance, a belief that the Holy Ones, the Elect of Israel, the 'Son of Man collective' as Schonfield describes it, would perform an atoning work by their faithfulness to the Law.[3] In sectarian circles this same function was applied to a messianic personality, the Just One, the singular Son of Man. And there was, as we have seen, the Joseph mystery. This mystery was directly related to northern Palestine, for the name Joseph is synonymous throughout the Old Testament with the northern Kingdom. Schonfield's hunch is that the Joseph figure as a Suffering Just One is related to the Syrian Adonis-Tammuz cult.[4] But so integrated had such beliefs become that it was possible for Jesus to speak of himself as the 'good shepherd' without raising the spectre of Adonis-Tammuz in anyone's mind. The term 'Son of Man', as used by the sectaries, and by Jesus, was developed by the Essenes, and belonged to the sphere of Jewish mystical teaching referred to as the Archetypal or Primordial Man,[5] although as Geza Vermes shows, the same term could be used simply to denote the speaker.[6]

A key book used by the sectaries was the *Similitudes of Enoch*, a section of the Enoch collection of documents which circulated among the Saints. An antediluvian patriarch, Enoch had walked with God and had been physically translated to heaven. Understandably, Enoch was a hero. The origin and date of the *Similitudes* is uncertain. Schonfield speculates that it is not pre-Christian but Jewish-Christian, or perhaps a product of northern Nazarene-Essenism not in use in the south. Whatever its origin, or date, its contents are worth studying. For in the *Similitudes* we find not only apocalyptic and predestinarian scenarios suspiciously similar to that of Revelation and the Pauline epistles, we have the Son of Man concept *united* with the Just One and the

Messiah of Righteousness present in the mind of God before the creation of the world – a familiar enough notion to any Christian. But this figure is neither divine nor pre-existent, and that in spite of the texts which seem to suggest just that. The Son of Man is the Messiah as *idea* in the mind of God, and as such embodies *all* Messiahs, which in essence reflects the 'eternal principle of righteousness exemplified in all the Just Ones'.[7] It does not suggest, as Christians erroneously came to believe, that the Messiah was either a pre-existent divine soul or, in some incomprehensible fashion, God himself residing in his own mind as the Messiah and about to split off and descend to planet Earth.

Dr Schonfield says simply that Paul, during his time in Arabia, acquired his inspiration from such documents and developed his idea of a heavenly Messiah who incarnated in the earthly Jesus. And Jesus too continually echoes the *Similitudes* with statements about the Son of Man as judge sitting on the throne of his glory – his statements resound with regal imagery. These apparently distinct concepts – the Suffering Just One and the Glorious King – are united by Jesus, and Schonfield neatly captures the importance of this when he says 'It took a Nazorean of Galilee to apprehend from the Scriptures that death and resurrection was the bridge between the two phases. The very tradition of the land where Adonis yearly died and rose again seemed to call for it.'[8]

Paul's little twist of perception relates to his habit of imbuing ecstatic texts with literal meaning – at least, this is how it appears at first glance. Now for someone supposedly educated at the feet of the great teacher Gamaliel the Elder, this was a puzzling habit. But perhaps understandable when we realize along with Marcello Craveri that his boast to be 'an irreproachable Pharisee' is actually quite odd, and that he had shown himself again and again to be 'remarkably removed from the Pharisaic mentality'.[9] In fact he was so far removed from that mentality that the Ebionites (the most extreme Jewish group of early Christendom allied to the Nazarenes is through James the Just) actually accused him of not being of pure Jewish blood.[10] Proud of his Roman citizenship, he Latinized his name in 47 CE from Saul to Paul in honour of Sergius Paulus, the Roman Governor of Cyprus, and was from the very beginning uninterested in upholding the finicky customs of his co-religionists.[11] And something of Rabbi Gamaliel's egocentric and eccentric behaviour may also have rubbed off on this self-proclaimed Hebrew of the Hebrews, for it is said of him that he once wrote a prayer of blessing to the creator for a beautiful heathen girl he saw at a street corner. And more extraordinary still, he was fairly permissive about sexual matters. Given the task of testing the virginity of a bride by a suspicious bridegroom, he apparently made her squat over the bunghole of a wine barrel and then smelled her breath to see if the scent of wine could be detected. So was Paul a Pharisee? Indeed, was he even a Jew?

In *The Nazarene Gospel Restored*, Robert Graves and Joshua Podro describe Paul as an opponent and persecutor of the Nazarenes, and mention the allegation in the *Clementine Recognitions* that it was he who threw James the Just (Jesus' brother) down the 15 steps of the Nicanor Gate in the Temple. They also record that this same Paul, previously named Saul, became a convert to the Nazarene faith after either a vision of, or a *meeting with*, Jesus post-crucifixion.[12] This echoes Acts, where Barnabas declares that Paul 'had seen the Lord in the way, and that he had spoken to him'.[13] The context of this meeting is interesting. Saul-cum-Paul undergoes hysterical fright on being confronted by a very bold Jesus en route to Damascus, is struck with temporary (hysterical) blindness as a result, and becomes a convert. Referring to the Damascus journey, Graves and Podro write:

> It is far more likely that Saul's illegal raid into 'strange' territory (Acts 26:2) was made with the sole object of arresting Jesus, news of whose re-appearance in Damascus had reached Jerusalem. If he had succeeded in handing back his prisoner to Pilate for a second crucifixion, the Nazarene movement, which was founded on the knowledge of Jesus' continued existence in the flesh . . . would have collapsed in ridicule.[14]

They also record that in his *Ecclesiastical History*, Eusebius declares that James the Just (leader of the Nazarenes) was eventually martyred because he testified to Jesus' being physically alive after the crucifixion.

Like many another, Graves and Podro are suspicious of Paul's claim to have been either a Pharisee or the son of a Pharisee. His native city, Tarsus, had been predominantly Greek, and the Ebionite account of him was that he was Greek through and through – an account quoted by Epiphanius in his *Heresies*.[15] So it is in fact highly unlikely that he was, as he so vehemently claims, a Hebrew of the Hebrews, and a member of the tribe of Benjamin, for he quite obviously delighted in his Roman citizenship, and this fact alone undermines these claims.[16]

This raises the question of how Paul paid for the privilege of becoming a Roman citizen. Graves and Podro suggest that he helped himself to the alms collected for the Ebionites, and that he 'charged it to his expenses under the heading "Provisions for honest things in the sight of men out of this abundance, which is administered by me"'.[17] His being a Roman citizen certainly fitted in with his general attitude of being 'all things to all men', and his being a 'Jew among Jews' and a 'Gentile among Gentiles' either bespeaks a broad, healthy mind or an opportunist of the first ilk.

Paul's home city was basically Greek and a centre of Stoic philosophy. His Epistles suggest a Jewish education of Grecian slant, and his Old Testament quotations are apparently recognizably Septuagint in origin – even to the extent of following divergences from the Hebrew original. His language and style of thought is Greek, and he admits in Corinthians[18] that he *became* a Jew when among Jews. What this means in exact terms is difficult to gauge, but whatever its meaning, his background, education and proclivities suited him admirably for the job of taking Jesus' message of the coming Kingdom of God to the Gentiles. What he would do with this message would at first annoy James the Just, and then infuriate him, as this new theology of the 'Christ' began to cast an ever darkening shadow across the path of Israel's God.

CHRISTOLOGY AND THEOLOGY

The difference between Paul's new Son of Man *christo*-logy and the Messiah *theo*-logy of the Nazarenes led by Jesus' brother James, is one that must be explored if the twist in Paul's thinking is to be understood. Paul was well aware of, and in total sympathy with, the orthodox interpretations applied to the Messiah of Israel, but for some curious reason decided to enlarge the concept and bring it dangerously close to the idea of the dying-and-resurrecting pagan saviour Adonis-Tammuz. The question is, knowing the dangers in such a move, and considering his claim to have been rigorously trained in the Law, why did he do it? What could have driven him to such a revolutionary reassessment?

The answer to this question most probably lies hidden in his late appointment as an apostle. As an apostle 'born out of season' – that is, nominated as an apostle of Jesus by Jesus in what is described in the New Testament as a 'vision' – Paul was odd man out and highly suspect in the eyes of Jesus' Nazarene followers. Having become apostles on the occasion of Pentecost, these Nazarenes could not quite believe their ears when informed that their relentless persecutor Saul of Tarsus had changed sides. With warrants in his pocket for the arrest of the Nazarenes in Damascus, Saul had apparently undergone a life-transforming experience. It was hard to believe, but the miraculous had seemingly taken place. It may never be exactly known what happened that day, but that Saul was given a whole new set of marching orders is certain. From that moment onwards he was a different man. The persecutor becomes an apostle of the very Messiah he had considered a dangerous fake, and the already rolling history of that Messiah and his followers begins to bend, in his hands, in an unexpected direction.

THE MIND OF JESUS

Rudolf Bultmann would not approve, but that is not our concern. What Jesus thought and believed is of the utmost importance, and we can gain a certain insight into what he believed by comparing his words and actions with the beliefs of his day – the beliefs he so often disparaged and scoffed at. Paul the 'outsider' must have felt a certain affinity with Jesus, for Jesus too was an 'outsider', and that in spite of his central messianic role. To say that Jesus' behaviour was at odds with what many Jews expected of their Messiah would be an understatement: he was not of the expected traditional mould and markedly at odds even with the Essene sectaries' notions of a 'Holy One'. On the one hand he steadfastly created the circumstances whereby he could fulfil the prophecies and be recognized as the Messiah, but on the other confronted and criticized the very people who were trying to attract God's attention by strictly observing the Law of Moses. Allowing for the fact that only *some* of the Pharisees were hypocrites, the question is, why? Why turn on those who were trying to attract God's attention through living blameless lives? And why did he himself disobey the Law of Moses yet talk of having come to fulfil it? Did he in some fashion mean that he had come to complete it? What was going on in the mind of Jesus to make him act in this contradictory fashion?

It has been suggested by some scholars that there are two Jesuses in the gospels – a meek and mild one, and a militant one – and that these two figures have been uncomfortably collapsed into one another. But that may not be the case, or at least not the case in quite the way they suggest. It may be more accurate to say that there is only one Jesus, but that he slowly underwent a change of mind and personality. Jesus may not have thought of himself as the Messiah of Israel at the beginning of his ministry, but progressively realized that the responsibility for such a role was his and his alone. Or it may be that he saw himself specifically as the regal Messiah but soon underwent the trauma of having to accept the role of Suffering Servant (the priestly Messiah) due to the untimely death of John the Baptist. That he must have been scared of what lay ahead of him, of what was expected of him, goes without saying. This is most probably the reason that in the garden of Gethsemane he cries out to God in deep anguish to be released from his mission: the event was just around the corner and his nerve was in danger of giving out.

And rightly so. He was thinking of the brutality of the event ahead of him, of the fact that he would have to undergo actual crucifixion to atone for Israel's sinful state. On the one hand he was a shield; on the other a destructive sword. When the moment came, the Romans would not survive. Israel would be triumphant and he would be king, a priest-king of the order of Melchizedek. The world would be transformed in that moment. Not only would the yoke of subjugation to Rome fall away, but the heathen nations would immediately recognize Israel's greatness, the fact that she was a Holy Nation to which they should come for spiritual succour. War and violence and suffering would be no more – the Kingdom of God would have arrived in all its splendour.

This raises an interesting question. When did Jesus expect this glory and honour to descend on him? Immediately after his crucifixion and supposed resurrection? Were the Romans simply going to evaporate, or were they going to be militarily engaged in the same moment as he walked out of the tomb? Or was there a sequence of events to be gone through – a sequence ending with a massive Zealot attack on the Romans at an unspecified date? This would explain why Jesus' brother James was willing to argue doctrinal points with Paul and to continue to view Jesus as the legitimate Messiah of Israel *after* the crucifixion. There was no conception of failure at this point – the divine plan was still potent and in place. In spite of his being rejected as the Messiah by what was probably a substantial number of Jews and sectaries, Jesus' crucifixion and rumoured resurrection was still held by many to be an authentic messianic event which would fairly soon reveal itself as a divine intervention in human affairs. The Qumran Essenes were of the belief that *after* the Holy War with Rome there would be a period of Renewal, but that it would have to be backed by meticulous observance of the purity codes. God would respond and the Kingdom of God would materialize, but only as a result of festivals celebrated and temple sacrifices made. Some have speculated that this might have been the reason that James the Just forced Paul to cleanse himself in the Temple and donate to the Nazarite cause.

Jesus had completed his Messianic Mission, survived to tell the tale, and was waiting in the wings for his crown of glory. Everyone connected with the Nazarenes knew this. His brother James knew it. All twelve disciples knew it. Mary Magdalene certainly knew it. And if we are to accept what might be New Testament hyperbole, some 500 others knew it. But much more importantly, Paul knew it – for had he not talked with the Just One directly and received a new and startling commission? Thirty years would pass before Rome would decide to invade Judea. During this long and difficult time all the characters in this extraordinary drama would interact in equally extraordinary ways, and I think it certain that they each must have been delighted when Rome eventually made its move. Now, at last, they would see their God in action.

A SHADOW TAKES ON SUBSTANCE

In Luke's gospel Jesus turns up after his supposed death on the Cross and literally terrifies the disciples out of their wits – shades of Paul's later reaction. They can't believe it. He is there with them in what appears to be his physical body and they know that that simply cannot be. He had died on the Cross. There had been witnesses. He had been buried. So the only rational explanation was that they were dealing with a spirit, a ghost, an apparition of some kind. It must have amused Jesus to see their consternation. In fact he remarks on their reaction by asking what is troubling them. Now if this isn't a tongue-in-cheek statement, nothing is. And it is revealing too in that it shows Jesus to have had a sense of humour – an important little something denied him by the medieval Church. One can almost see the smile on his face; a mere trace of a smile. And no wonder. He had attempted what looked like the impossible and carried it off. To prove the point of his physicality, his next move is to show them his hands and his feet and get them to touch and feel his body for themselves. When even this doesn't quite convince them, he adds a final proof: he asks them for meat and proceeds to eat what they give him. But it is perhaps his next statement which is the more important, for it rather proves the point that *everything* had been planned down to the smallest detail. 'These are the words that I spake unto you, while I was yet with you, that all things must be fulfilled, which were written in the Law of Moses, and in the prophets, and in the Psalms, concerning me.'[19]

Jesus was fully conscious of all the prophecies concerning the Messiah, and had made very, very sure that everything was carried out just as written. And it should be realized that Jesus was physically present in that room; to think otherwise is to miss the whole point of the exercise. Jesus simply cannot make it any plainer: 'a spirit hath not flesh and bones, as ye see me have'.[20] This man did not suddenly and miraculously materialize in their midst – he had the door opened for him. When Jesus turns up as an old white-haired man and talks to John in some kind of ritual setting in the book of Revelation, what took place in the upper room that day is in essence recaptured down to the last detail. 'Behold,' says Jesus, 'I stand at the door and knock: if any man hear my voice, and open the door, I will come in to him, and will sup with him, and he with me.'[21] And it is this that has to be kept in mind on each and every other occasion: he is *physically* there. He is not a phantom. He is not a spirit. He is not a ghost. And neither is he some kind of apparition with the ability to alternate between physicality and some other less dense state. He is a flesh and blood man still in the process of healing from the horrendous wounds of crucifixion. This in itself is an interesting point: the marks of crucifixion are visible. But the text has perhaps been tampered with at this point, for Jesus says 'Behold my *hands* and my feet', so continuing the myth that he was nailed to the cross through the palms of his hands. This is now known to have been impossible – a body secured to a cross through the hands would not have been able to sustain its own weight. So is the whole text spurious? Probably not. It is more probable that a little editing has been going on by the compilers, an editing which has him appear in the room as if by magic, and keeps the nails through the hands for the sake of what Burton L Mack would probably call 'story continuity'. And anyway, it was not the first time Jesus had been mistaken for something other than what he was. The story of his supposed walk on the waters of Lake Gennesaret culminates with the crowd's being so astonished to see him suddenly appear from the direction of the shoreline (they had thought he was not going to turn up) that they considered him an *apparition*: they 'supposed it had been a *spirit*', Matthew and Mark tell us.[22]

This particular 'appearance' story ends with Jesus' going as far as Bethany with the disciples – a considerable walk for a recently crucified man, although the Dead Sea Scrolls scholar Dr Barbara Thiering speculates that his feet were not pierced. And an even more remarkable event for a being just pretending to be real. Also a little too convenient – for it is at this point that Jesus, like Enoch, is physically translated to heaven. Or are we to believe that he suddenly switched off his physicality and became the spirit he had earlier denied he was? There is something wrong here. Any good journalist could spot the re-location device a mile off. The compiler/editor simply had to get Jesus out in the open for such an extraordinary feat of levitation. Much more difficult to have him ascend through the ceiling of a room and at the same time go through the necessary transformation process en route. And so up he went, into heaven, to be with . . . himself? Or might it be that he simply underwent, in their presence, some form of ecstatic experience which transported him far beyond ordinary consciousness? Paul talks of being *caught up* to a third heaven, but he doesn't mean it literally. And if Jesus was capable of such mental transformation, might such a state of mind not allow a crucified man to function *as if* uninjured? As a way of speaking, an 'ascent to heaven' was common coinage in mystical circles.

Prior to his physical appearances to eleven of his disciples inside a building, there is another very interesting appearance story set on the road to Emmaus. As two of Jesus' followers walk along discussing the terrible events that have taken place, a mysterious stranger joins them, overhears what they are saying, and asks for an explanation. With the innocence of children they divulge everything that has happened, and the stranger reveals himself to be none other than Jesus in person. This story does not ring true. There is no reason to doubt that there were two followers of Jesus walking to Emmaus who met Jesus either en route or on their arrival, or that they discussed the crucifixion, but to accept that they opened up to a complete stranger without reservation, even to the extent of talking about Jesus' body having disappeared from the tomb, is too much to take on board. These were very dangerous times. King Herod had earlier had spies and innumerable detectives in his pay, and because his heirs were of the same suspicious ilk there is no reason to believe that spying on the populace had ceased. Pilate too had his own spies. Afraid of rebellion amongst the Jews and Galileans, Pilate had eyes and ears everywhere. So no one in their right mind would have divulged what these followers of Jesus are supposed to have divulged to a perfect stranger, particularly as Jesus had been identified by the Romans as a Zealot and crucified for that reason. And to believe for one minute that it was Jesus in person and that they did not recognize him is simply preposterous.

Once again the hand of the compiler, the editor, can be seen and felt. Yes, Jesus was alive. Yes, he linked up with two of his followers either en route to Emmaus, or in Emmaus itself, but like the men in white robes at the tomb identified as 'angels' by the women, and later as a 'vision of angels', the rest of the story is simply heavy-handed embroidery. What is of interest is that Jesus again stresses his awareness of what Moses and the prophets had to say about the messianic event. We are told that he expounded *all* the Scriptures concerning himself, and that he *ate* meat and bread.[23] This man was bent on changing attitudes towards himself, attitudes which prior to the crucifixion had resulted in his being rejected by his own disciples. Such conversations were not gentle reminders, they were the acts of a teacher sorting out students who had neither properly understood nor believed what

st told them. So the words 'did not recognize him' may
ɔfer to *claims rejected*.

account starts with the women, and certain others
d) who came to the tomb early in the morning. To their
amazement, the stone that had covered the opening has been
rolled aside, and the tomb is empty except for two figures dressed
in white robes who tell them that Jesus has risen. They add, quite
sensibly, 'Why seek ye the living among the dead?' The women
head straight back and tell the disciples, *and* other persons, what
has happened, and are met with blank disbelief. The disciples, all
eleven of them, treat what the women have to say as 'idle tales',
and dismiss their announcement as nonsense. Peter seems to be
the only one to take them at all seriously. He rushes off, gets
to the tomb, has a look around, and finds that the body really has
disappeared. We are told that he 'wondered in himself' about
what had happened to Jesus' body. In Matthew's version, Mary
Magdalene and another Mary actually run into Jesus on their way
back to tell the disciples about the empty tomb. They touch him,
and he tells them to tell the disciples that he will meet them later
in Galilee. A little later on we learn that this meeting had been
prearranged. In John's gospel a slightly different version of the
story is told: Peter is beaten to the tomb by 'the disciple that Jesus
loved', and there is a personal meeting between Jesus and Mary
Magdalene where she is told not to touch him.

This account carries John's indelible gnostic signature. Jesus
takes on a heavenly persona not evident in the other gospels, and
only near the end of the account is Thomas allowed to touch the
nail prints in his 'hands', and the spear wound in his side. Jesus
then shows himself to the disciples at the Sea of Tiberias, where
he takes the trouble to build a fire, bake fish and supply bread for
his disciples who are out fishing. This section ends with an
extraordinary statement:

> And there are also many other things that Jesus did, the which, if they
> should be written every one, I suppose that even the world itself could
> not contain the books that should be written.[24]

If this verse refers, as it seems to do, to things done by Jesus *after*
his Resurrection, then he was either very, very busy before his
Ascension at Bethany, or the remark refers to the *long life* he is
not supposed to have had.

THE IMPORTANCE OF THE
RESURRECTION

The Resurrection story is, as Christians realize only too well, of the greatest importance. Referring to the tragedy of the crucifixion, the Jewish scholar Joseph Klausner remarks that Christianity would not have been possible without its 'epilogue'. The Resurrection is therefore very important indeed, and Paul leaves us in no doubt about its importance when he says: 'if Christ be not risen, then is our preaching in vain, and your faith is also vain.'[25] It would seem that everything hangs on the Resurrection – and rightly so. The gospel of Matthew gives us the whole story. We are told how the chief priests and Pharisees inform Pilate that Jesus ('that deceiver') had said that after three days he would rise again. And so it is proposed to Pilate that he put a guard on the tomb, and that it be sealed with their seal in case Jesus' disciples decide to steal the body. This, they tell Pilate, would compound the problem. If the people became convinced that Jesus really had risen from the dead, the last error would be worse than the first. But of course things did not work out for the priests and Pharisees: the body of Jesus disappeared in spite of these precautions. And so the story of his disciples' having really stolen the body is put around, and the guards are incomprehensibly let off the hook in spite of having failed in their duty.

That the disciples did not steal the body is certain. If they had, the whole basis of their belief in Jesus would have been undermined. There would have been no 'joy' in such an act, and certainly no joy afterwards. In a word, there would have been no reason to continue with what was no more than a charade. Yet they did continue, and the reality of their joy cannot be ignored. Jesus was alive, very much alive, and the mystery of his being alive set the disciples alight. This in itself suggests two things. First of all, if the disciples had been really in on what Jesus was up to, if they had really been privy to all that was going on prior to the crucifixion, then they would not have been surprised, indeed 'terrified', by his suddenly turning up the way he did. Can you imagine the scene? There's a knock at the door, and when it's opened they find the man they know to have undergone the horrors of crucifixion standing there large as life.

In Matthew's gospel we are told that the disciples travel to

Galilee and meet Jesus at a prearranged spot. Then comes a series
of statements worth looking at.

> And when they saw him, they worshipped him: but some doubted.
> And Jesus came and spake unto them, saying, All power is given unto
> me in heaven and in earth. Go ye therefore, and teach all nations,
> baptizing them in the name of the Father, and of the Son, and of the
> Holy Ghost: Teaching them to observe all things whatsoever I have
> commanded you: and, lo, I am with you alway[s], even unto the end
> of the world. Amen.[26]

Commenting on these very verses, the Jewish scholar Joseph
Klausner remarked in 1926 that they were 'replete with the
Pauline spirit'.[27] And indeed they are. Here we have a Jesus
of power speaking, a majestic Jesus claiming without a flicker of
doubt that it is no longer the Law of Moses that they must heed,
but what he himself teaches. This is not ordinary messianic
Judaism, it is sectarian heresy of some kind – and some of the
disciples recognized it as such. Not everyone 'worshipped' Jesus;
some held back.

When we clearly identify what it was that the disciples
doubted, then the text takes on a ring of authenticity: Jesus'
Messiahship was being questioned. And perhaps because
the message was no longer just for Israel, but now also for the
Gentiles. This, along with Jesus' acceptance of 'worship' must
have worried some of these Nazarenes. It certainly wasn't his
being there physically that now bothered them: his flesh and
blood reality had already been proved to them beyond reasonable
doubt. Following the words 'but some doubted', Jesus does not
again talk about his not being a spirit, or about his being a flesh
and blood man; instead he reinforces the idea of his Messiahship
by talking of the power given to him in heaven and on the earth.
He has fulfilled the prophecies and completed his Mission. Along
with the disciples he too now awaits the imminent arrival of the
Last Days. And the promise 'I am with you alway[s], even unto
the end of the world' has nothing whatsoever to do with a
disembodied Jesus ruling from heaven and returning at some
unspecified date in the distant future. It has to do with a
physically alive Jesus promising to be right there with them when
the Romans are defeated and Israel is set free. This is not a text
for the distant future: it is a text within which the Jewish
expectation of the *soon to be experienced* Last Days is being spelt

out loud and clear. To murky the waters with heavenly explanations is to entirely miss the point.

PAUL'S HEAVENLY VISION

Paul deals with the Resurrection story in what appears to be a straightforward manner. He tells us that Jesus was seen by Cephas (Peter), then by the twelve, then by around 500 of his brethren at once, then by his brother James, and latterly by himself. He seems to get a bit mixed up and mentions the 'apostles' as having seen Jesus second last after having said that the 'twelve' had seen Jesus directly after Peter, but we won't quibble over that.[28] And neither will we quibble over his not mentioning Mary Magdalene, or the other women who saw and physically handled Jesus. What concerns us here is Paul's description of his experience of Jesus on the road to Damascus. When explaining to King Agrippa why he has been accused by the Jews and eventually arrested and delivered to the Romans, he details his previous opposition to Jesus and his followers, and then describes his interaction with Jesus on the road to Damascus as a 'heavenly vision'. Before dealing with this vision, however, it is necessary to put Paul the apostle into a clear perspective – for next to Jesus himself he is the most important figure in the history of the Christian Church, a fact with which few Christian scholars would disagree.

First of all, there is the role played by Saul prior to changing his name to Paul. He tells King Agrippa that his manner of life from his youth has been to live as a strict Pharisee, and that everyone who knew him during those years would testify to the truth of this claim. He then states that he has been wrongfully accused and arrested, when all he has done is remind the Jews of the promises of God as given to the twelve tribes. Then suddenly he mentions the resurrection of Jesus, and this indicates that it was what he had to say about the resurrection that had got him into trouble with the Jewish authorities, not his general teaching about the Messiah as spoken of by the prophets. Doubling back to the kind of man he had once been, to his role of 'persecutor', he explains that he has not only had followers of Jesus locked up in prison (including women, it later transpires), and had them forced to blaspheme the name of Jesus through torture, but that he has also been instrumental in harassing them in the synagogues and having them put to death. Then comes the claim that his hatred of these Nazarenes drove him to persecute them from city to city, and that his actions were backed by warrants of authority from the chief priests of the Temple. All in all, an impressive description of his own fanaticism, a fanaticism now engaged in the opposite direction due to a personal encounter with Jesus.[29]

Paul refers to this encounter as a 'heavenly vision', and it is supposed by Christian scholars that he meant just that and no more. But when one looks at the transcript of what Jesus said to Paul during this heavenly vision, one cannot help but wonder at its content. And there is also the context, the geographical location and the time of day to be considered. It is truly remarkable that this heavenly vision comes to Paul not only in broad daylight but at midday. What a strange time for a vision. No dark secluded corner this. We are led to believe that Saul and his arresting officers are trudging along the road to Damascus when without warning they are visited by a light brighter than the midday sun. Scared out of their wits, the whole party falls to the ground in fear. And then the voice of Jesus is heard, speaking not Aramaic (his mother tongue) but Hebrew, the language of the Scriptures, the Law and the Temple. Jesus comes straight to the point in this difficult-to-speak language which only the highly educated had mastered, and which was not used for common everyday purposes. 'Saul, Saul,' says an obviously exasperated Jesus from somewhere or other, 'why persecutest thou me? Is it hard for thee to kick against the pricks?' Saul is bewildered; he asks for the identity of the person speaking and is informed that it is the very Jesus whose followers he has been hounding. And then Saul is told to stand up, and is there and then commissioned as a disciple of that same Jesus he hates, and given orders of a strange and novel character – to take the news of Jesus as resurrected Jewish Messiah to the Gentiles.

What a head-scratcher this heavenly vision is: it is full of twists and turns and complications and unexpected deviations. One moves from reference to reference sensing a real story, a real happening, a real intervention in the life of this fanatic, but in the end one falls back unconvinced in spite of the energy and time taken to create the notion of a supernatural event. In the final analysis it is simply all too silly for words. Yes, Paul met Jesus, perhaps on the road to Damascus, but it sounds more like a hijacking than a heavenly vision, more like a carefully executed plan by a group than a spectre speaking out of thin air. Two discrepancies between the three accounts of the same event in the book of Acts reveal much, and Paul's later development of the doctrine of 'physical resurrection' in the Last Days gives the show away – the Jesus he had interacted with was without doubt flesh and blood and bone.

The first few verses that describe the heavenly vision in Acts 9 more or less correspond with what we learn from Acts 22. Then the story goes completely off the rails with a series of mistakes. In mentioning the people travelling with Saul on the road to Damascus, Acts 22:9 tells us that they 'saw indeed the light, and were afraid; but they heard not the voice', whereas Acts 9:7 says 'And the men which journeyed with him stood speechless, hearing a voice, but seeing no man.' In Acts 9:7 we are told that Paul's followers 'stood speechless' during the whole event, whereas in Acts 26:14 everyone falls to the earth in fear. The writer of Acts 9 has not got his facts straight. Either that or we must presume that Paul's memory is faulty – an unfortunate weakness in someone we are being asked to treat with a grand seriousness.

And then there is the havoc caused by Paul in Jerusalem, where it is said that he had the whole city in an uproar.[30] Why? Because of what he was preaching. He later admits that what he was preaching was what the Jews considered to be overt heresy. 'But this I confess unto thee,' he says, 'that after the way which they call heresy, so worship I the God of my fathers'.[31] And when he is being treated for blindness in Damascus due to his overpowering vision (or hysteria at Jesus turning up as bold as brass), someone called Ananias informs him that Paul has been chosen by God to directly 'see' the *Just One* and to 'hear' his voice – the 'Just One' presumably being Jesus, as Dr Schonfield suggests. So a second meeting with Jesus is on the cards.[32] And Ananias knows what he's talking about, for we are told earlier[33] that Jesus appears to Ananias in a vision and calls him by name.

Once again Jesus has something very concrete to say, something pertaining to the moment. 'Arise,' says Jesus, 'and go into the street which is called Straight, and inquire in the house of Judas for one called Saul, of Tarsus: for, behold, he prayeth,. And hath seen in a vision a man named Ananias coming in, and putting his hand on him, that he might receive his sight.' And so Ananias immediately jumps to his feet and runs to the house where Saul is, and . . . Not quite. Ananias in fact does something quite incomprehensible: he *argues* with this supposed vision of Jesus by telling Jesus what he already knows only too well. Paul is dangerous. He has warrants in his pocket for the arrest of people just like Ananias.

What an extraordinary reaction. Is this man so used to having visions of Jesus that he has become blasé? And is the extra vision in which Ananias is seen by Saul prior to his actual arrival really necessary, or just more supernatural padding to further conceal the fact that Jesus is not dead at all but right there in Damascus with his finger on the pulse of everything that is going on? People simply do not argue with visions sent by God; they argue only with people in natural situations, or with imaginary beings in their mind. A seeming contradiction to this is Peter's arguing with the Lord in a vision concerning unclean beasts,[34] but this is so obviously a contrived story, an imagined event, that it does not warrant consideration.

Acts 26:16 carries the whole vision business one step further, for Jesus spells out to Saul the exact reason for his vision, and that reason is that he *intends to keep on appearing to Saul in visions*. He says: 'I have appeared unto thee for this purpose, to make thee a minister and a witness both of these things which thou hast seen, and of those things in which I will appear unto thee.' This is to say that Jesus and Paul are going to be in regular contact. Now to believe in visions is one thing, but to believe in visions of such an obvious utilitarian nature is to be uncritical to an unbelievable degree. No thinking person could possibly accept such nonsense. The realm of non-time within which such things are seriously reported to happen is, by nature, neither so literal nor so opportunistic. We are dealing here with physical events, and the reason Jesus is being so secretive about his whereabouts is obvious: if the Jewish and Roman authorities realized that he was still alive, still in control of a large number of followers (over 500 in Galilee), he would become the centre of a massive manhunt which in the end could not fail but capture him.

Paul met Jesus face to face; his commission to go to the Gentiles was direct. Imagine Paul's surprise, his utter amazement, his religious awe, when he realized that Jesus was not dead but very much alive and in control of a large and well-organized Operation Last Days. There is no disputing this. There were, as Paul already knew from bitter experience, Nazarenes in almost every major city and village. They were daily being encountered in the synagogues and even in the Temple itself. And what were they preaching? That Jesus was alive. Everywhere the story was the same: Jesus was alive and the Last Days were closing in fast. As Paul says to King Agrippa, 'this thing was not done in a corner.'[35] Festus confirms this in his speech to King Agrippa when referring to Paul's accusers. He says that when 'the accusers stood up, they brought none accusation of such things as I supposed: But had certain questions against him of their own superstition, and of one Jesus, which was dead, whom Paul affirmed to be alive.'[36]

Paul must have been flabbergasted when Jesus turned up – indeed, so taken aback by the fact that he was physically alive as to undergo instant conversion. Or perhaps it was just the shock of being taken by surprise, confronted by the very man he had been sent to arrest. Boldly taking the initiative, Jesus, in conjunction with an armed following had not only stopped this fanatic in his tracks, he had so amazed him that he changed sides. So thought Graves and Podro, and their scenario is not without merit. Under conditions where it seemed to Saul that he and his officers were certain to be killed, a Jesus replete with the scars of crucifixion confronting him when he least expected it must have made a mighty impression – in fact, so great an impression that Saul became hysterically blind. Perhaps that was when Jesus realized that Saul could be turned, that he was ripe for conversion. To be led away blinded by terror and expecting death, but to survive and be treated with kindness must have seemed like a miracle to Saul. And as it all began to sink in and Ananias talked to him about Jesus and his purpose, he must have collapsed inside and become open to what the Just One would eventually advocate.

SIX

THE ARABIAN CONUNDRUM

The book of Acts as a patchwork quilt of fabrication, fact and fancy, the probable doctrinal discoveries of Paul while in Arabia, and the necessity of breaking the taboo against suspecting that Jesus planned and physically survived his crucifixion.

Kamal Salibi, historian and specialist on the modern Middle East, is a Christian from Lebanon. His book *The Bible Came From Arabia*, published in 1985, caused quite a stir in academic and political circles. A radical reinterpretation of Old Testament geography, Salibi's book revealed startling linguistic evidence which controversially suggested that Judaism had originated not in Palestine but in western Arabia. It is not my purpose to follow Salibi's complex and well-documented argument to source – that is quite beyond my expertise – but to pick up on comments and observations made by Salibi in a follow-up book entitled *Conspiracy in Jerusalem*. Published in 1988, this book also challenged biblical scholars, but for reasons very different from his first challenging analysis of the Old Testament. This time it was the New Testament that was under fire, and Salibi's insightful eye and critical reading of New Testament texts had Christian scholars eyeing him with the same distrust and amazement as Jewish scholars had done years before. Salibi was homing in on some uncomfortable facts which for too long had been swept under the scholarly Christian carpet.

PAUL IN ARABIA

One of these uncomfortable facts was Paul's visit to Arabia after his conversion – an incident picked up on by Dr Schonfield in *The Passover Plot*. With his usual sharpness, Schonfield says of the *Similitudes of Enoch*:

He [the Messiah] is named and hidden from the beginning in the secret thoughts of God, finally to be revealed in the Last Times as the Ideal Man who will justify God's creation of the world. In this sense he is the Second Adam, answering to the Light Adam of the Nazorean-Mandeans, and the Nazorean-Ebionite 'mankind figure invisible to men in general'. From such teaching, probably while he was in the borders of Arabia, Paul acquired the inspiration from which he developed his concept of the heavenly Messiah who had incarnated in the earthly Jesus.[1]

Salibi too is of the opinion that Paul got much of his inspiration for a new theology of messiahship in that neighbourhood, but pushes the argument much further by drawing our attention to the little-mentioned fact that Paul's claim to have visited Arabia after his conversion utterly contradicts what is claimed for him elsewhere in the New Testament.

Speaking of his own conversion, Paul stresses that immediately afterwards he did not go up to Jerusalem to meet the apostles but instead went into Arabia for *three years*.[2] Three years? What did Paul find to do in Arabia for three whole years? And where exactly in Arabia did he go? Back to Damascus he comes, eventually, with whatever it is he has found out, or found, and only then does he travel up to Jerusalem to meet the apostles. Well, not quite. He goes to Jerusalem specifically to see Peter, with whom he stays for 15 days. The only other apostle seen by Paul during this time is Jesus' brother James – the flesh and blood brother which, for doctrinal reasons, the Catholic Church cannot ever admit he had. It is interesting to note that this blood relative of Jesus, like Paul himself, is a bit of a latecomer, perhaps even a gate-crasher. Virtually unknown one minute, he is the chief of the apostles the next – and with no prior credentials, it would seem, to his name. Or perhaps his name amounted to the best credentials possible.

As if expecting to be contradicted by someone, Paul lays unusual emphasis on his having gone to Arabia, and not to Jerusalem immediately after his meeting with Jesus. In his Galatian epistle he says: 'Now the things which I write unto you, behold, before God, I lie not.'[3] Fourteen years will pass before he again visits Jerusalem (fourteen years without recognition of his apostleship by the Nazarenes), and it is during this second meeting that he is finally accepted by James as apostle to the Gentiles – an apostleship given to him *by Jesus in person*. Salibi's important question at this point is, why does Paul nowhere explain why he went to Arabia, and why didn't he later write about that journey?[4]

The story of Paul's supposed journey to Jerusalem not long after his conversion, and his supposed meeting with the apostles who, we are told, were afraid of him,[5] again raises the question of compiler interference with the New Testament text. Everything seems of a piece, but isn't. Salibi informs us that some scholars have assumed that the book of Acts was written with a Pauline bias, but says that this is not necessarily the case. Information from varying sources, and mostly of an indirect nature, have been combined with one direct account of Paul's preaching voyages. So the bias varies, as is detectable, with the sources used. This would account for the fact that Acts, although mostly about Paul, what he believes and what he does, contains many areas where conflict and contradiction are only too evident between Paul, Jesus' brother James, and the original Nazarene apostles. And there was conflict – of that there is no doubt. The fact that Paul swears before God that what he says about his going straight to Arabia is not a lie can only mean that some other story was already circulating about him.

This 'other story' is of course the story of his miraculous conversion on the road to Damascus, his being healed of blindness by Ananias, and his immediate trundling off to Jerusalem to submit to the authority of James and the apostles. Paul does not deny getting his commission straight from Jesus, but he makes no reference to Ananias or the road to Damascus, or to what happened to the Temple officers he had with him who either heard, or did not hear, the voice from heaven, while lying either flat on their faces or standing up. What he does mention is the fact that there is another gospel of Jesus floating around, and that his Galatian Christians have been seduced into believing it instead of his own gospel. He gets quite fired up about this alternative gospel, and goes as far as to say 'there be some that trouble you, and would pervert the gospel of Christ.' And then, 'though we, or an angel from heaven, preach any other gospel unto you than that which we have preached unto you, let him be accursed.'[6] This other gospel was most probably the Nazarene gospel as preached by the apostles in Jerusalem (Nazarene sectarian teachings heavily laced with orthodox Judaism), so the gulf between Paul and these other apostles can well be imagined.

The fact that Paul's journey to Arabia has been carefully re-arranged into another story suggests that the Nazarene apostles of Jesus had something to hide, that they knew something they did not wish anyone else to know, and that Paul believed he had more chance of finding out what that something was by going to Arabia than to Jerusalem. This also suggests that he knew a little about what he was looking for, and that he had information of some sort concerning Jesus and his Mission which only such a journey could complete. Or it might just be that he was considered 'unqualified' by Jesus to speak in his name until he had been properly schooled in the intricacies of Nazarene tradition and doctrine. The fact that this journey has been scrambled beyond recognition seems to suggest that the Nazarene apostles of Jesus wanted to deny Paul the right of possession, the right to claim equality with them on the grounds of knowing what they knew about Jesus. It goes without saying that the information gained by Paul in Arabia was important; the question is, what exactly was it? What did Paul end up knowing that allowed him to construct his amazingly elevated Christology? Three years was a long time for this would-be apostle to stay out of sight, out of the limelight, and when he eventually surfaces and goes to Jerusalem, it is with a truly remarkable confidence. Offering the apostles a universal vision to replace their ethnic one, Paul impudently announces a 'gospel of the uncircumcision' and faces up to Jesus' brother James with a baffling bravado.[7] Well, not quite baffling – Jesus was James' elder brother, it has to be remembered, and because he was *still alive* had the dynastic right to appoint whomever he wished. James may not have liked the idea of Saul-cum-Paul's joining the ranks, but he could not veto Jesus' decision.

That Paul considered his own authority as good as the special authority claimed by the Jerusalem apostles is everywhere evident, and that he even considered them unequal to himself in authority and substance of teaching can be seen clearly when he says that the leaders of the Nazarene community 'added nothing to me'.[8] This impression is later reinforced when he speaks of 'false brethren', or 'spies' who infiltrate his Galatian Church to witness the 'liberty' in Christ Jesus which they enjoy. This 'liberty' is obviously Paul's lenient attitude to circumcision, and much else, which in turn raises the question of how this Pharisee of the Pharisees ever came so to reverse his attitudes to the Law of Moses. Salibi comes to the rescue here by observing that the narrative in Acts begins to speak of 'Saul',[9] continues with this name, then suddenly changes to 'Paul' by way of device. 'Then Saul (who also is called Paul), filled with the holy ghost, set his eyes on him.'[10] The changeover is virtually unnoticeable, a simple piece of editing which perhaps allows two people to be seamlessly collapsed into one. Salibi suggests that Acts possibly confuses the identity of Paul with someone called Saul who was a student of Gamaliel, resident in Jerusalem, and persecutor of the Nazarene followers of Jesus. He even toys with the idea that the name Saul might be an outright invention.[11] Robert Graves and Joshua Podro are of the opinion that Paul was not Jewish. These possibilities are backed by scholarly suspicions that some of the Epistles were not written by Paul, or at best contain only fragments of his writing, so allowing for an overall tampering with the texts. And because Acts too has been 'repaired' into existence from many sources, and there are substantial contradictions between Acts and the Epistles, what appears to be a straightforward series of stories has to be handled with great interpretative care.

But whatever Paul's background, he was, according to Dr Schonfield, a theological genius, and this suggests that he was a trained thinker, and possibly a Pharisee as he claims. Ultimately, it is his thinking which concerns us; his 'vision' of things sets the pace of our comprehension. On this score, there is a tantalizing verse in the first epistle to the Corinthians where he says, 'we speak the wisdom of God in a mystery, even the hidden wisdom, which God ordained before the world unto our glory.'[12] And then in the next chapter he adds: 'I have fed you with milk, and not with meat: for hitherto ye were not able to bear it, neither yet now are ye able.'[13] Over and above Paul's laxity in observing the Law of Moses, there is also a teaching concerning Jesus which is not immediately given to converts. This teaching – this 'meat', as Paul calls it – is a 'hidden wisdom' which he can only hint at or speak of in disguised terms. That this hidden wisdom is what he discovered in western Arabia, is pretty certain. And it is the possession of this hidden wisdom which eventually allows him to present himself before the apostles in Jerusalem as a doctrinal equal.

But there is a problem here. If Paul had truly discovered a secret known only to Jesus' original followers and family, why then did they reject him when he eventually turned up? And why is he persecuted by these same followers over the next 14 years for preaching a gospel with which they are supposed to be in basic agreement? Is there perhaps something wrong with Paul's interpretation of the secret wisdom? Is it missing an ingredient or two? Or is it simply that Paul, in his fervour, in his enthusiasm, has misunderstood this secret wisdom? If Saul and Paul are not the same person, if they have been tacked together for credibility's sake, then a literalizing of metaphorically exuberant secret texts is possible. But if Saul and Paul are one and the same, then we are confronted by a trained theological thinker who decides, or is pushed, into reframing that secret wisdom for the sake of a new and unexpected cause – the rapid conversion of Gentiles to an expanded form of Judaism.

NEW WINE IN OLD BOTTLES

Paul tells us that Jesus directly commissioned him to go to the Gentiles, and this information is probably reliable for the very reason that it is at variance with what we know of Nazarene wishes. If there was a difference of opinion between Jesus, his Nazarene followers, and his family members (particularly James), it must have been on exactly this point. For reasons which were probably political as well as religious, Jesus eventually decided to carry the message of his Messiahship, his world-saving act on the Cross as the Suffering Servant, to the Gentiles. He knew that with a little twist they would understand and respond. The Jewish hierarchy had finally rejected him because he scoffed at what they considered to be important. His only followers had been the Nazarenes, certain other sectaries which we glimpse from time to time in the gospels, and disparate 'Jesus groups' which had formed as a result of his preaching in town after town. Mysterious figures flit in and out of his life like ghosts, and from the tomb itself announce his miraculous return to physical life. Elevated to the rank of glistening angels in one gospel, they are more aptly described in another as 'men in white robes'.

From the moment of his return from Arabia, Paul's life is interrupted quite regularly with 'visions' of Jesus talking to him. These visions, like his vision of Jesus on the road to Damascus, or in Damascus itself, are quite likely to have been based on actual physical appearances by Jesus. For obvious reasons, Jesus was in hiding and could no longer risk going to Jerusalem. But he was not totally dependent on his brother James and the Nazarene Party – he had hundreds of followers elsewhere, and if Acts is to be believed, eventually thousands (Acts 4:4). It is quite possible that many of these followers were Gentiles, or Gentile converts to Judaism. Herod had invited large numbers of Gentile trades-people to settle in Judea, and many may well have responded to both Judaism and Jesus' auxiliary messianic message due to its strong Galilean flavour. This in turn would have swayed Jesus to consider a separate mission to the Gentiles, for as a Galilean he had lived among them all his life. As a result he would have felt some affinity with them in spite of his being of a Jewish family with sectarian connections – perhaps even more so because of his sectarian connections. Joseph Klausner captures the spiritual conditions of the time when he says:

> To understand Christianity, i.e. the teachings of Paul and his successors, and to understand the victory and growth of Christianity during its first two hundred years, a knowledge of Hellenistic Judaism is very necessary since it, alone, accounts for the origin of the Trinity and the 'word' as God, and the introduction of Greek elements into the Jewish Nazarene system.[14]

As with Craveri's earlier statement about the Jews' not having a doctrine of redemption, this is all very true, but similarly it does not allow for the influence of Essene thinking on Paul – the sectaries had some amazing doctrinal ideas up their sleeves.

With the elevation of his brother James to prominence in the Nazarene Party after his supposed death, Jesus must have literally targeted Saul as a potential convert and future missionary – and what better way to bring this persecutor of Nazarenes to his knees than to reveal himself to him *in the flesh*. Paul's curious doctrinal notion of eventual *physical* resurrection for all Christians after death probably sprang from the shock of that moment. Is it again Jesus' sense of humour we can detect when he commissions this fanatic to bring Gentiles into the Kingdom?

But it is evident from the gospels that Jesus had not always thought of the Gentiles as potential converts – in fact the reverse seems to have been true. Fatigued from constant teaching, he sent the disciples out to preach the coming of the kingdom of heaven, and expressly told them, 'Go not the way of the Gentiles, nor to any city of the Samaritans. Go only unto the lost sheep of the house of Israel.'[15] But shortly afterwards, to escape from his enemies, he himself went to the Gentile Tyre and Sidon with his disciples. And post-Resurrection (Acts 1:8), he specifically tells his disciples to witness in Judea *and* Samaria. However, when implored by a Gentile woman to cast devils out of her daughter, Jesus' reply is brusque and unbending, and makes him out to be a true Jewish nationalist – or perhaps that is just what the writer-editor wants us to think: 'Let the children first be filled,' he replies dismissively, 'for it is not meet to take the children's bread, and to cast it unto dogs.'[16] Matthew's gospel has Jesus add, 'I was not sent except to the lost sheep of the house of Israel.'[17] The woman's reply is that of a mother who must overlook insults and fend for her child. 'And she answered and said unto him, Yes, Lord: yet the dogs under the table eat of the children's crumbs.'[18] The nationalist in Jesus is apparently overcome by the sheer wit of the woman's reply, and he heals the girl from where he stands.

What is important here is not the healing but Jesus' attitude to the Gentile woman – it is the attitude of a nationalistic Jew. Joseph Klausner considers this statement by Jesus to be historical, and reminds us that things were not going well for Jesus at this point: he had been rejected over and over again by his own people and delivered himself of an ugly tirade against certain towns and cities for their unbelief.[19] Klausner says:

> Such bitterness shows clearly that his condition was becoming worse; he saw no progress in his work: he is indignant and curses. Such words have in them something of the severity . . . of an Isaiah or an Ezekiel: they show not the least trace of that peculiar 'tenderness' and 'unconditional forgiveness'. Jesus was a Jew, educated on the severe indictments of the Prophets, and at times he followed their lead: he is by no means that type which the Christians have depicted for themselves – one who forgives all; who, when offended, offends not again.[20]

Klausner then speculates that it may have been around this time that Jesus taught the parable of those bidden to the feast or wedding. When the important guests did not turn up, the 'way-farers, the poor and indignant, the blind and the lame, the evil and the good alike, were summoned'.[21]

The scribes and Pharisees and the pick of the nation had rejected him, so he was forced to invite publicans and sinners and harlots into the Kingdom of God in their place – or, more exactly, Jewish dregs and Gentiles. Jesus' next move was to return to

Galilee by way of Decapolis – that is to say, via the 'Ten Cities'. These ten cities were inhabited by non-Jews (except for Beth-Shean) and were in Transjordania. If it is at this point that he visits Gadara, then it is here that he drives devils out of a man called Legion and allows them to enter a herd of pigs. Because pigs were not reared by Jews, Jesus must certainly have been in the thick of Gentile territory.

But perhaps the most telling episode in the gospels concerning Jesus' attitude towards a new beginning for Judaism is the occasion on which he is rebuked for not fasting like John the Baptist. His answer was that you cannot sew a piece of new cloth on an old garment, or put new wine in old bottles. This was to say that John's methods were of the old school, whereas his methods were of the new. New wine would burst old bottles, just as new cloth would tear away from old cloth. The old external forms of baptism and fasting and group repentance had to be broken up to make room for a teaching which was *personal*. It was no longer 'Israel' the collective that would usher in the Last Days, it was the repentant individual aware of his or her responsibilities before God. The old had to be cleared away for the sake of the new, and as Jesus witnessed the best of the Jewish nation turn against him, he began to turn from them towards the poor and the enslaved, and sheep not of the Jewish fold – the Gentiles. The abolition of the ceremonial laws and the opening of the doors to uncircumcised Gentiles would come later, after the crucifixion, and Paul would be the man chosen to initiate this heretical move.

James obviously did not at first agree with the direction in which his brother Jesus wanted to take the Nazarene Party, but belatedly accepted him as the Messiah of Israel after he had undergone the horrors of crucifixion and shown himself to be capable of ritualistically carrying the messianic burden to its ferocious conclusion. Like Paul the mad persecutor, he could not easily overlook that fact – or the even more amazing fact that his brother was still alive. It simply had to have been God's will, surely? And everything was fine on the theological front (relatively speaking) until Paul turned up with evidence that not only had Jesus been the Messiah of Israel but that he was now somewhat more than a man. That had been too much for this devout Jew to swallow. Yes, he was a sectarian, a Nazarene-Ebionite leader (the Ebionites, probably as a result of James' leadership, believed that Jesus was born in normal fashion) with mystical views at variance with the orthodox Pharisees and Sadducees, but to perceive and acknowledge his own flesh and blood brother in the same elevated way as Paul was more than he could bear. Regal Messiah of Israel Jesus might be, but to set him up as some kind of transcendent being worthy almost of worship was utterly unacceptable. Paul was guilty of heresy, and had to be straightened out.

There is only one recorded meeting between Jesus and his brother James after the crucifixion, and we are understandably given not a single detail of what was said or discussed. James, it would seem, is dispensable. He is not in line with Jesus' post-crucifixion intentions, and his rejection of Paul must in some sense have been a rejection of Jesus himself – but not of Jesus' Messiahship. James would have continued to believe in Jesus as God's chosen vessel in spite of Paul's demand to be recognized as the apostle to the Gentiles at Jesus' instigation. In James' mind, Jesus himself might have been doctrinally suspect, but that did not change his messianic standing; he was still the regal Messiah, and James' senior in the Nazarene movement. Of course the Gentiles would be part of God's kingdom, but that would come later, after the Glory had descended on Israel and the Romans had been swept into oblivion. The Gentiles would come then, kingdom by kingdom, to acknowledge Israel as God's chosen people, and share in Israel's bounty. But there was no need to go out and drag them in, no need at all. And if they begged entrance to the Jewish faith, then let them in – but only by way of circumcision and obedience to the Law of Moses. That was James' stance, and he would not budge.

PETER HEDGES HIS BETS

Confronted by the persuasive Paul, Peter, on the other hand, was all at sea. He would eventually side with Paul, or at least *seem* to do so as a result of scribal interference. But for the moment he hedged his bets. And Paul must have been aware of Peter's wavering spirit before going up to Jerusalem – why else seek out Peter instead of Jesus' brother James? Paul undoubtedly saw Peter as the weak link in the Nazarene chain. Paul would later attack Peter for hypocrisy and weakness and call him a 'false brother'.[22] Picking up on this theme, Joseph Klausner describes Peter thus:

He seems to have been enthusiastic and imaginative, energetic and warm-hearted, but thoughtless and not profound, lacking the stamina of a real reformer and one who must endure to the end.[23]

And in Acts we read that the elders of Israel viewed Peter and John as 'unlearned and ignorant men'.[24]

Over the course of two weeks Paul and Peter must have talked long and hard about what had to be done to comply with Jesus' wishes, and in the end agreed that the Gentile converts to the Nazarene Way would come in very handy as a source of money and manpower if the Romans had ultimately to be faced. Peter would not have been against the idea of a large Gentile infusion – he himself lived like a Gentile, and preferred the Gentile manner of life in spite of a basic conservatism.[25] But he knew he would have to face up to James, and that must have made him quake in his shoes. He was afraid of James, and the other disciples seem to have been of similar temper. It is a telling point that James does not properly appear in the gospels. Jesus' mother, his brother James, and his other brothers and sisters are given no role to play as he trudges towards Jerusalem and the Cross. At one point the whole family turns up and attempts to take him home because they think he has gone mad. And perhaps he had, for who in his right mind could consciously offer himself up as a human sacrifice and believe that it was a sensible act? Or was there another reason?

Rudolf Augstein touches on what James may have believed in his book *Jesus, Son of Man*. He says:

> Under the influence of the gnosis which had flooded in from the East over the whole inhabited world, including Palestine, the man Jesus, who was not raised up to be the son of God until his resurrection, as even James may perhaps have believed, became the son of God from the beginning of time.[26]

And Paul too must have believed something like this. Jesus was no longer just Jesus; he was *the risen* Jesus, and as such a *son of God*. Before his crucifixion he had been an ordinary man with an extraordinary Mission; after his crucifixion he was an extraordinary man for the very reason of having fulfilled his Mission. And to fulfil it, he had to physically survive. This is to say that the idea of the dying God in the minds of the sectaries had taken on new significance, an elevated significance based, it can only be assumed, on the survival of the subject. Pagan dying gods had died once a year, every year, and that had been the end of them. This version demanded that the victim survive to lead the people into the Glory of the Last Days – pagan belief had undergone a dramatic transformation, a literalization that would skew paganism itself in a whole new direction. According to Bultmann, the mystery-gods of the Hellenistic world were gods who suffered, gods who continued in 'the form of the sacraments of the Christian religion',[27] and Jesus' every indication prior to delivering these very sacraments to the disciples in the upper room was that he would survive Roman punishment and meet up with them at a *prearranged* place in Galilee. The only possible explanation for such a rendezvous is that Jesus had to physically get there like everyone else – phantoms simply have no need of utilitarian arrangements made prior to their earthly demise.

THE LEAP OF REASON

Jesus' commissioning of Paul as apostle to the Gentiles, and his subsequent meetings with Paul in secret, or in the presence of chosen followers, carries us back to Paul's reasons for going to Arabia and not up to Jerusalem as one would have expected. And the length of the visit is also important – three years is a considerable length of time. So what was Paul up to during that three-year period? Was he meditating and preaching to the local inhabitants, as some Christian academics suggest? Or was he searching for something – parchments, perhaps?

Kamal Salibi is of the opinion that Paul did eventually lay his hands on secret documents concerning a Jesus-like figure in Arabia, and that it was these documents, these 'parchments', that he asked to be brought to him as he languished in prison awaiting his order of execution from the Romans. The parchments, which were obviously of the greatest importance to Paul, probably contained the blueprint of his advanced Christology, 'the wisdom of God in a mystery, even the hidden wisdom' to which he refers in his Corinthian epistle.[28] 'Why did he want them?' asks Salibi. So that he might destroy them, is the probable answer.

The problem at this point is not in accepting that Paul may have found secret documents in Arabia concerning a Jesus-like figure, but in fully appreciating and accepting the fact that Jesus was alive and fully in control of events – a fact we have striven to

rom the numerous gospel references post-resurrection. But
have to make a leap: not a leap of faith but a leap of
... — the leap that will carry us from mythology into reality.
Christian scholars will see this leap in reverse, but that is to be
expected. With all our might we have to somehow break the
taboo against thinking that Jesus rose from the dead and face
the narrative of the gospels square on. We have to break the
taboo of only hearing what we have been brought up to believe –
that 'flesh and blood' does not mean exactly what it says – and
accept that 'flesh and blood' does mean precisely what it says. The
taboo against the realization that Jesus planned and physically
survived his crucifixion is so firmly rooted in our minds that
it takes time for its opposite to fully register. But when it does,
when the penny finally drops and the probable truth sinks in, the
effect is as startling, indeed as numbing, as it must have been for
Paul himself.

But is this possible? If we are not Christian, then not believing in
the Resurrection as a divine event is only too easy. But if we are
orthodox Christian, we have to do something quite spectacular:
not only do we have to slip mental gear and accept the fact that the
Resurrection was a literal event and not a divine happening, we
also have to face the truth of our own minds and admit that
we probably never really believed in the Resurrection as a divine
event anyway – and then face the disturbing fact that we now
have to treat that event as something that really happened.
Suddenly, unexpectedly, the Jesus we so comfortably and easily
accommodated is no longer a dead phantom inexplicably roaming
around in a real body soon to be transmuted: he is a flesh and
blood man with whom it is necessary to deal in real terms, the
terms of history. On the other hand, evangelicals and fundamentalists, bound as they are to the literal belief that Jesus'
Resurrection was simultaneously physical and divine, have to find
the courage to question that belief and realize that the fundamental
physical laws that govern our world today were equally valid in
the first century. When Jesus' survival of death is appreciated in
those terms, it cannot be viewed as anything other than a lucky
escape.

It is not at all surprising that Paul made resurrection the
cornerstone of his new gospel, indeed the cornerstone of his very
life, for Jesus the Nazarene was living proof that the God of Israel
had worked a mighty wonder on behalf of Israel and the whole

world. How could Paul doubt it? Like the disciples he had been confronted, *fait accompli*, with an admittedly scarred but indisputably alive Jesus. There was no arguing with this fact. And after the first unbelievable encounter, the first nerve-shattering confrontation with this hypnotic figure, all doubt was dispelled – this Jesus was dishing out orders and reasoning according to the Prophets just as he had always done. The only problem – particularly for James and his coterie of followers – was dealing with Jesus' claim that he was now a transcendent being, that 'all power had been given to him in heaven and in earth'.[29] The more conservative of the Nazarenes could not accept that claim, and that in spite of the fact that it was legitimate for Jews to see their Messiah as *son of God*. Jesus had changed, taken on a curious air, a majesty born out of his suffering, out of his experience of himself as the Messiah of Israel, and not everyone could go along with his grandiose perception of things.

THE NAZARENE SUCCESSION

Jesus' brother James became chief disciple, or leader of the Nazarene Party (also sometimes referred to as Ebionites or Nazarites) after the crucifixion. A severe ascetic, James put a tight rein on Jesus' disciples, and must have been a bit of a problem for those of them who preferred Jesus' more relaxed attitude to the Law of Moses. Eusebius (quoting Hegesippus) speaks of James as one who neither drank wine nor strong drink, ate no flesh, never cut his hair, clothed himself in cotton and never in woollens, possessed but one garment, and spent much time fasting and praying in the Temple.[30] In Acts, James takes Paul to task on his attitude to the Law of Moses and pointedly suggests not only that he give money to the Nazarite cause, but that he enter the Temple with these Nazarites and purify himself in accordance with the teachings of the Pharisees.[31] And Paul, in his epistle to the Galatians, remarks with equal pointedness that when James was present, both Peter and Barnabas refused to eat with Gentile Christians, something they had been quite willing to do when he was not around.[32] Klausner remarks that the only thing separating James 'the righteous' from the Pharisees was his regard for the 'Suffering Messiah as the Redeemer and Saviour, and in supposing that the Messiah had already come'.[33] This is to say that it was James, and not Paul, who was the Pharisee of the Pharisees, and as we shall see later, probably carried much more authority in sectarian eyes than New Testament specialists have ever suspected.

But there was more to the Nazarene Party than met the eye. Their Messiah had, after all, been condemned by the Jews as a heretic and executed by the Romans as a zealot, and a similar fate was in store for Jesus' brother James. Considered subversive by both the ruling Sadducees and the Romans, the Nazarenes continued to be persecuted, and in 44 CE Peter and John were arrested, flogged, and on pain of death ordered not to speak again in the name of Jesus. In 62 CE James, along with other Nazarenes, was arrested and charged with 'deserting the faith' by the ruling Sadducees, and killed. Knowing James' piety, the Pharisees protested.[34] Hegesippus, writing in the second century, reports that the last words of James were the prayer 'I beseech thee, O Lord God and Father, forgive them, for they know not what they do.'[35] After his death James was replaced by Simeon, the son of James' mother's sister, Mary the wife of Clopas, and what remained of the Nazarenes continued in Jerusalem until 65 CE, then fled to the city of Pella on the east side of the Jordan prior to the Roman invasion. Salibi tells us that after Simeon's death, other members of James' family, including two grandsons of his brother Judas (or Jude), continued to succeed as 'Bishops' of Jerusalem.[36] Talking of this family dynasty, Dr Schonfield says illuminatingly, 'by appointing again not an apostle but a kinsman of Jesus they showed their determination to re-establish a government in readiness for the return of King Jesus.'[37] There is therefore little doubt that these 'Bishops' of Jerusalem were in fact a dynastic bloodline, a dynasty claiming sacred legitimacy because of a blood relationship to Jesus.

From Pella the Nazarene remnant moved north-eastwards, eventually making their way to the Tigris-Euphrates basin. In this relatively safe area they preserved their traditions for centuries.[38] Eusebius and Epiphanius bear witness to the fact that the Nazarenes survived and that numbers of Jews joined them.[39] And from the historian Julius Africanus (160–240 CE) we learn that the Nazarene 'heirs' took pride in their Davidic descent and circulated the genealogy which now stands at the head of Matthew's gospel.[40] Jesus, according to the gospels,[41] and to Paul,[42] was the first-born of many brothers, and had at least two sisters. In his *Ecclesiastical History*, Eusebius of Caesaria (340 CE) speaks of grandchildren of Jesus' brother Jude who were living in Galilee during the reign of the Roman Emperor Domitian (81–96 CE). According to Eusebius, the descendants of Jesus' family (*Desposyni*) eventually became dynastic leaders of various Christian Churches, and continued so up until the time of the Emperor Trajan (ruled 98–117 CE).

Picking up on Eusebius' statement, Richard Leigh writes:

> A modern Catholic authority recounts a story which brings them up to the fourth century – the time of Constantine – and adds that the Bishop of Rome [Pope Sylvester] is said to have met personally with eight Desposyni leaders – each of whom presided over a branch of the Church – at the Lateran Palace . . . They are reported to have requested (1) that the confirmation of the Christian bishops of Jerusalem, Antioch, Ephesus and Alexandria be revoked; (2) that these bishoprics be conferred on members of the Desposyni; and (3) that Christian Churches 'resume' sending money to the Desposyni Church in Jerusalem, which was to be regarded as the definitive Mother Church.[43]

Their requests were of course ignored.

Julius Africanus speaks of Herod the Great's burning the registers of aristocratic Israelite families because he himself had no such blood in his veins. Then he says,

> A few careful people had private records of their own, having either remembered the names or recovered them from copies, and took pride in preserving the memory of their aristocratic origins. These included the people . . . known as *Desposyni* (i.e. the Master's People) because of their relationship to the saviour's family.[44]

Leigh adds that the burning of the genealogies to which Julius Africanus refers was more probably perpetrated by the Romans after the revolt of 66 CE. And it is a telling point that the Emperor Domitian (81–96 CE), according to Eusebius in his *Ecclesiastical History*,[45] ordered the execution of 'all who were of David's line' so many years after that event.

So it is ironic indeed to find Paul underplaying the importance of the genealogies awarded to Jesus' family in the gospels as 'those legends and long lists of ancestors, which only produce argument'[46] – did he perhaps feel threatened by the Davidic line because of his own disgraced Benjaminite ancestry? Or was he himself not a Jew, and therefore not inclined to speak of such matters? Or did he perhaps know something about those genealogies that robbed them of their importance?

Simon Peter was not a descendant of David, yet is recorded as having been directly commissioned by Jesus to be the leader of the Nazarenes after the crucifixion.[47] As already noted, Marcello Craveri thinks this highly unlikely due to the fact that the other gospels do not register such an event – particularly as the gospel of Mark is thought to contain Peter's teachings. When the time comes it is Jesus' brother James, second in the sacred Davidic line, who assumes the mantle of leadership. Later Christian tradition will refer to James as *Iakobos Iostos* (in Latin *Justus*), rendered in English as 'James the Just', or 'James the Righteous' – meaning someone who strictly upheld the Israelite Law. Salibi notices, however, that in the Semitic languages the terms denoting 'justice' and 'righteousness' also denote 'legitimacy' or 'lawfulness' of succession. This then makes James' title both a possible description of his character and also, by definition, an indication of his lawful hereditary succession to the Nazarene leadership.[48]

So did James short-circuit Jesus' wishes and force Peter to stand aside? Or was Peter merely a temporary leader relieved by James at the first opportunity? This is quite possible; and the fact that Peter seems to have been second in charge is suggestive of his having been 'displaced' by James for one reason or another. It is almost as if James, of whom we hear virtually nothing in the gospels, suddenly turns up after the crucifixion, reminds everyone of his family credentials and steps into his dynastic role. And it is truly remarkable how Jesus' disciples seem not to have really grasped the fact that he was heading for the cross. This suggests that the disciples may not have been properly in Jesus' confidence, not fully central to his needs, and that there was another circle of followers who were more fully aware of his intention right from the very beginning of his ministry. The question is, who?

The ecclesiastical historians bear witness to the fact that the original apostles and elders and relations of Jesus were eventually in control of the *whole* Church, and that Jewish Christianity considered Pauline Christianity a heretical offshoot. Writing of this period, Schonfield unravels the intricacies of the situation when he says:

> We have to appreciate the difficulties of the Nazoreans. The Simeonite government, although it was the legitimate Christian authority, was not in a position effectively to exercise control of Christian affairs. By

reason of its Davidic leadership and strong Messianic conviction Nazorean Council was marked down as anti-Roman, and could exist and function somewhat precariously in the East. This crea' vacuum fatal to Christian coherence under the post-war conditions, which had to be filled if Christianity in other parts of the Empire was to survive.[49]

And so, slowly, the Roman Church assumed the mantle of Christian leadership, and produced the necessary propaganda to undermine and finally replace Nazarene dynastic authority. Schonfield caustically remarks: 'According to the view which prevailed, the Catholic Church of the new orthodoxy was the inheritor of the true tradition of the Apostles, an assertion which illustrates the power of a lie if it is a thumping big one.'[50]

THE SAMARITAN EYE-OPENER

During my attempt to unravel what was going on between Paul and the Nazarenes, I happened upon Michael Goulder's highly detailed essay 'The Two Roots of the Christian Myth'.[51] Captured by the title, and half expecting Goulder to claim the Nazarenes as one of the two roots underlying that myth, I was surprised to discover that what he had identified as the other root was not Nazarene but *Samaritan*. I did a double-take. Samaritan? How could that be? As far as the Jews were concerned, the Samaritans were *personae non gratae* by reason of their being descendants of colonists imported by the Assyrians during their occupation of Palestine. Although professing Judaism, the Samaritans nevertheless would have nothing whatsoever to do with the Temple at Jerusalem, and accepted the Jewish Scriptures only up to the time of Moses, and no further. As Goulder points out, the Jews believed that God was active in history, whereas the Samaritans believed that God had withdrawn from history – perhaps because they felt that they had been abandoned by God to the mercy of the Assyrians. As a result of this view, the Samaritans rejected the whole Jewish prophetic corpus, and their theology – which was based on a personal revelation of God through Scripture rather than a historical intervention by God – reflected this stance.[52]

Delicately tracing a path through Samaritan beliefs, Goulder reveals an astonishing array of ideas held by the Samaritans which without doubt must eventually have influenced Paul in the creation of his own highly complex vision of Jesus in the role of 'Divine Man'. Five features are cited:

1 God is experienced not through history but through revelation of Scripture;
2 God's revelation was in the form of 'secrets' and 'mysteries' and formed a 'wisdom' or 'knowledge' of God known only to an élite;
3 God is a duality;
4 God manifested himself and *stood by* Moses as a 'physical incarnation' (Joshua?); and
5 God would some day send a prophet like Moses.

This is a very truncated version of Goulder's observations, but it suffices to show the similarities between Samaritan theology and what Paul eventually came up with. For it is evident that Paul did not quite see things this way at the beginning, but slowly came around to a version of Samaritan teaching as a result of inter-acting with their missionaries – missionaries preaching a Jesus more exciting than his own. This is not to gainsay Nazarene harassment of Paul through spies and undercover agents: it is to present a three-pronged, rather than a single-pronged, theory of influence. Paul's theological system, as it developed, reveals input from sources Jewish, Arabian and Samaritan, and this helps explain its strange and sometimes incoherent development. From somewhere in Arabia Paul arrived back with ideas quite at odds with that of Nazarene beliefs about Jesus. From the Samaritan missionaries he augmented his Arabian findings and evolved a Christology which eventually eclipsed the historical Jesus altogether. And from a Jesus waiting in the wings for God's Glory to descend on Israel and initiate the Last Days as a result of his mighty ritualistic effort on the Cross came a certainty that the Kingdom of God was just around the corner.

But it is Simone Pétrement who puts the finishing touches to this set of influences on Paul. Observing that the sect of the Nazarenes was linked to that of the Dositheans, she tells us that the eponymous Dositheus was himself an object of worship. She also states that although considered a Samaritan heretic by many scholars, this same Dositheus (whose name means 'gift of God') is more likely to have been a Jew, indeed the name may represent a title for Jesus himself. Dosithean beliefs were of the same type as those of the Ebionites, and the Ebionites and Nazarenes are known to have been closely related in belief and practice. Pétrement speculates that this name or title may have been given to Jesus by Samaritan Christians, and she backs up this startling point of view by pointing out that Dositheus was:

1 Jewish and not Samaritan;
2 that he was 'Christ' for the Samaritans;
3 that he claimed to be a saviour figure;
4 that his disciples believed him to be alive and not dead;
5 that he prescribed baptism or baths for those wishing to join his faith;
6 that he had been a disciple of John the Baptist and had succeeded him;
7 that he was the founder of the Ebionites;
8 that the Dositheans were also called Nazarenes; and
9 that the Dositheans were Christian heretics, or, more precisely, that they were among those constituting the *transition between Jewish heresies and Christian heresies* [my italics].[53]

To my way of thinking, this extraordinary similarity between Dositheus and Jesus the Nazarene may run deeper than mere reflection. It might well be that what we have here is Jesus himself surfacing under another title, rather than a name, for obvious reasons. For it is interesting to note that there are only two passages in the whole New Testament where the title 'Gift of God' appears, and both passages are linked, as Pétrement points out, with Samaria. And the very fact that Simon Magus and Paul are also, on occasions, interchangeable names may point to an intentional mixing of identities for the express purposes of camouflaging what was actually going on.

SEVEN

PRIMORDIAL CHRISTIANITY

The existence of an Arabian Christianity centuries before Jesus, the problem of the New Testament Jesus being partly composed of a previous Jesus-type figure, and the fact that Jesus did not consider himself co-equal with God.

The Koran has it that there was an Arabian Christianity centuries older than that of the New Testament, and directly aligned with the Nazarenes, then called *Nasara*.[1] According to Kamal Salibi, this earlier form of Christianity survived in its original Arabian home until the coming of Islam, and was the basis of the New Testament Christological form developed by Paul. But as it turns out, Paul, during his extended stay in western Arabia, seems to have unwittingly accepted doctrinal information from a splinter-group of the Nasara which just happened to be heretical – at least, that's how it appears at first glance. Having obtained insights (perhaps even parchments) concerning the Nasara's doctrinal system, Paul creatively merged Nasara esotericism with Jewish/sectarian messianic expectations and came up with a Messiah-figure of greater stature than that expounded by the orthodox Nazarenes. The Koran, in speaking of this early form of Christianity, roundly condemns a section of the Nasara for maintaining that God is not One, but part of a divine Trinity,[2] and also makes a clear distinction between the Israelites (*Banu Isra'il*) and the Jews (*al-Yahud*).

The Israelites are recognized as 'special', or 'chosen', and the Jews as followers of biblical monotheism and the laws of Moses as interpreted and developed by post-exilic rabbinical Judaism.[3] The Nasara, or early Nazarenes, are conceived of as a sister community to the Jews, and not merely as an offshoot of Judaism. This is an important point, for it means that Nazarene Christianity was not a runaway Jewish sect but in early times an altogether different religious development parallel to Judaism, and quite possibly the heart of the whole sectarian phenomenon eventually called Essean-Essene. In this scheme of things, the Nazarenes and Ebionites and Zadokites and Nazarites and all the other opposition groups (this even included a branch of the Sadducees) were not a raggle-taggle conglomerate of religiously out-of-focus sects and cults, but rather a highly organized body of religious opinion brought to doctrinal completion at the time of Jesus, and probably organized on a military level if some of the Scrolls are to be read literally and not as imaginative constructions. This 'completing' – and to a certain extent 'merging' – of doctrinal niceties among the sectarian opposition groups was underpinned by a manic desire to keep the Law, and this reveals what Eisenman and Wise have termed a 'mindset of extreme apocalyptic "zeal"'.[4]

This raises the interesting possibility that the great mystical leader of the Qumran Essenes, the Teacher of Righteousness, was himself a Nazarene, and that Jesus, over and above his pretensions to the throne of Israel, was either this great teacher in person – as Schonfield seems to suggest – or a teacher of similar background and authority. The Nazarenes would then have been the spearhead of the sectarian groups, the doctrinally sharpened tip of a general messianic movement. But things of course went wrong for Jesus, terribly wrong – unless 'rejection' was part of the divine purpose, and in some mysterious fashion consciously built into the messianic pattern itself. The Jewish hierarchy did not respond, and the urbane, cosmopolitan Jews of Judea simply could not accept that this strange Galilean with his little band of ignorant disciples could possibly be their awaited Messiah. On the one hand, the priesthood wanted to delay any such madcap exercise and make absolutely sure of victory, and on the other, the educated Jewish élite were more than happy with the Roman occupation in spite of its grassroots brutality. For the scribes and Pharisees, Jesus' open-ended attitude to the Law of Moses set their teeth on edge, and his talk of having come to 'complete the Law' made them fear for his sanity. It was one thing to gossip expectantly about the coming of the Messiah; it was quite another to be faced with someone who actually believed that he *was* the Messiah. And in that Jesus continually attacked nit-picking attitudes to the Law, and regularly broke the purity codes so dear to the sectaries, the idea that he himself might have been the Essene Teacher of Righteousness seems highly unlikely.

ISSA

The leader of the ancient Nasara, or Nazarenes, was called Issa. When rendered into Greek, this Arabic name can come out as *Iēsous*. When the Greek name *Iēsous* is translated into Aramaic, it comes out as the equivalent of 'Jesus'. And this in spite of the fact that the names Issa and Jesus are not the same name in Arabic. In the Koran, the name Jesus is *Jeshu* (standard Arabic *Yasu*), not Issa. The connection, apparently, is in the anomaly of transliteration, where both names end up in Greek as *Iēsous*, Jesus.[5] This is not to say that the Jesus of the New Testament was some kind of fiction based on Issa, but that these two figures, because of many curious similarities of background and storyline, were eventually collapsed into one another to denote both a divine mystery and an apostolic succession – a direct link between the Nazarenes of Jesus' time and the ancient Nasara of western Arabia where Salibi convincingly places the historical activities of the monotheistic Israelites. With infinite patience, Salibi shows that Israelite history did not take place in Palestine but in the western Arabian province of Hijaz and Astir, bordering the Red Sea. Due to migrations of Arabian Jews/Israelites from western Arabia in earlier times (the result of invasion), the names of many towns and villages from the Hijaz had been transferred to Palestinian locations for sentimental reasons – including the name for the whole area as well. And so we end up with two Galilees and two Nazareths, and a number of other telling duplicates which help cement Salibi's point into place. On the basis of these anomalies and other difficult to refute proofs, Salibi suggests that Jesus himself was from western Arabia.

BENEATH THE TEXT BUSINESS

Before considering this claim, and its ramifications, it should be pointed out that the Jesus of the gospels is often composed not of flesh and blood but of esoteric exegesis in relation to the Old Testament, which sometimes alters the surface story of his real personality and behaviour. The Old Testament sources for such textual manoeuvres are generally quoted by the writer-compilers of the gospels, but sometimes they are not, and one has to fathom what is going on beneath the text. This 'beneath the text' business is very important when attempting to interpret the story of Jesus. Yes, there is a real Jesus in the gospels; but there is also a visionary Jesus – the archetypal messianic Jesus who existed solely in the minds of those creating the story. And the story is 'true' even when it does not tell the historical truth, for to the writer-compilers the truth about Jesus was also the truth of what they believed had been promised about him as the Messiah. So the gospel story accommodates these 'belief stories' as if they are actual history, and on occasions Jesus himself can be seen to control situations so as to form a correspondence with what was expected of him. These were the 'signs' of the Messiah, either given directly by Jesus in words or acts, or later added to his messianic story to substantiate further his authority and authenticity. So it is obvious to scholars that Jesus has been 'retextured' in more than one way, and on more than one level – and as we will shortly see, his historical background in far-off Galilee hides further surprises.

As with the work of Dr Schonfield, the discoveries of Kamal Salibi have earned him not praise (as one would hope and expect) but angry condemnation from both Old and New Testament scholars. He remarks bemusedly in his introduction to *Conspiracy in Jerusalem* (1988), 'None of these scholars has so far advanced a single item of direct or even circumstantial evidence to prove me wrong.' And a few lines later he adds: 'In any serious historical inquiry, one must do what a good coroner does: listen to all the gossip, but start the actual cross-examination from a clean slate.'[6] Salibi's 'clean slate', however, necessitates turning to the Koran for assistance.

The Koran states that the people of Israel were organized into a religious community by Moses, and that later two other messengers were sent to them: Ezra, then Issa. Ezra's followers became the Jews; Issa's followers became the early Nasara – Nazarenes. 'Each of these two communities,' says Salibi, 'came to revere its special apostle as a son of God.'[7] The Koran seems to place the mission of Issa as latter-day prophet of Israel around the fifth or fourth century BCE, and roundly condemns those followers of Issa who imagined their leader to be divine.[8] In general terms, Issa sounds remarkably like the gospel Jesus.

Born of a virgin called Mary, Issa was thought of as a miraculous being who reflected in his human person not only the 'Holy Spirit' but also the divine *kalimah*, the prophetic 'word'.

This Issa performed miracles, raised the dead, alleviated the rigours of the Mosaic Law, had followers who wore 'white robes', and was a consecrated or ordained person. It was also said that Issa had probably been crucified, that he had been taken up into heaven, and that he would undergo a resurrection, after which he would pass judgement on humankind. All in all, a series of remarkable coincidences, considering that Issa is Arabian and belongs to the fourth century BCE.

The political history of the Israelites ended with the destruction of the kingdom of Judah by the Babylonians in 586 BCE. Taken into captivity, the Israelite exiles were finally given their freedom in 539 BCE when the Babylonians were themselves conquered by the Persians. As a result, large numbers of Israelite exiles were allowed to return home, and it is at this point that Ezra the prophet's career is highlighted. Ezra, who had returned from Babylon the year before, helped with the reconstruction of Israelite society, and through his teaching and preaching laid the foundations of a new religious development: Judaism. Working from an account of Issa and Ezra in the Koran, Salibi tells us that Issa (separated from Ezra by over a century, it should be remembered) was probably a Sadducee, a follower of the original Israelite monotheism, and that he must have reacted strongly against Ezra's earlier innovative reforms. For Issa apparently claimed exactly the same descent as Ezra on his mother's side, and this suggests that both men had been of the same priestly aristocracy.[9] Because the history of Judaism for the next 300 years is a virtual blank, the exact repercussions of this struggle for the priestly seniority of Issa over Ezra are not known. But with the help of Koranic material, something of that lost period can be pieced together.

In about 400 BCE Issa began preaching a liberal interpretation of Israelite monotheism at variance with that of Ezra. Those of Issa's home region who followed Ezra's now highly developed school of thought – Judaism – flatly rejected what this new prophet had to say. Others did however accept Issa's teachings, and they came to be known as Nasara – Nazarenes. Salibi assumes that this choice of name came about because Issa's first major preaching success was probably among the inhabitants of the Arabian village of Nasirah – Nazareth. Remembering that the names Issa and Jesus are one and the same in Aramaic when translated from Greek, we are left with a historical conundrum:

what is the actual nature of the inferred connection of Jesus to this Issa-Jesus? Similarity, and no more? Coincidence? Is it mere coincidence that Issa had a mother called Mary? A virgin birth? A crucifixion and resurrection? An ascension? If only coincidence, then how to explain Issa's 'Nazarene' followers, and the astonishing fact that there exists in the region of the Hijaz both a 'Galilee' and a 'Nazareth'? Salibi suggests that four centuries after Issa the Jesus of the gospels left this Arabian Galilee and arrived in Galilee of Palestine with his eyes set on the throne of Israel. Recognized as a legitimate descendant of David – an Israelite of the old school, one might say – this Arabian Jesus then put his political and religious Mission into operation. Dr Schonfield, quoting Matthew Black, states that the 'oldest root of the Christian movement in "Galilee" is to be sought in a group of dedicated Nazarites, sectarians who continued the ancient Israelite institution of the lifelong Nazarite'. He then goes on to say: 'We have every reason to hold that the family to which Jesus belonged was nurtured in this tradition, and much of his teaching confirms this.'[10]

But like Issa before him, Jesus had a much more liberal religious attitude – the strict Nazarite way of life was not for him. His brothers, particularly James, would carry on the Nazarene-Nazarite tradition handed down to them from the Nasara (the orthodox line), but Jesus would break away from this religious form and develop – much to the consternation of his family – an altogether more open and daring religious policy: a policy dangerously near to that of the heretical Nasara splinter group. Moving freely among the people, he repudiated Nazarite segregation and taught a more personal system of communication with God. And in place of Nazarite strictness to the Law of Moses he advised a Sabbath made for man and dietary freedom. But perhaps his most daring, his most revolutionary, opinion was that the 'secrets' of the Saints, the 'hidden wisdom' of the sectaries, should be made known to the people – in fact, proclaimed from the rooftops! To the old Nazarene way of thinking, this would have made Jesus a dangerous teacher – in fact, a false teacher, an apostate Messiah. But he was of course following through on what was said of the Son of Man in the *Similitudes*, where Enoch says: 'This is the Son of Man who hath righteousness, with whom dwelleth righteousness, and who reveals all the treasures of that which is hidden'.[11]

The same section describes this Son of Man as 'the light of the Gentiles'. In that the *Similitudes* is suspected of having been written by the northern Nazarene Essenes, what constituted 'righteousness' and 'good religious policy' was obviously still under debate within that fraternity. Schonfield eventually makes the precise connection we require between the *Similitudes* and Paul's Christology when he says: 'From such teaching, probably while in the borders of Arabia, Paul acquired the inspiration from which to develop his concept of the Heavenly Messiah who incarnated in the earthly Jesus.'[12]

The difference between Paul's and James' systems of belief concerning the nature, and stature of the Messiah seems to link directly into the ancient Nasara community's splitting into two factions – one orthodox, the other heterodox – and the distorted reflection of this split among the Nazarenes and other sectarian groups of northern Palestine. It is this difference in Nasara belief systems which, centuries later, will produce the tension and persecution of Paul by James and his faction, plus those of Jesus' original disciples who had reverted to orthodoxy under James' austere guidance. Paul would adopt what appeared to be the heretical camp's theological point of view, and Christianity would be under way. According to the Koran, a special 'book' written in Aramaic (the lost Nazarene gospel, in all likelihood) had been divinely delivered to Issa.[13] Schonfield tells us that the Nazarenes were in possession of 'a Gospel written in Aramaic of which fragments have been preserved, and produced much other literature partly known to us',[14] and Simone Pétrement in her definitive statement on Gnosticism and Christianity says, 'The Jewish Christians had a particular Gospel, primarily derived from Matthew. They rejected Paul's epistles, who was for them a "Greek", that is, a pagan.'[15] Some of these Nazarene writings would have been available to the gospel writer-compilers. Is this then Paul's 'secret wisdom', his 'meat', the propagation of which will eventually lead to the formation of a Church that will replace the authority of pagan Rome with the authority of a Jewish Messiah turned pagan god? In *The Nazarene Gospel Restored*, Robert Graves and Joshua Podro shed light on this situation. Paul, they tell us, in conjunction with Gentile God-fearers of Syria, Asia Minor, Greece, Italy, and *a small but influential body of Samaritan converts*, 'shaped the Nazarene tradition to their own convenience'.[16]

Over 200 years later, the Emperor Constantine, as initiate of the Sol Invictus cult, was to have only token trouble convincing Christians that Jesus had been *wholly* God in human form. The point of a sword and the threat of falling off a cliff will bring most waverers round to his point of view – a point of view not at that time accepted by the bulk of Christian churches strewn across the then civilized world. In 325 CE, the Council of Nicea would decide, by vote, that Jesus is God, not a mortal prophet, and from that moment anyone who disagreed with this finding, or any book offering a view at variance with this finding, would be classified as 'heretical'.

It is likely that as a result of his Arabian journey, 'parchments' concerning Issa's background and the teachings developed about him would have come into Paul's possession. Either that or he was 'schooled' in ancient Nazarene doctrine, and out of this experience created a new and controversial gospel around Jesus *and* Issa. Whatever the case, parchments related to the Nasara do seem to have surfaced after Paul's death, and it is probable that they were used by the gospel writers to complete the fusion of Jesus and Issa and promote what were undoubtedly ideas *not* of mainstream Nasara belief. The question is, was Paul responsible for what eventually happened? Scholars feel sure that there must have been another information source used by the gospel writers to complete the gospels, and the lost Gospel of the Nazarenes, or some other version of it (Samaritan?), seems likely to have been that source. So was Paul's 'secret wisdom' composed of the heretical notions of the Nasara splinter group? Everything seems to point in that direction – particularly Paul's own teachings concerning Jesus as the 'Christ'. But it may just be that to take this line is to do him an injustice, for there is a distinct possibility that Paul's teachings were grievously misunderstood by the Gentile leaders of the Church who came after him. Paul, on his own admission, held back on divulging his 'secret wisdom', preferring to feed his Gentile babes with 'milk' rather than 'meat' – one must suppose messianic Judaism and sectarian notions stripped of strict adherence to the Law of Moses. And there is little doubt that it is this very 'secret wisdom' which made the Nazarene hierarchy in Jerusalem reject him when he presented his theological credentials. The question is, why? What was it about Paul's version of things which so disturbed Jesus' flesh and blood brother? For 14 years James and his Nazarene faction would endlessly persecute Paul wherever he went. But in the end, due to the logistics of space and time, Nazarene influence would wither and Paul's highly successful missionary campaign would win the day – James and his followers would strike a compromise with Paul, and the ban on him as a Jesus-appointed apostle to the Gentiles would be lifted. Well, almost. There were no telephones in those days; it took time for a change of mind to get around. And, strange to say, after Paul's arrest in 58 CE, his teachings were again strongly opposed by the Jerusalem authority, and many Pauline Churches defected to James and accepted orthodox Nazarene doctrine.[17]

THE ARCHETYPAL MAN

The truth of the matter seems to be that the difference between what Paul taught, or wanted to teach, and what James believed, was a difference of degree rather than a difference of kind. James did not believe in the virgin birth; neither, so it seems, did Paul. James did believe that Jesus was the regal Messiah by right of his Davidic descent; Paul also believed this, but preferred to overlook this aspect and concentrate on Jesus' right to 'priesthood' not by lineage but by ancient standards linked with Melchizedek as priest-king. James as Jesus' 'heir' considered himself the arbiter of who did what, when and where during Jesus' absence; Paul considered his direct appointment by Jesus as apostle to the Gentiles as giving him all the authority he required. Now among reasonable men, such differences would not have caused the problems detectable in Acts and the epistles – so what was the degree of difference that so profoundly separated them?

The answer to this question seems to lie in how they perceived and interpreted the Resurrection and the leadership. Both men obviously believed in the physical resurrection of Jesus, for both had interacted with an *alive* Jesus post-crucifixion and burial. But Paul's conception of this risen Jesus was radically different from that held by James. James the 'Just', James the 'Righteous', James the 'orthodox Jew' vehemently defended by the Pharisees prior to his death, was not mystically inclined – he was an austere man of the Law, an 'externaliser' of the truth. When James detected how Paul read the Resurrection event, he must have drawn back in horror. For although himself a sectarian leader, a

Nazarene-Ebionite with declared Nazarite sympathies – in effect an Essean-Essene or 'Holy One' – his underlying orthodoxy was such as to stop him considering the resurrection of his brother Jesus as anything other than an event promised by God and brought about by the ingenuity of man. Yes, Jesus was alive. Yes, Jesus was a Messiah of Israel, a Suffering Servant as promised in the scriptures. Yes, it was truly remarkable that this brother of his had found the will, the strength, the determination to undergo such an ordeal – particularly in the light of his attitude to the Law of Moses – but to push Jesus into the mould of the 'hidden wisdom' of the Nasara, to make of him the Archetypal Man of Israel, the Light Adam of Essene conception, and spread this abroad among the Gentiles was to openly invite doctrinal disaster: the Gentiles would not be able to understand such metaphors.

Accepting Paul's right to go to the Gentiles (it was expected that the Gentiles would benefit from the inauguration of God's Kingdom on Earth), James nevertheless rejected his interpretation of Jesus' importance – it was simply too much for his orthodoxy to bear. James' own epistle clearly separates him from the Pauline vision that faith in Jesus was all that mattered. He rejects this claim and points out that without 'works' faith is meaningless. Between the 40s and the 60s, James, as leader of the Jerusalem Community, insisted on complete obedience of the purity laws for *all* Jews drawn to the sectarian cause. And so the book of Acts portrays the relationship of Paul and James as strained, but the truth of the matter is that they were at loggerheads, their doctored writings revealing a veritable war of words.

THEOLOGICAL ADJUSTMENT

In the second century CE the Jewish Mishnah records the attitude of Pharisees and Rabbis to the 'secret doctrines' of Pharisees of the early period. So dangerous were these doctrines considered that rigorous prohibitions were set in place to stop anyone dabbling in or meddling with them. Dr Schonfield records the appropriate Mishnah passage for us:

> Men are not to expound unlawful unions with a company of three, nor the Lore of Creation with two persons, nor the [Heavenly]

Chariot [i.e. in Ezekiel] with one; but if a man do so, he must be a wise man, and one who has much knowledge on his own account. Everyone who meddles with these four things that follow, it were better for him if he had not come into the world: they are, What is Above and What is Below, What is Before and What is After. And everyone who does not revere the glory of his Maker [ie detracts from God's Unity and Incorporeality], it were better for him if he had not come into the world.[18]

It was the eventual belief of those who followed Jesus that the Archetypal Man, the vast universal figure of the invisible Messiah, had incarnated in Jesus. Adam in his sinless state, it was believed, was a being of transparent light whom sin eventually made opaque. Jesus, during his transfiguration, had momentarily revealed himself as a 'being of light', a second Adam. Schonfield says: 'The account of the transfiguration . . . is here expanded to emphasize the composite personality of Jesus in the capacity of Messiah, not as God and man, but as Archetypal Man and earthly man.'[19] According to one version of the Nazarene-Ebionite teaching, Jesus was 'begotten of the seed of man' and chosen as the vessel into which the Messiah would enter in the likeness of a dove.[20] Another view was that the incarnation of the Light Adam, the Archetypal Man, took place in the womb. James' problem with all of this, as a strict Nazarene, would not have been whether such ideas were true or untrue, but that such ideas should not be handed over to Gentile converts who would misunderstand and utterly distort such delicate teaching. Schonfield, in completing his observations concerning Jesus as Archetypal Man and *not* God as man, posits what I believe to have been James' intuition of the Christian Church's future in clear and precise language when he says:

This was something the majority of the Christian theologians who were converts from paganism did not apprehend, and accordingly they misunderstood and misinterpreted the New Testament records. The Church today, still labouring under the credal follies of its Councils from the fourth century onwards, has not got round to making the theological adjustments which are called for.[21]

This is to say that Paul's vision was a perfectly honourable one, but an inherently dangerous one. He himself admits that he is having problems finding anyone among his Gentile followers capable of comprehending his 'secret wisdom', and it is probable that he never at any time pushed these profundities on to anyone. The question of why Paul wanted his 'parchments' brought to him as he languished in a Roman prison is, I think, as Salibi suspected, that he wanted to destroy them. Such material in the wrong hands, he knew would constitute a disaster. And it was as he probably feared. The Greek-speaking writer-editors of the New Testament took up the highly esoteric teachings that were made available to them, peppered the gospels with them, and reduced what had been a majestic archetypal vision recording the deepest aspirations of the human spirit to the level of a rather gaudy comic book. The same mistake as made by the heretical Nasara splinter group was being made a second time, but its repercussions on this occasion would not be local but universal. Of course the surface veneer of myth and marvel may, as Dr Thiering suggests, have been intentional – that is, not so much a misunderstanding as a camouflaging of damaging information about Jesus.

Dr Schonfield draws our attention to the fact that the Essene and other Jewish mystics were highly influenced by dualistic Iranian ideas from the sixth to the fourth century BCE, and this corresponds exactly with what Salibi says about the growth and distribution of Nasara beliefs in relation to the Arabian Issa. Iranian dualism was obsessed with Light and Darkness as opposing forces, and its deity Mithra was defined as a projection of God, named Ahura-Mazda. Mithra was the divine made visible *in light,* and could be represented by the sun. As such, Mithra was a 'mediator' and a 'saviour' of mankind – a fact which, in conjunction with a similar belief system developed in Syria, would allow Constantine in 325 CE to happily view Jesus and the sun god as compatible: identical beings expressed in different geographical locations and at different times. As a high initiate of the Sol Invictus (Invisible Sun) cult, Constantine would legitimize Jesus not as the Archetypal Man of Jewish esotericism but as *wholly* God, God manifest in the flesh as 'light of the world'. Not everyone present at the Council of Nicea would agree with Constantine and his theological backers, but the day would be carried by threats, and the Church's literalist theological course would be firmly set.

ALICE IN THE LOOKING GLASS

Dr Schonfield emphasizes that 'neither before nor since Jesus has there been anyone whose experiences from first to last have been so pinpointed as tallying with what were held to be prophetic intimations concerning the Messiah. The nearest comparison available to us is that of the Teacher of Righteousness of the Dead Sea Scrolls.'[22] This suggests that Jesus knew exactly what it was he had to do, step by step, to make his Mission a success – a success to the extent that he would get himself crucified. For there is a curious reversal of logic evident in his thinking, and in his actions – a reversal that implied: When you fail, you will win. To become the 'rejected man' of prophecy, Jesus had to be rejected by the Jews, and he was. To successfully become the Suffering Servant he had to get crucified, and he was. And to become the resurrected Lord of Glory he had to escape death, and he did. From there on everything had ironically to be downhill to reach the pinnacle of accomplishment he sought. There is something of 'Alice in the Looking Glass' about this – everything is back to front.

If the Jews had responded to Jesus, if they had accepted him as their Messiah and risen as a man to back him against the Romans, he would not have been a legitimate Messiah. He had to get rejected, and by hook or by crook that is exactly what he managed to do. Schonfield wraps up this curious situation with the words:

> It is not difficult to understand how Jesus could have arrived at a comprehension of what the Messiah would experience. He evidently accepted that assured results were obtainable . . . and a prophetic blueprint of the Days of the Messiah was the outcome of his investigations. The Scriptures thus disclosed to him the character of his mission, how his message would be received, his fate, and his subsequent appearance in glory as king and judge of all nations.[23]

Yet he seems to have tried very hard to actually succeed at the same time as he was successfully failing – perhaps because he believed his rejection had to be authentic and not contrived.

Exhausted from his teaching efforts, he first sends out 12 disciples (the number of the tribes of Israel), then 70 (the number of the heathen nations yet to be called). But it is all to no avail; he is successfully heading for the Cross exactly as predicted. In phase one of his ministry, Jesus carefully follows the recorded prophetic blueprint and presents himself as the Teacher of Righteousness of the Last Days. Making his headquarters at Capernaum by the Sea of Galilee, he fulfils prophecy.[24] Speaking to the people in parables, he fulfils prophecy[25] – although it was also expedient for him to speak in disguised terms because of a security system introduced by Herod the Great. To have openly admitted that he was the Messiah at that point would have been to announce himself as the legitimate King of Israel and invite immediate arrest. In phase two of his work, he turns his face steadfastly towards Jerusalem, begins to seriously instruct his disciples in what his secret intentions are, learns of John the Baptist's death, and is assured by this sign that he is still on track. As from that moment, says Schonfield, 'it was demanded that to comply with the conditions of his fate he must increasingly reveal himself as the Messiah and abandon his incognito.'[26]

This raises the question as to what the 'Nazarenes' were doing all this time. The disciples would eventually be classified as Nazarenes, but as they followed Jesus from town to town it is evident that they did not at first know what he was up to, and only later began to realize the nature of his Mission. Bit by bit he opens their eyes to his particular messianic intentions, and the penny eventually drops. So where are the Nazarenes? His mother and brothers appear at one point and try to take him home because they think he has gone mad, but he rebukes them, rejects them, and goes about his business with a steely will. They do eventually seem to come round, but is it they who flit almost invisibly in and out of his life when he finally turns towards Jerusalem? Or is it perhaps some other band of sectaries – a breakaway branch of the Essenes from Qumran? The men 'in white robes' who announce his being alive after the crucifixion sound like Essenes, and his suddenly having many hundreds of followers as from that moment suggests not converts but compatriots, not new followers but some kind of retinue or small army. So maybe the Nazarenes, in spite of their obvious importance as the background from which Jesus came, and their crucial role after the crucifixion in establishing the Jewish strand of the Kingdom yet to come, were, after that horrific event, of less importance to Jesus than one might suppose.

THE ATHANASIAN ERROR

And so we come to the climax of it all, the Passover meal in the
upper room, the Garden of Gethsemane prayer, the arrest and
crucifixion, the burial and resurrection. Like a play or novel, the
story of Jesus has all the highlights necessary to hold one's
attention, and no less so the hour prior to his arrest. There is in full
evidence a deep, deep fear in Jesus' mind concerning the ordeal
ahead of him as he enters the Garden of Gethsemane, but the
mechanics of the situation are peculiar. His disciples, full of
Passover lamb and wine (the 'four cups' of Passover tradition), are
half-asleep and apparently oblivious to the dangers of the moment,
to the imminence of his arrest. Jesus is deeply depressed and nervy
– sick to the very heart, one might say. He takes Peter, James and
John (his favourites) and goes off to pray. 'Tarry ye here, and
watch,' he tells them, but does not tell them what to watch for.
Then comes his heart-rending prayer, interrupted no fewer than
three times by his observation that his favourites are asleep. On the
third occasion he gives up on them and leaves them to rest. Then
suddenly it is all happening, and he is rousing them and telling
them that Judas and his captors have arrived. What a moment that
must have been. One minute asleep; the next facing a well-armed
Civil Guard. With blind veneration the disciples had followed him
to this point, promised undying fealty, but when the moment of
dread reality comes – the moment of stark truth bereft of dream
and romance – they desert him and flee for their lives.

Mark's gospel spells things out quite clearly. Jesus and his
disciples were virtually ambushed by 'a great multitude armed
with swords and staves'.[27] Even as Jesus tells his half-asleep
disciples that Judas and the Civil Guard have arrived, they are set
upon and set to flight. The text is explicit: 'And immediately,
while he yet spake, cometh Judas . . . and with him a great
multitude'.[28] The disciples immediately take to their heels – the
bit about Peter slicing off someone's ear is a ludicrous insertion –
he would have been cut to pieces for such an act. The text of
Mark is glaringly corrupt at this point: it has Jesus upbraiding the
Civil Guard for coming with swords and staves at the very
moment his own disciple is supposed to have produced a sword
and lopped off someone's ear! No, Peter fled for his life like
everyone else, but 'followed him afar off'.[29] And when we are told
that Peter trailed the Civil Guard into the palace of the high priest

and unsuccessfully tried to pass himself off as a palace servant, his three denials of Jesus in that moment – in spite of verses which suggest otherwise[30] – cannot be read as the result of a sudden moment of weakness, or cowardice. Denial was the only sensible course; it was not a betrayal. To have admitted discipleship would have been to exhibit useless heroics, invite certain arrest and death. Why run away and then let the cat out of the bag? The real question is: did Jesus really expose his disciples to danger when he took them to Gethsemane? Why didn't he mentally prepare them for his arrest? Did he consider them expendable? Did he take Peter and James and John aside, separate them from the main bunch so that they could more easily escape detection and possible capture? It is possible. Peter obviously escaped, and we know that James and John lived to tell the tale. But so apparently did all the others, and one cannot but suspect an intrigue.

Dr Schonfield has it that the Civil Guard were only interested in capturing Jesus; that the disciples were unimportant small fry.[31] So it might be that Jesus, through Judas, had arranged what he hoped would be safe passage for his disciples, and that he refrained from telling them to heighten the effect of his being taken – he was after all setting up a 'drama' which he wanted to be remembered in precise detail. There is some evidence for the 'safe passage' theory. The kiss delivered by Judas clearly marks Jesus out to avoid arresting the wrong man, and the answer to Jesus' question 'Whom seek ye?' narrows whom they sought down to only one person – himself. If it had been a free-for-all, they would have scooped up everyone and identified the ringleader later.

But more importantly, the Jesus of Gethsemane reveals not only his organizational skills, he also reveals his human frailty in the face of a looming reality full of terror and pain, his capacity for depression and fear, his perhaps hysterical nature – we are told that he sweats blood, and this is a known medical condition suggestive of a super-sensitive nature in a state of violent emotion.[32] But over and above all of this he inadvertently reveals how he perceived himself in relation to God, and it is this more than anything else which marks the Gethsemane story out as significant. What he reveals is that he, Jesus, is an ordinary man, a man of flesh and blood truly shaken by what confronts him. The moment of truth has arrived, and his spirit does more than waver – it quakes. But it does more even than this, for Jesus' prayer in Gethsemane is full of doctrinal errors, mistakes in self-interpretation which would have earned him the stake a few hundred years later. It is obvious from this prayer that he does not consider himself God made manifest in the flesh – in fact, the very opposite. The Messiah he may be, the one chosen to undergo the supreme ritual for the sake of Israel and the world he may be, but at base he is a man of flesh and blood and no more. 'All things are possible unto *thee*,' he prays, implying that all things are not possible to himself. And then, 'not what *I will*, but what *thou wilt*,' signifying submission to God, not the completion of a purpose of his own making.[33]

T D Doane remarks that Jesus 'never for a moment pretended to be co-equal, co-eternal or consubstantial with God'.[34] And later, on the cross, the words '*My God, my God! why hast thou forsaken me?*' will further divorce him from this ridiculous pagan overlay – for how could Jesus as God forsake *himself*? Doane follows through on this very observation by reminding us that whenever occasion arose Jesus acknowledged subservience to God by admitting both 'inferiority of knowledge' *and* 'inferiority of virtue'. Only the Father knew the day and hour of the Last Judgement; only God was 'good'.[35] To overlook or attempt to explain away such statements is to be dishonest. To accuse others of not properly understanding what Jesus meant, or to accept illogical theories of a double-nature and goodness knows what else, is to insult the intelligence of reasonable men and women and make a laughing-stock of scholarly pursuits.

Both James and Paul would have been astonished to see what the later pagan Church Fathers eventually did with Jesus the Arabian/Palestinian Jew. 'The sublime theology of the primitive Christians was gradually corrupted and degraded by the introduction of popular mythology, which tended to restore the reign of polytheism.' So says T W Doane.[36] The Creed of Athanasius (member of the first general Council of Nicea) asserted that the true Catholic faith could be defined as follows:

> That we worship *One* God as Trinity, and Trinity in Unity – neither confounding the Persons nor dividing the substance – for there is one Person of the Father, another of the Son, and another of the Holy Ghost, but the Godhead of the Father, and of the Son, and of the Holy Ghost *is all one*, the glory equal, the majesty co-eternal.

This was of course to overlook, as Dr Schonfield points out, that 'Paul's Christ is not God, he is God's *first creation*, and there is no room for the trinitarian formula of the Athanasian Creed.'[37] even Athanasius himself had trouble with his own definitio he later writes that concerning the divinity of the Logos, 'the more he thought the less he comprehended; and the more he wrote the less capable was he of expressing his thoughts.'[38]

To enforce this piece of incomprehensible verbalism the Council of Nicea then attached an anathema to it, so making it binding on the whole Christian Church. The anathema ran as follows:

> The Holy Catholic and Apostolic Church anathematizes those who say that there was a time when the Son of God was not, and that, before he was begotten, he was not, and that, he was made out of nothing, or out of another substance or essence, and is created, or changeable, or alterable.

All in all, a tight little package which set the inevitable ball of heresy rolling, the flames rising, the cries and screams of innocent human beings into the fetid air of dank prisons. Because a Church Council composed of people like Athanasius had said so, Jesus was no longer the Jewish Messiah, the Suffering Servant of Isaiah, the Archetypal Man and Light Adam of the *Similitudes*, he was the alien Jewish God shoe horned into a physical body and let loose as a refurbished pagan deity of monstrous proportions.

EIGHT

THE NEW TESTAMENT REVISITED

The theory that the New Testament contains a concealed history,
the further theory that Christianity did not grow out of Judaism,
and the existence in the synoptic Gospels of a three-tier Jesus.

I met Dr Barbara Thiering fleetingly during February 1991, having previously written to invite her to lecture before the Tasmanian Society of Editors. She was unfortunately unable to do so due to international engagements, but was friendly, interested in our request, and as I happened to be in Sydney invited me to an evening lecture she was giving at the University. I attended this lecture, and was suitably impressed.

Barbara Thiering is a small, white-haired lady of neat appearance who glistens at you over spectacles. But behind this almost innocent façade she is a tough-minded academic who completed university in 1951 with a first-class honours degree in modern languages, developed her interest in religion with a master's degree in theology, and followed this up with a PhD in 1973. She joined the School of Divinity in 1976, and, at the time of writing, lectures in Old Testament Hebrew and feminist theology. On Palm Sunday 1990, Australian television (ABC) broadcast a documentary by Thiering entitled *The Riddle of the Dead Sea Scrolls*. The result was nationwide controversy. In 1992 she published *Jesus the Man*, and the controversy intensified. To say that she has blown the lid off New Testament scholarship would be to state the obvious – and that even if she is eventually proved incorrect in some of her claims. Two earlier books – *Redating the Teacher of Righteousness* and *The Gospels and Qumran* – set the pace of hypothesis and revelation, but it is yet to be seen whether Thiering's detailed theories will cancel out as fully reliable. One thing is certain, however: in conjunction with R H Eisenman and Morton Smith and their equally adventurous ideas, she has opened a whole new chapter in New Testament thinking, and not even collective prejudice will be strong enough to close it again.

So what is she saying that is so different, so challenging, so disturbing to biblical scholars? What is it about her theories that made some of these scholars treat her like an intellectual leper during the 1990 ABC television programme? Well, according to Thiering's basic premise, the surface story of the gospels and the Acts of the Apostles conceals another story – a historically exact story relating to Jesus' daily journeyings, his associates and family, and his contact and interaction with the Essene sectaries. The Church preaches (and more or less believes) the cover story, the surface story we are all familiar with, but this story deliberately conceals, through a device called *pesher*, information which is markedly different from, indeed dramatically at odds with, the surface story. This *pesher* device is a technique adapted from Old Testament methods of interpretation characteristic of the scribes at Qumran, and used by the writers of the gospels and the Acts to safeguard the true history of Jesus and his followers. And just as Dr Schonfield believed Jesus to have been directly influenced by the *Similitudes of Enoch* and by other such writings, Thiering believes the gnostic literature found at Nag Hammadi in Upper Egypt in 1945, and the *Clementine Recognitions* and *Homilies* of the late first century CE, are also relevant to an understanding of Jesus and his mission.

But this is only the start. Dr Thiering links Jesus directly to the Essene sectaries, and believes the Dead Sea Scrolls to be intrinsically connected to the gospels and the Acts of the Apostles both in date and substance – a connection either doubted or vehemently denied by most biblical scholars. Many of these scholars agree that the gospel story should not be accepted literally, that the stories of miracles and suchlike are the result of legend and no more, so when someone like Thiering comes along and suggests the existence of an *exact* history lying hidden within this welter of apparent legend and myth, they find it difficult to take her seriously. How could such a thing be? The gospels are after all separate entities with all the faults and failings one would expect – corrupted text and suchlike – so to say that beneath this perfectly comprehensible muddle lies historical coherence and consistency is simply too much to accept. And anyway, *pesher* (plural *pesharim*) was a system of interpreting texts to suit a belief system, not a secret code lying within a text.

The answer to this question in particular is given by Thiering in *The Gospels and Qumran*. Aware of the kind of objections that will arise, she writes,

> The essential assumption of the *pesharim* concerns the *language* of the Old Testament. Arising from a definition of prophecy as primarily foretelling the future, and also from their doctrine that their own community was the focus of divine revelation, they held that the prophets used language in an unusual way, with two levels of meaning.[1]

So it seems that the prophets, because divinely inspired, were talking on two levels, but only to certain people – those who could understand the mystery or *raz* contained in the words. Certain words carried double meanings, and the singular or plural exactly defined whether one was talking about a particular person or the followers of that person. The word 'righteous', for instance, was to be accepted in its general meaning but also as referring to the Teacher of Righteousness, who was *the* Righteous Man of the divine creation. Each and every time this word was used, in whatever context, this underlying *raz* or mystery was to be apprehended – but only by those who understood the code. Needless to say, this produced situations in which it was extremely difficult to work out what the *raz* was referring to, for it was a method which decoded through a system of 'belief in codes', and not through any actual code, which is how many New Testament scholars interpret the gospels. The *raz-pesher* was a completely different type of coding from that of Schonfield's Atbash cipher, which was an actual code hidden within certain difficult to understand words like 'Taxo'.

Dr Thiering's claimed discovery concerning the New Testament is that she has identified *intentional pesher*, a code created with the express purpose of avoiding the kinds of problems which arose with Old Testament texts. The authors of such *pesharim* have apparently *created* the gospel stories to operate on two levels of meaning: one for general consumption, the other to convey information of an exact historical nature. In these new scriptures large numbers of *raz* are used, each with a definite meaning. Thiering says that anyone in possession of the 'lexicon' will end up with the same interpretive result. Now this is clear and precise – as clear and as precise as one can possibly get – so what's the problem? Is it that her method has been thoroughly tested and found wanting? Is it that other evidence so completely disallows her supposed discoveries that there is no need to test her hypothesis? I think not. There seems to be scholastic reluctance when it comes to testing her hypothesis. Either that or it is simply assumed that what she has discovered is no more than an imaginative construction.

Off the cuff rebuttals made by certain scholars during her television programme on the Scrolls seem to confirm this. N T Wright in his book *Who was Jesus?* castigates her for creating 'an exegetical circus stunt'.[2] Tough words. But Wright is no slouch; he backs up his accusation with pages of criticism, and one cannot but feel uneasy about some of Thiering's ideas in the light of what he has to say. J H Charlesworth is of a similar opinion:

> Astounding are the claims of Barbara Thiering, an Australian. She contends, with Eisenman, that the Dead Sea Scrolls have been misinterpreted. She concludes that the Righteous Teacher 'worked at Qumran about 26–30 AD'. She argues that the history of the Righteous Teacher 'and his rival corresponds to that of John the Baptist and Jesus'. The Dead Sea Scrolls, she claims, reveal that Jesus was born at Qumran and did not die on the cross.[3]

Sound as some of N T Wright's points seem to be, and genuine as Charlesworth's amazement obviously is, I cannot help but feel equally uneasy about Wright's plea to utterly dismiss Thiering's work as without value. Too much of what she has written seems to fit the general pattern of observations made by other scholars interested in, and convinced of, a direct Essene connection with Christianity. So I think we should give this adventurous thinker the benefit of the doubt until future evidence either confirms her findings or sends her back to the drawing-board. And because the observations of N A Silberman in his book *The Hidden Scrolls* (an excellent and witty read for anyone interested in scholarly disputes) rather suggest that a reassessment of dates on the Teacher of Righteousness is at hand,[4] and scholars like Robert Eisenman and Michael Wise also detect *pesharim* functioning within the New Testament, perhaps more attention should be paid to the dating techniques around this Essene-type phantom of the opera.

Commenting on how her work has been received by orthodox Christian scholars, Dr Thiering insists that her methodology has not been given a chance to prove its worth. She writes:

The experiment of using this technique of interpretation is repeatable, and those who undertake to repeat and continue it will find an enjoyment and illumination that is very rare indeed. They will find nothing less than the historical Jesus, in the place where, ironically, he has been thought to be least likely to be found, in the gospels and Acts of the New Testament.[5]

As with the highly detailed studies of Professor Salibi, it is not my intention to attempt a detailed survey of Dr Thiering's contribution: that would be an impossibility. My intention is simple and straightforward – to pick up on what she has to say when it forms a coherent pattern in conjunction with my own findings and conclusions. This makes sense, I think. Coherence and consistency are often the hallmarks of possible truth, a pointer to the fact that something substantial is being described. Like a complex jigsaw, the features of a historical problem can be slowly built up out of pieces of information which interlock properly. But as is sometimes the case with jigsaws, pieces are found already locked together which allow one to rapidly complete a section, and in so doing create the conditions to choose correctly, and immediately, future pieces. I've never known anyone yet who did not take advantage of such fortuitous interlocking. There is also of course the possibility that pieces interlock quite perfectly but on closer study reveal that the picture they create is disjointed.

The studies of Dr Thiering are fascinating and daunting and sometimes perplexing, but they are never, never boring. Surprise after surprise surfaces, and one gets a sense of a real Jesus emerging, a Jesus involved (as one would expect) in full-blown political intrigue, religious aspiration and cultic expression. A man of his times, and a man ahead of his times, Jesus was no simpering preacher advocating meekness and mildness in the midst of brutality and fanaticism. He was a convinced sectarian (Nazarene-Essene) working methodically towards a new definition of the religious life. What he had to say was to some blasphemous, to others liberating. As the leader of a splinter group of Nazarene-Essenes, he would attract criticism and hatred from both the priestly caste and the sectarians, and this would lead to his betrayal and crucifixion. But he would not die; he would survive and continue his unique ministry.

In Dr Thiering's scheme of things, Jesus' brother James remained with the Jewish Christians after the crucifixion, and did not accept as facts either the Virgin Birth or the Resurrection, or for that matter that Jesus was the last and final Messiah, the archetypal Messiah of the Last Days. James knew only too well that their common father was Joseph, that the Resurrection had been an event contrived by his followers, and that Jesus' claims of regal and messianic authority could be disputed due to the irregularities of his birth. The two brothers did not get on, and James at first would not 'recognise' Jesus as leader, a term familiar after the crucifixion in relation to certain people who met Jesus, but meant to indicate *rejection*, not *mistaken identity*. James would, however, come round (like many another) and eventually accept Jesus as leader – but only after the death of John the Baptist. Jesus, says Thiering, was conceived during his parents' betrothal period before legal marriage, and was born during March, 7 BCE. In 29 CE he joined with the twelve apostles, all Hellenists (I presume by inclination, like Peter), and opposed John the Baptist who, like James, held the doctrine of the Hebrews. Ever the innovator, Jesus introduced new doctrines (new wine), and proclaimed himself a 'priest-king'. By doing so he taught the priesthood of all believers, the free admission of all members (including Gentiles), and did away with the Essene gradings of birth, race, sex or physical condition. Opposed by those who believed in Jewish orthodoxy, he was called the 'Wicked Priest', and the 'Man of the Lie'.

The group to which Jesus belonged (Nazarene-Essene) split into two parties: the 'Figtree', who wanted to oppose Rome by force of arms, and the 'Vineyard', who wanted peace with Rome. When the Vineyard lost its leader (John the Baptist), priestly leadership was conferred on Jesus who, it should be remembered, cursed the 'Figtree' and caused it to wither – in other words, to lose adherents. The Vineyard itself then split into two parties – one western Christian, the other eastern Christian – and these factions were eventually led by Paul and James, Jesus being on Paul's side. Dr Thiering describes this process as 'a series of steps with a progressive narrowing resulting from divisions in the parties until only the Christians survived in western and eastern form'.[6] So goes the Thiering saga, in cameo, and at one glance it is easy to see why her academic peers are up in arms.

But there's more, much more. Dr Thiering proposes that the Teacher of Righteousness was Jesus' contemporary, not a figure belonging to a much earlier period, and that Jesus was his doctrinal rival. As such he caused a split in the Essene Party, and a breakaway group of some proportions formed around him. Considered carefully, her reasons for challenging the Teacher's period of operation seem sound enough, so it is up to scholars to properly refute her claim that the dating methods used were inadequate, or that the work of other scholars which confirm her basic point of view are also in error. She will without doubt cause monumental problems if her theories work out, but that surely is the whole point of pertinent scholarship – the breaking of new ground, not just the perpetual polishing of the status quo.

But Thiering's most important point is probably her observation that before such a powerful group would go to the length of writing a new scripture, they must have believed that they had something of importance to write about – in fact, a new revelation equal to that of Moses. And the fact that there was a hidden message within this new scripture reinforces the idea that they believed something momentous had taken place in their own lifetime. This something, it seems, was the appearance of *two* Teachers of Righteousness, the one called Jesus having a policy of social and religious restructuring which quickly split the Essene Party into rival factions. Advocating a relaxing of the Law of Moses, and dramatic changes to the processes of initiation, this new Teacher instituted startling reforms and directly challenged the authority of the original Teacher. This, in essence, was the hidden message of the four gospels, a message of astonishment which often filters through to the surface text. But it was also a record of the on-going completion of prophecy: predictions which primarily concerned Israel and not the Gentile world.

In terms of the coming Kingdom of God, the Gentiles were of secondary importance, Israel of primary importance because of her long-standing relationship to the one true God. But this particular part of the hidden message of the gospels records not prophetic success but a series of failures in prophetic judgement – failures followed by extensions of time for the purposes of adjustment. These adjustments, however, turned out to be no better than the original interpretations, and slowly but surely the expected time of the Last Days was shuffled into an indeterminate future. The gospels with their so obvious messianic hope were composed before the final disillusionment with prophetic interpretation set in, and when these hopes too were finally dashed (in relation to the Kingdom of God's appearing on Earth), the hidden message of religious aspiration and political certainty *allied to Israel and its future* ceased to be relevant to the quickly growing Gentile Church. The 'Figtree' was long since discredited; the 'Vineyard' had split into two and formed the orthodox eastern Jewish Church and the unorthodox western Gentile Church. The eastern Church, holding to the traditional values of the original Teacher of Righteousness, recognized James and his successors as Messiahs (Christs). The western Church, having no longer any use for the now defunct history of Jewish reforms and expectations hidden within its sacred books, preached the surface text as truth, and finally suppressed knowledge of the sub-text because it had neither meaning nor value to its predominantly Gentile adherents. As time went by, knowledge of the sub-text disappeared, leaving only the surface text to be grossly misunderstood by Gentile Fathers of the Church whose pagan backgrounds allowed them to make a god out of Jesus and, by the fourth century, to elevate that god to the role of Supreme Deity.

The word *pesher* was apparently used in the Old Testament to mean 'interpretation of dreams',[7] and the surface story of the gospels is a dreamlike series of events which ought to be 'interpreted' and not simply 'believed'. To 'believe' in the surface story of the gospels is to believe in dreams, whether we accept Thiering's sub-text theories or not; to build a life on such dreams is to be in the clutches of a reality turned inside out and upside down. This is without doubt the underlying reason for the decrepit spiritual climate of the Western world in relation to Christianity, a spiritual climate which in essence is no more than ancient pagan superstition awarded the status of a divine truth – an *unquestionable* divine truth. There is no sidestepping this. It is something that most people instinctively feel, and it has systematically undermined our collective and individual ability to properly relate to the *alien otherness* of God. There are levels of reality about which we know virtually nothing because our spiritual teachers are, on the whole, only concerned with the trivia of belief systems and not with the exploration of spiritual dimensions. Either literalist in their interpretation of scripture or atheistic to the extent of using Christianity as no more than an ethical system for reasons of crowd control, our disparate clerics (in conjunction with modern philosophy) studiously avoid and ignore the real spiritual questions: Who am I? What am I? Why am I? Am I?

THE ISRAELITE DYNASTY

To get all of this into a proper perspective, a clear focus, we must now return to a statement made by Professor Salibi. Referring to the Koranic story of Issa in which a careful distinction is made between the monotheism of the ancient Israelites and that of the Jewish faith as introduced through Ezra, Salibi says:

> The story clearly depicts Judaism and the original Christianity of the Nazarenes as different departures from the original religion of Israel, and this suggests a new vision of the origins of Christianity as a sister religion to Judaism, rather than a runaway Jewish sect, as has long been the common view.[8]

These are explosive words. To follow them through is to come upon a new interpretation of Israelite/Jewish history not yet considered by Christian scholars.

This new interpretation is shadowed in the work of Dr Thiering, although she herself states that the Christian Church originated from an ascetic movement within Judaism. But when talking of the ancient Israelites, she backs Salibi's point of view by saying:

> The former royal family had lost the throne in the fifth century BC, but at once a party of loyalists formed around them, dreaming of their restoration, and of the return of Israelite society of old. This was the historical reason for the formation of the Essenes. They intended to restore not only the Davids but the high priests of the family of Zadok who had held sway with them. There were still many elements in the country who believed that only a David could be the true king.[9]

Quoting the *Clementine Recognitions*, Dr Schonfield writes:

> The first schism was that of those called Sadducees, which took their rise almost in the time of John. These, as more righteous than others, began to separate themselves from the assembly of the people. By Sadducees the writer here appears to mean the Zadokites, members of the same Essene sect as those at Qumran, who called themselves the 'sons of Zadok' and deliberately segregated themselves to follow the Law strictly and avoid pollution.[10]

He goes on to tell us that Jesus is referring directly to these 'Sons of Zadok' when he says 'From the days of John the Baptist until now the kingdom of heaven suffereth violence, and the violent take it by force.'[11] This was to suggest that the Essenes of his time were attempting to storm the Kingdom of God and initiate the Last Days by their strict way of life. In saying this, he not only recognizes their existence, their religious influence and political importance, he also separates himself from their narrow religious aims. A Nazarene-Essene he may be, but he will split the sectarians in two and form his own visionary party.

As noted in Chapter Four, the name 'Nazarene' referred to a community whose members thought of themselves as preservers of the *true faith of Israel*, and that as northerners 'the Nazarenes were opposed to the Judean, or southern, traditions which, they believed, had falsified the Law of Moses.' So said Schonfield, and here is the crux of the matter. Through the Essenes, and Jesus as the Davidic Messiah, the religious traditions of the ancient Israelites resurfaced, and this traditional belief system was not only seriously at odds with Judaism, it also carried along with it a legitimate king for Israel which made it political dynamite.

This priest-king-cum-Messiah of the Qumran Essenes belonged to an entirely different religious tradition from that of the expected Jewish Messiah. The Messiah of the Essenes was of the ancient order of Melchizedek, the priest-king to whom Abraham deferred, and who by definition was greater than the Levitical priesthood which stemmed from Abraham as Levi's ancestor. Hence the rejection of Jesus as the Messiah by the Jews – he was not properly the 'Jewish Messiah' in their eyes. Schonfield, when talking of the Nazarenes, refers to them as a *family dynasty*, and adds that Jesus' brothers constituted 'a dynastic blood-line, a dynasty claiming sacred legitimacy because of a blood relationship to Jesus'.[12] Regarding them as a menace, rabbinical Judaism tried to ban the Nazarenes, the Essenes, and all Last-Day fanatics from the synagogues around 90 CE.[13] And in relation to the ancient Israelite institution of the lifelong Nazarite (Jesus' brother James followed this strict and unbending way of life), Schonfield says:

> We have every reason to hold that the family to which Jesus belonged was nurtured in this tradition . . . But his reading of his messianic mission led him in many matters to turn his back on it, which may well have been a cause of friction with his family.[14]

This fits exactly with what we know of Jesus' life: he was rejected both by the Jews and the Nazarene-Essene Party, formed a splinter group, and after the death of John the Baptist managed to more or less persuade the Nazarenes (and his family) to accept him again. This is to read between the lines of the gospels in conjunction with Jewish history, custom, tradition and myth, and when we align our findings with the findings of Dr Thiering, we find that they match remarkably well. For the surface text does in many places seem to reflect the hidden sub-text of Thiering's studies, and common sense and a shaking loose from religious taboos is sufficient to allow the semblance of the basic picture to emerge.

The Essenes were 'the old aristocrats, who longed for a return to the great days of Israel, when a David was on the throne and a Zadokite high priest was in the temple'.[15] Professor Salibi tells us that Issa, according to the Koran, was a 'Sadducee' (Zadokite), and therefore a strict follower of the original Israelite monotheism. He then reminds us that in the Hebrew Bible Ezra is described as a descendant of Aaron,[16] and that the Koranic Issa also claimed the same descent on his mother's side. Both men, in their own separate periods of time, were apparently descended from the same priestly aristocracy and had equal claim to religious authority. Dr Thiering says 'There were still many elements in the country who believed that only a David could be a true king.'[17] Salibi agrees:

> There were Israelites of different sects in the country who were unhappy with the plight of their race and yearned for the promised coming of the Messiah, or Christ: the Son of David, who would restore to them their lost dignity as a people by re-establishing the historical Israelite kingdom.[18]

This Israelite Messiah was expected to be of David's house. But there were also Israelite sects who allowed for the idea of two Messiahs – one of the house of Aaron, the other of the house of David – the Essenes of Qumran were such a sect.[19] But the gospel of Luke seems to sort everything out, implying that Jesus' mother was of the house of Aaron by making her cousin Elizabeth of that very house. The verse is quite specific in its inference: 'and his wife was of the daughters of Aaron, and her name was Elizabeth'.[20] If this is correct, then Jesus was not only a potential king of the Davidic line, he was also – like Issa – a priest of the Aaronic line, and as such a full-blown priest-king in his own right with the extra backing of Melchizedek.

The Pharisees, in the tradition of Ezra, upheld a broad

interpretation of Israelite monotheism. The Sadducees (even in the time of Jesus) upheld the original monotheism of the Israelites which was strict and unbending and religiously limiting. But Jesus did not follow either school, at least not with any consistency; he turned that original monotheism on its head by introducing a personal note, a note of personal responsibility in the face of Truth, and the Sadducees and Pharisees and those Essenes of strict Sadducee/Zadokite caste rejected both his new teaching and his claim to the throne of Israel outright. So Jesus wasn't just a potential priest-king, he was also a social revolutionary who attempted to single-handedly shift the whole religious and political direction of the Jewish nation.

Dr Thiering says that a social revolution was implied in what Jesus did. When he 'turned water into wine', this was his way of replacing the rigid system of Essene initiation with a method that did away with baptism and allowed all members to partake of the Drink of the Community – which was wine. From that moment 'all adult members of Jesus' following, whether married, Gentile, women, physically handicapped, racially different, slaves or free, could come to the communion rails and receive the bread and wine'.[21] This kind of attitude, in conjunction with many other reforms – such as the ordination of priests who were not of the tribe of Levi – was the reason for his downfall, his rejection by the sectaries and the Jews. But beyond all of this lay the Cross as a future event of cosmic importance, for if he survived to tell the tale there would be a complete reversal of fortune on the religious, the political, and the social fronts – at least, so he hoped.

THE NAZARENE GOSPEL CONNECTION

A proof in reverse for Paul's having found written materials about Issa in Arabia, and therefore a direct link between the ancient Israelite faith, the Nazarene-Essenes and the Christian gospels, is produced by Salibi through an analysis of the gospels of Luke and John – an analysis we need only touch upon to illustrate the point. Taking his information from the now lost Nazarene gospel known to us from the Koran, Luke quite obviously reproduces Issa's Christmas nativity story (the virgin birth), but does not specifically say that Mary was of the house of Aaron – perhaps

because the other gospels failed to give her a priestly lineage. But
Luke gives the game away through carelessness: he leaves in the
part about Mary and Elizabeth being cousins. So the probable
reason for none of the gospels' giving Mary a Levitical lineage
was because they knew she was not of that bloodline, and
preferred not to complicate the issue with further improbabilities
– Thiering's interpretation certainly does not mention a Levitical
background for Mary.

We are then made aware of the fact that textual criticism
recognizes a sudden faltering in the style of Luke's fluent Greek
during the Christmas narrative, followed by a sudden resumption
of the previous style when the story of the virgin birth is complete.
This suggests that Luke was translating from a written source –
probably in Aramaic – and that the change in style is because
he was quite literal in his transposition from the one language
into the other. Paul does not make this mistake. He slurs over the
idea of a virgin birth and does not even name Jesus' mother.[22]
Corroboration for the idea that the Nazarene gospel was used in
such a manner is supplied by Robert Graves and Joshua Podro
in *The Nazarene Gospel Restored*. They write:

> The introduction to *Luke* and the accounts quoted by Eusebius from
> the early second-century writer Papias . . . show that all the Gospels,
> except the patently fictitious ones, were based on notes taken by
> Greek-speaking converts from the Aramaic Gospel orally current
> among the Nazarenes; and that each evangelist, as Papias reports,
> 'interpreted them as best he could' – that is to say, uncritically and, in
> general, with studied ignorance of their historical background.[23]

But for Salibi it is John's gospel that gives the show away. John
refers to Jesus as the Logos, or 'Word', and speaks of a
parakletos, or 'Comforter'. According to the Koran, both of these
concepts belonged to the Nazarene gospel of Issa, the Aramaic
gospel that contained a virgin Mary and a Holy Spirit; an Issa
who performed miracles but did not strictly adhere to the Law
of Moses; an Issa who was considered by some to be not just a
son of God, but God *in person* (a belief roundly condemned in
the Koran); an Issa whose followers were called Nasara or
Nazarenes; and an Issa who was crucified, brought back to life,
and who ascended to God and was expected to return. So it is not
difficult to see where the gospel writers got much of their
enchanting source material.

Working from this Arabian gospel, and from other religious materials of a more heretical and mystical type, Paul had constructed his theologically elevated Jesus and walked the tightrope of being understood too literally by his Gentile converts, and at the same time rejected by his Nazarene fellow-travellers who preferred a more restricted and sober text. Only too aware of what Christian scholars would make of such a view, Salibi countered objection to his use of Koranic material with: 'most of the material it presents is highly original. It is therefore reasonable, at least tentatively, to proceed on the assumption that the Koranic story of Issa preserves an independent tradition concerning the origins of Christianity.'[24]

THE SALIBI/THIERING PROBLEM

The question is, could a hidden sub-text such as described by Dr Thiering remain consistent when the surface text had been literally peppered with borrowings from an Arabian source? Does this not make a nonsense of what she claims? The answer is, I think, No. If, as Thiering suggests, this hidden sub-text was created step by step during the writing of the gospel manuscripts, the code carefully and precisely placed or highlighted in the surface text to point unerringly to what lay within, ultimately it did not matter in the least where that surface text came from, or of what it was composed – the trick was to simply keep a surface story going which contained enough of the truth to make it a decent vehicle or carrier for the historical truth – a story capable of holding the attention of the 'uninitiated'. Thiering does say, however, that the claims of a virgin birth, the miracles, and the Resurrection, are not myths or traditional legends, as some scholars hold, but cover-stories for actual happenings. Her saying this does not constitute a problem – in fact it confirms the point of view stated above. Yes, these stories have been carefully used to carry a message, and the scholarly notion that they are *only* legend and myth is incorrect. However, the fact is they might well reflect *actual* Arabian myths and legends which simultaneously point to historical connections between the Nazarenes and the Arabian Nasara.

But what of Salibi's well-substantiated claim that there existed in western Arabia, specifically in the Hijaz, an original Galilee, a

Nazareth, a Bethsaida, and a number of other towns and villages which exactly duplicated those to be found in Palestine? Well, there are two sides to this question, and both are interesting. One is that the place-name 'Nazareth', for instance, is thought never to have existed in Palestine at all. Marcello Craveri informs us that Nazareth had never been mentioned before it was cited by the gospel writers, and that the name does not appear in the writings of any of their contemporaries. Richard Leigh is of the opinion that Jesus was not from Nazareth and says that an overwhelming body of evidence indicates that it did not exist in biblical times. In fact, with others he relegates its existence to the third century.[25] Michael Grant reflects the confusion around this question by telling us that it has been proposed that 'Nazareth may be a synonym for all Galilee'.[26] And Salibi notes that the historical existence of Nazareth as a town in the Palestinian Galilee is very poorly attested for the period of Jesus.[27] Dr Thiering adds a whole new and unexpected dimension to the question when she reveals that she has uncovered an unusual usage of place-names in her *pesher* code which also produces two Galilees, two Nazareths, two Jerusalems, etc.

In Professor Salibi's view, place-name problems were simply the result of migrants from the Arabian Hijaz giving the names of their towns and villages to locations in Palestine out of pure nostalgia. Thiering's discovery of double place-names, on the other hand, she relates to the Essenes' establishing their own 'Temple' at Qumran, and following this up with a series of place-names which either denoted a real location or a Qumran mirror-equivalent, or alternatively again a person carrying a title amalgamated with a place-name. All very complicated, but revealing. And also tantalizing. For as Thiering observes, there had once been on the dry bed of the Wadi Kidron a building called Nazara (an alternative form of 'Nazareth', she says), and if we believe that Nazareth did not actually exist as the gospels describe it, then it could well be that this Nazara on the Wadi Kidron is a mirror reflection of the Arabic Nasara which referred not so much to a place, but to a *sect* – the sect of the early Arabian Nazarenes who were themselves a reflection of the ancient Israelite sect of the Nazarites. This river-bed Nazareth, on the steep side of which the Magnificent Christian monastery of Mar Saba is built, is equated by Dr Thiering with the place where Jesus was brought up,[28] but the words 'brought up' do not signify a town or village in the normal sense: they signify a sectarian hide-away where Jesus was *schooled and prepared for his dynastic mission*. And Jesus' brother James was also 'brought up' there to be a Nazarene/Nazarite, as was John the Baptist. As children, Nazara (Nazareth) was their collective wilderness home.[29]

THE KORANIC JESUS

The next step in the unravelling of this puzzle is a difficult one, but immensely rewarding when taken. It carries us back to those mythical stories of virgin nativity and miracles as found in the gospels, having their counterparts in the lost Aramaic gospel of the Nazarenes as cited in the Koran, and put forward today by the more literalist Christian interpreters of the New Testament as signifying the divine basis of the Christian faith. The main question to arise concerning this literalist attitude is, why does it exist? We have to try to answer this question before getting down to the business of placing the 'marvel' aspects of the gospels in a sensible context. So what is it about these simple stories that makes them so important to the scheme of salvation? Is it really necessary to believe that Jesus' mother was a perpetual virgin, and that Jesus worked miracles, for someone now to qualify as 'Christian'? Is the curse/taboo on 'adding to' or 'taking away from' the book of Revelation, and by associative inference the whole of the New Testament, to be believed in unbendingly to the extent that all critical work on the New Testament should be either abandoned or dramatically modified? Is this what Christians of a literalist frame of mind really believe? It seems so, terrifying as it may sound.

So what is going on? Why are some Christians so dogmatic, so unreasonable in the face of reason? Well, I think there is an explanation. In fact, I think there is a perfectly logical reason for this apparently illogical attitude – a logical reason even for scriptural insistence that everything be left just as it is. This reason is not allied in any way to a wish in the mind of God, but the result of the fact that the writers and compilers and guardians of the scriptures from the earliest days knew that they contained a hidden linear history which would be upset or lost if gross alterations were made to the text. Thiering is probably right. The text is internally alive, and this aliveness had to be protected at all cost. The 'command' not to interfere with accepted canonical texts would have been passed on from initiate to initiate until the use for such knowledge became obsolete due to the failure of prophecy – but the echo of the command would have continued. I think this is the obvious answer – obvious because it also explains why certain books were considered to be 'inspired', and others 'uninspired.' There were lots of perfectly good texts around, but they did not contain the inner sectarian breath, the *raz-pesher* which elevated them to the level of divinely-inspired Scripture. This too would explain the idea of 'dictated Scripture', the screwy notion that every word, every grammatical nuance has its place in an overall strategy of divine communication. As Barbara Thiering has shown throughout her extraordinary investigations, every word had indeed been weighed and carefully pressed into the service of the sectarian dream.

Next to arise is the question of how virtually identical 'marvel' stories could arise in both the canonical gospels and the Arabian gospel of Issa. A fluke? No, this was no fluke. The story of the virgin birth and of the miracles in the canonical gospels were not plucked out of thin air: they were lifted directly from the Nazarene gospel and cleverly edited into place. And their inclusion was not because of naïvety: they were selected precisely because they reflected the ancient past of the Nazarenes as Nasara. Such stories linked past to present, present to future, and secretly pointed to rituals of initiation and rites of passage engaged in by the Nazarene-Essene sectaries of whom Jesus was a breakaway leader. This is to say that Jesus was engaged in the performance of such rituals and initiations. Dr Thiering reveals that Jesus was personally responsible for introducing dramatic changes to the forms of ritual and initiation revered by the Nazarene-Essenes (there is veiled evidence for this view throughout the New Testament), and that he eventually paid a high price for his meddling. Professor Morton Smith is also of the opinion that Jesus initiated his followers, and that some kind of night baptism was used by Jesus to impress his authority on their minds.

But it is only through an examination of the mutual content of these ancient writings that the highly detailed observations of both Salibi and Thiering can be satisfactorily correlated and made to yield scholastic gold. Aware of the problems he faced in trying to convince Christian scholars of his Arabian thesis, Salibi argued for 'difference' as well as 'similarity'. He pointed to there being seven major differences between the Arabian Issa of 400 BCE, and the gospel Jesus of 30 CE. On seven counts the Jesus of the Koran (Issa or Isa, translated into Greek as *Iēsous*) is utterly different from the gospel Jesus (also *Iēsous*), and this shows that the Issa story is not merely the gospel Jesus by another name, but that two historically similar identities have been collapsed into one another. He says of this situation:

> It has been commonly assumed that Muhammad, ignoring the standard Arabic form of the name of *Jeshu* as *Yasu*, opted instead for the Greek form of the name, which he freely transliterated back into what he thought was its Semitic original, thus transforming the *Iēsous* of the Greek gospels into the Koranic *Isa*. This, however, could not have been the case, because Muhammad belonged to an Arabian environment where Christianity was an established religion of long standing, and where many local Christians – Nazarenes and others – could have advised him on what the founder of Christianity was actually called.[30]

So why the verbal sleight of hand?

For the sake of clarity, I'm going to designate the Issa of the Nazarene gospel *Iēsous 1*, and the Jesus of the Christian gospels *Iēsous 2*. For what seems to have happened is that these similar yet dissimilar figures have somehow found their way into the Koran as one person, and this observable fact allows us to legitimately speak of an *Iēsous 3*. According to Salibi, 'Christian scholars tend to view what the Koran says about the person and mission of Issa as a garbled version of canonical or apocryphal gospel accounts.'[31] For Christians, such an interpretation can be the *only* interpretation, for if the reverse were true, the Jesus of the New Testament would become no more than an Issa look-alike, a projection from the past which could be discarded as having no historical validity. This is obviously not the case. *Iēsous 1* (Issa) is a real historical figure in the Arabia of 400 BCE. *Iēsous 2* (Jesus) is an equally real historical figure in the Palestine of 30 CE. But *Iēsous 3* (Issa/Jesus) is a phantom created out of the other two, and it is this phantom which has led some scholars to surmise that Jesus never existed at all. *Iēsous 2* is the flesh and blood Jewish Messiah; *Iēsous 3* is the altogether bogus Jesus which Christian literalists wish to keep intact because of a long-standing post-hypnotic suggestion to that effect – a 'command' for which the underlying reason has long since been lost.

The problem is, *Iēsous 3* (the phantom Jesus who healed and
walked on water and raised the dead) carries just as much weight
in Thiering's *raz-pesher* code as the more credible Jesus of
everyday life. And as there is now little doubt that the canonical
gospels have been heavily influenced by the content of the
Nazarene gospel of Issa, and Thiering's hidden sub-text reveals
the Nazarene-Essene movement at work throughout the New
Testament, then it can be said with certainty that the Koranic
version is not so much a scrambled version of Jesus the divine
incarnation with Issa, but rather a revealing few frames of the real
historical Jesus as found in Thiering's hidden sub-text intentionally aligned with his ancient Arabian roots. Intentionally?
Yes, intentionally. As Salibi points out, Muhammad would not
have made this kind of translation mistake – he would have had
advisers. These advisers were obviously Nazarene descendants in
possession of the authentic story of Jesus' life, a story that
included the origins of the Nazarenes as Nasara.

There is little doubt that the Aramaic Nazarene gospel of Issa
(*Iēsous 1*) was the principal document used by the writer-
compilers of the New Testament to add the 'marvel' aspect to the
gospel narratives; the correspondences are simply too great to be
ignored. And waffling on petulantly about a divine incarnation in
the face of such evidence is patently absurd. The meek and mild
miracle-worker of the gospels is a bogus Jesus, a surface Jesus
whose actual miracles were courageous reforms of religious and
social customs which cut across sectarian and orthodox practices.
His views were revolutionary; his daily acts and statements
challenged the authorities; his messianic pretensions terrified the
careful and the cautious.

NINE

THE JEWISH-ESSENE BACKGROUND

*Getting the family relationship of Jesus and James into focus,
sorting out Jesus' attitude to the Essenes, and understanding the
dynamics of Jesus' mystical vision in relation to Shekinah.*

The Talmud and Midrash underwent rigorous censorship in
the Middle Ages, but the excised parts of these early Jewish
books still exist. These omissions, in their original Aramaic and
Hebrew, were first published in English by R Travers Herford in
his book *Christianity in Talmud and Midrash* in 1905. In *Jesus of
Nazareth*, a scholarly assessment of Jesus as he appears in these
censored writings, the Jewish academic Joseph Klausner picks his
way through the minefield of vituperation and polemic against
Jesus and presents him as he believes he really was. Dr Klausner's
study of Jesus' life, teachings and background is both thoughtful
and fair, and reveals what can only be described as a revolutionary figure.

It should be mentioned, however, that in the introduction to
The Nazarene Gospel Restored, Graves and Podro record that
Klausner's work 'reads at times like that of a Lutheran theologian
who has acquired an exceptional knowledge of the Talmud and
the Midrash'.[1] The influence of Christian theology on Klausner is
evident to these writers, and they are surprised that this Jewish
scholar should ignore the Nazarene dynasty which, under James
the Just and Simeon Cleopas, headed the Church in Jerusalem,
and fail to mention that the original Nazarene Church was only
gradually discredited by Gentile Christian libels. I agree; this is a
serious omission. But on most other levels Klausner's observations about Jesus and the New Testament in general have stood
the test of time and scholarship.

Born in Russia in 1874, Dr Klausner entered the University of
Heidelberg, studied philosophy and Semitic languages, and for his
PhD wrote a thesis on Jewish messianic ideas during the first two

centuries CE. As a result of his subject matter, and the particular period chosen, he also covered the origins of Christianity and the growth and development of the Christian Church. In his introduction, Klausner has this to say about Jesus:

> From a man's disciples, and even from his disciples' disciples, it is possible to draw conclusions about the original teacher. Had there not been in Jesus' teaching something contrary to the 'world outlook' of Israel, there could never have arisen out of it a new teaching so irreconcilable with the spirit of Judaism.[2]

Jesus, he concludes, may not have deliberately set out to teach a faith directly against Judaism, but what he taught had within it the germs from which there could develop not only a non-Jewish teaching but also an anti-Jewish teaching.[3] It is interesting to note Michael Goulder's comments on anti-Semitic elements in the New Testament, elements of thought described by Goulder as 'metaphysically anti-Semitic'. This is well put, I think, for it captures the essence both of the Samaritan version of Jesus' teachings, and of that of the heretical wing of the Nasara who may well be behind what was basically an injection of gnostic-type conceptions into early Christianity. Goulder also notes that an infusion of some such teaching explains why the Church evolved a full-blown Gnostic wing in the second century.[4]

Dr Klausner observes that Jesus was condemned and put to death as a seducer and beguiler, a scoffer and sorcerer who encouraged the people to abandon the Jewish faith. But his more important observation is the undeniable contradiction between the idea of Christianity as an offshoot of Judaism and the fact that Judaism did not succumb to Christianity – Judaism continued down its own path in spite of Christianity, and did not veer from its original beliefs. So although Christianity resembles Judaism, Judaism does not resemble Christianity. So what does? At the heart of this question lies the little-talked-of separation of Judaism from the old monotheism of the original Israelites, the old Israelite religion from which the Essenes developed the *Way* of the wilderness, the 'Way' which Jesus himself claimed to be. It was the 'Way' that was basically at variance with Judaism, and it seems certain now that Christianity is a reflection, or more accurately a *reworking*, of that many-pronged wilderness tradition.

Remarking on this state of affairs, J H Charlesworth attempts to clarify the situation by reminding us that:

Some excellent scholars erroneously thought that if Jesus was influenced by the Essenes he would have had to visit Qumran. They then rightly claimed that there is no evidence to warrant the hypothesis that Jesus was in the Qumran community. They incorrectly concluded, therefore, that Jesus could not have been influenced in any way by the Essenes.[5]

The main consensus in biblical scholarship seems to echo these sentiments – that is, most scholars agree that Jesus was not a part of the Qumran community – but they do now agree that he was influenced by the Essenes. There are, however, voices at variance on this matter – the Dead Sea Scrolls scholar Robert Eisenman's for one. Professor Eisenman has quite another story to tell. He is of the opinion that just about every passage in the Qumran *Habbakuk Commentary* should be interpreted in relation to the life and teachings of Jesus' brother James, head of the Jerusalem Nazarene movement, and contends, along with Dr Barbara Thiering, that the Qumran writings have been misinterpreted.

As we saw in Chapter Three, John the Baptist is thought to have been an Essene; others have considered James' devotion to the Law an indication of Qumran-Essene-type behaviour; and the fact that Jesus seems to have taken over from John suggests at least an alignment with ideas of Essene origin. And because Jesus' initial stance as John's replacement is thought to have included the rite of baptism, and ritual purification by water was an Essene rite of great importance, it is not precocious to suggest that John and Jesus and James were probably in sympathy with certain elements of Essene thinking. But none of this actually puts Jesus into the Essene camp, of course – it does not make him into an Essene. What it does do, however, is remove the problem of having to keep Jesus and the Essenes utterly apart – *that* has been a problem hindering biblical scholarship for many, many years. Jesus the scoffer, the beguiler, the supposed sorcerer who encouraged the people to abandon certain elements of the Jewish faith was without doubt not only aware of the Qumran Essenes, he was also at times an advocate of some of their principal teaching.

There are a number of important overlaps between what Jesus taught, and what the Qumran Essenes believed. One such overlap is that Jesus and the Essenes both believed that redemption was now under offer to the poor. However, as we saw in Chapter Three, 'the poor' was a technical term for the Essenes themselves, as was 'the poor in spirit'. So was Jesus referring directly to the Essenes when using these terms? Perhaps not. I sense that he was playing a verbal game. But it must be admitted that he certainly seems to have had them at the back of his mind. Then there is the fact that both Jesus and the Essenes placed considerable emphasis on prayer, going well beyond the requirements of the Temple. He seems to have agreed with the Qumran *Rule of the Community* that prayer was more important than sacrifice, that the 'offering of the lips' was greater than living creatures put to the slaughter. And then there was his use of the term 'Holy Spirit', used technically at Qumran, but not to be found in the Old Testament in a New Testament sense.[6] One could multiply such evidence endlessly, but suffice to say that there is now sufficient proof to show that Jesus was well aware of the Qumran Essenes, and that many of his ideas and reactions to Judaism can be directly linked to the Qumran mentality. J H Charlesworth is again worth quoting: 'It is conceivable that Jesus may have inherited it [the term "the poor ones"] from the Essenes, with whom he could well have discussed his concept of God's kingdom.'[7]

But the exact opposite can also be postulated, and convincingly. There was much about Jesus that the Essenes would not have liked, and might even have hated. If directly concerned with him, his attitude to diet, to the Sabbath, and to ritual purity would have driven them crazy. In fact the Qumran Essenes followed rules for purification much stricter than those followed by the Jews, and their penal code even included the death penalty for breaking certain purity laws.[8] Jesus, on the other hand, continually crossed the purity boundaries by associating with people deemed unclean and unworthy in Essene estimation – just as Paul would do later. He kept on breaking the rules, and had he been an Essene would have been severely punished for his behaviour. The Jews with their more lenient purity laws found Jesus difficult enough to handle, but the Essenes would have found him utterly impossible to deal with. He broke the Sabbath rules about work, and healing, mixed with the wrong people, drank wine in perhaps too great a quantity on occasions, mixed with women, lepers and prostitutes, and was even critical of sacred Scripture.[9] Flying in the face of Qumran Essene rules and regulations in what seems a quite intentional manner, he drew near to madmen, lunatics, simpletons, fools, the blind, the deaf and the maimed. Such people were excluded from membership by the Qumran Essenes – Jesus dealt with them daily. When he went in for attack, it seems he attacked not Jewish Law but quite directly the laws of the Qumran community which were severe and unbending. In fact, if he had been part of the Qumran community he would have been 'hanged on a tree' (crucified) according to laws in the Scrolls themselves. And that, oddly enough, is exactly what did happen to him, but at the hands of the Romans.

Modern consensus in scholarship is satisfied with its view that Jesus, although aware of the Essenes, was not himself an Essene. They are happy to have finally resolved the problem of Essene influence on Jesus and done away with the problematical notion that he might have been of that persuasion, and training. But have they? It seems to me that there is still a large question mark hanging over this issue. Jesus' teachings, indeed his whole approach, although individual and ultimately at variance with the Qumran vision, leans too heavily in that direction on other levels for it to have been merely subsidiary, and his arrowing in on Essene closed-upness is not so much a major difference as it is a negative connecting factor. The New Covenant of Christianity is too close in spirit to the New Covenant of the Qumran Essenes to be mere coincidence – a *personal* pact with God did not equate with Judaism. And because we now know that Jesus referred to the Essenes on quite a number of occasions without actually naming them, and that he was apparently angry with them because of their narrow-minded religious philosophy, and that the Herodian party who harassed him may have been the Qumran Essenes by another name (as is now believed by some scholars),[10] I would like to suggest, along with Dr Barbara Thiering, that he may have been a member of that community – indeed, a high-ranking member who split the Qumranites in two and ended by paying the community's price of death on the cross.

Paolo Sacchi, Professor of Old Testament at the University of Turin, says that 'it appears that Jesus' formative background was of an Essene type.'[11] This observation, in conjunction with what is cited above, brings us to a rather critical question. If Jesus was of possible Qumran Essene background, does it not stand to reason that his brother James came from the same background? And if Jesus was a high-ranking leader who split the Qumranite community in two with an almost diametrically opposed set of doctrines, wouldn't his brother also have been a high-ranking

member of the same Brotherhood holding the opposite set
of doctrines? And if Jesus, as the elder of the two brothers had
dynastic rights linked to King David, would not his desertion of
the Qumranite cause have intrinsically threatened the outcome
of that cause, sort of knocked it out of balance? As Jesus' younger
brother, James was second in command, and this incontrovertible
fact is seen as such after the crucifixion when James, and not
Peter, takes over the reins of the Nazarene Party. So what am I
suggesting? I'm suggesting what Professor Robert Eisenman
suggests – that James may well have been the Essene Teacher of
Righteousness, the rigorous keeper of the Law of Moses who
would face down Paul and demand that he become ritually pure.
Here, then, is the possible divide between Jesus and his brother,
the divide Paul attempted to heal at Jesus' instigation. Dr Hugh
Schonfield teeters on the edge of this when he speculates that
Jesus was himself the Just One mentioned in Acts, for it may be
that the split in Essene ranks was due to the fact that both James
and Jesus claimed to be the Just One of Israel.

An anguished cry will rise from almost all Scrolls scholars at
such a suggestion. Preposterous nonsense! Unlearned drivel! An
idea utterly without foundation! Really? Are you sure? Are you
really sure? Or is it just that such a theory would cause too much
of an upset to the status quo if it turned out to be correct. As an
idea it is *only* an idea. It is not blasphemy, and it is certainly
not subversive. It is *possible* history, that's all. As Burton L
Mack says:

> Myths, mentalities, and cultural agreements function at a level of
> acceptance that might be called sanctioned and therefore restricted
> from critical thought. Myths are difficult to criticise because
> mentalities turn them into truths held to be self-evident, and
> the analysis of such cultural assumptions is seldom heard to be
> good news.[12]

Indeed. And the response to Robert Eisenman's suggestion that
James was the Teacher of Righteousness has for many scholars of
the consensus attitude been to reject his suggestion for perhaps
that very reason. Ultimately, as Stuart Sutherland states in
Irrationality: The Enemy Within, 'the desire to conform, of which
on most occasions we are not even aware, can lead to highly
irrational behaviour.'[13] By saying this I am not declaring that
consensus thinking is automatically irrational: that would clearly

be an idiotic suggestion. All I'm saying is that a fear of being out of step with one's peers can hinder creative thought.

In spite of the initial shock of identifying James with the Teacher of Righteousness, I think such a theory really does have merit. It would explain the gulf between Jesus and his brother James, and it would explain the growing concern of Jesus' whole family in the gospels as the doctrinal tack he took became more and more evident. Yes, they thought he was mad, and may eventually have considered him not only mad but so dangerous that he had to be stopped at any cost. Dynastic families have always had their problems – there's nothing new or novel in that. And the fact that James and Jesus seem to get back together again after the crucifixion does not disallow this suggested scenario, for the understanding they seem to have reached was obviously a strained one. Jesus, we are told, had *one* meeting with James after the crucifixion. From then on it is Paul who takes up the task of negotiation. And the link between Paul and Jesus is strong – in fact, Paul's whole religious strategy is stamped all over with Jesus' disregard for authority and his belief that the Law of Moses had to be translated into a more bearable code of practice. When this negotiator speaks, he speaks with an authority that cannot be explained except in terms of delegation. Like a Roman officer carrying the command of the Emperor, Paul must have dictated Jesus' terms to James through Peter – terms stamped all over with the authority of Jesus as regal Messiah. As such, Jesus was not only James' messianic equal, he was also his dynastic superior, his elder brother who had miraculously escaped death on the cross. Utterly outmanoeuvred, James' reputation must have taken a hammering in the eyes of the Essene sectaries, for by rights Jesus ought to have been dead, but wasn't, so signifying God's approval. This is perhaps why James sets up shop in Jerusalem: he may have been in disgrace with his former Essene colleagues. Or it may again be a case of mirror-reflection, the 'Jerusalem' mentioned actually being its Qumran equivalent.

There are real differences between Jesus, the early Christian community as founded by Paul, and the Qumran community, but there is also an intrinsic sameness which I believe springs from the one being a reworked version of the other – a reworking in the sense of Jesus having kept for himself the best aspects of Qumran life and doctrine. He did not throw out the baby with the bathwater; he renewed the Essene Covenant with Israel's God.

The Jewish scholar Yigael Yadin was of the opinion that Jesus was anti-Essene. I agree; I think he detested them. And the fact that he seemed so fond of other aspects of the same community only strengthens my suspicion that he had originally been part of it. The Christian community, one could almost say, was the Qumran community in reverse – it was openness and joy, not seclusion and hatred. Jesus pulled up the blinds, so to speak, and the room was filled with light. So much so that the supposed Sons of Light (Luke 16:8) revealed the dark side of their natures and used their crippled understanding of spiritual things to bring him down. Yes, the Romans had to do the deed, but it was probably the Qumran Essenes who arranged the deed, the deed that would ultimately backfire on them in the most unexpected manner. Referring to Professor Lawrence Schiffman of New York University in his book *The Hidden Scrolls*, N A Silberman tells us that for Schiffman the Qumran Essenes do not represent 'an evolutionary stage in religious development or an inspiring example of national resistance, but a disturbing example of religious pathology'.[14] Or as Jesus so delicately puts it in Luke's gospel: 'the children of this world are in their generation wiser than the children of light.'

THE TANNAIM AND THE AMORAIM

So is there proof of any of this in the Jewish sources? Is there even circumstantial evidence to back up such an extraordinary set of theories? I think there is. Old editions of the Talmud contain only a few references to Jesus, and these are virtually useless due to their disputative and abusive tone. This is to say that the stories of Jesus which survived outside of the canonical gospels were turned into subjects of ridicule, the content perverted into what Klausner calls 'blameable acts'.[15] The gospels had it that Jesus was not born of a human father but of the Holy Spirit; the Talmud asserted that yes, Jesus was born without a father, not as a result of the Holy Spirit but because of illegitimacy. According to the gospels, Jesus was a healer and miracle worker; according to the Talmud, he was what Professor Morton Smith believes him to have been, a sorcerer. The gospels described Jesus as promoting true religion over rote-learned precepts; the Talmud referred to Jesus as a 'scoffer against the words of the wise'.

The problem facing anyone genuinely interested in what the

Jewish writings have to say about Jesus is that of differentiating between the statements handed down by the Tannaim and the Amoraim. The name *Tannaim* belongs to the authorities of the first two centuries CE, *Amoraim* to those in authority from the third to the fifth century. The teachings of the Tannaim are to be found in the Mishnah, the Baraitoth and early Midrashim. The teachings of the Amoraim survive in what is termed the Gemara and later Midrashim. Dr Klausner tells us that statements made by the Amoraim have virtually no historical importance, but that *some* historical importance may be attached to those made by the Tannaim where open controversy is not detectable.[16] Professor Sacchi views the Mishnah – in spite of Christian tampering – as the best literary witness to Pharisaic thought contemporary to Jesus.[17] In the time of the Tannaim – the successors of the Pharisees – Jesus' disciples had already formed a separate sect which denied many of the religious principles of Judaism; the Tannaim were accustomed to coming into close religious contact with this sect. Sect members had even had to face the embarrassment of having to reject the new Jewish Messiah Simon bar Kokhba and undergo scourging as a punishment for not renouncing Jesus. If Jesus had been dead there would have been no need for his disciples to keep up such a charade.

In an early Talmudic statement, the earliest known in Hebrew literature dealing with Jesus, Rabbi Shimeon ben 'Azzai says: 'I found a genealogical roll in Jerusalem wherein was recorded, "Such-an-one is a bastard of an adulteress".'[18] Klausner, after exhaustive efforts to prove other suggestive texts inadmissible, allows this one through as beyond doubt a reference to Jesus. Why? Because the term 'such-an-one' was probably introduced into the passage when Christianity was widespread and they could no longer openly mention his name in a derogatory fashion. By way of further explanation, Klausner uses the phrase 'by reason of the anger of Minim', signifying those Jews rightly or wrongly suspected of a leaning towards the new Christian heresy. And he is also of the opinion that ben 'Azzai's statement may have resulted from hearing Celsus' claim that Jesus was illegitimately conceived during Mary's espousal. Ben 'Azzai refers to an *esheth ish*, the terminology used to indicate a married woman, for in the time of the Talmud, espousal was in all respects equivalent to marriage among the Jews.[19] This naturally backs Dr Thiering's point concerning the conception of Jesus, but that is of course made in the completely different context of the *pesher* code, the hidden sub-text of the gospels rejected by almost all Christian scholars, and refers to the Qumran Essenes, not to Jews in general. The *pesher* reveals that opinion was split among the Essenes on the issue of legitimacy, one party accepting Jesus as legitimate, the other rejecting him as illegitimate. Because the throne of Israel was at stake, one begins to understand the tension between Jesus and his younger brother James, and between the Essene parties who wished to place a David on the throne of Israel.

BETROTHAL AND ESPOUSAL

The intricacies of Essene 'betrothal' or 'espousal' are described in Thiering's magnum opus, *Jesus the Man*. For the Essenes, celibacy was the most appropriate way of life; marriage and sex were considered unholy. The Dead Sea Scrolls reveal a religious order of considerable severity – although some members did recognize that without some form of marriage the race, and therefore the order, would die out. The highest and most holy level of the Essene order lived a life within the closed walls of Qumran, had all property in common, brought up abandoned and illegitimate children, owned nothing, and totally renounced marriage. For obvious reasons, Essenes of high birth were of the same opinion as some of the lower ranks, and as the order itself had come into existence for the express purpose of preserving the great Israelite dynasties of the Davids and Zadoks, marriage had to be accommodated in spite of the order's Cathar-like rejection of it as an institution. The potential priests and kings of these high-ranking families practised sex only to have children, and for the most part remained apart from their wives after a trial marriage of three years to allow for possible procreation, but underwent a permanent marriage thereafter if procreation took place. A betrothal period of some years was the first step, and it was during this waiting period that the unthinkable sometimes happened – the bride, who was actually a 'nun', conceived. Under such circumstances *a virgin had conceived*, for the woman was still legally a virgin although no longer physically intact.

Jesus of Nazareth is mentioned by name in an early Baraita, and not quite in condemnation. A first-generation disciple of

Jesus' is said to have met up with Rabbi Eliezer (the Great), had a conversation with him about something Jesus had said about harlots and latrines, unconsciously repeated this statement many years later because he had liked it, and as a result ended up on a heresy charge. The name used for Jesus in parallel passages is Yeshu ben Pantere or Yeshu ben Pandera rather than Jesus of Nazareth, but as Klausner points out, the name 'Pantere' or 'Pandera' was widely used by Jews from an early date as the reputed name of Jesus' father. Christian scholars are of the general opinion that this Talmudic passage is a late addition, but Klausner disagrees. He estimates Rabbi Eliezer as being around 60 years of age when arrested for heresy, and suggests a birth date between 30 and 40 CE for this famous Jew.[20] This would mean that Rabbi Eliezer met Jesus' disciple around 60 CE.

What is of interest here is the name *Yeshu ben Pantere* or *Pandera*. This pseudonym occurs in several Baraitoth from the end of the first and the beginning of the second Christian century. Origen, quoting Celsus, tells of a rumour that Jesus' father was a soldier called Pantheras, whereas Origen himself says that James, the father of Jesus' father Joseph, was called 'Panther'. By this means Origen was able to explain why Jesus the son of Joseph was called 'ben Pandera' or 'ben Pantere'. The idea of Jesus' father's being a foreigner, or a soldier, is a view utterly rejected by Klausner. The legend of Jesus' having no father and a virgin mother had, in his opinion, more than likely resulted in a linguistic anomaly – the Greek word *parthenos* ('virgin') being scrambled into the name Pandera or Pantere. The Jews had constantly heard that the Greek-speaking Christians referred to Jesus as 'Son of the Virgin', and in mockery had renamed him 'Ben ha-Pantera' – son of the leopard. After many years the origin of this mockery was forgotten, and the mockery itself continued as a proper name. Because Pandera/Pantere were not Jewish names, it was assumed that Jesus' father had been a foreigner. In relation to this question, Professor Salibi notes that in Arabic the term 'son of a lioness' (*ibn al-labwah*) is an expression of insult commonly heard in Egypt.[21]

In the Talmud, Jesus is a Jew who has gone religiously astray. He is a transgressor of the Law and a scoffer against the words of the wise. He is a seducer and a beguiler. He is someone who ridiculed the Jews for 'straining at a gnat and swallowing a camel', and he is seemingly of the opinion that he had come to fulfil the Law. From Jesus' own words it was deduced that he had not come to do away with the ceremonial laws – but the gospels spoke of their annulment by Jesus, and this inner contradiction was pounced on by the Tannaim, so making Jesus a liar on top of everything else. As we saw earlier, he kept company with the ignorant class, sinners and women, and even rejected his own mother and family when they tried to dissuade him from the path he had chosen, the path that would split the Nazarene dynasty down the middle. He healed on the Sabbath whether the illness confronting him was dangerous or not, plucked ears of corn on the Sabbath (which the Pharisees considered 'work', and therefore taboo), and in general upset the religious authorities just about every time he appeared or opened his mouth. So again we must ask the question: to whom or to what did he owe religious allegiance?

THE ESSENES

It is interesting to note that the Essenes embodied the moral socialism of the prophets, and that Essenism is described by Dr Klausner as 'the first social Utopia'.[22] It is also interesting to note that the Catholic Church has recently admitted on film that the early Church must have been influenced by the existence of the Essenes – a belated doubling back on previous statements adamantly against any such influence.[23] At its best, Essenism embraced all the positive characteristics of socialism: equality and community of possessions. Klausner saw in Christianity a great deal that was Essenism. This Jewish scholar was also of the opinion that John the Baptist, the forerunner of Jesus, was an Essene in his whole manner of life, and that Jesus' brother James lived like an Essene.[24] So is this where Jesus got his basic value system? Were the Essenes his early mentors and teachers? Is Barbara Thiering right when she classifies Jesus as a high-ranking Essene who split the Essene party in two?

The Essenes had their own sacred writings, and from ancient books learned the medicinal power of roots and the quality of stones. They also laid special store by the names of the angels, and anyone joining or brought up in the sect had to swear not to divulge either the names of the angels or the contents of the sacred books. (It should be noted that the Samaritan Christians were enamoured with Bethel where Jacob had his vision of the angels ascending and descending.) By means of the concentrated study of the angelic names, the Essenes attained the vision of the *Shekinah*, and as a result believed themselves capable of seeing into the future. The *Book of Enoch* is thought to be of Essene origin for the very reason that it has so much to say about angels, secret remedies and 'secrets of the Law', and it is also considered the ultimate source of both practical and theoretical Kabala.

So it is again interesting to note that angels, or what appear to be angels, pop up at Jesus' birth and Resurrection. It is an 'angel' who announces to Mary that she is about to conceive, and it is an 'angel' or 'angels' who announce that Jesus has been physically resurrected. This is to say that people *dressed in white* and *called* 'angels' attended both of these events, and this description fits not only with the gospels themselves but with a statement in the Koran concerning the followers of *Iēsous 2*. The disciples who followed *Iēsous 2* are described as the 'people in white' (*al-hawariyyun*), or those who 'assume white clothing as a party badge'.[25]

Joseph Klausner's book *Jesus of Nazareth* is an important source of information on Jesus' life, teachings and background because it is so well researched, so detailed, and so fair. Translated into English in 1926, it stands as a timeless work of scholarship. That it was massively ahead of its time can be detected on almost every page, and the fact that it notices the parallels and similarities between Christianity and Essenism removes it from the accusation of merely jumping on a popular bandwagon. That is not to say that other writers of that era had not also noticed such similarities – this was certainly so – but Klausner's contribution is without doubt a sober and sane approach guided by properly handled evidence. And the fact that Dr Klausner was Jewish makes his work all the more acute, all the more important, all the more pertinent when it is remembered that Jesus was a Jew, not a blue-eyed Gentile. So in writing of other scholars who also noted the Christianity-Essenism connection, Klausner is extremely careful.

One such scholar is Graetz, one of only three Jewish scholars to have written complete works about Jesus known to Klausner, and of whose contribution he says, 'It is, both in form and style, the work of an artist; and in many respects it is not yet antiquated.'[26] Graetz's *History of the Jews* (which included a section on Jesus) was published in 1905, and contained observations similar to that of Klausner's concerning the parallels between Christianity and Essenism. This history is mostly concerned with the Jews, but when it finally turns its attention to Jesus and his teachings, it reveals both a sense of humour and an eye for subtlety. On the side of humour, Graetz denies scholarly status to both Renan's and Strauss's books on Jesus, and refers to these works as 'modern gospels'. On the level of subtlety he homes in on something already noted by Thiering: that Jesus 'assumed nothing more than the principal features of the Essenes, particularly the love of property, community of goods, dislike of oaths, power to heal those possessed of devils, lunatics and the like'. But he then explains what he means by 'healing' – and this is the major point, for it is exactly Thiering's thesis of the healings standing for something else. Graetz says:

> The deaf, the blind and the sick whom Jesus healed, and those whom he raised from the dead, were, in actual fact, simply the ungodly and sinful, the publicans and harlots, to whom he preached the living words of God and showed a new way of life which should cure their spiritual defects and revive their dead souls by his loftier moral code.[27]

Graetz does not deny that Jesus actually healed those afflicted with nervous illnesses, but argues that it was Jesus' 'spiritual healing' that was new. In all other respects Jesus was a respected teacher. And in conjunction with Klausner, Graetz is also of the opinion that John the Baptist was an Essene in every way, and that Jesus' brother James had all the habits of an Essene.

So what do we have? We have a Jesus who carried within his teachings *the principal features of Essenism*; a Jesus whose brother had *all the habits of an Essene*; a Jesus whose relative John the Baptist was *an Essene in all his manner of life*; a Jesus who healed the nervously ill, but who more importantly *cured spiritual defects, revived dead souls and raised them to a loftier moral code*; and last but not least a Jesus who was the *embodiment of political oppression under the Romans* and *of the messianic hopes* which grew stronger at that time.[28] These are the considered opinions of two Jewish academics, and they are also the opinion of some modern scholars no longer able to ignore the blatant and undeniable correspondences between Jesus, the early Christian Church, the Essene community, and the political reality in which Jesus found himself. Dr Thiering may not be absolutely right in all of her intricate interpretations of the gospels according to the hidden *raz-pesher* code (the code, if it exists, must surely have been disrupted in places), but it only takes a modicum of imagination to translate and relate Graetz's findings to what she has identified as community 'orders' within the Essene movement, and the elevation of these orders through 'initiation' to levels unacceptable to both the stricter Essenes and the Pharisaic Jews, to conclude that Dr Thiering and Professor Eisenman are on track as far as the real historical Jesus is concerned.

SHEKINAH

But we must now double back to the word *Shekinah*, the vision of which was attained by the study of the angelic names and, I presume, through the process of contemplation and prayer – the Samaritan Christians had special 'exercises' through which knowledge could be attained.[29] One translation of the Shekinah was as the 'divine presence', a description borrowed from the Temple where the Lord chose to cause his name to dwell. The Shekinah was a kind of light reflected from God: it had no separate existence. The Godhead could not directly approach humankind, but the Shekinah could approach it and touch it with its rays. In this way the Shekinah was the reality or basis behind all things revealed to human beings as an experience. The Shekinah was not yet thought of as an 'emanation' but as an indescribable abstraction full of poetic grace and tenderness.

The next step was reached with the inclusion of the 'voice of God' – not a literal voice, not material speech, but a kind of echo parallel to the idea of a reflected light in relation to the Shekinah. This was the 'Word', the Greek *Logos*, or, in Aramaic, the *Ma'amar* – that by which the word was created. The Ma'amar was the 'working instrument' of the Deity, and mediated between that which was wholly spiritual and that which was of the material world. In the beginning the incomprehensible 'word' was uttered by God, and the Ma'amar brought all things into existence.[30]

And the angels too constituted a medium between the spiritual world and the material world. Wholly spiritual, but not original, having no body and therefore no desires or vices, they existed to

carry out the 'word' of the Godhead, and were therefore emissaries for both good *and* evil. There were 'ministering angels' and
'destroying angels'. The ministering angels, or 'angels of the
presence', were seven in number. The *Book of Enoch* and
the Talmud record large numbers of angel-names, and the names
of 'angel formations', and there is little doubt that certain
initiated Essenes – a select few – were in possession of these names
and aware of the 'powers' attached to them.[31] Dr Klausner, in
speaking of these angels, has this to say:

> Of those mentioned in the Talmud may be noted: Metatron and
> Suriel, the prince of the Presence, Michael, Gabriel, Uriel (perhaps
> identical with Suriel) and Raphael, the first two of which are
> mentioned in the book of Daniel. Later we hear of Sandalfon, Domah
> the angel of the winds, and Yurqami the prince of hail – popular
> imaginative creations of various periods – while 'Rahab' prince of the
> sea, and 'Laila' the angel of conception, are only academic creations
> based on some Scriptural passage. Among the 'angels of destruction'
> an important place is held by Asmodai (an old Persian name) and
> Samael, the personal name of Satan, which in post-biblical times
> became his general title, and Lilith, the flying night-demon, taken
> from the name of a terrifying night-bird.[32]

I've quoted this passage in full for two reasons: because it is
singularly fascinating, and because it reveals the kind of mental
world in which the Essenes lived – the psychical and
psychological atmosphere that surrounded them as they went
about their daily business. They had some strange ideas; they had
some wonderful ideas. They had gone far beyond the magical
literalisms of the past with their idea of the Shekinah as the first
hypostasis of the Godhead, but were still allied to that past
through their belief in devils and demons and spirits which were
no more than the primitive heathen gods demoted and hidden
away in the unseen world. And in the gospels that unseen world is
spoken of, and we have Jesus expelling spirits and devils from the
sick in accordance with the belief-structure of his day – beliefs
that he himself held to be true. Incantations and sorceries and
'spittings' were considered the antidote to such forms of illness,
and although strictly prohibited by both the Torah and the
Mishnah, these forbidden techniques were sought after by
the common people. Some sages were not averse to a little
'whispering' or 'spitting' over a wound (Jesus used spittle on at
least one occasion), but such conjurations were frowned on by the

religious authorities, and Jesus seems to have relied more
touch than anything else.

Marcello Craveri details what joining the Essene sect mea___ ...
practical terms:

> Admission ... was determined by the result of a rigorous examination
> in which a master of the order sought to ascertain the earnestness of
> the candidate. Acceptance was followed by one year of probation as a
> neophyte and two years as a novice, during which the new Essene
> accompanied his older colleagues in their journeys through the
> surrounding countryside, where they performed works of charity for
> the poor and treated the ailing. Little by little, the novice learned the
> magic words that were to be pronounced in order to drive demons
> out of the body of which they had taken possession, the ritual
> gestures and empirical medical procedures to restore the sight of those
> afflicted with cataracts, mouth-to-mouth breathing techniques to
> revive the unconscious.[33]

All in all a very interesting grocery list, and as we will see, the
same kind of format as used by first and second-century Christian
Gnostics to vet new entrants.

By the time of Josephus the Essenes numbered 4,000 members
– not exactly a small sect. They lived in Palestine, mostly in
villages, but were also to be found in towns, as Richard Leigh and
J H Charlesworth have shown, and there was a 'Gate of the
Essenes' in Jerusalem. In the time of Pliny, they were to be found
mainly in the wilderness of En-Gedi, near to the Dead Sea. They
had common dwelling places, ate their meals at one table, and
after two probationary periods were taken in as full members
and sworn to secrecy concerning the hidden teachings and the
names of the angels. Dismissal was complicated. A court
consisting of 100 members had the authority to dismiss anyone
who had broken community laws, and such a dismissal was the
equivalent of social death – a severe and unrelenting ostracism
similar to excommunication as practised by the later Roman
Church, and reflected perhaps in the Lazarus story as Dr Thiering
suggests. And even death could be meted out under certain
circumstances: the Temple Scroll discloses that crucifixion was
practised by Jewish authorities against their own people.

Each community had a 'treasurer' whom members obeyed
without hesitation. This treasurer looked after the common
property given to the order by new members. Everything was
shared, even clothes. And if members travelled to another town, a

fellow Essene from that town attended to their needs on arrival. A white garment was given to each new member, together with an apron to be worn during bathing. Along with this white garment and apron came a hoe with which to dig a hole when satisfying the call of nature, and a cloak to cover the act itself. This image was perhaps borrowed by Paul when speaking of the unrighteous having 'no cloak for their sin'. According to the Talmud this was to avoid dulling 'the orb of the sun', and was also related to not restricting 'the goings of the Shekinah'. Members of the Essene order, or Party, did not take oaths but held that yea is yea and nay is nay, as did Jesus' brother James. And most importantly of all, those who married *separated from their wives once they were pregnant*. To overcome the problem of sustaining the order, children of parents sympathetic to Essenism were brought up by the community, and orphans, and illegitimate children were taken in and trained according to the system. Once again we see a direct correspondence with the *pesher* revelations of Dr Thiering.

Considering the mystical nature of the Essenes, it is not surprising to find that their idea of the Messiah was also an entirely mystical one. The Pharisees, on the other hand, although they did not actually deny the mystical aspect of Messiahship, were unwilling to allow belief in the Messiah to turn into an uncontrolled visionary exercise. Yes, the Messiah was coming, but it was not their responsibility to 'hasten the end' or follow some miracle-working sage and lead the whole nation to unnecessary destruction. The Sadducees were of a similar cast of mind concerning politically dangerous individuals, and gave no credence whatsoever to the post-biblical writings and imaginings of the Essenes – whereas the Zealots were all for pushing the Romans as far as possible to inaugurate the Kingdom of God through direct violence.[34] This was why the religious authorities rejected Jesus: they saw in him a wayward Essene with a sharp tongue who would inadvertently bring the wrath of the Roman Empire down on their heads.

Because Jesus was not a Pharisee, and certainly not a Sadducee, and quite obviously not a violent revolutionary in spite of the odd sword or two among his followers (one or two swords were allowed by the Romans for the defence of travelling groups), it stands to reason that he was in some way connected to the Essenes – there was simply no other foundation party to which he could belong. The fact that he was a Nazarene only confirms this point, for as we saw earlier, the Nazarenes and the Nazarites and the Ebionites and the Zadokites were all part of the Essean-Essene, the Holy Ones of Israel who had chosen separation from the Jerusalem Temple because its priesthood did not properly follow the Law of Moses. So Dr Klausner is again accurate when he places Jesus in the Essene camp and says, 'The mystical and moral messianic belief of the Essenes was nearest that of Jesus, who, in the end, abolished its political aspect and made it purely mystical and ethical.'[35] A simple statement carrying an almighty punch – for if it is true, then Jesus must have caused a veritable riot in the Essene camp, once again confirming Thiering's basic interpretation of Jesus as a renegade Essene, and Eisenman's contention of a serious difference of opinion between James and what appears to have been Jesus' chief apostle, Paul.

That Jesus gave the Pharisees and Sadducees a hard time cannot be denied, and that he probably gave the Essenes just as hard a time is only just beginning to be realized. This was a man of passionate belief, a man of action, a man who believed himself fully qualified and positioned to challenge the religious leaders of his time. He was educated in the Law, could swap witticisms with the best Jewish minds, and as a child had perhaps even been an intellectual prodigy capable of engaging in debate with his elders. Whatever the truth, he was certainly charismatic, self-assured, well-informed and wilful. Only a cast-iron will could have seen him through the ordeal of trial and crucifixion; only a charismatic, self-assured and probably regal personality could have attracted so many people to his ideas, beliefs and aims. And only a strong intellect backed by a well-stocked head could have combated the high learning of his religious peers. This was no half-baked revolutionary with a rabble behind him: it was an individual of clear mind and strong heart who wished to inaugurate a revolution on both the religious and social levels of his culture and time. This is what is so attractive about him – one can sense the passion in him boiling away as he tries to make his often doltish disciples understand his insights and long-term plans. He is special, and he knows he is special. He can see only too clearly that his religious peers have become bogged down in narrow-minded, nit-picking practices, and as a Galilean with a deep sense of space and freedom he wants to reveal what he has personally found out about God – that He does not live in a box labelled Religion.

Dr Klausner neatly sums up the religious situation at the time of Jesus when he says:

> In every system, as time goes by, the secondary comes to be regarded as primary and the primary as secondary; the most exalted idea has associated with it, disciples who distort it and transform it, and so there is aroused the indignation of the better against the worse disciples and the dispute is not with the system or the teaching but with fellow partisans who have greatly damaged the system to which they adhere. This happened to the Law of Moses in the time of Jeremiah, to Christianity not long after Jesus, and to the teachings of the Buddha.[36]

And this is exactly Thiering's point with regard to those who castigate her for all sorts of wrongdoings re Christianity – they have simply lost sight of what real Christianity is about and become bogged down in dogma and doctrine and dodo-mindedness. It was not Jesus' intention to create a religion which set person against person – it was his intention to make people free of dogmatic, doctrinally-driven religious ideas. There was neither Jew nor Gentile in his scheme of things, neither male nor female. There was equality on all fronts. The nit-picking had to stop. The emotional blackmail had to stop. The holier-than-thou attitude had to stop. *That* was his existential message.

Emotional blackmail is the most pernicious of the clubs used to bring someone to doctrinal heel. Evangelicals and fundamentalists bludgeon outsiders with their personal testimonies about Jesus' saving grace, his life-changing and body-healing capacity, his nearness and present-day aliveness. Or, in the case of some Catholic charismatics, they simply bore one to death with their veiled insinuation of a (wink-wink) deep spiritual life to which only they have access. When confronted with the more basic religious hysteria of the evangelicals and fundamentalists, orthodox Christians tend to slip-slide away into the safety of Wittgensteinian silence, and this silence in the face of literalisms run mad allows intelligent protagonists to be turned into spiritual dunces. I suppose it is less painful than faggots lit around one's feet, but it is still a dastardly way to treat what are mostly sincere, well-informed and thoughtful individuals who often take Jesus' historicity and credibility more seriously than those who claim to be his most ardent followers. If confronted by those same literalists today, Jesus would, I am sure, react in exactly the same manner as he did all those centuries ago when faced with the religiously constipated – he would attack them with stinging gusto.

JESUS' MYSTICAL VISION

There was, on just about every level, more to Jesus than most Christians realize. This man broke the rules time and again, and he broke them not just because he was a naughty boy, or because he was God masquerading as a human being, but because he possessed a penetrating insight into the nature of reality. The gospels have gone through a long process of addition and deletion, and a sixth-century manuscript known as the Codex Cantabrigiensis contains sufficient additions and differences to show that the gospels as now presented do not represent unchanged original texts. Some of these additions throw light on Jesus' motives, on why he thought what he thought and behaved the way he did, and one in particular reveals a penetrating mind to whom everyday events were much more than merely everyday events.[37]

In the gospel of Luke[38] there is the story of how Jesus and his disciples were confronted by the Pharisees for plucking ears of corn on the Sabbath, rubbing them in their hands, and eating them. When challenged on this, Jesus' reply is clever and puts these austere teachers in their doctrinal place. But as an addition to this particular passage the Codex Cantabrigiensis appends the words: 'On the same day, having seen one working on the Sabbath, he said to him, O man, if thou knowest what thou doest, thou art blessed, but if thou knowest not, thou art accursed and a transgressor of the Law.' This statement, straightforward as it may seem at first glance, is in fact the equivalent of a stick of theological dynamite.

So what did Jesus mean by this strange statement? Did he mean that to break the religious laws of his day necessitated a mind trained in, and armed with, a detailed knowledge of the Law? If that was the case, then the common people, the publicans and sinners and harlots and slaves whom he seemed so fond of did not stand a chance. And as he was obviously talking to a worker, to someone so poor that he had to take the chance of being caught working on the Sabbath, to challenge him on not having a detailed knowledge of the Law would have been churlish. So what was he talking about? Was he in fact talking about the Law at all? Breaking the Law is mentioned not as a something in its own right but as a result of something else, that 'something else' being not just the attitude carried during an act but the *intrinsic awareness possessed* in alignment with attitude and behaviour. What he seems to be saying is this: If you do not have a distinct and present-minded awareness during an act, any act whatsoever, then whatever it might be it is automatically accursed because it does not follow this basic law of authentic perception. Without this intrinsic level of awareness, this present-mindedness, this *authentic seeing of reality out of one's own presence and the presence of God through the Shekinah which touches and imbues all things with a hidden grace and tenderness*, then behaviour and attitude and statement and belief and everything imaginable is in a fallen state. If this is indeed what Jesus meant by these words, it constitutes a revolutionary insight. According to Robert Eisenman and Michael Wise, 'the study of the seemingly forbidden subject of "Being" or "Existence"' was part of the Essene secret mysteries.[39]

The gospel of John speaks of Jesus as the 'Word', or as it is in Greek, *Logos*. By describing Jesus as the *Word made flesh*, the gospel writer is vastly and quite illegitimately developing the original idea of the Shekinah, the incomprehensible presence of God made manifest as an indescribable abstraction full of poetic grace and tenderness, and with a twist of his theological wrist produces not just an ephemeral light, ray or emanation (all classified as heretical by the later Church) but a human being acting as *Shekinah in person* – the most heretical notion of all. This is where the whole physical-incarnation-of-God fiasco has its origin, and from this point onwards the idea is developed beyond the bounds of decency and becomes a recognizable heresy in relation to Judaism.

In Samaritan theology this hypostasis is spoken of as 'Glory'; in Paul's system it is termed 'Wisdom'; and in Jewish Terminology it is 'Shekinah'. Paul, in spite of modern interpretations of his Christology, does not equate Jesus with God. He is without doubt God's agent, but at the end of the day 'he is to give up his delegated authority so that God will be all in all.'[40] Jesus' sonship to God is not described as a 'divine nature', but as a result of divine creation, election and obedience of will. As Schonfield is at pains to point out again and again, Jesus is the Archetypal Man, the archetypal Son of God. And as Frances Young so astutely observes, 'When Paul wrote: "God was in Christ reconciling the world to himself," he is unlikely to have envisaged a Nicene conclusion.'[41] As we saw earlier, because the Godhead could not directly approach man, man eventually learned how to approach God though the opening up of his perception of reality – the reality or basis behind all being (Shekinah) as revealed to human beings as an experience. Next came the 'voice of God' – not literal or material speech but an 'echo' of something mysterious and far away – and with this the idea of reflected light, the first attempt to form a link or line of communication between God and material creation. But with one almighty leap the Greek compilers and editors of the gospel of John transform Jesus from being a teacher who blasted aside the hypocrisy of his age into something he himself would not have tolerated: a pagan literalization of a subtle Jewish concept of profound significance.

THEOLOGICAL DEVELOPMENT

Speaking of this exact development in the theology of the early Church, Frances Young asks two questions: (1) how is the exalted Jesus whom we worship as Lord related to the one and only God? and (2) how is God related to the world? These are difficult questions, and Frances Young does not shirk her theological duty in attempting to describe or answer them. In an essay entitled 'A Cloud of Witnesses' she tackles the main issue of Jesus' divine incarnation and admits that Church thinking on this matter is divided. But on the question of New Testament content she is certain: the New Testament 'does not provide directly revealed information about his [Jesus'] divinity, and the notion of God being incarnate in the traditionally accepted sense is read into, not out of, the Pauline epistles.'[42] Fair enough. But she is also aware that Jesus was perceived in many ways by many people. People searched for categories to explain him, but never found one that was completely adequate. This search for an adequate description led some to honour Jesus through worship, but even then he was distinguished from God in both his risen and his earthly states. And although never confessed as God, he was nevertheless interpreted as standing for God, and was the focus through which

'God is revealed to those who respond'.[43] Tricky stuff. Then, talking of the many confessions concerning Jesus' status, Young begins to close in on her subject with more and more daring, and a picture pertaining to reality begins to emerge.

For those wishing to hold on to the idea of Jesus as a direct manifestation of God in spite of much New Testament evidence to the contrary, and no direct New Testament statement to that actual effect, the argument that the gospel writers were groping their way towards a full understanding of who Jesus was is noted to have been no more than a way out of a dilemma. According to this methodology, there was a 'gradual dawning of the full truth about the person of Jesus Christ, a development steered by the providence of God and inspired by the Holy Spirit'.[44] Frances Young refuses to buy into this, and understandably so, for it is a veritable licence to print incontrovertible truth. She comes back with the observation that the development of doctrine in the early Church was 'culturally conditioned and determined by the course of controversy and debate, not to mention factors such as politics, personalities and the chances of history'.[45] Inadequate argument and distorted interpretation of scripture was used to uphold Christological positions, and compromises resulted which created 'blind alleys of paradox, illogicality and docetism'.[46] And then Frances Young uses the same loaded term used by Dr Klausner with reference to the Shekinah; she says:

> Within Judaism, the 'hypostatization' of Wisdom or Torah did not seem to undermine monotheism, since ultimately it was a kind of periphrasis [an indirect, roundabout method of expressing oneself] used to circumvent the implications of direct contact between the transcendent God and the creation; true it had a positive function in this respect, but a faith so theocentric could never allow it really to challenge God's 'monarchy', his ultimate originality and sovereignty.[47]

It was not so much that 'providence' or the 'Holy Spirit' had nudged Christians into the realization that Jesus had been much more than an ordinary man, it was the ideas current at the time (Jewish, Arabian and Samaritan) that eventually produced such a notion and thereafter the creation of a deliberate theological stance. The idea of 'Messiah' among the sectaries had sometimes teetered on the edge of theological disaster – but the idea of 'Christ' in Christian thinking directly violated the unity of God and produced an unsolvable theological riddle. The Jewish notion of Shekinah as the first hypostasis (reality or basis behind all being) had been hijacked and changed into a concept which, from the time of Constantine, would literally conjure heresies out of thin air by its very existence – the Church of intolerance and prejudice and holier-than-thou certainty had appeared.

But more important still is Young's observation that the whole incomprehensible muddle of Trinitarian argument obscures the very thing it was supposed to reveal: 'a meaningful account of God's self-revelation in Jesus'.[48] Because the Fathers of the Church eventually admitted that the relationship of God to his creation was an inexplicable mystery, it was also 'less than true to this insight to regard their theology, and the philosophy on which it was based, as timeless and unquestionable'.[49] Religious compulsion based on past observations of Jesus as a truly remarkable individual had produced such ideas, but the evolution of these ideas was another matter altogether – history showed them to have been largely determined by a particular cultural environment.

Frances Young's next question has within it the heart-rending cry of existential despair, the authentic cry of an individual facing the facts without flinching: 'How is it then that we go on living in this way?' she asks. 'Are we all schizophrenic?'[50] And then comes the big statement, the acceptance of responsibility which the Church at large constantly shirks: 'Most of the time we in fact make little attempt to integrate two world views which must be related in some way and yet appear so incompatible.'[51] The Christian lives in more than one dimension, we are told, and has a responsibility to attempt to integrate what looks like incompatible models of reality. It simply is not enough to live exclusively by one or the other, or advocate that this is how a life should be conducted. We have both a spiritual *and* an intellectual responsibility to attempt the impossible, to hold steady in the face of apparent defeat and, if I may extend Frances Young's categories somewhat, define as best we can not only the nature of the problem but the nature of the nature that is posing the problem. It is, I think, at exactly this point that the Church utterly fails the people, because instead of pursuing human nature to its core, *to the base line where human experience consciously touches the boundary of being*, it throws a bridge of cheap sentiment across the existential gap and attaches it to nothing more than the posts of ethical and moral correctness. In that ever-recurring moment, that ever-slipping frame of existential reference sacrificed to the banality of petty rules and regulations (the Qumran Essenes at their worst), the possibility of a real spiritual understanding disintegrates and is replaced with systems of energyless belief. It was this kind of thinking that Jesus fought against with all his might, and it was those who held to this kind of thinking that had him crucified.

TEN

THE HUMAN DILEMMA

The dilemma of what constitutes a spiritual life, the problem Christian's have in appreciating and admitting to the dynamic role of myth in their own religious constructions, and the Church's problem of dismal doctrines blotting out the light it claims to have.

At the end of their insightful book *The Jesus Conspiracy*, Holger Kersten and Elmer R Gruber add an Afterword which neatly sums up the spiritual dilemma facing everyone born within the confines of Christendom. This dilemma is the claim of the Churches that a real spiritual life can only be kick-started through the acceptance of Jesus Christ as Saviour. According to Christian teaching we are faced with an unavoidable decision: the acceptance or rejection of Jesus' atoning blood sacrifice on Calvary. As individuals there is absolutely nothing we can do for ourselves; it has all been done for us. To believe otherwise is to be in direct contravention of the will of God, to worship *ourselves* instead of God. There is only one direction in which a spiritual aspirant can travel, and that is into the arms of Jesus.

To put it in such terms is of course to sentimentalize what is believed to be a high spiritual process – but this is right and proper, for that is what Christianity has ultimately done to Jesus: reduced him to the level of a rather gaudy picture-postcard. And yet rejection of this cardboard figure carries a dire penalty – everlasting death tinged with the possibility of torture. I say a 'possibility' because Christians seem to be unsure about unbelievers 'roasting in hell' these days. To use a euphemism, anyone holding a different belief system is 'lost', no matter how exemplary his or her life. Pauline Christianity is the Way, the Truth and the Life; all other paths, quests and theories which contradict the Pauline manifesto are as nothing. To reach the goal and purpose of life, the heart of what it means to be a spiritual being, the essence of authentic spiritual life, we must needs go through Jesus as blood sacrifice.

A real spiritual life is simply not possible unless founded on that hour or two of mental and physical anguish. There is nothing we can do, or think, or experience which can in any way contribute to this final redemptive act. Nothing more is needed. As our representative before God, Jesus has done everything necessary. It is, as he cried out on the cross, 'finished'.

This would be a great relief if it weren't for the fact that it is a form of theological insanity – an insanity based upon an interpretation of an historical event run riot – a man of flesh and blood grotesquely elevated not just to the level of a deity but to the level of the Supreme Deity. This claim, dragged into existence by the Council of Nicea and viciously upheld over the centuries, is the basis for the Christian belief that ordinary human beings who wish to comprehend the meaning of their individual lives can do so only through an act of faith – a blind 'leap into the arms of Jesus' which crosses the gap of discontinuity between God and themselves. But this leap of faith, this flinging of the self across the abyss of human despair and need, should perhaps be renamed the 'leap of folly', for as Jesus was just an ordinary man, the leap of faith is no more than the little self accomplishing by theological sleight of hand the very act of self-idolatry banned by Christian teaching. Reinhold Niebuhr (considered the most significant theologian produced by mainstream American Christianity in the twentieth century) was a great exponent of the 'leap of faith', of short-circuiting the self's petty attempts to storm the citadel of God. But even he failed utterly to notice that the very Jesus he held up as God's expression of final revelation was no more than a grotesquely inflated human personality – the very thing he warns us against in a punchy little essay entitled 'The Self and its Search for Ultimate Meaning'.[1]

Don Cupitt notices this slip into idolatry when writing of the Christ of Christendom.

> An example of the consequent paganization of Christianity was the agreement to constitute the World Council of Churches upon the doctrinal basis of 'acknowledgment of our Lord Jesus Christ as God and Saviour' – and nothing else. Perhaps it was only when Christocentric religion finally toppled over into the absurdity of 'Christian Atheism' that some Christians began to realize . . . Chalcedonian Christology could be a remote ancestor of modern unbelief, by beginning the process of shifting the focus of devotion from God to man. It could not put up any resistance to the focusing

of piety upon the glory of the incarnate Lord rather than the glory of God, and then upon the humanity of Christ, and then upon humanity in general. On the contrary, it appeared to legitimate a cult of humanity.[2]

This not only confirms my own 'leap of folly' proposition, it develops it further and allows us a glimpse into the darker areas of theological repercussion and social spin-off. In an inverted, ingrown-toenail kind of way, the Christian faith has itself created the climate of rampant secularism threatening our age. God has assumed human form and the ultimate mystery and unity of God has collapsed into a concept agreeable to the little self – the literal, rationally-minded self which can leap backwards and forwards between belief systems with extraordinary dexterity.

Oddly enough, it is the Shroud of Turin with its astonishing full-length image that has probably contributed more than anything else to this state of affairs. Christian depictions of Jesus seem to have emerged as a direct result of the Shroud image's being discovered, and by its very existence the Shroud legitimized what previously had been considered taboo – images of the sacred. As these images multiplied, this taboo against depicting God in any way whatsoever was forgotten, and the result was a focusing of attention on Jesus and away from the great mystery of God's *alien otherness* – that which takes one's breath away. And again it is Constantine who acts as the pivot between the one view and the other: Christian art prior to Constantine was low-grade and uncertain, but after Constantine elaborate and aesthetically pleasing. In fact, Constantine's sister is known to have written to Bishop Eusebius of Caesarea requesting a portrait of Christ, a request summarily rejected by this generally obsequious prelate because even he could not go against Church opinion – such objects were simply considered idolatrous.[3] Don Cupitt identifies the main issue when he says of the fourth century:

> Christian art was emerging as part of a complex process by which Christianity was very extensively paganized in its faith, worship, organization and social teaching. The period during which the classical doctrine of Christ was being framed was also the period in which a largely pagan iconography of Christ was developed; and these developments were both of them profoundly influenced by political needs and pressures.[4]

It is ironic indeed that the Shroud of Turin, the Church's greatest relic (now considered to be a fake by the Catholic Church, but not by all outsiders), should on the one hand appear to substantiate the historical existence of Jesus and his being alive after the ordeal of crucifixion, and on the other have become an object of such veneration after his death that it eventually broke the taboo of sacred image production and instituted the very idolatry of the human despised by the early Church. How odd of God, one might say. For if this is the case – and the case it seems to be – then the whole edifice of Christian thinking, grounded as it is on the idea of Jesus' being God made manifest in flesh, is fatally flawed at its core, at the point where what is human strikes its roots into the divine. Jesus had his roots struck in God, of that there can be no question, but there's a massive difference between having one's existential roots struck in God and being *mistaken for* God. Yes, it is perfectly feasible to see God in another human being, to sense God in another human being, to be confronted by God in another human being – but it is not at all feasible to say that that human being *is* God, not even when that human being is as close to God as it is humanly possible to imagine.

The theocentric beliefs of the Jewish nation carried the notion of God witnessed in man to dizzying heights, but it did not at any time treat as literally true its daring flights of language. This is what separates Judaism and Islam from post-Constantinian Christianity, and it is this well-entrenched and ultimately absurd notion which has bred endless conflict across the centuries. Dr Hugh Schonfield was well aware of this problem, and I repeat what he said about it in the introduction to *The Passover Plot* without apology:

> The modern dilemma of Christianity is patent and stems from a creed which down the centuries has so insisted on seeing God in Jesus Christ that it is in danger, as is now evident, of being unable to apprehend the existence of God without him. Far too many Christians do not know God in any other way than through Jesus. Take away the deity of Jesus and their faith in God is imperilled or destroyed.[5]

There is a sense in which it is necessary for the Jesus who died all those centuries ago to die a second time, not for the sins of the people but for the sins of the Church who made of him more than he ever wished to be. And so we have a double conundrum on our hands, the conundrum of a Jesus who returns not as a fulfilment of prophecy but in the form of a controversial artefact (the Shroud of Turin), and the conundrum of a Jesus who must now be theologically laid to rest so that Christianity can take its next major step – the step of rediscovering its deep links with Judaism and Islam. Why Islam? Because Islam as born in the Hijaz mountains of western Arabia, and that was the home of the ancient Nasara, Christianity's primary identity before Paul's too elaborate, and perhaps only half-digested theological system fell into the hands of the Greek-minded Fathers of the early Church. But before this can happen the Church has to admit, both to itself as a priestly hierarchy and to its many, many followers, that it has to rethink Jesus back into being an ordinary man engaged in an extraordinary mission. Without such a move the future of the Church is bleak – indeed, sealed on a downward path that leads only to extinction.

The idea of man become literally God was a foolishness brought about by religious, political and social pressures of a decidedly mundane nature, and this rather obvious fact should be faced. Don Cupitt's observation that developments in Christian thinking during the fourth century were profoundly influenced by political needs and pressures is strongly supported by Dr Schonfield.

> Christianity survived and flourished at the cost of change and accommodation . . . It is not a pretty story, for all the nobility, sincerity and idealism of many associated with it. Here with the lid off we can see this religion in the making, not without vision and a sense of revelation, but substantially as a result of competing influences and pressures, conflicts, intrigues, sufferings and disillusionments.[6]

This is the cold, hard truth of the matter, the unavoidable truth, the truth that must out so that Christians can gain not only a proper historical perspective on Jesus as self-appointed Jewish Messiah but also a glimpse of how their relationship to God can change from anthropomorphic projection back to that of *alien other* appreciated in silence.

APPROPRIATE AND INAPPROPRIATE MYTHS

The idea floating around in Christian intellectual circles that the doctrine of the Incarnation is a 'necessary myth' is in itself a form of myth – but which form? Maurice Wiles handles the question of 'myth', its many meanings and possible relevance, with some dexterity in an essay entitled 'Myth in Theology'. Running the gamut of myth as 'deliberate creation' through to 'unconscious religious enthusiasm', Wiles ducks this way and that and then admits that 'Insistence on a very precise definition of myth usually turns out to be part of a Pyrrhic victory in which the author succeeds in proving the points he wants to make about myth by the simple process of making them true by definition.'[7] Well said. But there is also, he tells us, the problem of a deep division in Christian thinking concerning even giving consideration to the word 'myth' when examining the make-up of the gospels or the doctrinal decisions of the later Church Councils.

Past reaction by many English divines to the notion of myth in relation to the Old Testament, never mind the New Testament, verged on apoplexy when the question was raised in the 1800s. To such thinkers myth was a 'deceit', a 'falsehood', an attempt to hoodwink. Yet 1889 saw B Powell remark positively in myth's favour with this definition: 'a doctrine expressed in a narrative form, an abstract moral or spiritual truth dramatized in action and personification; where the object is to enforce faith not in the *parable* but in the *moral*'. But he goes further. 'Every dogma is more or less a myth, as it is necessarily conveyed in analogical language and anthropomorphic action'.[8] Then came Bultmann and the whole demythologizing of the Bible controversy which reached its height in 1941.

Wiles then tells us that myth should not be confused with legend or fairytale. Myth proper is 'a pictorial way of expressing truths which cannot be expressed so readily or so forcefully in any other way'.[9] Quoting Norman Pittenger, Wiles reveals to us that 'the incarnation of God in Christ and the Atonement wrought by him are in a different category'[10] from, say, the myths of the Creation and the Fall and the Last Judgement. There is a serious hesitation in describing Christ's incarnation and Resurrection as 'myths'. Pittenger's point is that Christ's incarnation and Resurrection took place in historical time, not before it or after it. What Jesus did he did in history. But what he did in history is of course related to us in a 'metaphorical' or 'mythological' form, and this is how it must be when attempting to relate the realm of the human to the realm of the divine which, ultimately, is beyond description. Wiles accepts this as an argument not without force, but then quotes Wolfhart Pannenberg. Pannenberg's notion of myth in relation to the life of Jesus carries the argument one step further, for he notes that it is *contrary to the nature of myth itself* to speak of God as identical with a human being who had historical existence. Myth, in its fullest, richest, most meaningful and legitimate form cannot in all conscience be forced into the straitjacket of an historical event. This is to say that the substance of the myth – the very nature of deity expressed in a pictorial way – was directly linked to historical events, which is a rupturing of the whole idea of myth as something archetypal, something applicable to *every* age.[11] To reduce the myth of God in Jesus to a point in time is to automatically disqualify it as a myth and make nonsense of its transcendent quality – it is to make it parochial. This, according to Wiles, is the heart of the problem.

So is there any way in which a link can be set up between myth and history? Can historical facts be allied to myth? Can we make 'truth claims' at the same time as we 'affirm myth'? These are the questions Wiles asks, and he answers by directing our attention to Alasdair MacIntyre's writings about Platonic myths, myths about which 'truth claims' cannot be made. Myths, says MacIntyre succinctly, are either 'living or dead', but never 'true or false'. Myths cannot be refuted, because to refute a myth is to treat it as a hypothesis in history. Wiles does not agree; he considers this 'too sweeping a judgement'. So do I. But he does agree that it is extremely difficult to apply categories of truth and falsity to myths with confidence.[12] What Wiles prefers is the concept of myths being either religiously *appropriate* or *inappropriate* – that is, linked to the overall idea that the universe is of a certain nature. If the universe is self-contained and self-evolving, the Creation myth is 'inappropriate'; but if it is ultimately dependent on a transcendent creative source, then it is 'appropriate'. But because myths, like poetry, can have more than one meaning on more than one level, or even on the same level, we can speak of myths as *more* or *less* appropriate, depending on what we think them to be appropriate to. This is of course to say that something can be 'appropriate' without necessarily being 'true' on all levels.

What interests Wiles (and myself) is the transcendent quality of myth. Something dynamic is going on in mythic configurations which, like quicksilver, runs through one's fingers. As suggested earlier by Wiles, appropriate myths should reflect the grand background of existence – which suggests to Wiles that 'There must be some ontological truth corresponding to the central characteristic of the structure of the myth.'[13] What we have here is a suspected 'resonance' between myth and reality, a resonance between myth and being (or existence) which somehow filters all contingency, yet somehow relates to specifics at certain points – at least, that's how I read it. This, as Wiles admits, is to allow for a wide range of interpretations of central myths in relation to the Christian faith, but he goes on to argue for interpretations which do not abandon the ontological basis of myth.[14] I have no problem with such a demand. But is it not also true that certain literalist interpretations of mythic events in the gospels may actually violate that ontological base more than those which seem, at first glance, to radically undermine it? Get it wrong and existence itself could be distorted to an alarming degree.

When all is said and done, it may be the unbeliever who does the myth more justice than the believer, and that in spite of an approach which *appears* to be inappropriate in relation to Christianity and its origins. The central characteristic of the structure of the Christian myth may resonate, in general terms, with ontological reality, but that does not make it automatically 'relevant' or 'true' or even 'necessary' at the mundane level, at the level of phenomenal existence. Why? Because a myth pushed too far cancels itself out; it annuls its general quality of appropriateness when it moves beyond its energy quota. Orthodoxies and their literalist offshoots are composed of such energyless myths – hence the heavy reliance on emotion and sentimentality and blackmail. Energyless myths are therefore no more than clichés, and David Crystal's definition of a cliché in *The Cambridge Encyclopaedia* enables us to understand what this might mean.

> In clichés we see fragments of language apparently dying, yet unable to die. Clichés emerge when expressions outlive their usefulness as conveyors of information. They are dying not from under-use, as with the gradual disappearance of old-fashioned words, but from over-use . . . And yet they survive, in a kind of living death, because people continue to use them, despite complaints and criticisms. They are, in effect, lexical zombies.[15]

In the eyes of devout Christians, it would be a radical undermining of the Christian vision to state that the incarnation myth cannot be directly linked with Jesus the Jewish Messiah in a literal, historical sense. For many that would be a truly 'inappropriate' interpretation of Jesus' nature and mission. But because the opposite is in fact a direct negation of the unity of God, a negation that neither Judaism nor Islam has ever been able to condone, the question of whether such a vision may be deemed 'parochial' cannot be avoided. The doctrine of Christ's incarnation is a strangely incoherent vision which, outside of pagan worship and derailed Jewish occultism, does not properly fit into the universal scheme of things, the ontological base which seems to underpin reality at *all* levels of expression. It is indeed, as Powell suggests, the 'moral' of the parable, not the parable itself, that is all-important – God is not a literalist. To continue to push energy into the view that Jesus was literally God is to push an inappropriate metaphor, an inappropriate myth, much, much too far. But more than that. It is to support a conception of things which was not even appropriate at its inception – the Nicene Council simply got it terribly wrong.

Burton L Mack's insightful description of how myths, mentalities and cultures interact is also worth repeating. 'Myths, mentalities, and cultures go together,' he tells us, in preparation for a stark truth we may not wish to know about.

> Myths are celebrated publicly in story and song. Mentalities are nurtured just beneath the surface of social conventions by means of unexpressed agreements. Myths, mentalities, and cultural agreements function at a level of acceptance that might be called sanctioned and therefore restricted from critical thought. Myths are difficult to criticise because mentalities turn them into truths held to be self-evident, and the analysis of such cultural assumptions is seldom heard as good news.[16]

Here, then, is the transition of myth from ontologically charged truth to emotionally charged cultural opinion, a stepping down of energies to such an alarming degree that the outcome cannot be anything other than false disclosure.

A RADICAL SHIFT IN PERCEPTION

In *Resurrection: Myth or Reality?*, Bishop John Shelby Spong writes:

> One can artificially resuscitate the dead corpse of yesterday's religious conclusions only so many times. Eventually they will not hold air.

This is the moment in which either a new starting place is found or the final chapter in the history of a long, but now exhausted, faith story is written.[17]

Bishop Spong is the Episcopal Bishop of Newark in the United States, and like few others of his ilk he has faced the religious challenges of the twentieth century head-on. Aware of the formative influence of Jewish traditions on the early Church, he argues for an interpretation of gospel writings in line with Jewish Midrashim, legends and myths. N T Wright does not agree with Spong's use of Midrash in this fashion, and I have to admit to being uncomfortable with the use of Midrash in such an all-encompassing manner, but I have the greatest respect for Spong's thinking on every other level, and take my hat off to his courage in the face of constant attack.

One of Bishop Spong's principal observations is that the 'pew-sitter' has been left far behind by the advent of biblical higher criticism, a form of biblical research and interpretation born in nineteenth-century Germany, and the root of the liberal Protestant alternative to literalism. Posing more questions than it can answer – or is willing to reveal in accessible everyday language – present-day Christian scholarship attempts to *protect* believers from ideas and concepts that might undermine their faith. Clergy are not encouraged by their teachers to speak from the pulpit of what they have learned behind seminary walls, and are directed to preach the old, old story as if nothing dramatic has taken place in either nineteenth- or twentieth-century scholarship. And so the gap between pew-sitter and academic grows ever wider, and Church people automatically split into 'liberal' or 'conservative' camps, each viewing the other across a tension-filled gap. For in spite of academic aloofness and censorship by the clergy, the truth of what is going on cannot be altogether hidden – intelligent men and women simply do not stand about idly, they find out what they want to know for themselves.

In the Roman Catholic tradition this distrust between conservatives and liberals has grown alarmingly and resulted in some scholars being silenced, harassed, and even removed – Hans Küng and Matthew Fox being just two of many. But as Bishop Spong points out, Protestant Christianity has fared no better. Protestant Churches have split into mainline and literalist camps, and this split has produced a wide range of religious opinion. But there is a third category of Christian – one that I would term the

'secularist' – and the secularist mode of thought is almos
from the liberal as the liberal is from the literalist a
conservative. The secularist camp is composed of
Christians who have stepped over the boundary line into atheism,
their faith having been steadily eroded as Jesus lost power, status
and divinity. And so, quite understandably, the literalists react,
pushing their mode of interpretation to extremes to save
themselves from this contagion, this 'visionless vision'. Closing
minds and ranks to all modern scholarship, the literalists
successfully safeguard their faith and the emotional charge
they draw from it, but lose out on the psychological balancing
factors which make of existence not a closed scheme but an
open invitation.

Dr Schonfield's point that if Jesus' divinity is damaged or
erased, then the ability of many Christians to apprehend the
existence of God is imperilled, or even destroyed, and this is seen
in the life of secularists and in the life of many a literalist who
suddenly loses faith. For God is not so easily approached when
Jesus as human intermediary is removed, and one could almost
say that God is *too* easily approached when his *humanity*
becomes the imaginative go-between. Christians of a literalist
bent approach God not as 'alien other', as 'fathomless father', as
'that which cannot ultimately be defined' or described, they
approach God as Jesus-the-historical-personality-who-loved-
little-children and are left with a *human being standing in for
God*. This chatty and terribly cosy relationship that literalists
have with Jesus *as* God is very, very comforting (it can even
be life-style-transforming), but it does not in its own right
carry individuals beyond their own ecstatic personalities, their
own emotionally-driven spiritual vision of what it means to
be Christian.

On the other hand, secularist Christians have all but lost their
sense of the existence of God through the removal of Jesus as
divine being and are really atheists in disguise, non-believers who
pay lip-service to the Christian faith because it helps hold the
status quo in place. Conservatives also worship the status quo,
have a tendency towards being politically right of centre, have the
capacity to accommodate biblical assertions of a highly debatable
nature without actually resorting to literalist methods (they
would accept the Creation and the Fall as myths, but not the
Incarnation or Resurrection), and when called upon for support

by Christian liberals against literalist attack, almost inevitably show a lack of intellectual courage and seem to back the literalists. Is it any wonder that literalists look askance at liberals and secularists and conservatives? And is it any wonder that liberal Christians – those who have had their experience of God strengthened rather than diminished through Jesus' returning to a less dominant role – should find the other three groups downright difficult to deal with?

For reasons not quite the same as my own, but certainly parallel in intention, Bishop Spong asks the same fundamental questions:

> Does Christianity depend on a grave that was empty, on a body that has been resuscitated, on angels that descend in earthquakes and roll massive stones away from the mouth of a tomb, or on a figure who can disappear into thin air after the breaking of bread? Does it not bother the literal believer that the details of the Gospels are as contradictory about what happened after Jesus' death as they are about what happened at the time of his birth? Is this not the last frontier?[18]

For uttering such words people have been tortured and burned in the past. Today, things are little different: the courageous are either verbally bludgeoned to death on radio and television talk shows by clergy whose intellectual dishonesty is often blatant and occasionally frightening, or they are awarded withering smiles by those same illegitimate custodians of the Christian faith. I say 'illegitimate' because in spite of their insignia and titles they are predominantly locked in a mind-set that has all but stifled the faith they claim to love so much – the faith that is dying under their very noses. Doomed to disappear if its vital spiritual energies are any longer wasted in upholding a religious vision composed of allegorical surface stories reduced to fixed truths, Christianity is crying out for apologists to help cut the ship of faith free from its literalist and semi-literalist mooring.

With his usual pithiness, Reinhold Niebuhr tells us that 'Biblical faith must remain a commitment of the self rather than a conclusion of the mind.' And then, 'Commitment is not possible without the prerequisite of repentance because the darkness about the meaning of its existence is due not so much to the finiteness of the self's mind as to the pretensions of its heart.'[19] This raises all kinds of questions, but suffice to say that 'repentance' cannot be made into a catch-all philosophy to which we must all blindly respond, and 'commitment of the self' begs the question of what it is one is committing oneself to. A commitment of the self to something greater than the self – if this is what Niebuhr is referring to – may indeed be necessary, indeed vital, for the little self to fully comprehend the larger self, but that commitment cannot properly be made unless it is sensibly backed by the finite mind. For once again, when all is said and done, 'repentance of the heart' does not require anyone to believe in the virgin birth, or that Jesus walked on water, or that he was God incarnate – in fact, *not* believing in such things may well be a corrective spiritual step in alignment with myth and its resonance with being. And repentance for a guilt of the human heart linked to some Original Sin is, if taken literally, a repentance built on the misnomer of *intrinsic evil*, an evil conjured into existence through a supposed act of disobedience to the will of God by beings designated our first parents. Rescued from the literal mind, the Genesis myth intimates not a 'Fall' but a *change of focus*, a dramatic development in human perception, a perceptual and conceptual leap which carried the human race towards its first great evolutionary hurdle – self-consciousness. The naming of the beasts had started.

The evolution of human perception to a point at which individuals became psychically separated, then isolated, then cut off from their intuitive level and driven to despair in their most cherished relationships, demands a better explanation than that supplied by the Christian Church. To be told that it is all the result of our first parents' having sinned against God and having passed on some kind of contagion is an insult to the finite intelligence which even Reinhold Niebuhr could not completely ignore. So what is the answer? What happened way back then to cause this existential hiccup to surface later as an intimation of intrinsic evil? Are we collectively guilty of some deep psychical misdemeanour? Or is it just that our ancient ancestors could not evolve without first creating *a gap in perception* across which to consciously stare – a creative gap that would rapidly grow until a complete sense of separation from 'world' and 'other' erupted and took centre stage. What a moment that must have been for those individuals who first broke through into the realm of complete self-consciousness (for it cannot be assumed that everyone went through this experience simultaneously). There must have been a vanguard – and if a vanguard, then individuals of curious capacity looked upon by others as veritable gods.

THE AUGUSTINIAN KNOT

But we have to jump forward to the fourth and fifth centuries to get this whole business into perspective, to see the Adam 'myth' transformed into clear-cut conceptual form. Destined to shed its mythological guise and assume supposed theological clarity at the hand of Augustine, the Adam and Eve myth underwent literal translation and became the backbone of the doctrine of Original Sin which would dominate Christian thinking for well over a thousand years. But Augustine did not have it all his own way. When making his move from 'myth' to 'doctrine', from flexible pictorial idea to hard text, from humanity conceived as made in the image of God, and therefore intrinsically good, to humanity conceived of as intrinsically evil due to Adamic contagion, he met with stiff opposition. For at one stroke he did away with three centuries of insistence on human beings' having free will (the very basis of the gospels), and argued that only his jaundiced view of human nature would 'liberate men from themselves'.[20]

In her book *Augustine, Philosopher of Freedom*, Mary T Clark may argue that Augustine did not deny the existence of free will as a faculty in historical man after the Fall, and that his main denial was the existence of a 'perfect freedom to do good',[21] but at the end of the day it was the former, and not the latter, notion which seems to have held sway, and the point may only be a semantic one anyway. The real point is that Innocent, Bishop of Rome, through fear of losing episcopal authority, accepted Augustine's interpretation over the alternative view put forward by Pelagius, and the idea that episcopal authority was necessary to ensure human salvation became an idea never again to be dislodged. So great was the controversy roused by this debate that riots took place in the streets of Rome in 417 CE between supporters and opponents of the doctrine of Original Sin. For Augustine's reversal of the concept of human freedom went against the grain of many a Christian, and would later condemn as heretics those who upheld the Church's earlier belief that God had gifted humanity with the will to make moral choices. Gregory of Nyssa's view that the soul was self-governed would soon be defunct, and the Rabbinic tradition which saw humanity as made in the living image of the Universal King would fade away with many another shadow of Jewish influence.

Yet all of this was in a way unavoidable, for the transplantation of Pauline-cum-Roman Catholic Christianity from Asia to Europe, from its Galilean birthplace into the Western Graeco-Roman world of science and philosophy, meant that its background mythology would inevitably undergo analysis and discussion, and that the ill-defined notion of 'hereditary weakness' to be found in the book of Genesis be variously interpreted by thinkers. For as is now known, psychological balance or imbalance governs our decision-making processes, and religious history is studded with examples of dismal doctrines foisted on the religious community by individuals of highly suspect emotional and intellectual balance. I am not suggesting for a moment that Augustine was mad or that his doctrine of original sin was political expediency in theological guise – the facts state otherwise – but it cannot be disputed that the Church did derive its enormous power over the individual by embracing this particular idea, and Augustine's *Confessions* do reveal a mind inordinately preoccupied with sin, or to be more exact, sex.

In his 1924 Bampton Lectures, Norman Williams describes Augustine's influence on historical Christianity thus:

> A giant personality such as his might be expected to have the effect of warping and drawing out of proportion the thought of his age, much as the passage of a comet near the solar system has the effect of perturbing and distorting the orbits of the planets.[22]

There is perhaps even more truth to this metaphor than Norman Williams realized, for it could be argued that Augustine distorted ancient truths and helped kill off recognition of the natural resonance between myth and psyche, and that we are still suffering the consequences. But why such a dreary view? Perhaps because he had experienced his own will as impotent against the ravages of sexual desire. Seeing his own will as divided against itself, but interpreting this as his will in the hands of an 'enemy', he excused himself at the personal level and concluded that the enemy was *human nature*, the nature bequeathed to him as a son of Adam. Human freedom was a lie, the desire to master one's own will an aberration. Adam and Eve may well have had free will to start with, but they used it to eat of the fruit of the tree of good and evil and from that moment chose self-will as their master instead of God. This seems to have been the crux of Augustine's thinking, the heart of his vision – self-will was a human capacity used *against* God. The will to master one's will, to bring it under control was for Augustine not a natural right given to man from God but in a curiously contorted fashion the very basis of his incapacity to do the will of God. Free will, self-autonomy and self-government were illusions of the soul which made a mockery of God's all-powerful existence.

Augustine's vision of human nature as 'fallen' from the very start was basically a heretical idea that caught on because the Church was temporarily under immense pressure from Gnosticism. The spear-head of the Gnostic movement was the powerful Marcionite Church (a natural outgrowth of Christian Samaritan theology absorbed and adapted by Paul), which threatened to replace the established Catholic Church with its own esoteric version of Christian teaching. This very real threat led to a speedy development within the Church of the canon of the New Testament, the baptismal Creeds and the universal episcopate through systematic expositions of orthodox Christianity. The Fathers of the sub-Apostolic Church may have argued for humanity's intrinsic goodness and freedom, and the New Testament may have vaunted the freedom of the individual over that of the power of the state, but with the Marcionite heretics breathing down their necks Catholic thinkers were forced to examine and delineate what up until then had been 'mysteries' hidden from profane eyes.[23] Self-defence was the name of the game, and a rapid consolidation of Christian doctrine was the result. Prior to this period the fixed doctrinal conceptions with which we are all familiar simply did not exist – and that in spite of Paul's writings. The infant Church had carried a generally diffused and often confused body of doctrine, and it was not until around 130 CE that Irenaeus began to frame systematic expositions of Church thinking.[24]

And how modern Irenaeus was in his thinking concerning what Elaine Pagels calls the 'politics of Paradise' can hardly be imagined – Augustine must have shuddered to read this early Church Father in full flight. With one stroke Irenaeus destroys Augustine's jaundiced view by pointing out that if the serpent had truly tempted Eve, God was Himself the author of sin. And there was equally no sense in blaming the serpent's ability to speak on some demon, for if that had been the case it was a trick demons would never have ceased to use in their deception of human beings. This, and other similar rationalizing criticisms to be found in the writings of Irenaeus concerning the Fall story reveal a mind fully cognizant of the story's allegorical sense. He may treat the existence of Adam and Eve as a literal event, but he is in no way fooled by the veiled language of the text – he is (on this occasion) more interested in moral than parable, in reading between the lines than slavishly accepting a myth as historical truth. It is a pity he did not use this ability to recognize allegory when dealing with the ideas of the Christian Gnostics. In a careful exposition of Irenaeus' point of view, Norman Williams goes as far as to say that Irenaeus's Adam belongs, 'in respect of his moral status, to the category of *hominidae* or "sub-men" rather than to that of *homo sapiens*; but for the fact that his early home was an extra-mundane "third heaven", he might pass for the immediate progenitor of the semi-human race of Neanderthal.' And Williams isn't finished; he adds:

If this primitive Hellenic-Christian conception of man's primaeval state had never been overlaid by the Rabbinical imagination as to Adam's supernatural perfection and splendour, later Christianity might have been spared even the appearance of a conflict with Darwinism.[25]

The canonization of the New Testament led to the promoting of the Fall doctrine. From the realm of 'pious opinion', the individual documents of the New Testament were elevated to the level of divine oracles. Paul's letters, particularly the First Epistle to the Corinthians and the Epistle to the Romans, once given the status of divinely inspired texts, delivered up doctrinal exactitudes of not too exact formulation, and the end result was unchallengeable dogma that no one really understood. But as we have seen, this was almost unavoidable due to the very real threat of the Gnostic ideas that were displacing the still-evolving notions of the orthodox Church. Or as Norman Williams puts it: 'The still young and tender Church developed, as it were automatically, a hard protective shell of armour, doctrinal and institutional, to safeguard the principle of its life against the vast, creeping, impalpable menace of Gnosticism.'[26] Compelled to face the question of the ultimate origin of evil because of the Gnostic belief in a *necessary* evil, Christian thinkers resuscitated the neglected idea of the Fall in Paul's teachings, and with the advent of Augustine this virtually ignored aspect of Paul's curious vision exploded onto the scene fully evolved and admirably suited to safe-guarding the Christian mind from Gnostic influence. From being merely letters to the Churches, Paul's highly individualistic communications in writing were elevated to the same level as the ancient Jewish scriptures, and from there on in his theological creations – in conjunction with the rest of the New Testament's curious story-line – took on the ring of absolute truth in spite of contradictions, anomalies, and the basic problem of mythology masquerading as history.

THE SALVATION MYTH

According to orthodox Christian interpretations of the New Testament there was nothing 'ordinary' about Jesus the Nazarene: he was quite simply God made manifest in a human body at a particular point in historical time. Everything he said was extraordinary. Everything he did was extraordinary. Everything about his life was extraordinary. He was mystery. He was love embodied. His time on earth was a revelation. His death on the Cross was a momentous cosmological event. And because he was God and the founder of the Christian Church, those who believe in him share in this extraordinary penumbra of power and wisdom and truth. Ordinary everyday life is quite without meaning and value unless set within the context of his having been here on this planet, and to live a life outside of the fold of the Christian Church is to be bereft of a real spiritual life even if one belongs to some other religious community.

There are now many variations on this theme, but at base, and in spite of a certain embarrassment at its own self-centredness, the Christian Church continues to conceive of itself as 'special', as 'privileged', as 'chosen' to not only complete the Jewish revelation of the one true God, but fundamentally to stand over all other religious visions, whatever their origin or age. Needless to say, this is not accepted by the other major religions. Judaism does not consider itself the poor relation of Christianity, and down the centuries Islam has adequately shown its rejection of supposed Christian superiority.

Professor Burton L Mack finds the fact that Christian mentality is caught up in things unique, original, charismatic, miraculous,

radical, transformative and apocalyptic an interesting phenomenon. In fact, he suggests that this way of seeing, interpreting
and dealing with the world is the direct result of the New
Testament story. There is nothing 'ordinary' in the story of Jesus'
life and death. And so the symbols for solving the critical
problems of everyday life, instead of belonging to the level of
the daily round – the round of repetitious labour, chitchat,
negotiation, compromise, folk wisdom and ordinary humour –
are forced into the mould of New Testament strategies, and end
up as 'breakthroughs', 'victories' and 'transformations'. Sound
familiar? Christian mentality is therefore ever dependent on such
radical symbols, and all other attempts to create a spiritual vision
are considered banal if they do not in some way measure up to
this explosive mixture.[27] But perhaps this scholar's most
important observation is that 'the disclosure of a myth is deemed
academic as long as the myth belongs to somebody else.
Recognising one's own myth is always much more difficult, if not
downright dangerous.'[28] Here, in a couple of sentences, lies the
heart of the matter. For if the gospel stories can be explained by
means other than the historical – by reference, say, to 'myth' –
then Christians are going to have to renegotiate not only the real
and imaginary worlds contained in the gospels but also recognize
that the supposedly banal everyday reality of non-Christians may
not be as meaningless, or as pointless, as it seems.

To contemplate the meaning of one's life in tranquillity is, by
definition, to contemplate it shorn of fear, self-loathing and small-
mindedness. Marcello Craveri draws our attention to Jesus'
injunction to live in peace, in harmony, in brotherhood, and there
is no doubt whatsoever that in Jesus' mind the attainment of the
above required real personal effort, not a blind following of
dogmatic instruction from the past, or an equally blind belief in
enchanting stories. Everything about his teaching reinforces this
view. Religion at its best is 'personal', 'intuitive', 'interior': a
moment-by-moment realization of the presence of God *in*
creation, *in* events, *in* others. And so the Kingdom of Heaven is
like leaven hidden in dough – you hide it there until the whole
lump is leavened. That is to say that the Kingdom of Heaven is a
spreading and transforming influence from within – something
that modifies with a tempering element. To say that Jesus was not
concerned with esoteric doctrine would be an understatement.
His parables are not *secret recipes* for the initiated, as some would

like to think, but rather *simplifications* for the express purpose of communication. He did of course instruct his disciples privately, but never intended to burden the common people, or his disciples, with parables beyond their capacity to understand. Yet he himself made the mistake of expecting too literal an outcome from his endeavours because of what he conceived of as his obedience to God's will, because he had accomplished an astonishing ritualistic act by an act of will. Temptation and torture he might have overcome, but his expectation that God would miraculously cancel the flow of history and force the pagan world to its knees proved to be an utter fallacy – God as *alien other* remained aloof.

It was at this point that some of his simple parables began to pose a problem, for they advocated a way of life that was simply not tenable. Believing that the Last Days were imminent, that God would somehow initiate the Kingdom and make the Romans disappear when he had completed his Messianic Mission, Jesus caused confusion among the ordinary people by telling them to take no heed for tomorrow. This was fine for his disciples and for himself (they could live on stolen ears of corn, on the charity of others), but for the working poor such advice, if taken literally, would have been a disaster. Jesus saw a new world order just around the corner – the poor saw only more of the same, and then some. The poor were right.

Robert Graves and Joshua Podro highlight this attitude in their restored Nazarene gospel:

> After Jesus's departure, his disciples still organised their lives on communistic Free Essene lines and hourly expected the end of the world. Nazarene converts sold all their property, ceased to ply trade, spent as much time as they could praying in the Temple, enjoyed only spiritual relations with their wives, and lived in a continuous state of religious ecstasy.[29]

And Paul, faced with brethren who had taken Jesus' injunction to stop work too literally, had to rescind Jesus' teaching on the Kingdom's imminent appearance and instruct them to quietly get back to earning their own bread – reality was back in place.[30]

That was a telling moment. And it was soon reinforced by the destruction of Israel, the annihilation of the Jewish people and the collapsing of a dream – it sometimes takes a lot of suffering to destroy a dream. The New Testament makes no mention of this national disaster; it carefully glosses over the bloodshed and carnage and with sleight of hand changes the destruction of the Temple into a prophecy created in hindsight. So what happened to Jesus in that moment? The controversial Dead Sea Scrolls scholar Dr Barbara Thiering suggests that he had been on the move, visiting Christian communities and helping to hold things together, and that he probably died in Rome of old age.[31] Graves and Podro are of a similar opinion: 'No historical evidence survives for determining Jesus's subsequent movements and eventual decease or apotheosis, unless Suetonius's statement in his [*Lives of the*] *Caesars* (Claudius, 25) – reading *Chrestos* as *Christos* – refers to him: "Claudius expelled from Rome the Jews who were in a state of continuous tumult under the instigation of Christ."'

Suetonius quite obviously thought that 'Chrestos' was alive, well, and living in Rome. And because there is no record of another Messiah's surfacing between 41 and 54 CE with such a title, this causes Graves and Podro to speculate that 'it is at least possible that Jesus himself ventured into the lion's den.'[32]

But there must have come a point when it was obvious to everyone, including Jesus, that the game was up, that his claims had been false, that he was not God's chosen vessel in spite of early successes, just a man of flesh and blood who had seriously miscalculated due to the beliefs he held. What a terrible moment that must have been – a moment of agony perhaps greater than that of the crucifixion itself. A moment of perceptual clarity greater than any theological speculation or insight. A moment of unvarnished truth: God does not acquiesce in the vain imaginings of the human heart.

PART TWO

The Boundary of Being

PART TWO

ELEVEN

THE GNOSTIC LEGACY

The Jewish-Samaritan impasse, the Christian-Samaritan mix-up, and the Gnostic idea of the orthodox Christian-cum-Jewish God as no more than the manic human ego let loose in history.

Gnosticism had a conception of man and God quite at odds with orthodox Catholic Christianity. Its name derived from the Greek word *gnōstikos* (pertaining to *gnōsis*, 'knowledge'), this rival teaching is believed by most scholars to predate Christianity as a religious system, and to have taken on Christian symbolism sometime during the first century. Considered by some a religion in its own right, Gnosticism's roots are traced to pagan sources such as the *Corpus Hermeticum* and the *Oracula Chaldaica*, and even back to first- and second-century Jewish mysticism. This is an important link. Although later closely identified with Christianity, this system of knowing God had characteristics seemingly foreign to Christian tradition, and was considered syncretistic.

Following the thinking of Reitzenstein, many scholars continue to be persuaded (with modification since 1950) that the principal element in this syncretism was ancient Iranian 'salvation' doctrine combined with Greek Platonic dualism. However, in his study of Iranian Sufism, Henry Corbin slams the ease with which many scholars use the term 'syncretism', and suggests that it is 'often a substitute for reasoned argument'.[1] Corbin's point is that what scholars take for syncretism is in fact the attempt by spiritually astute minds to restore a lost philosophy to its rightful place, a philosophy that must surface again and again if we are to have an authentic knowledge and experience of God.

One major difference between Gnosticism and orthodox Christianity was the Gnostic objection to the atonement. Christ was considered primarily a 'revealer', and his atoning sacrifice was thus flatly rejected as *unnecessary*. This led some Christian

Gnostics to negate the humanity of Christ, and spurred the Church Fathers – especially Irenaeus – into emphasizing the reality of the incarnation. Rejecting (as did the Samaritans) the world as the place where God worked out his plan for the salvation of mankind through the process of history, they caused the early Church to react with a 'theology of history', so aligning them with the Jewish idea of history as God's experiential blueprint for salvation. And believing that the human race was divided into 'spiritual', 'psychic' and 'material' classes, the Gnostics also caused the Church Fathers to jump in the opposite direction and applaud free will and personal responsibility – a conception of man's relationship to God later rejected and pushed into reverse by Augustine's doctrine of Original Sin. This is to suggest that the development of orthodox Catholic doctrine was largely due to the Church's reaction against Gnosticism, the Church Fathers struggling to keep ahead as Gnostic influence began to infiltrate every nook and cranny of the body of Christ.

Gnosticism saw the unconscious self of man as identical to the Godhead, but fallen due to being born into the material world – a world utterly alien to real being. But there was a way out of this dilemma. Through interior revelation one could link back into one's origin, essence and transcendent destiny, such a revelation being part of initiation into secret doctrine. Unlike Greek philosophical enlightenment, and Christian revelation, Gnostic revelation could not be attained by way of philosophical reasoning or history functioning as a transmitter of the Divine Plan through Scripture, but by visionary experience. Such experience answered to an intuition of the mystery of the self, and revealed that the Jewish creator-God Yahweh was no more than a demiurge, the Gnostic God being found only in depth and silence beyond name or predicate.

An important aspect in relation to Gnosticism is Encratism. Encratites were members of an early Christian sect which abstained from meat, wine and marriage, taught the heavenly origin of the soul and 'knowledge', and knew of no division in the Godhead. The theory behind Encratism was deeply rooted in early Christianity, is believed to have been older than classical Gnosticism, and is thought to have served as the origin of Gnostic speculation. Some scholars are of the opinion that this Encratic background to Christianity eventually allowed Gnosticism to parasitically attach itself to the primitive Church.

Rudolf Bultmann suggested that a pre-Christian Gnostic myth of a 'Saviour' had influenced Paul's Christology *and* John's Gnostically-oriented New Testament gospel.

Up until recently, scholars rejected the idea that the Dead Sea Scrolls contained such a myth, but Dr Schonfield has shown there to be a direct link between the third-century Mandeans, the first-century Nazarenes, and the Essenes of the Dead Sea Scrolls through his analysis of the Mandean *Sidra d'Yaha* (Book of John the Baptist) and the Aramaic *Genesis Apocryphon* discovered among the Scrolls.[2] This opens up an interesting avenue of research. The 'Saviour' myth plausibly stems from the lost gospel of the Nazarenes – the gospel of the Nasara which was based on ancient Israelite monotheism, and of the Nasara who, as Professor Salibi has shown, split into two sects, one with the heretical belief in a man (Isa/Issa) become God, the other with this same Issa as no more than a prophet of God. Corroborating factors are the striking doctrinal parallels that exist between the gospel of John in the New Testament and that of third-century Mandean beliefs now closely aligned with the Nazarene sect. And it is important to realize that the Essenes are considered by some scholars as forerunners of Gnosticism, so confirming the fact that groups such as the Nazarenes, the Nazarites, the Ebionites and Zadokites were all part of one doctrinal movement deserving of the title Essean-Essene.

Another group influential on Gnostic thinking and development were the Merkaba mystics of Palestinian Judaism. Developed in the very midst of Judaism, Merkaba mysticism lent its concepts and terminology to Gnosticism, and perhaps influenced those later practitioners of Gnostic life-style to reject the 'atonement' of Christ as an insult to the unity of God. For Jewish Gnosticism remained staunchly monotheistic and preserved the distinction between even the most highly evolved man and the transcendent God of their fathers. But something happened to break this ancient conception of the unity of God, and we are suddenly presented with what looks very much like heretical notions sprouting at the heart, or very near to the heart, of Judaism – notions of man become divine (or transformed), as in the case of Simon Magus, a Jewish heterodox teacher from Gitta in Samaria who proclaimed himself to be 'that power of God which is called Great',[3] and who came up with the startling notion that evil was due to a break in the Godhead – an idea that was eventually to pervade all other Gnostic systems. Although he perceived himself to be a divine incarnation, Simon Magus was quickly cut down in size by the writers of Acts, reclassified as nothing more than a cheap magician, and relegated to the religious scrap-heap.

THE SAMARITAN CHALLENGE

But this is too neat a summation of Simon's life and beliefs. As Michael Goulder describes in his essay 'The Two Roots of the Christian Myth', Luke's reduction of Simon from divine incarnation to mere magician is a ploy to justify his eventual acceptance into the Church – blasphemy had to be smoothed away to make of Simon nothing more than an unusual sinner come to repentance.[4] But Simon's claims to divinity are not so easily erased – in fact, the whole Samaritan scenario is much more complicated than Acts would have us believe. As noted in Part One, the Samaritans were a mixed population of Israelites and descendants of Assyrian colonists, and although professing a form of Judaism, slowly broke religious ties with both Galilee and Judea over the centuries. This break with Judaism also meant a break with the Temple cult at Jerusalem, and resulted in the Samaritans' building an independent temple on Mount Gerizim at the time of Alexander. It is thought that the Samaritans organized themselves as a schismatic community when the Jews, viewing them as mongrel stock, refused their assistance in the building of the second Temple. The schism intensified, however, when the Samaritans established their own temple on Mount Gerizim around 322 BCE. Viewing themselves as of a single, homogeneous race, they claimed that they were actually the descendants of the Ten Tribes, utterly denying that the latter were ever deported *en masse* to Assyria as the Old Testament relates.[5]

Together with the Jews, many Samaritans were deported to Egypt and, under the heel of Antiochus IV Epiphanes, they were compelled (with the Jews) to give their sanctuary over to the worship of a heathen god. While in Egypt the two nations continued their rivalry in Alexandria, marking their antagonism to each other as deep-seated, if not ineradicable. But it was only when the Jews embarked on a blatant policy of expansion under the Hasmoneans that open hostility seems to have broken out, resulting in the destruction of the Samaritan temple by John Hyrcanus I in 129 BCE. From that moment the Samaritans found themselves sandwiched between the Jews and the Romans, and it was not until their enemy was subjugated by the Romans in 63 BCE that Samaria was liberated and allowed to look after her own affairs by the Roman governor Gabinius. Later, however, and in spite of past treatment, Samaria would support the Jews against Vespasian, pay the price by being massacred, and suffer equally with the Jews the oppression perpetrated by Hadrian. Their traditional writings burned by the Roman conquerors, they seem to have shared in the Jewish dispersion, setting up Samaritan synagogues throughout the Empire.

Once again a little-mentioned New Testament group turns out to be much more important than first suspected, and, as we shall see, much more powerful and influential in early Christian affairs than is presently realized or admitted. Church tradition and sections of the New Testament suggest that the Samaritan Christians were a strongly-constituted first-century group who not only gave Paul many a headache, but also had the Jerusalem-based Nazarenes on the doctrinal hop. Working from a slightly modified version of the Jewish Pentateuch in which the Samaritan sites of Shechem and Bethel are featured instead of Jerusalem, and the command is to worship God on Mt Gerizim or Mt Ebal, the Samaritans rejected those scriptures that were anti-Northern and cut off their revelation with Moses. And so history stopped for the Samaritans, and with the stopping of history came the demise of that view which said that God worked out his grand design and purpose through history. This constituted, as Michael Goulder points out, 'an important theological cleft'.[6] God had withdrawn from history, therefore the whole Jewish prophetic corpus had to be rejected. Goulder sums up this situation by saying that because God could not be experienced through history, he was instead experienced through *revelation* in relation to early Scripture.[7] These are the magic words: Samaritan theology was on its way to being a Gnostic vision, a personal rather than a collective experience. There would be an elite, and even exercises by which knowledge of God could be attained.[8] A liturgical composition by Marquah (fourth-century material believed to reflect early Samaritan theology) reads, 'Respond to the light within you, and it will develop until it is one with the Light.'[9]

So what of Simon Magus' claim in the 30s BCE that he was 'that power of God which is called Great? Was he taken seriously? Had he simply borrowed the idea from Paul's evocation of Jesus as Son of God? Apparently not. Goulder draws our attention to Justin's statement that Simon was eventually worshipped in Rome by other Samaritans as a god, and goes on to reveal that there are good theological reasons for accepting Simon's claim to have been uniquely based in Samaritan religious ideas prior to the appearance of the Pauline Mission.[10] It was perhaps this very factor which attracted many Samaritans to Paul's already highly elevated idea of Jesus as 'Son of God' – they would have sensed a resonance with their own religious teachings and listened with interest. The only problem was in selling the Samaritans Jesus' lineage, his death on the Cross and his Resurrection, for King David 'was the arch-apostate who had set up worship at Jerusalem'.[11] And because there was no notion of a messiah in Samaritan thinking, and they had not even heard of Daniel or the Son of Man, and they did not believe in a resurrection after death (an afterlife), the idea of a resurrected Jewish Messiah trying to resuscitate the Davidic monarchy would have been of no interest whatsoever. So why did they respond so readily to Christianity? Why were the early Christian missionaries to Samaria so successful? And why, eventually, did Jesus specifically instruct his disciples to preach the gospel in Samaria?[12]

Simon Magus, it is thought, was primarily attracted to Christianity because he was enamoured by the apostle Philip's magical powers. His reasoning, it is assumed, was that as Philip's disciple he hoped to learn the origin of Christian magic. This does not ring true. And neither does his sudden and inexplicable conversion, or his proffering of a fee to Peter for the secret of how to confer the power of the Holy Ghost on others. And neither does his repenting after a reprimand from Peter, or his fading discreetly into the woodwork never to cause bother again. Sectarian literature reveals the opposite: Simon again assumed his power role in relation to God. This is reflected in Acts through the tussle Paul later has, or appears to have, with Samaritan Christian missionaries (Hebrews) whose teachings about Jesus are even more highly imaginative, and certainly more successful, than his own – teachings perhaps allied to Samaritan Gnosticism and Simon's success as a separate hypostasis of the Godhead. As revealed in sectarian literature, Paul's eventual problem in relation to Samaria must have been that the Samaritans saw Simon as Jesus' equal – in fact, they appear to have believed that the same spirit animated both men. This is to say that Philip and Paul did not preach anything even resembling Jesus the *Jewish* Messiah to the Samaritans,[13] they simply jumped on the bandwagon of Samaritan Gnosticism, attempted to displace the *god* Simon with the *god* Jesus, and ended up with the anomalous situation of *two* Sons of God – a double hypostasis (in the Jewish sense of 'reflection' of God) that must have been very embarrassing.

That Simonian theology did influence Paul's thinking cannot be doubted – and that in spite of the fact that he already had a head start with ideas drawn in all likelihood from the heretical Nasara. Michael Goulder captures Paul's mentality when he says: 'One of Paul's most admirable qualities is his flexibility, his ability to steal the opposition's clothes while they are bathing.'[14] Paul will eventually begin to exhibit Samaritan thinking in his Christology: the pre-existence of Jesus the Messiah and his role as hypostasis, along with theories of 'mystery' and 'knowledge', *gnosis*,[15] and what was flatly rejected by him at the start because of difficulties with Samaritan missionaries[16] will appear later as self-evident and orthodox[17] – orthodox to the extent that it will underpin the Gentile Church's notion of orthodoxy in the future. Oddly enough, this orthodoxy of the future will take upon itself the right to classify as 'heretical' questions by intelligent Christians as to exactly where one should draw the dividing line between the man Jesus and his relationship to God, and out of a necessity to sidestep such questions will arise the need to deify Jesus and canonize the New Testament corpus. From there on, paradoxically, Paul's basically Gnostic beliefs will be used to stem the spread of Gnosticism and will result in a totally muddled and topsy-turvy theology which the Fathers of the Church and obdurate Church Councils will struggle to enforce with greater and greater severity. And John's gospel, written according to Michael Goulder for a 'Samaritan Church-membership',[18] will carry this Gnostic teaching all the way with his *Word become flesh*.

The taint of anti-Jewish sentiment in Gentile Christian thought is most certainly the result of their having spliced Samaritan and heretical Nasara theology together, for both religious parties sprang from ancient Israelite monotheism, and both regarded Judaism as a false – or at best a wayward – perception of God's purpose. As we have already noted, the Samaritans had undergone centuries of Jewish belligerence and subjugation, and had suffered dreadfully as a result of coming to their aid against Vespasian. Classed as mongrel Jews, they had been treated as poor second-cousins and made to feel singularly unwanted. Separated from Jewish life both intellectually and emotionally, they had created a religious vision based on personal revelation instead of collective sensibility, and the result was a theology of transcendence connected to the religion of the ancient Israelites, and directly influenced by some of the old Israelites living among their half-caste brethren in Samaria who were carrying a teaching developed centuries earlier by the Nasara precursors of the Nazarenes. Disguised virtually beyond recognition, Issa the Godman was alive and well and about to be reinforced as the central focus of Pauline-Petrine Christianity.

For Paul, the 'Lord was at hand'.[19] His return was just around the corner, so to speak. Goulder says of Paul almost wonderingly: 'He never lost faith in the primitive Galilean eschatology.'[20] Is it any wonder? Jesus *was* just around the corner. In every single chapter of 1 Thessalonians Paul refers to Jesus' *imminent* return. But it is in his first Epistle to the Corinthians that we find him waxing strong and confidently over the issue.

> If there is no resurrection of the dead, then is Christ not risen; And if Christ be not risen, then is our preaching vain, and your faith is also vain. Yea, and we are found false witnesses of God; because we have testified of God that he raised up Christ: whom he raised not up, if so be that the dead rise not. For if the dead rise not, then is not Christ raised: And if Christ be not raised, your faith is vain.[21]

I cannot believe for a second that Paul simply created a fantastic bit of theology around Jesus and then believed it as if it were real. That would be to insult the man's considerable intelligence. He believed in the *physical* resurrection of Jesus, of that there can be no doubt. And that he considered this physically resurrected Jesus as 'transformed', there also can be no doubt. In his scheme of things, 'flesh and blood' could not ultimately inherit the Kingdom of God *just as it was*. Something dramatic had to happen before the mind and physical body could be regarded as ready for God's Kingdom. There would be a moment in which those waiting for the Kingdom to appear would be suddenly and unexpectedly *changed*. The Last Trump would be blown, in the twinkling of an eye the dead would come back to life in new spiritual bodies, and those alive and waiting would be similarly transformed – that is, cleansed of sin and limitation.[22] Jesus' followers would be transformed; the world would be transformed; and into this transformed world would step an already transformed Jesus.

But it never happened – at least, not as hoped. The Last Trump went unheard. The Kingdom of God did not suddenly materialize. The dead were not raised incorruptible. The living followers were not suddenly changed in body and in mind. And so the return, or more accurately the 'revealing' of Jesus, never took place either. The days simply stretched into years, into decades, and the Jesus of the gospels grew old like everyone else. Dr Schonfield draws down the curtain on Jesus' Messianic Mission with the following words:

> He had no control over what lay beyond, and in much that he anticipated he was mistaken. The Church had to face before long the acute problem of the postponement of his expectations, and dealt with it rather lamely and unconvincingly by largely spiritualising them. The dogma of his deity did not allow it to be admitted that he had been in error.[23]

In *The Passover Plot*, Schonfield reveals that in ancient Samaritan eschatology there is a direct link between the Day of Judgement and the events at Sinai. There would be thunders and lightnings and heavy cloud, and a great fear, and 'a mighty sound of a trumpet'.[24] But of much greater interest is his linking of the Samaritans with the Nazarenes. The Nazarenes, as part of a rich and disparate community (Essean-Essene), regarded themselves as

> the 'maintainers' or 'preservers' of the true faith of Israel. This claim was shared by the Samaritans, inhabiting Samaria (Shomron), who represented themselves as the *Shamerine*, the 'custodians' or 'keepers' of the original Israelite religion in opposition to the Judeans. The same may be said of a pre-Christian sect of Nazarenes (Aramaic *Natsaraya*) described by the Church Father Epiphanius.[25]

A few pages further on Schonfield again touches on the interesting topic of Nazarenes and Samaritans. 'Epiphanius, whose pre-Christian Nazarenes in the north have an affinity with the Samaritans, was convinced that the Essenes derived from the Samaritans.'[26] The plot thickens.

Not only do we now have the Nazarenes and the Samaritans directly linked in historical intention, we have the added factor of the Essenes being themselves perhaps of ancient Samaritan origin. Drawing the strings of his argument together, Schonfield then directs our attention to the fact that the Essenes are not mentioned in the gospels or the Acts, and suggests that any such reference would be needless if the primitive Christians as Nazarenes came within the framework of what is termed Essenism. This statement completes the necessary connections between Nazarenes, Samaritans and Essenes, and allows us to legitimately surmise (along with many others, it now transpires) that the gospels do not accurately reflect Jesus' relationship to the Samaritans or to the Essenes. For it is exceedingly odd that Jesus should instruct his disciples to keep away from the Samaritans, but at the next turn of events do exactly the opposite; that he should openly admit Messiahship to a Samaritan woman, hide this fact from the Judeans, and at Jerusalem be taunted with being a demon-possessed Samaritan; and that there should be a 'good' Samaritan and a 'grateful' Samaritan in Luke's gospel, both stories suggesting *bad* Jews and *ungrateful* Jews. There is a definite bias in the gospels towards the Samaritans, and this probably reflects a Samaritan scribal touch.

Robert Graves and Joshua Podro add fuel to the suspicion of a bias towards the Samaritans when they write:

> Yet in the interpolated Matthew xxi. 43, Jesus promises the Kingdom of God, the rightful inheritance of Israel prophesied in *Zechariah* and *Daniel*, to 'another nation'. Not to all nations equally, but presumably to Samaria, where, according to Acts viii. 14 and ix. 31, the Nazarene faith had flourished before the time of Paul's conversion.[27]

And it is again worth remembering that Jesus eventually instructs his disciples to go to the Samaritans with the gospel, so reversing previous orders.

Barbara Thiering's hidden *pesher* code in the New Testament has much to say about Simon Magus and his relation to Jesus, but it would require too much by way of explanation to properly delve into this material. Suffice to say that she identifies Simon not just as the leader of a Gnostic sect but as the head of a missionary order, and describes him as 'a man of extraordinary gifts who could attract followers to his version of the doctrine, an amalgam of liberalised Judaism and Greek philosophy and science'.[28] Dr Thiering's studies actually connect Jesus and Simon – that is, she contends that they knew one another and interacted as sectaries. Considering that we have already discovered that the Nazarenes, Samaritans and Essenes had historical and theological links, this is not too difficult a proposition to accept. Their claims were eventually very similar, and the two figures were certainly related in Samaritan thinking. It may well be that as her *pesher* reveals, Simon eventually conducted a rival missionary campaign for the hearts and minds of the Gentiles.

In her study of Gnosticism, Dr Elaine Pagels records Irenaeus' evaluation of Simon as the 'father of all heresies', and this certainly reflects early Church thinking on the matter, although in itself it is an exaggeration. Samaritan religious ideas were a threat because they were so attractive, and it would seem that Paul progressively counteracted Samaritan successes by incorporating their theology of 'mystery' and 'knowledge' into his own quite elaborate Nasara-based system. Christian scholars will bridle at such a suggestion, but as Karen Armstrong contends in her highly readable *History of God*, Gnostic thinking was not 'an entirely outrageous cosmology',[29] a sentiment quite obviously shared by Paul as evident in the development of his thinking.

THE GNOSTIC PARADOX

In *The Gnostic Gospels*, Dr Elaine Pagels asks an important question: 'Why did orthodox tradition adopt the literal view of resurrection?'[30] She goes on to suggest that one reason may have been the practical effects on the Christian movement. The bodily resurrection of Jesus served a political function: it validated the apostolic succession of bishops. This was due to the fact that after his Resurrection Jesus claimed to have *all* authority in heaven and on earth, a claim not made before the Resurrection. A good point, and one validated early on by the behaviour of bishops towards their flocks. But a parallel reason may have been that when the gospels speak of Jesus' body after the Resurrection as 'spiritual' and not 'physical', what we're dealing with are Gnostic-cum-Samaritan infiltrations which the Roman Church wished neither to recognize or stress. There are many discrepancies between the gospel accounts – some arguing for a fully physical Jesus who ate and drank, who could be touched, others suggesting a spiritual body which could not be touched. And the strange argument by some early Fathers that Peter, and not Mary

Magdalene, was the first to see Jesus after his Resurrection is flatly contradicted by scripture. Mary, who would later figure so grandly in Gnostic literature is given pride of place and named as not only the first to see the risen Lord, but the one to communicate the news of his Resurrection to the Twelve – the suggestion that Peter was first evidently due to a desire to keep the episcopal succession from Peter to the fore.

Michael Goulder's observation that the Samaritan Christians were much more influential than previously thought, that they were a 'powerful section of the first-century church, and that their movement grew into Christian Gnosticism in the second',[31] allows us to conjecture that they too provided writings which were eventually incorporated into the New Testament. Burton L Mack's Book of Q certainly upholds the idea of there being numerous 'Jesus groups' involved. As with Acts, in which there are many levels of text and allegiance sandwiched together, the gospels too reflect differing theological notions awkwardly amalgamated – some of them likely to have been Samaritan-based. In a letter to Victor, Bishop of Rome, Irenaeus warns that Gnostic writings are circulating among his congregations. Florinus, the author of these writings, apparently claimed the prestige of being a priest – so even the clergy were involved in spreading Gnostic ideas and challenges.[32] Now Irenaeus condemns these early second-century gospels as forgeries, but he ought also to have widened his condemnation to include many first-century gospel documents already thoroughly edited and made to speak the language of Catholic orthodoxy.

Adventurous to a fault, these Gnostic Christians of Samaritan and other backgrounds refuted the Roman Church's already consolidated institution of bishops as unquestionable leaders, took to having their own meetings without episcopal permission, and in general attempted to create a much more relaxed atmosphere. Jesus' own teachings and behaviour were more to their liking, the already rigid framework of ecclesiastical authority being rejected on the grounds that the true Church constituted two or three gathered together under the direct supervision of spiritual forces and energies – not overseen by some self-appointed external regulatory body that had to be obeyed without question.

That the orthodox Catholic Church was only one of two streams of Christian thought and practice is obvious when the texts of the Nag Hammadi scrolls are consulted. Accusing orthodoxy of being fake, of having no real spiritual life because of a reliance on dry dogma and fixed beliefs, the Gnostic Christians proclaimed themselves the true Church, described their membership as 'Sons of Light', and in doing so echoed the self-designation of the Qumran Essenes. By 200 CE these two bodies of religious opinion were facing one another across a theological divide about as deep as can be imagined – the Gnostics arguing for a qualitative assessment of new members (as did the Essenes), the orthodox allowing anyone in who would confess the creed, accept the ritual of baptism, take part in worship and obey the clergy without question. By way of contrast, Gnostic demands on a candidate were stringent, each candidate being evaluated 'on the basis of spiritual maturity, insight, or personal holiness'.[33] To stifle any attempt at charismatic upheaval within the orthodox fold, Ignatius, Bishop of Antioch, had this to say:

> Let no one do anything pertaining to the Church without the bishop. Let that be considered a valid eucharist which is celebrated by the bishop, or by the person whom he appoints . . . Wherever the bishop offers [the eucharist], let the congregation be present, just as, wherever Jesus Christ is, there is the catholic church.[34]

This tied things up quite neatly: only a 'heretic' would consider Christ to be present if the bishop wasn't there. The door of authority and episcopal power had shut quite firmly in the faces of those who believed that Christianity signalled intrinsic freedom of the spirit.

Writing in 180 CE, Irenaeus, Bishop of Lyon, speaks of 'heretics' boasting that they have many gospels, and that these gospels have been distributed as far as Rome, Gaul, Greece and Asia Minor. Elaine Pagels states that the suppression and burial of banned Gnostic literature (the Nag Hammadi scrolls) was 'part of a struggle critical for the formation of early Christianity'.[35] The Nag Hammadi texts discovered in Egypt in 1945 by an Arab peasant belong, according to Dr Pagels, to the beginning of the Christian era, and the *Gospel of Thomas* in particular is dated by Professor Gilles Quispel at around 140 CE. However, Dr Pagels quotes Professor Helmut Koester of Harvard as suggesting that the Thomas collection, although correctly dated by Professor Quispel, probably includes older material even than the gospels themselves.[36] This is an interesting remark, for it gives further substance to Mack's *Book of Q* theory that there was an original collection of sayings by Jesus similar to that of Thomas' gospel – a group of sayings around which the gospel stories were written. Dr Pagels also notes that by the time of Constantine, orthodox Christianity, previously victimized by pagan law enforcement, came to command those same forces of oppression and used them to confiscate heretical books and denounce those who owned them.

With the same dismissive certainty, the Church of England declared the *Gospel of Thomas* a dud in 1962. H E W Turner and the former Bishop of Birmingham, Hugh Montefiore, classified the text as without value when compared with the canonical gospels.[37] Yet it is quite possible that this sayings-source was used by the gospel writer-editors along with Mark's gospel, as Tobias Churton states in his book *The Gnostics* – an interesting overview of early Gnostic activity written to accompany a Channel 4 television series.[38] Churton's reasoning was that the *Gospel of Thomas* was a sayings-source used by the Jewish Christian Church in Syria before the composition of Luke and Matthew (*circa* 70–90 CE), and that this unusual narrative was not then considered apocryphal. This is an important observation – the term 'apocryphal' was later used to rubbish perfectly good texts deemed unsuitable by the orthodox Catholic Church – that is, contradictory to their by then carefully defined purpose. Pruned out of existence by Athanasius, these more-than-likely primary source documents were relegated to the theological and historical dustbin by those seeking to establish Church authority.

There were of course very good reasons for such moves against the Gnostics. With its multiple variations in ideas and doctrine, Gnosticism was a real headache for those attempting to define what exactly it was that Christians were being called to die for. A *martyr* was etymologically a 'witness', and as Churton points out, it was necessary to 'know the exact truth to which the deaths bore witness'.[39] It was all very well inventing novel schemes and words to describe obscure interior experiences of so-called 'truth', but such experiences were far too complicated and personal, too subjective and arbitrary, to vie with the belief that Jesus had been the Son of God and that he had died for the sins of the world. This was the 'truth' that mattered, not some airy-fairy nonsense imagined or dreamed or ecstatically conjured into existence by charismatic groups lacking doctrinal order and discipline. This

was what changed lives, rescued souls from destructio
brought social order to a disordered and dangerous society

So thought Irenaeus, Bishop of Lyon, and he wrote a r
five-volume refutation of Gnostic heresy to prove the point.
Churton draws our attention to the reasons underlying such an
attack, and with the help of Elaine Pagels suggests that the
Western Christian movement outrightly rejected mystical
tradition for reasons of stress. In fear for their very lives,
Christians were continually under threat of persecution, potential
arrest and public execution, and so had to be able to clearly
identify who was on their side and who was not.[40] Unlike
convinced orthodox Christians who had placed their faith in
Jesus as the 'Christ', who believed that the salvation of their very
soul for all eternity rested on their unflinching declaration of him
by name, the Gnostics were able to shuffle their sentences and
come out of most confrontations looking like just another pagan
philosophical school. Unable to tolerate such slipperiness, and
deeply threatened by Gnostic willingness to juggle symbols
and swap one definition for another, the Church hardened its
attitude and finally determined to eradicate all Gnostic influence
within its sphere.

THE GNOSTIC VISION

But was Gnosticism all flipperty-flapperty nonsense as the Church
and a substantial number of scholars would like us to believe?
Was there nothing in it at all? Paul certainly seemed to think
there was something in the Gnostic approach to personal
revelation – in fact, he contradicts Iranaeus' notion of revelation
only coming to the Christian *after death* by making experience of
revelation a cornerstone of the Corinthian Church. Having 'the
mind of Christ' allows the Christian to 'know the mind of God',
he tells us straight out. The First Epistle to the Corinthian Church
is an eye-opener in terms of Gnostic influence, for in it Paul spells
out as 'natural' what the Church will eventually reject as
'unnatural' – that is, as disorderly spiritual behaviour. Churton
reminds us that many scholars believe Paul to have faced a
Gnostic outlook at Corinth,[41] and it may well be by way of saying
that he himself has experienced personal revelation in the Gnostic
mould that makes him talk of 'someone' who experiences being

'caught up to the third heaven'. Unspeakable words are heard, and visions and revelations. But Paul is cagey: he knows there are dangers involved – ego inflation, division among members – and warns that unless there is an underlying love to temper such experience, then it is worthless. Churton ties all of this together when he says:

> It would not be long before the visionary would become suspect in the Church and a substantial part of the spiritual gifts which Paul's Churches enjoyed would be downgraded, and, in the case of the Gnosis, excluded altogether.[42]

This is to basically agree with Karen Armstrong's contention that Gnostic thinking was not 'an entirely outrageous cosmology' – and it is revealing that the psychologist Carl Jung is quoted by Gilles Quispel as having said that the Gnostics already knew what he had spent all of his life trying to find out about the human psyche.[43]

Gainsaying Gnosticism as a meaningless conglomerate of ideas and symbols not related to Christianity, the French scholar Simone Pétrement takes on those who hold this view and lashes back with a direct statement:

> In separating Gnosticism and Christianity our scholars have not allowed us to understand Gnosticism. Their hypothesis is not only unilluminating but renders unintelligible a large number of Gnostic writings. What they offer us as the meaning of these writings is in fact fanciful doctrine, almost entirely irrational, and one wonders how people could ever be led to imagine it. These same scholars admit, however, that they cannot explain the birth of Gnosticism, even by Judaism, from which it differs even more than from the Church's Christianity.

Pétrement continues with the amusing and pointed suggestion that Gnosticism must then have fallen from the sky 'completely formed, about the time Christianity appeared'.[44] Appalled by books and articles on this question replete with references but full of 'inexact or unfounded statements',[45] Pétrement states that we simply cannot be sure that Gnosticism was not initially Christian. And in alignment with my own researches, Pétrement captures the sequence of probable historical events in relation to Judaism, Gnosticism and Christianity when she says: 'Gnosticism sprang from Judaism, but not directly; it could only have sprung from a great revolution, and at the time when Gnosticism appeared, such a great revolution in Judaism could have been nothing other than the Christian revolution'.[46]

In his Gnostic storehouse of a book, *Fragments of a Faith Forgotten*, G R S Mead talks of 'indirect' documents on the Gnostics – that is, those polemical writings of the Church Fathers against the Gnostics which came to underpin established orthodox Catholic teaching. Up until 1853, these refutations of Gnosticism were scholars' only means of entry into this vast and complex subject, but with the translation of the *Pistis Sophia* by Schwartze in that year, everything changed. Mead remarks on this state of affairs by way of warning:

> Our indirect sources of information . . . came through the hands of the most violent opponents of the Gnosis; and we have only to remember the intense bitterness of religious controversy at all times, and especially in the early centuries of the Church, to make us profoundly sceptical of the reliability of such sources of information.[47]

He goes on to tell us that the early Fathers of the Western Church were less capable of understanding the philosophical and mystical problems which so concerned the Eastern communities, and that their grasp of Greek and oriental thought was limited. And then he draws our attention to a very important historical fact: we have no single refutation of Gnosticism from the first century, and only Irenaeus' massive attack on Gnosticism in the last decade of the second. As from that point, all future refuters based their criticisms of Gnosticism on Irenaeus' highly compact, highly muddled and highly exaggerated commentary. But two lost works against heretics are known to have existed during those early centuries – one by Agrippa Castor, the other by the apologist Justin Martyr. Mead remarks that if Justin's extant works are anything to go by, then his telling of the gospel story was probably at variance with the canonical gospels as we now know them, and this may well have been the reason for the disappearance of his work against the heresies – it probably 'threw too strong a light on the pre-canonical controversy to make its continued use desirable. This may also be the reason for the disappearance of the work of Agrippa Castor.'[48]

Sorting his way through the muddle of names and accusations, through the use of 'every art of hostile criticism',[49] Mead tells us that it is impossible to obtain anything but a distorted picture of these Gnostics 'whose greatest sin was that they were centuries before their time'.[50] And then he touches on the interesting topic of the Samaritans. On referring to the precursor of Simon Magus, Dositheus, he tells us that he was probably an Arab, and that in Arabia 'there were many mystic communities allied to those of the Essenes and Therapeuts.' Then for good measure, he adds: 'One of the gospels used by Justin, under the general title *Memoirs of the Apostles*, states that the "wise men" came from Arabia.'[51] Once again the Arabian connection is made, and on this occasion Arabian 'wise men' are linked directly to the Qumran Essenes and the Egyptian Therapeuts. This is to say that in the Dosithean-Simon Magus tradition one major source of the pre-Christian *gnosis* (revelation) was from Arabia. Then, quoting the Tübingen school of German studies, Mead makes a very interesting suggestion – Simon Magus is quite possibly *the legendary symbol for Paul*. Noting that there is a remarkable similarity of doctrinal points being contested in the conflict between Simon Magus and Peter, just as there is between Peter and Paul, Mead accepts the Tübingen school thesis and leaves us with an interesting and highly plausible theory: someone is trying to distract our attention from a debate between Peter and Paul, or to be more exact, between the Nazarene-Ebionite and Pauline-Gnostic camps.

So it perhaps is not so much that Samaritan Gnosticism influenced Paul, but that Paul was himself a full-blown Gnostic of Samaritan ilk. The Petro-Pauline controversy, as analysed and put forward in Part One, concerned the difference between Nazarene orthodoxy led by James and Peter, and that of Paul's fast-developing theology of revelation. A compromise between those radically different systems would eventually be made by the gospel writer-editors, and the symbol of everything Gnostic and forbidden (Simon Magus) would be put into the Act's story to camouflage the fact that Paul was the Church's first great Gnostic heretic. This theory would explain why the story of Simon Magus and Peter's confrontation does not ring true – it is a probable fabrication planted in the rather convenient book of Acts to join together two inimical traditions.

In Mead's opinion, and in the opinion of many other scholars, Paul's letters date back to the middle of the first century. This fact makes it difficult to believe that he had any knowledge of the later historical gospels and their carefully constructed contents. For in his letters the historical Jesus evaporates and is replaced with

the Mystic Christ. As Mead points out, there are plenty of
tunities for him to refer to the canonical sayings and do
Jesus, but he instead relies on 'conceptions and technica
which receive no explanation, but are fundamental with the
handers-on of the Gnosis.'[52] Paul's mission cannot be read as
having had the same intent or purpose as the early Nazarene
mission led by James and Peter. He was exclusively concerned
with the gentilization of Nazarene Christianity and the breakdown of Jewish exclusiveness. Everything about his ministry
spells this out. He was a charismatic. His converts received the
Holy Ghost and acquired spiritual gifts. Christianity was a mode
of life, not a dogma. Fixed doctrinal ideas did not exist: everything was free flowing – the *Spirit* had the ultimate say. The first
'heresy' was Paul's doing away with circumcision; the rest
followed quickly. The Jerusalem Church – the Church of the
Nazarene sectaries – became a narrow-minded sect at loggerheads
with Paul's heterodox beliefs and practices. All of these points are
cited by Mead, and they reveal a Gnostic mentality, a Gnostic
vision, a Gnostic approach to just about everything.

So what exactly was it that the Gnostics had found out about
the human psyche that so infuriated the early Church Fathers and
so fascinated the psychologist Carl Jung? Well, for a start,
Gnosticism claimed that wisdom could not be attained by faith
alone, but by 'definite endeavour and conscious striving along the
path of cosmological and psychological science'.[53] One had to
gain a knowledge of one's own nature and work towards *a
purified will*. Jesus' brother James was of the same opinion,
and with precision spells out the difference between 'faith' and
'works' in his epistle. Gnostic pupils were saved from ignorance
by the power of their own *nous*, the Gnostic faculty of perception.
There was a dominion of the lower angels (the planet Earth), and
one had to learn how to free oneself from that domain. The claim
of the Gnostics was that a human being could become *a conscious
worker* in conjunction with the higher powers, or energies. On
reaching a certain state of interior perfection, or enlightenment,
the trainee Gnostic was said to 'rise from the dead' – that is, 'he
obtained possession of the unbroken consciousness of his spiritual
ego.'[54] Language was placed in the category of 'bindings' – what
Tobias Churton calls 'the great irreality which produces intoxica-
tion in us, drunkenness or sleep'. The Gnostic had to 'break
through this dullness of sense, to look through this whole fraud of

the world, this Deception which struts around in so many forms and under so many names.'[55]

Because the light and dark sides of human nature are sandwiched together, any attempt to quicken the spiritual nature inevitably quickened its darker, shadowy counterpart, and this led to a release of energies both helpful and unhelpful. Many Gnostic dabblers lost control of their sexual appetites for this very reason. The serpent of the Genesis story was a glyph for the Divine Will, and the uplifting of the serpent-rod of Moses in the wilderness symbolized the force which fashioned the universe and man – a force which he in turn could use. This energy could carry a human being to the heights of spiritual attainment – but only if the waters (energies) of the Jordan (the human biosystem) were made to flow upwards. Linked to the historico-legendary background of myths and religious and mystic romances, the learned Gnostic could read what appeared to be history and myth as tales of spiritual aspiration and attainment. This is to say that Gnostics attempted to read *soul-processes* into such events, whereas the orthodox were content with an intellectually created theology and a grocery-list of fixed interpretations.

THE GNOSTIC GOD

But by far the most interesting contribution made by the Gnostics was their conception of God. The Catholic orthodoxy would go on to accept and adopt the Jewish Old Testament as a divinely-inspired background for their own self-appointed Christian New Testament (a clever move driven by the need for legitimacy and the appearance of continuity), and with this move they would inherit not only the popular beliefs of Judaism, but also Yahweh the tribal God of the ancient Israelites as the ontological base of their new belief-system – a system which quickly deteriorated over the first two centuries to exclude the very principles of spiritual freedom advocated by Jesus as rebel teacher. For the Gnostics, however, Yahweh was not the transcendent God, the *real* God: he was no more than a system of energies which had created the universe. This made of Yahweh a mere demiurge, a creator of the world of sense and the senses, who, when worshipped, obscured in the mind all idea of, and cut off all connection with, a higher realm. This world was utterly alien to the *real* God, who for the Gnostics was not a divine being, personality exhibiting human characteristics, but rather th of depth and silence which could only be approached in depth and silence.

But what did this mean? Did the Gnostics literally believe in a creator-God 'out there somewhere' who was responsible for obscuring the higher realms? Was the Gnostic alignment of the Semitic creator-God Yahweh with this energy-driven demiurge of their imaginings a useful contribution to religious thought? The Jews and the Christians did not think so; they were mightily shocked by such an idea. For it not only demoted their mutually worshipped God, it also accused that God of arrogantly and falsely proclaiming itself to be the only God in existence when there was in fact another greater than itself. This, for the Gnostics, was the heart of the matter, and it is in this self-description of the Judeo-Christian deity that we can perhaps detect the basic, underlying principle of the Gnostic vision – the God who applauded and advocated ritual subservience and belief in rigid exterior forms rather than fluid interior forms was no more than the human ego indecently inflated and psychically projected. The God of 'depth' and 'silence' could not be equated with this travesty of everything spiritual, this God who could so easily instruct its devotees to murder in cold blood and believe in a dry, energyless religious path. As a system of perceptual and conceptual energies amalgamated into a limited and limiting psychic complex, Yahweh was no more than the culturally-encircled human ego unrestrained, manic, and let loose in history.

True as this may be on the psychological level, it of course represents only part of the story, for Yahweh is quite obviously more than a mere psychological complex – he is also the evolution of a potent idea of perfection intuited to exist by the early Hebrews, and developed in isolation over the centuries. Eventually carrying the persona of a protective sovereign, legislator and judge of human actions, this potent idea became progressively personified, and with this transition from the abstract to the personal there developed the notion of communication through such conveniences as Shekinah (the presence of God), *bath qol* (the voice of God), Ma'amar or Memra (the words of God), and *ruah* (the breath of God).[56] Other qualities were also added, such as the 'anger' of God, and the 'jealousy' of God. But the borrowed Hebrew God taken over by Christianity had also had added to it a neo-Platonic dimension, a philosophical overview which emphasized ultimate and absolute perfection as a pure abstraction which could not be attained by thought or scientific learning, but only through the emotions in the form of *revelation*.

Craveri sums up this situation with reference to the Gnostics:

> Gnosticism . . . represented an attempt to make the abstract concept of the neo-Platonists accessible without recourse to anthropomorphism. According to the Gnostic philosophers, God issued out of his silence and his depth by means of emanations called 'aeons', ~~lons~~ through which he established contact with the finite world.[57]

Craveri then states that later philosophical speculations attempted to bring order into the disarray, and that official theologians of the Church finally chose to accept the abstract idea of God as the Highest Good, or *absolute perfection*. But with this acceptance of a more abstract vision of God arose the problem of God's becoming nothing more than 'the contrast between the idea of God as perfection and man's recognition of his own perfection'.[58] Centuries later <u>Martin Luther</u> would sail dangerously near to this idea of God as a projection of man's own potential higher nature by stating that

> the divine being is nothing but man's own essence, freed of the restraints of the individual – that is, of the limitations of corporeality and of his own imperfect reality – and made objective: that is, contemplated and adored as another being distinct from himself.[59]

The problem for the Gnostics was that this absolutely perfect God of Christianity and orthodox Judaism was to them a limited vision, a truncated intellectual creation which when worshipped obscured and cut off all connection with the higher realms. This meant that ordinary human beings, caught as they were in space and time, were liable to imagine things into the mind of this perfect God, yet believe them to have come voluntarily from that primary source. Claiming divine inspiration through the Holy Spirit, Christian literalists interpreted their own deepest needs and desires as the nudgings of the Spirit, and began to build an edifice of theology aligned to personal opinion and political necessity.

To the Gnostics, this kind of behaviour was an illegitimate copying of an earlier state eventually accepted by Paul – the psychic state within which the gift of *gnosis* was obtained through approaching God as silence and depth. Ever surprising and novel and unique, this knowledge of God and self rested in the

IN-
YANG

realization that light and darkness could not be separated. To the
Gnostics, light without darkness was a lopsided vision created by
a lopsided bit of the psyche, namely the ego. The God of 'depth'
and 'silence' was experientially a God of light *and* darkness. To
make of that God only a figure of light was to invest energy in a
concept which must by its very nature backfire. Serious psychical
and psychological consequences could not be avoided if God was
reduced to the level of a perfect being devoid of creative darkness
– darkness was the necessary contrast whereby light became
visible. As metaphors for good and evil, light and darkness
functioned on a co-equal basis, and as such pointed to the
mystery of good and evil inhabiting a *timeless* space where human
definitions of good and evil, governed as they were by time, had
no relevance. And so a moment-by-moment Gnostic concern was
the *unmaking* of time, and this unusual idea was allied to the
Gnostic conception of God as a numinous duality of evil and
good united in what Stephen Hoeller has called 'a terrifying
and majestic divine hybrid, a veritable God-Devil whom Jung
calls *Abraxas*'.[60]

TWELVE

A TERRIBLE SECRET

The early Christian Gnostics' claim to have direct access to reality, the Church's misinterpretation of their claim to be 'knowers', and the idea of Jesus as the Jewish Messiah ironically resuscitated to combat the Gnostic idea of the 'archetypal' Christ.

Mature Gnostics believed themselves to be in possession of a secret so terrible, so devastating, so powerful, that it allowed the one who possessed it to cut through the religious and political conformity of their time. Believing themselves to be consciously 'awake' in an unusual, peculiar and unprecedented fashion, they devoted themselves to the task of opening up their inner lives in a manner unacceptable and eventually threatening to the early orthodox Church Fathers. Ever devising new and novel approaches to their God and his mysteries, they gave the impression of being at the mercy of unintelligible forces dangerous to social order and civil authority.

Taken aback by what appeared to be a veritable avalanche of ideas and symbols incomprehensible in their contradictory complexity, the early Christian Fathers of orthodox persuasion recoiled in horror. How could these people expect their pre-posterous notions to be taken seriously? What would happen to the Church of Jesus Christ if these Gnostic Christians managed to convince the rank and file that everyone and anyone could wander into the presence of God without going through the proper episcopal channels? Anarchy would result. Everything worked for, indeed *died* for, would come tumbling down if such unruly behaviour were allowed to spread unchecked.

This is, I think, a fair representation of how the early Church hierarchy eventually viewed the presence of Gnostic Christians in their midst. But what, I think, has been overlooked by most scholars is the fact that this devastating secret of the Gnostic Christians ran much deeper than mere 'world-denying' and 'anti-life' sentiments of a dualistic nature transmuted into a spiritual policy for daily life. It is certainly true that the Gnostic, on receiving the 'Light' through initiation, was 'effectively out of history',[1] as Tobias Churton so charmingly puts it, but this being 'out of history' had more to it than a surface change in social values and priorities. The orthodox Church may have failed in Gnostic eyes for the very reason that it was fast becoming a successful social phenomenon, that it had already negated its basic spiritual message by growing into an authoritarian institution, but the main Gnostic gripe was that the spirit of orthodoxy that infused Church leaders had effectively dismantled the possibility of their ever seeing or appreciating reality through eyes *opened to the nature of reality*. It wasn't just that the Gnostics saw things differently, that they had a different social focus, it was that they *literally* saw things differently. They had not just changed their attitude, they had changed their whole method of perceiving reality. Tobias Churton puts it this way: 'the Gnostics felt removed from ordinary perception.'[2] Believing themselves capable of detecting the obscuring and deadening effect that being locked in normal relations to visual and conceptual reality caused, the Gnostic Christians strove to liberate themselves from those dictatorial demands by a trick of perception, a trick with the most devastating results. Language and dogma and prejudice all had the capacity to obscure and deaden, but it was visual reality in particular, the realm of solid matter infused with shape and colour and pattern, which constituted the greatest enemy. To be resurrected from the dead was to wake up out of this seductive *dream of matter* into a new life, a life which allowed an often disturbing intimation of a deeper and more expansive self to erupt. Later, more complicated versions of Gnosticism would lose sight of this underlying secret, and what had once been a devastating tool or technique would be changed into a mere attitude carrying the dialectic that matter and material existence were intrinsically evil.

The suggestion that Gnostics possessed a powerful perceptual tool or technique which they used on the world may sound a bit fanciful to some, but as I later hope to show, some such capacity probably covers the issue of Gnostic revelation without having to bend or force that revelation into this or that esoteric camp. And I find myself in agreement with Pétrement that those who have so diligently translated these Gnostic texts for us, although specialists in their own right, are no more qualified than others to interpret their religious and philosophical meaning. This applies particularly to Christian scholars who, bound as they are to the Christian paradigm as it now is, seem almost incapable of appreciating the psychological and philosophical possibilities embedded in the early Gnostic texts. Once again it is Simone Pétrement who exhibits scholarly courage. Taking on those who have made a nonsense of Gnosticism for reasons which are themselves a nonsense, she says:

> What a picture of Gnosticism can be painted if we read certain books and articles! The authors are often very learned, often even very intelligent, but because they are a priori scornful of their subject, they really understand almost nothing. They present it in such a way that one can only make fun of it.[3]

And the reason for this outcome? Badly put questions and the fear of properly relating Gnosticim to Christianity. A blind spot one might say. And a seeming inability to properly understand Christianity itself. Extravagant the Gnostics may have been in the eyes of the early Fathers, but it cannot be denied that they possessed a capacity for creative insight, for a poetry of the heart which went far beyond the fabrications of their orthodox counterparts.

The Gnostics had, so it seems, gained access to a stream of energy deep within the psyche which, when it surfaced, blew preconceptions and authoritarian constructions to pieces. In his mysterious *Seven Sermons to the Dead*, the psychologist Carl Jung spells out the basis of Gnostic discovery, and we learn that what the Gnostics identified as the creative demiurge – the dualistically-minded God who created differentiation by creating the universe – is none other than what Stephan Hoeller calls 'the alienated human ego'. In his quite excellent book *The Gnostic Jung*, Hoeller draws the necessary parallel:

> The ego thus appears very much like an intermediary between the realm of extroverted action and the greater, unconscious matrix, within which Jung saw all external phenomena to be rooted. Like the Gnostic demiurge, the ego in its alienated, blind arrogance boldly but falsely proclaims that 'there is no other God before' it – that it alone is the true determinant of existence – and that the powers and potentialities of the unconscious are unreal or non-existent.[4]

The suggestion here is that through the medium of perception, through the five senses, the ego creates the universe and sustains that creation through continual acts of differentiation. Imagine the consternation of those around them when certain Gnostics revealed how to break the ego's grasp on creation, when they initiated others into the knowledge of how to stop the flow of differentiation and allow reality to be perceived without interference from the ego.

That this was the net result of their spiritual efforts is certain, and that it was based on some curious notion of the material world's being somehow responsible for the whole mess is evident throughout Gnostic literature. That it was not the world itself that they considered evil, or bad, but the effect of the existence of the world that was identified as the problem, is aptly shown by their attitude towards sex. Classified as sexual deviants by orthodox Christian writers, the mature Gnostics' vision of sex as 'sacramental' was confused with that of extremists and dabblers (you would think the Church had never had any of her own), and resulted in a condemnation applied en masse to the Gnostic movement. Finding the accusation of sexual deviance useful, this partial truth was regularly used by the early Fathers to disgrace advanced Gnostic practice in the eyes of the faithful, and, as they say, the rest is history. Basically, however, all these Gnostics were saying was that sexual intercourse was good for people – a simple affirmation of life and living which rapidly secured for them the wrath of a Church already travelling down the fearful path of enforced sexual abstinence.

But what of this disruptive energy? What exactly was it? And in that the Church Fathers got so apoplectic about it, can't it be assumed to have been a kind of madness, a shared delusional state not dissimilar to that of the Greek *Corybantes* so decisively castigated by Plato? I think not. There may well have been cases of severe psychic disturbance to confuse the issue, cases with certain similarities in behaviour or claim to make the Church Fathers appear confident in their condemnation, but I suspect even they were ultimately discriminating enough to know the difference between mental disturbance and the state of mind exhibited by their advanced Gnostic antagonists. I think this is the fact of the matter because these very antagonists would have exhibited a grounded ego in spite of unusual revelatory experience.

Writing of his own depth experiences, the psychiatrist Carl Jung tells us that like any psychotic's his conscious mind was often filled with mythopoeic imaginings which, although confusing to his patients when they experienced them, were to him manageable experiences due to the stability of his home life and the demands of his profession. He also tells us that although such experiences are considered risky and questionable by many, they are the path leading into the unconscious which should not be avoided. Considered the path of error, equivocation and misunderstanding, such a path may well give rise to unusual phenomena, but Goethe's injunction to 'dare to open wide the gate Past which men's steps have ever flinching trod' should be understood as the challenge we must *all* face before death strikes.[5]

There were also those who parodied the Gnostic way of life and caused real problems for the young Church – charlatans who pretended to be pure in heart and have knowledge so as to reap financial gain. But such people, although disturbing to the faithful, must again have been clearly distinctive in comparison with those Gnostics of high calibre to whom the demands of the living psyche were a daily experience. To make of them one indiscriminate mass is to reveal fear of a powerful rival, a contender strong enough in attraction and coherence to justify rejection at any cost. For Gnosticism was not some strange sect set up alongside Christianity, some advancing terror from outside. It was a direct expression of Christianity itself, the other half of the Christian psyche carefully integrated into the Church by Paul, but later rejected by the theologizing Fathers who saw Gnostic depth-experiences as a direct threat to episcopal and apostolic authority. Later, even a Church Father like Origen would be anathematized because of his moderate liberalism, a Gnostically-oriented liberalism passed on to him by Clement of Alexandria.

CLEMENT'S ALEXANDRIAN TEACHERS

Clement of Alexandria lived smack in the middle of Gnostic activity and knew some of the great Gnostic teachers. It has even been suggested that he himself was a Gnostic initiate in the light of the tenor of some of his more adventurous theological notions. G R S Mead records that Clements' works are:

for the most part free from those wholesale accusations of immorality with which the general run of Church Fathers in after years loved to besmatter the character of the Gnostics of the first two centuries.

He goes on to say that critics are now agreed that such accusations are 'unfounded calumnies as far as the great schools and their teachers were concerned'.[6] In a lost work entitled *The Outlines*, Clement is thought to have dealt with the higher problems of Gnosticism, and apparently attempted to put together a complete system of Christian teaching in three books much resembling the three stages of the Platonists: Purification, Initiation and Direct Vision. Later, in his *Miscellanies*, he would claim to be a 'true Gnostic', and as Henry Bettenson relates in his translation of the early Christian Fathers, founded this claim on the fact of 'an unwritten tradition, entrusted by the Lord to his Apostles and handed down from father to son',[7] an interesting choice of words in anyone's terms. The next paragraph opens with these telling words: 'Typical of Clement's Gnosticism is his contrast between faith and knowledge.' And so we not only have an early Father of the Church who claims to be a 'true Gnostic', and discriminates between 'faith' and 'knowledge', but a man who believes himself to be in direct contact with teachers in possession of knowledge originating with Jesus himself.

Clement apparently believed that faith, far from being the end of the affair, was that upon which knowledge had to be built: it may have to come first, but it had to be followed up with something a little more substantial. This knowledge was the contemplation of God and the discovery of the *divine likeness* in humanity. Each and every human being had the image of God within them, and this image was 'reason', the source of which was the Logos. Bettenson points out that Clement meant by this that the Logos had to be understood as working not only in Christianity, but also in 'Hellenic thought and in Jewish religious intuition'.[8] One could easily add Buddhism to this. The Logos bestowed the gift of possible truth on *all* cultures, on *all* religious traditions, and the real Gnostic should attempt to comprehend the shape and pattern of that universal truth wherever it might appear. That Clement's Alexandrian teachers were advanced Gnostics is evident, but it is his claim that their teachings were derived *from the Lord* that is of interest, for it suggests a two-pronged teaching tradition from the earliest days.

A letter of Clement's discovered by Professor Morton Smith in

1973, talks of a secret, apocryphal gospel of Mark and reveals what the *Encyclopedia of the Early Church* calls Clement's 'wider view of canonicity'. Clement's writings contain a vast and detailed knowledge of early Christian literature, and an equally impressive knowledge of Judeo-Hellenistic literature, of which his principal source was Philo of Alexandria. Aware of a teaching tradition alternative to orthodoxy's theological and historical stance, of traditions stemming from Jesus himself, Clement's sophisticated approach to Christian truth eventually got him into trouble – he knew things he was not supposed to know, thought things he was not supposed to think. Considered a saint up until the eighth century, he was dropped as such by Benedict XIV and left out of the Roman martyrology due to his having been Origen's teacher – the pupil's heterodox beliefs were seen to reflect the teacher's opinions.

Alongside the four gospels of the New Testament, numerous other Gnostic gospels were held in high esteem by many orthodox Christians, but it is probable that the secret gospel of Mark was quite literally secret, for Clement is of the opinion that *all* knowledge of its existence should be denied in spite of its authenticity. Why? Because the Gnostic sect of the Carpocratians had used this text to suggest that Jesus was personally involved not only in baptism (the canonical gospels do not refer to Jesus as a baptiser) but in curious all-night rituals involving nakedness. The Church's automatic response to such an image is 'Rubbish!' – but Jesus' probable interest in 'ritual' is attested to in the creation of the lost Nazarene gospel by Robert Graves and Joshua Podro, and the studies of Dr Schonfield certainly suggest that the crucifixion, burial and Resurrection were interpreted by Jesus to be rituals of profound significance. Clement rejected the secret gospel of Mark not because it contained such information, but because the Carpocratians used it for sexual purposes. Ever intelligent and creative, he went on to cite Greek philosophy (particularly the ideas of Plato) as a legitimate way to approach and understand Jesus as the 'Christ', and was himself eventually accused of Christological heresy.

The young Church, struggling to exist, and faced with problems of continuity and coherence, was turning into an authoritarian structure. But alongside it was a living tradition which refused to die, a tradition passed on by word of mouth *not* as a syncretism but as a 'secret', and quite beyond the reifying tendencies of doctrines too strictly sculpted for the collective. So to which carrier tradition was Clement referring? Tellingly, Bettenson completes his short introductory piece on Clement of Alexandria by associating his basically Gnostic vision with that of the teachings of 'Paul' and 'John' – a move quite in sympathy with our findings so far – and Stephan Hoeller completes the picture when he says:

> With the loss of Gnosis in the third and fourth centuries the Alexandrian spirituality of the Gnostics – and of the almost-Gnostics of the order of Clement and Origen – gave way to the literal-minded fundamentalism of the Nicene fathers, who came to substitute the physical Jesus for the spiritual Christ.[9]

What an interesting turnaround. Threatened by the Mystical Christ of Gnostic revelation, the Church spun back to the physical Jesus and made this dangerous Jewish messianic figure weighed down with history and a real physical existence the central focus of a personality cult, a cult which would turn Jewish, Syrian, Samaritan and Arabian aspects of the faith into a gigantic literalism; a Jesus wrenched out of the legitimate frame of Archetypal Man and made into an incomprehensible parody of the Supreme Deity. Henry Bettenson may call Clement's Gnostically-oriented contribution to Christian theology 'woolly-minded and unimportant',[10] but in spite of what is certainly a confusion of orthodox and heterodox notions peppering his thinking (Elaine Pagels detects three levels of the Gnostic pattern woven into his orthodox teachings),[11] I am quite certain he would have been forced to reject eventual Nicene speculations. For what up until that time had been basically free-floating ideas about God and Jesus and the nature of spiritual revelation turned rapidly into a straitjacket theology which encroached more and more into the very fabric of people's lives. The joy of having found a bright, lively and self-illuminating faith allied to real archetypal symbols resonating in the depths of consciousness was swapped for a handful of fairy stories – the Jewish Messiah was back in business, but for all the wrong reasons.

THE GNOSTIC CHALLENGE

Realizing that the Gnostics had been confronted with the primal world of the unconscious, and had somehow learned to deal with it, Jung studied what existed of their writings between 1918 and 1926. But so much time had elapsed, and so much recorded Gnostic experience had either been destroyed or simply distorted by the early Church Fathers that little could be rescued from the exercise. The link with the past had vanished; there was no way of determining how these Gnostics had viewed their own experiences.

It was recorded with disapproval by the early Church Fathers that the Gnostics had seemed to write a new gospel each day, but relentless suppression by these heresy hunters had successfully eradicated the possibility of ever knowing what such gospels had contained. Then suddenly in December 1945, in some caves in the Jabal al-Tarif mountain range in Upper Egypt, a whole collection of Gnostic codices were discovered by a peasant digging for fertilizer. Stephan Hoeller is of the opinion that this extraordinary collection of manuscripts would have been consigned to scholarly oblivion had it not been for Jung's intervention.[12] Alerted to the fact that five of the 52 discovered texts had been smuggled out of Egypt, and that they were for sale in America, the Jung Foundation in Zurich managed to purchase them, and in conjunction with the religious historian Gilles Quispel Jung got down to the task of discovering what they contained. What they contained was truly astonishing.

Elaine Pagels states that some of these 52 texts probably represent early forms of Christian teaching, and that we may have to 'recognise that early Christianity is far more diverse than nearly anyone expected before the Nag Hammadi discoveries'.[13] Although claiming to offer secret teachings, many of these texts include New Testament characters – Jesus and his disciples – and frequently refer to the Old Testament and the letters of Paul. According to these Gnostic writers, self-knowledge *is* knowledge of God: there is no difference between the self and the divine.[14] Illusion and enlightenment are the measures we must attend to, not sin and repentance. Christians during the first two centuries apparently carried a mixture of beliefs, some radically different from those held today, and group structures were not uniform. Much of the writing in the texts is in Christian terminology, reveals a Jewish background, and more importantly suggests *gnosis* to have been 'insight' into the nature of the self, not just 'knowledge' *about* the self. Ranging from instruction for mystical practice to secret gospels, myths, magic, poems and philosophical explorations, the texts afford a dizzying array of adventurous ideas and views contentious to modern-day Christians.

But what is even more fascinating is the fact that some of the Nag Hammadi texts denounce orthodox Christians as ignorant pagans and dumb animals who thought they were on Christ's side but who were unknowingly empty of the truth.[15] There is even the claim that the orthodox Church is an *imitation* of the true Church, a Church which 'reconciles its adherents to fear and slavery, encouraging them to subject themselves to the earthly representative of the world creator, who, in his "empty glory", declares, "I am God, and there is no other beside me." ' This particular text – *The Second Treatise of the Great Seth* – concludes with these startling words:

> Such persons persecute those who have achieved liberation through *gnosis*, attempting to lead them astray from 'the truth of their freedom'.[16]

Elaine Pagels suggests that these attacks indicate a late stage in the confrontation between the two sides, and has it that the battle lines had been drawn up by the year 200. Reminiscent of Paul's anger at discovering 'spies' and 'false brethren' influencing the beliefs of his flock, and of his having to confront Peter with being two-faced when it came to interacting with the Gentiles, these barbed statements of the Gnostic Christians against their bishop-controlled counterparts reveals an on-going controversy of such seriousness that it could only end in bloodshed.

The general definition of a Gnostic is that of a 'knower' rather than a *follower* of someone who knows. Gilles Quispel said that Gnosticism was neither a philosophy nor a heresy but a specific religious experience which manifested itself in myth and ritual.[17] Stephan Hoeller's definition of Gnosticism is that it is a mythological expression of an inner experience.[18] Elaine Pagels records the Gnostic conviction that whoever explores human experience simultaneously discovers divine reality.[19] Tobias Churton's approach is to see Gnostic myths as a kind of map of the mind's experience as it searches for the root of itself and its meaning.[20] In his introduction to G R S Mead's study of Gnosticism, Kenneth Rexroth tells us that what the Gnostics projected onto the screen of their profound ignorance as a picture of the universe was in reality a picture of their own minds.[21] G R S Mead's own general evaluation of Gnosticism's worth was that the Gnostic mind arrived at many conclusions which the Catholic Church gradually adopted only after generations of hesitation, and that it reached spiritual conclusions which even to our present generation seem premature.[22] And Carl Jung's notion was that the Gnostics had given birth, as it were, to original, and therefore primal, creations from the mystery of the unconscious.[23] The Church's view, on the other hand, is clear, precise, and damning: Gnosticism was/is a heresy which debases Christian doctrine, is influenced by the dark, devilish side of human nature, and carries within its tangled folds a mishmash of mythology and erratic thinking which, if taken seriously, will lead the seeker away from, rather than towards, God.

Gnostic Christians claimed that they were the 'true' Church, but it was orthodox Christianity that won the day due to its organizational capacity and its theological precision. The Gnostics simply weren't interested in running a Church of that type, or size, and theological precision was the last thing they were after. Credal beliefs, baptism and even martyrdom, in Gnostic eyes, were not conclusive proof that someone was a Christian – the Christian life was a qualitative process from deep within, not an external acceptance of ideas in the form of beliefs, no matter the emotional charge one might get from them. Elaine Pagels informs us that the 'bishops eliminated qualitative criteria for Church membership'[24] so as to unify the scattered Churches into a single entity: trying to work out the spiritual maturity of each entrant was simply an administrative impossibility. But only for a fast-growing institution, of course. The Gnostics, by comparison, could afford to indulge potential members with a detailed scrutiny of their spiritual seriousness. Anyway, special vetting procedures led to an élitist attitude among those chosen – better to risk admitting the many than to create too rarefied an atmosphere. In one of the circulating Gnostic gospels attributed to Peter, the apostle declared that enlightened Christians were able to discriminate for themselves between truth and falsity, a message roundly denied by orthodoxy. And the further one goes into this the more one is faced with a group of people apparently independent and free and deeply involved in the spirit of community through a shared knowledge of God and his Mystic Christ – not at all unlike the very early Church as described in the New Testament, and daringly modern in that they allowed women to officiate at their bishopless services.

THE GNOSTIC WOMEN

That the Church eventually got rid of its Gnostic population and destroyed its literature is attested to historically, and that it put great effort into removing every trace of this strangely independent and spirited body of Christian esotericists is well known. But why? What exactly was it about Gnostic teaching that so irritated and dismayed the Catholic Church? Was it their belief that there was a God greater than Yahweh? That it was possible to descend deep within the self and intercept, or be intercepted by, archetypal beings and intelligences emanating from the primal source of all being? Was it their sacramental vision of sex? Or their notion that good and evil were synonymous terms? Certainly it was all of these things. But it was perhaps their inclusion of a feminine principle in their acts of worship, and their allowing women to be priestly functionaries at their services which pushed the Church Fathers to a complete and utter rejection of everything they stood for.

I am indebted to Dr Pagels for recording Tertullian's outrage against the inclusion of women in Gnostic celebrations of the Eucharist. The quote is fascinating, and reminds one of the debate going on in our own time. 'These heretical women,' explodes Tertullian, 'how audacious they are! They have no modesty; they are bold enough to teach, to engage in argument, to enact exorcisms, to undertake cures, and, it may be, even to baptize!'[25] And the Gnostic teacher Marcus is given a hard time by Irenaeus for talking of the feminine element in the Divine Being, and of equating that element with the initiated Gnostic women who took part equally with men during services. Women even acted as priests in Marcus' Gnostic community. Dr Pagels informs us that women were considered equal to men among the Valentinians, and that the heretic Marcion scandalized his clerical peers by 'appointing women on an equal basis with men as priests and bishops'.[26] And it should be remembered that Paul's traditionally Jewish reaction to women is tempered by his recognition of women as deacons and fellow workers. In the early first-century Church, and in accordance with Jesus' own rebellious policy of treating women with respect and having them among his chosen followers, leadership was conferred on women, and they were accepted into the roles of prophets, teachers and evangelists.[27] This is to say that in the early first-century Church there was, as

Paul informs us, neither male nor female, and that the idea of the
Archetypal Man of Jewish messianic tradition (the archetypal
image of *all* humanity) was without gender.

In view of how the early Church functioned in relation to
women, and in the light of Paul's highly developed mystical
Christology in relation to the Samaritan Gnostics with whom he
was in overt sympathy, it is more than probable that those texts
which have him demote women are later insertions. By the end of
the second century a double image of Paul existed in the New
Testament – a contradictory image born from insertions by
orthodox editors. A final nail in this argument is Dr Pagel's
reference to Paul's greeting a woman as 'an outstanding apostle,
senior to himself in the movement'.[28] The actual verse in Romans
reads as follows: 'Salute Andronicus and Junia, my kinsmen, and
my fellow prisoners, who are of note among the apostles, who
also were in Christ before me.'[29] Now if that doesn't contradict
Paul's supposed debarring of women from the ministry, or from
any other executive post for that matter, I don't know what does.

Carl Jung's friend and confidant Gilles Quispel has said that
gnosis gave women the right to, and experience of, the self. In
view of the plight of women in Judaism during the first century,
that is quite a statement. In Gnostic communities, a high
percentage of women were given multiple rights eventually denied
to them by the official Christian Church – which rather suggests
by way of reversed argument that the unofficial Gnostic Church
was in fact very similar to, if not identical with, the original
Church. Too big a jump? Perhaps not. Everything seems to indicate that the growth of orthodoxy was the result of a few Church
leaders' consolidating their power base within the early
Church and eventually usurping the rule of community and
replacing it with the rule of clerical and episcopal hierarchy. This
would explain why Gnosticism was tolerated for so long within
the confines of the Churches themselves, why some high-ranking
clergy inexplicably belonged to Gnostic ranks, and why, later,
they attracted such a ferocious reaction from officialdom – a bad
conscience can sometimes incite the carrier to brutal behaviour.

As previously cited, Michael Goulder tantalizingly suggests that
there would seem to be 'a *prima facie* case from the New
Testament and Church tradition for claiming that the Samaritan
Christians were a powerful section of the first-century Church,
and that their movement grew into Christian Gnosticism in the

second'.[30] Again we have to work in reverse, for when we refocus the historical lens and travel back down the line of early Church development, we end up with the distinct possibility that the early Samaritan Church was *always* of a Gnostic frame (Essene based), and that this may well have been the original frame of reference, the frame for a split-off community of rebellious Essean-Essenes led by Jesus and organized into a community of believers (Churches) by Paul, his superb commander-in-chief of operations. Suddenly, unexpectedly, we are presented with a glimpse of an early Church which allows us to do what was previously unthinkable: to accommodate supposed 'apocryphal' texts concerning Jesus and his disciples into our thinking in a new way. In a review of Dominic Crossan's book *Jesus: A Revolutionary Biography*, Leander E Keck states that Crossan insists 'that the noncanonical evidence has as much right to be taken seriously as the New Testament Gospels'.[31]

One of the major clues in this accommodation is the important role played by women in Jesus' life and ministry. And when the Church's later conservative editorial overlay is removed from the thinking of Paul, we find what we would expect to find: Jesus' attitude to women firmly entrenched in this apostle's behaviour. Maintaining Jesus' practice of associating women actively with his mission, Paul's statement that in Christ there is neither male nor female *ignores*, as the historian Dr Michael Grant points out, 'his own anti-feminist assertions and echoes the views of Jesus himself'.[32] Ignores? An interesting euphemism. With Mary Magdalene to the fore in the gospel narratives, and a coterie of other women financially supporting Jesus and his disciples, a picture much at variance with normal Jewish practice looms into view. Dr Grant homes in on this point and tells us that Jesus' close association with women set him sharply apart from other Jewish teachers.[33] The basic Jewish attitude to women at this time was that they were inferior to men because they were a secondhand creation – men had been created *first*. And they were of course tainted with evil due to the direct attention paid to Eve by the snake (Satan) in Eden's paradise, and were twice-damned in that she had acted as a conduit for the transmission of evil to Adam through the wiles of temptation. In fact so great was Jewish religious prejudice against women that it was perfectly legitimate for men praying in the synagogue to thank God that they had been born male and not female.

Jesus' attitude to divorce is of interest at this point. Mark records that Jesus was utterly against divorce (Mark 10:2–12); Matthew suggests that he was willing to allow divorce under certain circumstances (Matt 5:31–32). At first glance, feminists may be tempted to think Matthew's recording of events the better of the two, but when these texts are more carefully considered it is Mark's and not Matthew's which comes out on top. Why? Because in those days life for a divorced woman was frightful; it was far better that she remain married. Because Mark's gospel is still arguably the older of the two, in spite of one scholar's attempt to undermine this belief, it can be said that Jesus' attitude to divorce was to women's benefit. And this is in accord with his general attitude to women, Dr Grant accurately captures this relationship between Jesus and the women who followed him when he says:

> As every gospel agrees, Jesus' female followers remained conspicuously faithful to him right up to and after his death, exceeding in loyalty and understanding not only the single apostle Judas who betrayed him but all the other apostles as well, including Peter who was declared to have denied him three times. Since this superiority of the women's behaviour was so embarrassing to the Church that its writers would have omitted it had it not been irremovable, there is every reason to regard it as authentic, setting the seal on the exceptionally close relations they had enjoyed with Jesus throughout his ministry.[34]

By the end of the second century the orthodox Church again allowed women to be dominated by men, and made of this a divine condition of Christian life not to be questioned. Some Gnostic texts holding Mary Magdalene up as important – indeed in some instances as a 'teacher' of the disciples – suggested that the orthodox community was challenged by the activity of women, and that Peter was looked upon as the conservative spokesperson for that orthodoxy.[35] The *Gospel of Mary* records that Mary Magdalene, because she was in possession of secret teachings from Jesus, instructed the disciples after the crucifixion and ran foul of a furious Peter who could not believe that Jesus would have secretly instructed a woman. This is an interesting passage: it gives one the impression of real events not recorded in the gospels, events which suggest that Peter's ignorance of what went on between Jesus and his female followers might have been due to his not being around very much. If truly as divided and uncertain in his religious and social opinions as he is accused, then it is quite possible that his relationship to Jesus was not at all as the gospels seem to state – the sense you get is that he was a bit of an outsider, and not a little cumbersome in his intellectual processes. And the very fact that he finally becomes the cornerstone of the later orthodox Church does rather suggest lost historical reasons for that choice. The pseudo-Pauline letters written presumably by orthodox Church leaders are probably a response to this kind of Gnostic gospel, for in them women are utterly excluded from any kind of role and made subordinate to men.

Apocryphal texts such as the *Gospel of Mary*, the *Dialogue of the Saviour*, *Pistis Sophia*, the *Gospel of Thomas* and the notorious *Gospel of Philip*, all paint a picture of Jesus quite at variance with the synoptic viewpoint. There are certainly areas of contact – in fact, quite a few – but the Jesus of the supposed apocryphal gospels is more a Jesus of the creative imagination, a Jesus whose teachings and very being are transposed into a series of archetypal allegories and vivid metaphors, a series of symbols resonating with deep psychological and religious significance. There are to be sure bits and pieces of actual history merged with politically contrived stories created to combat orthodoxy's stranglehold, but these are mostly obscured by dizzying journeys into the essence of being, and have to be carefully teased out of the fabric of Gnostic intentions.

Knowing only too well that Jesus had been an ordinary man with parents like everyone else, the Gnostics chose to concentrate on his role as Archetypal Man and Light Adam. Using his life, teachings, crucifixion and survival of death as a kind of ritual amalgamated with archetypal knowledge from the real, as opposed to the pseudo, mysteries, the properly trained and schooled Gnostics gained access to their own deepest psychological levels – levels which they dutifully recorded and correlated with the experiences of others. Whether or not they fully understood the extraordinary explosion of symbols which resulted is hard to say, but that they were on a meaningful and transformative track is confirmed by present-day evaluations of their texts. Christian apologists may claim that even the best of the Gnostics were no more than spiritual frauds and psychological maniacs utterly devoid of coherence and validity, but this is not an honest evaluation: the ideas and insights springing from the findings of these explorers of the human psyche is only now being realized to hold the key to the very sanity of our species. If we ignore these Gnostics, if we turn our backs on them and relegate them to oblivion, if we do to them now what was done to them then, we ignore our own capacity to be other than we now are.

THIRTEEN

MULTIPLE REVERSALS

The setting up of an Apostolic succession that never existed, the elevation of Paul's archetypal 'Christ' to the level of God incarnate, and the problem of the Jewish-Christian Church under James not actually being 'Christian' at all.

In Matthew's gospel (16:13–20) Jesus asks his disciples a question which reveals much about his reception by the people, and his disciples' comprehension of his mission. 'Whom do men say that I the Son of man am?' he asks. The disciples reply that some say he is John the Baptist come back to life, or that he is a reincarnation of Elijah, and others again that he is one of the prophets. Jesus pursues the question further and asks: 'But whom say ye that I am?' Simon Peter replies immediately that he is the Christ (the Messiah), and adds for good measure that he is also the Son of the living God. Jesus congratulates Simon for making this observation with the words 'Blessed art thou, Simon Bar-Jona: for flesh and blood hath not revealed it unto thee, but my Father which is in heaven', and proceeds, so it appears, to inaugurate Peter as the head of the Catholic Church yet to come. Promising Simon the keys of the Kingdom of Heaven, he then defines the use of these keys as Simon's right to make important spiritual decisions. With that out of the way he tells his disciples to keep their mouths shut about what they have just discussed, and over the ensuing days and weeks begins to reveal to them what his plans and expectations are for the future.

On hearing that he intends to go to Jerusalem, and that he fully expects to be arrested, tried and killed, Peter rebukes him for having such thoughts and is pounced on by Jesus for daring to contradict him. And this is no ordinary retaliation – it is a slap on the face to this disciple who is supposedly going to be the first official leader of the Church yet to come. 'Get thee behind me, Satan,' says Jesus stingingly, 'thou art an offence unto me: for thou savourest not the things that be of God, but those that be of men.' Harsh words, and a strange reversal considering the earlier promises.

THE PONTIFICAL MYTH

From being someone to whom God has personally revealed the role his own Son will play in Jewish history, Peter is suddenly demoted to that of someone who isn't in God's confidence at all. In fact, he is demoted to the level of someone purveying the intentions of God's opposite number, Satan, and is further castigated by being told that his evaluation of things belongs to the blind and uninformed realm of mere men. Quite a change-around if one takes these verses at face value. But if one strips them of hyperbole and hindsight insertions validating Simon Peter's supposed rise to pontifical heights, then one is left with a very interesting and devastatingly different scenario indeed. For it is obvious that these contradictory scenes harbour another message, a message rearranged and disguised to create an illusion – the illusion that Simon Peter was Jesus' favourite disciple. So favourite, in fact, that he would one day run the whole show on Jesus' behalf, and have the power not only to influence what took place on God's good earth, but even to influence happenings in God's good heaven. If such a claim weren't so diabolically serious, its sheer absurdity would induce unstoppable laughter. For it is only in Matthew's gospel that we find such claims – Mark records nothing more than that Peter calls Jesus 'the Messiah': all the rest disappears, except for the injunction to tell no man. Jesus is the Jewish Messiah plain and simple, and there is no mention of his being the Son of God. Peter answers the question properly without theological embroidery. Jesus launches immediately into the terrible things that will happen to him when they get to Jerusalem, and Peter's castigation by Jesus for not accepting this dread scenario is immediate and in the same context. There is no lapse of days or weeks between the two events – they are one event. Luke's gospel follows Mark's in simplicity, and makes no mention of the second incident; and John's gospel is silent on the whole issue.

J H Charlesworth's approach to what Jesus did and did not say in the gospels should be heeded at this point: his approach is intelligent and basic.

We shall probably come closest to arriving at what Jesus actually said and meant if we focus primarily on his words quoted in the New Testament, eliminating those that were created out of the needs and perspectives of his followers (or the 'Church'), and giving priority for authenticity to those that are found in more than one gospel tradition and cohere with other reliable Jesus sayings.[1]

Charlesworth's directive is that the question uppermost in our minds as we read the gospels should be: *What did Jesus intend to communicate?*

Jesus, in his own eyes, was the Messiah of Israel; that is now the consensus opinion of biblical scholars. In Matthew's gospel, Peter is aware of this fact some time before it is officially announced, or admitted. When questioned by Jesus as to his real identity, Peter names the name of the game and shifts the level of interaction with Jesus to a new and dangerous plateau. Jesus is no longer the simple teacher, he is God's chosen one. But not quite in the way expected. He is not a warrior, and has no intentions of becoming one. Messiah of Israel he may be, but he is a Messiah of a different stamp. I'm going to be put to the test in Jerusalem, he tells his disciples. They're going to arrest me, try me and put me to death – and you're all going to be in the thick of it. Peter is incredulous. Arrested? Die? What are you talking about? If you're the chosen Messiah of God then what you do is lead an army against the Romans, not go up to Jerusalem and put your head on the chopping-block! What you're saying is ridiculous. Jesus turns on Peter and stems his Zealot-like imaginings with one sentence: 'Get thee behind me, Satan.'[2] This was to say: Don't try to tempt me, Peter. That's not the direction in which I intend to go. Your reasoning is the reasoning of men; I refuse to lead my nation into a useless war which could only end with the destruction of the whole Jewish nation. If you want to follow me, if you really want to be my disciple, then you're going to have to stop thinking like that. Do you think I'm going to turn killer over night, make as nothing everything I've taught?

I am convinced that some such conversation took place between Jesus and Simon Peter. And I think the passages from Matthew, Mark and Luke reveal a Jesus who never really had it in mind to be a military leader. In Matthew's story of the Temptation in the Wilderness,[3] Jesus again uses the term 'Satan' to describe someone who is trying to sell him the idea of political power and military prowess. He is obviously talking to some Zealot-cum-Essene who wants him on side – but he won't have a bar of it. Every inducement is tried: land, titles, flattery. He does not respond. In the chapter prior to this he has just undergone his baptism at the hands of John. At the end of the wilderness story he is informed that John the Baptist is in prison. And immediately following this information on John's arrest comes the interesting fact that Jesus stumbles into Simon Peter and his brother Andrew. Without as much as a single question being asked, these two men drop their nets and go off with Jesus without a quibble. But John's gospel is much more explicit. The day after his baptism by John, Jesus returns to the same place, is recognized by John, and two of John's disciples overhear their teacher say, 'Behold the lamb of God',[4] an obvious tack-on considering what happens later. These two disciples go with Jesus to where he is staying, and spend the day with him. We learn immediately that one of these disciples is Andrew, Simon Peter's brother, and in a strange hiccup within the text, we are told that Andrew first goes and gets his brother Peter, and that he too wends his way to Jesus' house to spend the day with him. To get Peter to come along, Andrew tells him that he has found the 'Messiah'. There is at this point no mention of John's arrest and imprisonment, and on the following day Jesus begins to gather his disciples one by one.

There are two major points here. The first point is that Andrew and Peter are disciples of John the Baptist – at least, Andrew definitely is, and it is highly probable that Peter was of the same persuasion. The second point is that Andrew and Peter are well aware of Jesus' Messiahship right from the start. Andrew tells Peter outright: 'We have found the Messias, which is, being interpreted, the Christ.'[5] So it is fairly certain that Jesus remained in the same location for at least another few days, that he then heard of John's arrest, and that he then went to collect John's disciples and make them his own. They too must have heard the terrible news. There is no quibbling. Stepping into John's place as leader, Jesus asks his disciples one by one to follow him, and they agree. Why? Because up until that moment Jesus himself had been either a disciple of John the Baptist – as many scholars believe – or he had been John's adjutant, as Dr Barbara Thiering believes. J H Charlesworth comments on the situation thus: 'The following portrait of Jesus seems now to be widely accepted by many New Testament specialists. Jesus had some relationship with John the Baptizer, who certainly baptized him.'[6]

Whatever the case, Peter's acceptance of Jesus in that moment confirms him as having been a disciple of John the Baptist, and this fact earmarks him as a Jew of the wilderness tradition of the 'Way'. There was therefore nothing at all remarkable in Jesus' calling of the disciples: he was well known to them as a high-ranking member of the 'Way' who had to be obeyed. This plainly suggests that these stories have been tampered with, that the relationship of Jesus with John has been intentionally obscured, and that there was much more going on than anyone realizes. Jesus did not materialize out of nowhere – he was an important member of this wilderness movement and simply took over when John fell into the hands of Herod Antipas. And so another curious reversal takes place: from being a supposed stranger to John the Baptist, Jesus is revealed to have been this probable Essene's right-hand man.

The next problem to arise is John's attitude to Jesus. During his baptism of this supposed stranger, the Spirit of God is said to have descended on Jesus in the form of a dove.[7] And there is even supposed to have been a voice heard proclaiming Jesus to be the Son of God.[8] All in all, pretty convincing stuff. How could John eventually say anything other than 'Behold the Lamb of God' when Jesus turned up the following day? And yet from prison he sends messengers to Jesus asking him if he is Israel's Messiah.[9] Surely, as A N Wilson notes, 'If John had heard the voice of God declaring from a cloud that Jesus was the Messiah, he would hardly have found it necessary to dispatch messengers to confirm the fact.'[10] No, there's something drastically wrong with the manner in which this story is presented. Wilson suggests bewilderment on John's part, or perhaps even 'an overwhelming disappointment in his follower'.[11] In fact the message from John may not have been 'Are you the Messiah?' but rather 'Who do you think you are – the Messiah?' Wilson's interpretation of this event is that John's question was another version of the Wilderness Temptation – a kind of goad to make Jesus properly commit himself to the role of Messiah which, up until that moment, he had refused to do.[12]

But what of Simon Peter? As a disciple of John the Baptist Peter would have been of that school of thought which believed Israel had to repent of its sins before God would inaugurate the celestial Kingdom on Earth. And as a follower of the 'Way' of the wilderness he would have believed, in conjunction with the Essenes and the Nazarenes and the Ebionites and the Nazarites, that the existence of a holy remnant among the people might help swing the issue in Israel's favour. If not enough of the people repented of their sins, then perhaps the combined holiness of the 'Way' would be sufficient to tip the balance. On this score it is interesting that in Matthew's account of John's message to Jesus, Jesus should firstly hold John up as a very special human being, a veritable holy man; in the next breath demote him by saying that the least in the kingdom of heaven is greater than he; and then top it all off with what appears to be an utterly incomprehensible statement: 'And from the days of John the Baptist until now the kingdom of heaven suffereth violence, and the violent take it by force.'[13] Meaning what? Meaning that the desert sectaries were attempting to twist God's arm by a holiness so intense, so pure, so demanding, that He would not be able to ignore their efforts on Israel's behalf. Peter is castigated by Jesus for suggesting a return to the old desert 'Way' of seeing things, John's 'Way', the 'Way' of the Essenes and of his brother James, the 'Way' of the Zealots, the 'Way' of mere men trying to overpower God. And so the Nazarenes will come out against Jesus, and so too will the Essenes. And eventually Jesus' own disciples will be split in their loyalty to him as the oddity of his vision unfolds. Peter will remain undecided, however, and his indecision will cause both James and Paul problems in the future. Joining Jesus' brother James as co-leader of the Nazarenes in Jerusalem after the crucifixion, he will vacillate until confronted to his face by Paul. This confrontation, so great, so bitter, so important in its theological implications, will be later camouflaged by the writer-editors of Acts as a confrontation not between Paul and Simon Peter but, as suggested elsewhere, a confrontation between Paul and Simon Magus. A name is changed, and along with it the whole basic nature of Paul's Gnostic/Samaritan Christology is made to vanish into thin air – a later orthodoxy bereft of vision had gained control of something it neither understood nor wished to understand.

Peter's indecisive nature is perfectly captured in the story of Jesus' arrest in the Garden of Gethsemane. He flees for his life and 'follows afar off', then straight away denies all knowledge of Jesus three times. These are intriguing passages. The gospel writers have it that Jesus foresees this triple denial, and I think this obvious addition to the text reveals that Peter's denial of Jesus is also a rejection of Jesus' idea of Messiahship, if not a direct rejection of Jesus himself. Why else gild the lily to such an extent in Matthew's gospel with the quite obvious tack-on that Peter is a 'rock', and that the future Catholic Church will be built on this rock. Rock? Of all Jesus' disciples Peter is the least like a rock – and it is this rather obvious fact that had to be removed by the later writer-editors of the gospels to recreate (reverse?) Peter's character and kick-start the myth that he ended up running the show in Rome. Deny Jesus I certainly think he did – but I also think he rejected again and again Jesus' odd vision of Messiahship, and that quite a few of the disciples – if not all of them – eventually did likewise. There is something extraordinary about the behaviour of the twelve disciples after the crucifixion. It's almost as if they are in a stupor. That the reason for this was fear cannot be doubted. The upper room was not a place of joy and light: it was a priest's hole, and it was jammed tight with frightened men. And again Charlesworth asks the correct question: 'What did he [Jesus] think about his rejections, first by scribes, by some Pharisees, and then finally by his closest disciples and friends, including Judas and Peter?'[14]

A REJECTED JESUS?

When Mary returns from the empty tomb after the Resurrection and tells Peter and the others that Jesus had risen from the dead, they are utterly incredulous. Her words were to them 'as idle tales, and they believed them not'.[15] To check things out, Peter goes to the tomb either by himself or with John the beloved disciple, has a look around, and leaves not knowing what to make of the situation. Now this is all very strange. Jesus had spelt things out pretty clearly, we are told, and Peter in particular had been severely rapped over the knuckles for rejecting Jesus' prophecy that he would end up arrested and crucified. But more to the point, Peter and the others had been informed by Jesus that he would rise on the third day. And given the fact that he was correct about the other two happenings, one would think that expectations among the twelve might just have been a titch higher. Or is it just that they had disowned him in their collective attitude long before, and that his mental perambulations were of much less interest to them than one might suppose? Mary herself, on being confronted with a living Jesus at the tomb, is said not to have recognized him at first, and the same thing happens when the two disciples on the road to Emmaus are joined by Jesus as they walk. Didn't they recognize him? I suspect a corrupted text within which disciples who had problems recognizing Jesus *as the Messiah* are persuaded to change their minds on discovering that he has somehow physically survived crucifixion.

But there is one other point that must be made about the two disciples on the road to Emmaus. The writer of Luke names one as Cleopas (Jesus' father's brother), and Dr Schonfield surmises that the other was Cleopas' son, Simeon, Jesus' first cousin – not an unlikely choice given the interior tenor of the piece. In that Simeon went on to become elected head of the Nazarene community at Jerusalem after James' death, it is not difficult to see why the principle of 'rejection' would be at work. At that very moment James, possibly the Essene Teacher of Righteousness, had taken over as legitimate dynastic successor to Jesus while he was in hiding, and there were a lot of unresolved issues between Jesus, his brother James and other members of the family.[16] And this also helps make sense of the meeting itself, putting it into a proper political context, rather than an arbitrary materialization by a voluble phantom.

Schonfield tells us that until the time of the Roman invasion there were no fewer than 15 successive Bishops of Jerusalem who were Jewish. The *whole* Church at this time was composed of 'Hebrews'.[17] Catholic orthodoxy has suppressed and destroyed much of the evidence, but in relation to Jesus' family Hegesippus states: 'These are those who take the lead of the whole Church as witnesses, even the kindred of the Lord, and when profound peace was established throughout the Church they continued to the time of Trajan Caesar.'[18] Jesus was physically alive and in full possession of his faculties after the Cross, and it was this fact and this fact alone that would change the minds of those either unsure of, or adamantly against, his Messiahship. Like Paul, who turns from being a persecutor to a chief apostle, the Twelve are stunned back into being his disciples, and have to be *reschooled in the Scriptures* so that their lingering doubts can be removed – doubts which for some do not altogether disappear. When the Twelve eventually meet up with Jesus in Galilee and he presents them with the next level of his Messianic vision, some are still doubtful of his claim that he is the Messiah – particularly when he appears to invite 'worship' and offers no correction.

Everything about Peter is pushed into reverse in the gospels, and his supposed elevation to leader of the Church in Jerusalem after the crucifixion is a fiction neatly cobbled together in conjunction with the misinformation that the Jerusalem Church was actually the original Christian Church from which the present Catholic Church sprang. That is historical nonsense. The Church at Jerusalem was Nazarene-Jewish-orthodox, probably Essene, but not Christian. It was led by James, Jesus' brother, and Peter was at best second in command, but never at any time leader. (Peter is reproved by emissaries from James the Just, his superior, for eating with Gentiles at Antioch.) It was this Church which fought Pauline Christianity tooth and nail for some 20 years before disintegrating in the face of Roman invasion and Sadducee persecution. Paul, on his return from Arabia, avoids James because of his Nazarite-Ebionite conservatism and homes in on Peter who is the weak link in the chain of command. Negotiation and friction between the two theologies start right at this point. From there on it is a 14-year cat and mouse game, both sides writing letters of condemnation against each other. Finally exasperated by the Nazarene Church's intractable attitude over circumcision and Jewish dietary laws, and fed up with Peter's changes of mind over whether or not it is proper to eat with Gentile converts, Paul confronts him, and we have a highly probable reworking of this confrontation in Acts under the guise of a row with Simon Magus. Because this disguised section is also about the power of the Spirit, about gifts of healing and much else besides, we can conclude that Paul's argument with Peter went much, much deeper than mere Jewish religious customs, and that the eventual making of these two figures the very foundation of Catholic orthodoxy is totally fabricated.

TRIPARTITE PROBLEM

The orthodox Jerusalem Church of the Nazarenes was not really 'Christian'. The many Christian Pauline Churches were basically Jewish in orientation, but not in the least orthodox. And to complicate things still further, the eventual orthodox Roman Catholic Church of the late first century and early second was not Pauline – it was Petrine (conservative) with Paul's Arabian-Samaritan Christology of 'revelation', 'knowledge' and 'wisdom' reconstituted as a pagan literalism, perceiving Jesus the flesh and blood individual as God incarnate. Brought into alignment with a reinterpreted Judaism stripped of its basic laws and used as nothing more than an authenticating backdrop, the members of this new ultra-orthodoxy were dished up 'beliefs' in the guise of irrefutable truths, and inadvertently found themselves dying for these supposed truths because their own inner truth had been eclipsed by dogma and emotion run riot. As a young boy, Origen became so infatuated with the idea of dying for his Lord that his mother had to hide his clothes. Die he would have willingly done – run through the streets naked he did not have the courage to do!

In anyone's terms, Paul was a Gnostic Christian capable of great flights of theological inventiveness. He would not have condoned later Church thinking about Jesus' literal Godhead, and he certainly would not have gone along with the collapsing of his many individual and highly inspirational Churches into the grand, bishop-bound Catholic Church of the second century. Simone Pétrement says: 'Whatever the strangeness of some of the Gnostic writings, Pauline thought and Johannine thought are always to be found at their roots.'[19] Sandwiched historically between two orthodoxies, and in possession of a highly developed theology of transcendence spliced with the knowledge that Jesus had *physically* resurrected, Paul's extraordinary theological efforts have been forced into a conceptual straitjacket and used as proofs for a literalism about Jesus that had no foundation in everyday reality.

The Hellenized Christian Church eventually scrambled Paul's theological vision by shifting its base line, used this scrambled vision as the foundation for a new orthodoxy attached to Jewish Nazarene Church structures already in place, and then outlawed both the real content of Paul's theology *and* the legitimate Nazarene Church of Jesus' family and disciples – a 'Church' which in all likelihood was nothing other than a branch of the Qumran community. Dr Schonfield tells us that Catholic Christianity had excellent reasons for discrediting the Nazarenes, for calling them 'heretics'. For a start, they did not believe in the deity of Jesus, viewed the early Pauline Church as heretical, and similarly categorized the later orthodox Catholic Church at Rome as it emerged with its new interpretation of Paul's basic doctrines.[20] The Nazarenes, we are told, believed that Jesus had become no more than the Messiah at his baptism, and this damaging belief was fiercely denied by the new Church at Rome now claiming central authority.

The Roman invasion of Judea, and the destruction of the Temple along with the infrastructure of Jewish daily life effectively destroyed the influence of the powerful Nazarene Church at Jerusalem, so allowing the Church at Rome to replace it with a power structure and doctrinal vision of its own. Marked down as anti-Roman by the Romans, as anti-Christian by the non-Jewish Christians in Rome, and as anti-Jewish by those Jews who wanted nothing more to do with sectarian dreams and Zealot nightmares, the Nazarene council quickly lost its ability after the invasion to intercept and control Paul's Gentile Christians in the West. So hated were the sectaries by the rabbinists that a special prayer damning them – particularly those in 'white robes' (the Essenes and Nazarenes) – was composed to be used in public worship in the synagogue. The prayer ran 'And for sectaries let there be no hope.'[21] And Paul too found himself frozen out of Roman Christian life when finally brought to the capital prior to the Roman invasion of Judea. Schonfield remarks that Paul's earlier letter to the Roman Church 'was not calculated to endear him to that community . . . and when he reached Rome as a prisoner in chains . . . he found many opponents'.[22]

Paul's own letter to the Philippians speaks of those who 'preach Christ of contention, not sincerely, supposing to add affliction to my bonds'.[23] So everything was not quite as some would have us believe. And there is an additional remark made by Schonfield regarding Paul's problems in Rome which again raises the question of Peter's exact role in relation to Paul. He tells us firstly that there is no convincing evidence that the Roman Church was founded by Peter, and then draws our attention to the interesting second-century legendary tale that Peter only went to Rome 'to undo the harm done there by the teaching of Simon Magus'. Simon Magus? We are then told that 'Jewish Christians afterwards used this story to convey Peter's opposition to Paul, who is thinly veiled in their account by the figure of this enemy of Christianity.'[24] So here once again we have the idea of 'Simon Magus' being a code-word for Paul. Interesting. And all the more so when Paul's treatment in Rome is looked at in more detail. When speaking of his reception by this community, he says: 'no man stood with me, but all men forsook me: I pray God that it may not be laid to their charge.'[25]

Paul, at the mercy of Roman justice because he is a Roman citizen, arrives in Rome not knowing what to expect either from the Roman courts or from the Nazarenes in control of that small messianic community. But he quickly finds out. Virtually ostracized by this community of sectarian Jews, he is left to fret and fume and write about his treatment. Only three Nazarenes respond to his presence in Rome, and for that he is truly grateful. And then all hell breaks loose, for the Zealots have finally pushed Rome too far, and the might of the Roman Empire is brought to bear on the Jewish nation. Militant Judaism is obliterated by Roman fury. The Nazarene Apostolic Church at Jerusalem is scattered, communication with Rome cut off. The small community of Nazarene-led believers in Rome is devastated (64 CE), the Jewish element most likely being singled out for special treatment. The Nazarenes in the minority, their Jewish homeland reduced to rubble, and the Apostolic authority of the Jerusalem Nazarenes utterly silenced, the result is a mad scrambling for life and security. Later, when the dust has settled and life has returned to a semblance of normality, the non-Jewish remnant will begin to reassess their beliefs and attempt to put their Church back together again. For it is now obvious to Jewish and Gentile Christians alike that Jesus has failed in his Messianic Mission – the Kingdom of God had not come as expected – just the Romans, as usual.

TRANSITION TO ORTHODOXY

According to the writer of Matthew, the obliteration of the Jewish nation by the Romans was God's punishment for their rejection of Jesus as Israel's Messiah. And this notion is cleverly amalgamated with the idea that the Gentiles gained access to Israel's heritage as a result, so displacing the Jews. This is to say that the writer of Matthew created an East-West mix containing what Schonfield calls 'a formulation of something like a Christian orthodoxy'.[26] But more important to our thesis is an earlier reference to the discovery of the Nag Hammadi Library in Egypt, that collection of Gnostic manuscripts which so delighted G R S Mead and Carl Jung. We are told that scholars have strongly favoured the view that 'part of this material derived from Jewish-Christian sources that had reached Egypt from Palestine'.[27] The collapsing of Nazarene-Essene ideas into a Christian-Gnostic and Christian-pagan theological context is everywhere evident in Matthew's gospel, and this fact suggests that at the time of writing (the end of the first century) the Nazarenes had finally lost control of the Roman Church's general push towards the future.

And so with the other gospels. The writer of Mark is apologetic about Jewish nationalism, does everything to dissociate Jesus from that mind-set, and allows Pontius Pilate off the hook. Luke's gospel is similarly constructed, has the non-Christian reader in mind, skims over Church problems and reverses the notion that Christians were a subversive breed, integrates the Hebraic and the Hellenic into a single stream, and without a blush borrows freely from the Jewish historian Josephus and the book of Samuel. Biographical in tone, and more novelistic than historical in construction, this gospel whitewashes the Roman presence and 'skilfully manages to have the best of both worlds'.[28]

But it is John's gospel more than any other which reflects the full influence of ideas any Jew or Nazarene or Essene would have rejected outright – and that in spite of the fact that such ideas are integrated with perhaps the most accurate descriptions of Temple worship and Jewish ritual procedures. The writer of John's gospel is truly a split being, and this split, according to Dr Schonfield, is due to the probable amalgamation of John the 'beloved disciple' – an actual Jewish priest and close friend of Jesus present at both the Last Supper, the Cross and the tomb – with John the Elder, writer of the epistle by that name. This second John is no priest: he is in fact a Greek heretic of Gnostic persuasion who superimposes his divine Jesus on to John the beloved disciple's historical Jesus.[29] According to Irenaeus,[30] it is this John who leads the Nazarenes when they flee from Pella to Ephesus in Asia Minor. But this can't be right. John the Elder would not have been given elbow room in the Nazarene camp: his beliefs were Paul's beliefs – beliefs which had perhaps even outstretched Jesus' own high estimation of his own importance. And yet the Nazarenes, in spite of Jesus' close association with Paul, continued to believe that he was the legitimate Messiah of Israel, and may even have fled to the Gentile city of Pella because told to do so by Jesus. Quoting Eusebius, Graves and Podro record that 'Shortly before the destruction of the Temple the Nazarenes, "commanded by a divine revelation", left Jerusalem and settled in Pella in Decapolis.'[31]

The Nazarene Council held out against Paul's quite different Jesus for well over 14 years, and successfully converted many of his churches back to their particular view of the messianic mystery, which would without doubt have become the orthodoxy of the future had it not been for Zealot stupidity. The predominantly Jewish Church at Rome, considerably reduced in 64 CE as a side effect of the Roman invasion of Judea, 'swung over to espouse the Pauline spiritual gospel divorced from Judaism, which previously had been attacked and largely rejected'.[32] Before long, due to his non-political and non-threatening vision of Jesus as Messiah, Paul would be transmuted from theological villain into hero first-class – but not without cost to everyone concerned. A new orthodoxy devoid of subtlety, and infected with pagan notions of divinity replacing Paul's delicately constructed Christ as 'hypostasis' (reflection of God) would win the day and change the trajectory of the Church for ever. The Nazarenes, scattered far and wide, would succumb to 'new teaching and relationships with remnants of Baptist, Essene, Samaritan and other sects of "Saints" of the pre-war period',[33] and those advocating contemplative experience as greater than episcopal guidance would at first be reprimanded, then persecuted. And with the later change in Christian fortunes, those persisting in their stance for a Christ of 'revelation', 'wisdom' and 'knowledge', would be hunted down and killed, their writings destroyed, every memory of their existence reduced to a hiss of disapproval.

BACK TO BASICS

The only thing Peter is not in two minds about is Jesus' resurrection. The writer of Acts has him say:

> Him God raised up the third day, and showed him openly; Not to all the people, but unto witnesses chosen before of God, even to us, who did eat and drink with him after he rose from the dead.[34]

Elaine Pagels is astute when she says that 'the political implications of the doctrine of resurrection does not account for its extraordinary impact on the religious experience of Christians.'[35] She then quotes the theologian Jurgen Moltmann, who said that the orthodox view of resurrection suggested that human life could not be separated from bodily experience: if a human being came back from the dead, then he or she had to come back *physically*.[36]

The political implications of the Resurrection are obvious. What is not so obvious is that the impact of Jesus' physical resurrection on his disciples, and on Paul's individual consciousness, was the equivalent of a very powerful torch being turned on in a dark room. Shorn of its actual physicality, of its flesh and blood reality by no more than theological sleight of hand, the Resurrection was eventually Gnosticized into a spiritual rather than a physical event, but incomprehensibly allowed to retain a species of physicality by those who wanted the best of both worlds. Psychologically galvanized by Jesus' physical appearance after crucifixion and burial, the disciples of Jesus belatedly scrambled to his call and attempted to understand what had taken place. In fact, it could be said that they were themselves 'resurrected' from the dead: brought back from the stupor of disbelief and rejection and set free from their fear – their fear of being seen and recognized on the streets. In psychological terms they experienced an 'earthquake'. The grave of disbelief and rejection gave way to the joy of prophecy fulfilled and hopes for the future rekindled.

In his book *Jesus*, A N Wilson digs deep and nudges close to the main issue:

(1) the Resurrection in relation to the Jewish Church of Jerusalem;
(2) the Resurrection in relation to the cult of the apostle Paul as presented to the Gentiles; and
(3) the fourth gospels' Gnostic approach to the Resurrection, which is at variance with both the Nazarene and Pauline traditions.

A cult figure in all three strands of tradition, Jesus remains the 'Jewish Messiah' in the first, the 'mystic Christ' in the second, and although similarly a 'mystic Christ' in the third, one considered by A N Wilson to be different from the one espoused by Paul.[37] An interesting observation, for by this time Paul's overt Gnosticism has been watered down into the strange literalism of Jesus' being God's Son. But this theologically generated idea hides the disturbing fact that there is actually no real difference at all between Paul's mystic Christ and the mystic Christ of the Gnostics. They are not radically different forms. They have simply been teased apart and kept apart to ensure the success of the prevailing orthodoxy's authority.

Michael Goulder's study suggests differences between Pauline and Samaritan Gnostic theologies in the early days of Paul's mission to the Gentiles, but it is pretty clear from his developed Christology that these differences were eventually overcome. This is not to suggest that Paul's theology was eventually identical to that of the Samaritan Gnostic school; it is to say that these theological modes need not be separated to the extent that they are by Christian theorists – they belong together (just as it is now realized that Jesus cannot be legitimately separated from the Essenes), and ought to be left together. To set the record straight on this point is to liberate Pauline thought, properly separate it from Jewish Nazarene expectation, and at last reunite it with its still developing transcendent base. To do otherwise is not only to make a nonsense of transcendence, it is to scramble the possibility of present-day Christians' finding the connection between their religious faith and psychological reality. As Wilson remarks, 'St Paul understood what most Christians never realize, namely that the Gospel of Christ is not *a* religion, but religion itself, in its most universal and deepest significance.'[38] And Christians should not interpret this remark to mean that Christianity is somehow the top-dog revelation – that would be an utter travesty of what Wilson is trying to say.

To Paul, Jesus was the 'risen' Christ. This message, delivered to the Gnostically-influenced Corinthian Church enables Jesus to turn into a figure who has, in Wilson's estimation, 'outsoared history'.[39] And although in practical terms this means that Paul's Jesus was well on his way to becoming the 'mystic Christ', it should not be forgotten that Paul claims to have received the traditions concerning Jesus not from the Nazarene Church at Jerusalem under James, or from any of the disciples of Jesus, but *from Jesus himself*. He is quite explicit: 'For I have received of the Lord that which also I delivered unto you'.[40] The tradition being referred to is the Eucharist. Paul claims that Jesus himself initiated this ceremony; Wilson does not agree. He thinks it highly unlikely that Jesus the Jew would have instituted a ritual so in tune with the mystery cults of the Mediterranean.[41] In the light of what we have so far discovered about Jesus, however, the development of such an idea is not so strange. As a ritual, the Eucharist certainly had nothing to do with orthodox Judaism, but it had everything to do with sectarian ideas bolstered by pagan influences redeveloped in an atmosphere of rebellion against the more restrictive aspects of sectarian practice, and eventually amalgamated with Gnostic Samaritan trends. New wine in new bottles indeed, and a vibrant religious vision to go along with it.

Wilson goes so far as to suggest that Paul quite probably had contact with Jesus *prior* to the crucifixion. If true, this would explain a great deal that is otherwise inexplicable in relation to Paul's eventual conversion and assignment to the Gentiles as a missionary. As with the calling of John's disciples by Jesus, the calling of Paul would lose its mystery if these two figures had come face to face prior to the crucifixion. Battling backwards and forwards on the issue, Wilson the novelist and analyst presents a quite convincing case for Paul's having been present at the crucifixion, and as a result of what he witnessed being psychologically obsessed with the Cross as a symbol. In fact he goes much further and suggests that Paul may have been directly responsible for Jesus' arrest.

But there's a problem in all of this. If Paul really was a persecutor of Jesus and his Nazarenes prior to the crucifixion, and actually responsible for Jesus' arrest in Gethsemane, when exactly did he hear Jesus describe the Eucharistic meal? Trying to make sense of this point Wilson says:

> Paul tells us himself that he was a persecutor of Christians, and that it was a confrontation not with the Christians but with Jesus himself which changed his mind. A hypothesis which might make sense of this claim is that Paul did actually come face to face with Jesus during his lifetime.[42]

Fine. But when exactly in Jesus' 'lifetime' did Paul get the details of this most intimate of Christian feasts? Certainly not at any time before the crucifixion – the ritual was inaugurated only hours before his arrest. The verse in Corinthians[43] not only speaks of Paul receiving the tradition of the Eucharistic meal *from the Lord*, it also states that the Lord spoke of bread and wine in relation to the breaking of his body and spilling of his blood, and that he did not get this idea from the disciples. Paul the persecutor would not have heard those words uttered by Jesus before his crucifixion, so it stands to reason that he heard them spoken *after* his crucifixion. Unless of course one wants to call Paul a liar, or have it that this material has simply been added to 1 Corinthians to neatly round off a theology. Or that he really did get the information on the Eucharist from the disciples. Completely possible, of course. But I still think Wilson has a point – Paul knew Jesus, and the evidence of the whole New Testament points to Jesus' being alive after his crucifixion. This is particularly obvious in Acts where Jesus appears to Paul in a so-called vision at Corinth and gives him explicit directions: 'Be not afraid, but speak, and hold not thy peace: For I am with thee, and no man shall set on thee to hurt thee: for I have much people in this city.'[44] Very utilitarian. And who are the 'people' that Jesus already has in the Gnostic-ridden city of Corinth?

The evidence suggests an alive Jesus after the crucifixion, a Jesus who engages in 'information exchanges' with Mary Magdalene, the two disciples on the road to Emmaus, the congregated disciples hiding in Jerusalem, James his flesh and blood brother, Ananias, and eventually Paul. The later appearances are described as 'visions', but there is every reason to believe that this term simply disguises the fact that Jesus was there in person. And it is not too difficult to work out why this would have been done.

Consider the state of affairs described earlier. There were the Nazarene followers of the 'Way' at Jerusalem, the many Pauline Churches developing alongside the Gnostic Samaritan Churches with which they finally amalgamated in doctrine and practice, and the eventual emergence of the orthodox Roman Catholic Church after the destruction of the Temple and the bringing under control of Gnostic ground-roots Christianity. Cut off from its orthodox Nazarene base, the Church in Rome put itself back together again and made itself the centre of the Christian world, rethought its previous ties with the Nazarene mother-Church, and began to create a system of 'belief' around Jesus which carefully camouflaged historical events and placed the emphasis on the miraculous rather than the political. With Jesus really dead, Paul dead, Peter dead and the Nazarenes scattered and powerless, the scene was set for the introduction of a coherent religious policy which would smooth away the in-fighting, past politico-religious obsessions and Jesus' embarrassing sectarian connections. Skilfully editing Jesus' life and teachings into an acceptable shape for general consumption, the Jesus of history was all but transformed into Paul's Gnostic Christ, made immediately to ascend bodily into heaven to get him out of the way, and then allowed to illegitimately metamorphose into Jesus as God incarnate in human flesh. All in all a dizzying feat of theological sleight of hand and novelistic ingenuity which would bequeath to the future a religion vibrant with archetypes burgeoning to break out of an ethical and moral straitjacket.

FOURTEEN

THE EYE OF THE STORM

The Church sidesteps the embarrassments of history, pushes its doctrinal base to ever greater levels of absurdity, evolves inadequate theological tools and stolidly ignores the fact that Paul's original communities of spiritual freedom have been transformed into a repressive authoritarian regime.

Latin theology triumphed; rational exegesis died. Faith overcame reason; philosophy languished. Dogma replaced revelation; wisdom, knowledge and understanding atrophied. Authority displaced individual responsibility; community vanished. Impoverished, orthodoxy encased itself in a rigid ecclesiastical system which Alvin Boyd Kuhn suggests 'will perhaps never discern truly or acknowledge openly the ruinous price it has had to pay for its rejection of Gnosticism, which came close also to costing it the loss of Paul's redeeming contribution'.[1] Dr Kuhn is well aware of the historical intricacies and anomalies surrounding the teachings of Paul, the Nazarenes, the Gnostics and the early orthodox Roman Catholic Church in transition. He speaks of Latin theology crushing Gnosticism in the Church,[2] tells us that Paul's Christianity had nothing whatsoever to do with the Christianity of gospel history,[3] and rounds off his salvo with a stinging comment on the deadening effect of Christian dogma on the laity, and the fact that worship eventually 'degenerated to a meaningless automatism of habit'.[4]

Describing the situation which arose within orthodoxy, the acknowledged expert on Gnosticism Dr Elaine Pagels seems to confirm this degeneracy into automatisms of habit when she says:

But orthodox Christians, by the late second century, had begun to establish objective criteria for Church membership. Whoever confessed the creed, accepted the ritual of baptism, participated in worship, and obeyed the clergy was accepted as a fellow Christian.[5]

The Gnostic *Gospel of Philip* had a similar message. It said that many of the converts to orthodox Christianity went 'down into the water and come up without having received anything'.[6] The *Apocalypse of Peter* was even more direct, stating bluntly that the orthodox Church was an 'imitation Church', a 'counterfeit' for the very reason that it claimed *exclusive legitimacy*.[7]

Reduced to what Dr Kuhn has termed 'dead formalism', the Christian religion, hooked now on 'faith' rather than rational exegesis so as to sidestep the embarrassments of history, functioned progressively without relevant meaning and eventually donned the mantle of irrationality.[8] Inanity followed. And with the rise of inanity came that reduction in intelligence which allows intellectualisms to rule the heart. And so the 'free spirit' of the early Christians – what Dr Kuhn has called 'the dynamo of driving power'[9] all but vanished and left the Church in the hands of self-appointed authorities bent upon consolidating their power base by every means available. Not a pretty picture – and one complicated by the fact that certain free spirits were seriously threatening this edifice of unfounded certainty: the 'heretics', so it seemed, were everywhere. With 'faith' elevated above 'reason', there could only be one outcome: persecution. Centuries later, Nietzsche would come to hate Christianity for this very reason, for faith alone was supposed to produce infinite blessings from God, and this meant that 'belief' in whatever the Church designated as 'truth' was greater than individual efforts towards understanding.

The more absurd the belief, the greater the faith required. Life itself had no meaning beyond what the gospel stories seemed to purvey. Individual striving, on whatever level, and with whatever success, was an expression of Satanic wilfulness. The Church's early growing pains, so euphemistically described by Christian historians, were actually the screams of heretics, the dumb bellowings of intelligent human beings forced to the level of hurt animals. With the rise to political power of the Catholic Church on 28 February 380 CE, the heretics would be dubbed 'mad' and 'insane', their meeting places no longer known as churches, their punishment the vengeance of God and the exquisitely directed anger of men. Eventually Augustine would supply what Joachim Kahl has described as 'a theological justification for compulsory measures taken by the state against Christian minorities',[10] and the efforts of courageous individuals to return to a deeper and more demanding spirituality would be officially outlawed.

TRANSFORMED CONSCIOUSNESS

Dr Pagels tells us that most Gnostic sources agree that the 'lamp of the body is the mind', and she reminds us that Freud claimed to follow 'the light of reason'.[11] She also quotes numerous Gnostic texts in relation to individual striving, and reveals a wealth of material accurately describing profound psychological processes. For instance, the *Gospel of Thomas* warns those who dare venture deep into themselves that self-discovery will produce 'inner turmoil', and also states that the Kingdom of God is *within* the individual but it is also 'spread out on the earth', though we cannot see it. Dr Pagels remarks: 'That "kingdom", then, symbolises a state of transformed consciousness.'[12] But perhaps the most remarkable of the *Thomas* sayings attributed to Jesus is: 'If you bring forth what is within you, what you bring forth will save you. If you do not bring forth what is within you, what you do not bring forth will destroy you.' Dr Pagels' remarks are again worth recording:

> Such Gnostics acknowledged that pursuing *gnosis* engages each person in a solitary, difficult process, as one struggles against internal resistance. They characterised this resistance to *gnosis* as the desire to sleep or to be drunk – that is, to remain unconscious.[13]

The Gnostic Jesus says, 'they are blind in their hearts and do not have sight'. And the Gnostic teacher Silvanus is of the same opinion. In his *Teachings* he says: 'end the sleep which weighs heavy upon you.'

But was there really anything to Gnosticism? Did it have any substance at all? The orthodox Church certainly didn't think so. And if you listen to men of the cloth talking about Gnosticism today the general impression you get is that this highly complex system was nothing more than an excuse to believe in whatever bizarre notion might come into your head. Proof that this was still the generally held view by Churchmen was quirkily dished up to me when I turned on my radio this very morning. Tuning just fractionally off target in search of my favourite music programme, I heard the word 'Gnostic' and stopped in my tracks – it was a clergyman doing talk-back radio on the subject. Amused that I should have stumbled on to such a broadcast, I postponed turning on my computer. The result was enlightening. Sounding 'fair' and 'reasonable', the speaker seemed to double over backwards in his attempt not to utterly damn those modern groups which in his estimation resembled and represented ancient Gnosticism. And then with surprising speed he changed tack, proceeded to turn these supposed copies of the ancient system into a complete joke, and by doing so once again reduced Gnosticism proper to the level of kindergarten self-indulgence. It was quite a performance, and it was exactly the same performance as given by the Church Father Irenaeus in his massive refutation of Gnostic teaching and exploration written at the end of the second century. Because this mighty work came to underpin the attitude of all subsequent refuters, its historical reliability and relevance is obviously of great importance.

According to G R S Mead, Irenaeus' sources of information on Gnosticism were certain memoranda of the Valentinians belonging to the followers of Ptolemaeus, one short fragment ascribed to Ptolemaeus himself, and the memoir of a follower of Marcus. He claims to be directly expounding the teachings of Valentinus, but is in fact quoting a prior refuter. It is also known that some of the opening statements in his grand refutation of Gnosticism came from the same source as Clements', and that much of his criticism is based on unreliable oral communications. He also quotes from, but does not name, the *Gospel of Mary*, and the discovery of this work has enabled scholars to check up on Irenaeus' diatribe point by point. Mead does not mince words in describing Irenaeus' expertise. Referring sarcastically to him as 'the sheet-anchor of orthodox haeresiology',[14] he shows conclusively that this great Church refuter really didn't know what he was talking about. Writing at Lyons in Gaul, 'far away from the real scene of action',[15] the whole edifice of Irenaeus' refutation is revealed to be at best secondhand and at worse a scrambled-egg version of Gnosticism with its poetic flights of description highlighted at the expense of its considerable substance. Setting pace and form for the future, Irenaeus created a patchwork quilt of half-baked notions about Gnosticism, borrowed wholesale from the fantastic notions of popular rumour, and directly attributed such hearsay to the Gnostic Schools. Professor Morton Smith agrees.

> The cults founded by Simon of Samaria and by other miscalled 'gnostics' would probably be recognised as 'mysteries' had not their distinguishing traits been obscured by immersion in Irenaeus's 'gnostic' stew.[16]

Dr Pagels, writing of Eastern and Western religious traditions, states that ideas associated with Eastern religions 'emerged in the first century through the Gnostic movement in the West, but they were suppressed and condemned by polemicists like Irenaeus'. She then adds for good measure, 'Yet those who called Gnosticism heresy were adopting – consciously or not – the viewpoint of that group of Christians who called themselves orthodox Christians.'[17] Then after a little discussion on the many 'true' Christianities that have existed, particularly since the Reformation, she draws our attention back to the Nag Hammadi manuscripts and states:

> If we admit that some of these fifty-two texts represent early forms of Christian teaching, we may have to recognise that early Christianity is far more diverse than nearly anyone expected.[18]

Indeed. So diverse in fact that Irenaeus was up in arms about there being Gnostic gospels in wide circulation throughout Gaul, Rome, Greece and Asia Minor. The question is, what was actually in these so-called gospels to make Irenaeus and his fulminating successors so nervous? What was it about the Gnostic vision which so disturbed Christians then and still disturbs Christians now? Stigmatized as 'the first-born of Satan', the Gnostics were treated as spiritual lepers, their books destroyed, their leaders arrested and tried for heresy, their communities harassed and persecuted.

The Church Fathers tell us that the doctrines of the Gnostics had their foundation in Plato and Pythagoras, Aristotle and Heraclitus, and in the mysteries and initiations of the surrounding nations – in fact, in just about everything but Christ. So was there no actual connection with Christianity? Was Gnosticism just a parasitical body attached limpet-like to the body of the Faithful? Well, not quite. As we have seen from our survey of Paul's interaction with the Samaritan *gnosis*, and the evolution of his Christology in alignment with religious ideas from Samaria and Arabia, the Christology eventually borrowed from Paul by the emerging orthodoxy at Rome was replete with Gnostic images and conceptions which they timorously interpreted back into absurd literalisms – that is, the high, resonant key of _gnosis_ (knowledge in accordance with interior reality) was stepped down to a lower register (knowledge made subservient to fabrications of the intellect) and turned into a linguistic muddle. When merged with the heavily camouflaged history surrounding Jesus' life and teachings found in the gospels, this muddle took on stupendous proportions and began to turn into the topsy-turvy theological nightmare modern thinkers are still trying to make sense of. Having popped Jesus *physically* into the sky, orthodoxy got rid of the primary influence on Paul's conception of the 'mystic Christ', ended up believing its own manufactured propaganda virtually by accident, and then made it anathema for anyone to disagree with this cutely concocted system of compulsory beliefs. And it really can't be argued that all of this was done in innocence – *that* is academic foot-shuffling.

THE KINGDOM OF GOD

Jesus' ordeal on the cross and the ultimate failure of his Messianic Mission had, as one would expect, a radical effect on him. And because he had been no ordinary individual to start with, he not only recovered from this monumental setback, he incorporated it into his spiritual mission. For to be 'fully conscious' in the sense that I think Jesus was does not mean that he knew everything, that he understood everything, it just meant that he had the capacity to retain conscious attention to the extent that his failings, when they surfaced, could be dealt with quickly and effectively. The Kingdom of God was no longer something that would come down from heaven and manifest itself in physical reality because God wished it and a man had willed it into existence; it was now an *inner* Kingdom which could be realized by anyone as even the gospel of Luke attests. I think this is where the confusion arises among scholars concerning Jesus' conception of the Kingdom of God: he simply changed his mind (as he did about going to the Gentiles when the Jews rejected him), woke up and realized that he had been a touch too literal in his expectations. The Nazarenes believed that an earthly paradise lasting a thousand years would follow the pangs of the Messiah, and when this did not eventuate they suppressed Jesus' statements to that effect. So says Robert Graves, in conjunction with Joshua Podro, in *The Nazarene Gospel Restored*.[19]

I have no wish to glamorize Jesus the Nazarene, and I certainly have no wish to elevate him beyond what he was in himself – but neither do I wish to underestimate him. This was a powerful individual, a highly trained individual, an individual with a will of iron and a fine grasp of spiritual and psychological processes. But that he was a man of his time and culture there can be no doubt. He was not infallible – like the rest of us, he made mistakes. Like everyone, then and now, he had to 'learn' – and you can't learn without making mistakes. On one occasion he said to the disciples that he had 'meat to eat which they knew not of'. Some have interpreted this to mean that he had his own store of food – another tired literalism. I believe he meant that he had thoughts of his own that he could not share, would not share. This is the man that interests me, the one Bultmann had no interest in. If Jesus said a quarter of the things he is recorded as saying in the Gnostic gospels, then in anyone's estimation he was a remarkable individual. But I suspect more than a mere thinker, in spite of his having thoughts kept close to his chest. The Gnostic gospels reveal flashes of history which cannot be verified – no more so than many of the historical claims of the gospels – but as with the gospels, a hidden history of interaction and argument and tension and event can often be detected just beneath the surface.

It is now realized and acknowledged by most specialists that the many different forms of Christianity reigning today reflect only in a pale way the amazing diversity of the first two centuries. Since the end of the second century, Christians of all persuasions have confessed the Apostolic Creed and accepted the New Testament as a fixed canon of scripture. So there is in fact an exact system of agreement between today's Christian groupings in spite of surface tensions and the occasional outbreak of collective egocentricity. But there was nothing of a similar nature during the first one and a half to two centuries of the Church's early dynamic life. During those years of turmoil there were lots of gospels, and they were *all* taken seriously. The *Gospel of Thomas* and the *Gospel of Philip* and the *Gospel of Truth* circulated alongside Matthew, Mark, Luke and John, and were held in just as high esteem by many devout believers in Jesus. Some preferred this group of gospels to that group of gospels, but it was only with the turn of the second century that such gospels were standardized into today's canon and the many disparate Christian groupings were brought under the full control of bishops, priests and deacons. This trinity of authority-figures came to believe themselves divinely appointed to look after their communities, and eventually took it upon themselves to decide the exact nature of what should and should not be believed about Jesus and his Mission. The Roman Church then emerged in a leading role, decided that it had the power to veto community beliefs through the bishops, and after a bit of a struggle was grudgingly accepted as having that right due to its central position at Rome and its past close associations with Peter and Paul. Everything in God's garden was now neat and tidy.

Well, not quite.

As should have been anticipated by those who cut the gospels back to four, the many other gospels excluded from the canon were still held by many Christians to be perfectly respectable. And as much of community spiritual life was intrinsically linked to the contents of these more imaginative and exploratory texts, and there were teachers who specialized in their contents, the end result of Rome's standardization process was amazement and revolt. Prior to the announcement of a fixed scriptural canon, there had been a large and sprawling conglomerate of communities all in broad agreement that Jesus was the lynchpin of their spiritual search. After the announcement, many of these communities not only found themselves disadvantaged by Rome's textual curtailments, but discovered – when finally the news got through – that their particular textual proclivities had pushed them into the category of 'heretics'. What a shock that must have been. A little like waking up one morning and discovering that your particular shade of politics had been classified during the night as 'traitorous'.

Christians one minute, heretics the next, those so classified were defined into existence as 'Gnostics' – that is, as those who relied too heavily on 'knowledge' and 'wisdom' and 'revelation' rather than on 'faith' and 'obedience'. There then followed the accusation that Gnosticism was essentially non-Christian. To have a rich and vibrant internal spiritual life was simply not conducive to credal acceptance and obedience without question. As Dr Pagels shows, the investigations of the later orthodoxy attempted to trace and confine the origins of Gnosticism to Greek philosophy, astrology, mystery religions, magic and even Indian sources, and many of today's biblical scholars would like to keep this grocery list of influences in place.[20] This suggests a Church, then and now, trying to eradicate legitimate expressions of Christianity because they did not conform to dictated patterns of belief and ritual, not because they were intrinsically alien. Like all growing bureaucracies, the Church progressively organized itself into existence by measures of standardization and control, but at the same time organized itself out of existence as these ever-tightening measures displaced and eventually replaced Christianity's original vision. Basically, there were no such people as 'Gnostics', just Christians with a different appreciation of spiritual truth in relation to Jesus and his message.

Such a notion will not go down well with Christian scholars, but I think it has been adequately shown that there are very good reasons to believe that this, and not the standard line of argument, is the more probable. Paul's extraordinary Christology was taken over by orthodoxy and literalized, whereas those who properly understood that Christology throughout the communities knew that the standardized version of the faith handed out by Rome was an absolute travesty of deep spiritual experience. Decades of high-quality meditational practice among Christians was thrown out of court and made inadmissible as evidence for no other reason than that those holding the strings of power lacked the will and capacity to pursue the enlightenment of the mind and the heart into the depths of their own being. Satisfied with a surface mouthing of credal notions which quickly deteriorated into the fear-based complexities and pronouncements of Church Councils, this exponentially growing bureaucracy succeeded in dismantling its own inner life and replaced it with an outer shell of conformity and emotional instability. The psychopathology of a future Church which would repeatedly tear out its own living heart and eat it alive was firmly in place.

GNOSTIC CHRISTIANITY

From being viewed as a Christian heresy to being viewed as an independent religious movement and not a Christian heresy, Gnosticism became for some scholars a pre-Christian movement, and ended up as an attitude towards existence. But one view in particular – that of Walter Bauer (1934) – is described by Dr Pagels as having 'opened up new ways of thinking about gnosticism'.[21] Bauer's idea of Gnosticism comes very close to my own contention that this body of religious experimenters was not a Christian heresy at all but a legitimate expression of early

Christianity. He is ultra-careful in how he couches interpretation, but there is no mistaking what he is saying – the Gnostics considered themselves to be the original Christians, and classified orthodox Christians as 'false believers'.

With the discovery of the Nag Hammadi texts in 1945, numerous scholars applied themselves to the task of translating and interpreting these explosive writings. The resultant view was that Gnosticism was a 'widespread movement that derived its sources from various traditions'.[22] Some of the texts confirmed what the Church Fathers had said about the Gnostics' being highly imaginative, but much of the literature proved to be 'distinctly Christian'.[23] A few texts showed little or no Christian influence whatsoever, but because it is virtually impossible to date the Nag Hammadi corpus, and the texts showing little Christian influence are more probably late than early, the argument for a Gnosticism independent of Christianity cannot properly be upheld.

In his introduction to the The Nag Hammadi Library, the general editor, Professor James Robinson, states that the collectors of this library were Christians, and that many of the essays were composed by Christian authors. We are told that this is not at all surprising, for primitive Christianity was a radical movement intent on the reversal of values and the replacement of the known world with a utopian ideal. Jesus' followers reaffirmed the stand he had taken against authority, and for many he came to personify his own teachings. Robinson goes on to speak of how the original circle of Jesus' followers broke into two streams, one practical and one utopian, and of how the Church as a growing organization concerned itself with 'order,' 'continuity', 'lines of authority' and 'stability'. The only problem was that such concerns 'encouraged a commitment to the status quo'. Those of utopian persuasion saw the bureaucratic success of this highly organized Church as proof that it had gone off track, and its protestations were interpreted by the Church hierarchy as a serious threat. We are then told that Christian Gnosticism 'emerged as a reaffirmation, though in somewhat different terms, of the original stance of transcendence central to the very beginnings of Christianity'.[24]

James Robinson's interpretation of Gnosticism as being a version of the original stance of Christianity is a step in the right direction, but it is a step which continues to overlook Pauline

Christology (backed by Jesus) and the influence of *gnosis*-oriented Samaritan Christians on the formation of the early Church. And Robinson's next idea that 'changed circumstances' caused real divergences from original Christianity may in fact be quite inaccurate. This reflects R M Grant's idea that Gnosticism emerged due to the breakdown in religious beliefs (Jewish and Christian) after the destruction of Jerusalem in 70 CE, but I think this now questionable. Christian Gnosticism of the late first and early second, centuries certainly diverged from Nazarene teachings and the teachings of the emerging orthodox Church at Rome, but it probably reflected quite accurately Samaritan Gnostic tradition with its roots in Jewish Arabia and elsewhere.

Treading a careful path through this minefield of possibilities, Robinson talks of a 'departure from the original language' of early Christianity, and allows this 'departure' or 'divergence' to underpin and explain orthodoxy's rejection of the Gnostics and their final exclusion as heretics. But at the same time he is well aware of Paul's rejection of what he calls Christian 'Judaizers' (the Nazarenes), mentions their mutual rejection of him, and eventually states that the Christian heresy-hunters (the early Church Fathers) 'clearly identified Gnostics as Christians'. In spite of having nothing to say about the influence of Jewish Samaritan Gnosticism on Paul as a theologian, he does recognize that the Samaritans were both Gnostics and Jews, that they worshipped the same God as the Jews and the Christians, that they 'built upon Jewish or Old Testament traditions', and that the concept of a Christian Gnosticism is now firmly established.[25] We are next reminded that prior to the discovery of the Dead Sea Scrolls the Essenes were as unknown as the Gnostics were prior to the discovery of the Nag Hammadi library, and that the Persian-based light-and-darkness dualism of these Essenes 'then moved forward towards Gnosticism'.[26]

All the links and reasons and arguments for accepting that a widespread Christian Gnosticism more ably reflected the Christianity of Jesus than the credal notions of orthodoxy are now so clearly available to us that it is difficult to imagine specialists' continuing to deny them. And the fact that later there were non-Christian forms of Gnosticism sporting many of the same ingredients does not detract from this picture. Such a situation is quite in accordance with Gilles Quispel's proposal that Gnosticism originated in a potentially universal 'experience of the self' projected into religious mythology. The challenge concerning the origins of Gnosticism issued to historians by the German academic C Colpe, referred to directly by Dr Pagels, indirectly by Henry Corbin, and backed now by the observations of Simone Pétrement, suddenly becomes pertinent: infinite regress to ever remoter periods of time and culture afford us nothing – the history of Gnosticism takes up roughly where Essenism breaks off.[27]

Pétrement tells us that in 1950

it was acknowledged that Jewish elements were more important than Iranian elements in Gnostic myths, and especially when the Nag Hammadi discovery showed that some Gnostic works celebrated James the Just, the head of the Jewish Christians in the time of Paul, scholars were inclined to think that the opposition previously made by historians between Jewish Christianity and Gnosticism was a false opposition; that the Gnostics in no way felt themselves to be opposed to Jewish Christians, and that the latter were also themselves Gnostics, perhaps even the source of Gnosticism. It seems to me, however, that the earlier idea was closer to the truth. Jewish Christianity, in its beginnings at least, does not seem to have been Gnostic. Rather it represented an interpretation of Christianity very different from that of the Gnostics.[28]

I've quoted this passage in full because it contains a series of important observations which, when spliced with Schonfield's general thesis concerning the Nazarenes, and aligned with Kamal Salibi's contribution concerning the ancient Nasara, fold into one another and cease to be contradictory. First of all, Pétrement points to the fact that Jewish and not Iranian elements are more important in relation to Gnostic myths. Then she mentions the rather odd fact that some Gnostic texts 'celebrate' Jesus' brother James, whom she designates 'leader' of the Nazarene Christians. Then she points out that there was a reversal in scholarly opinion, so allowing Gnosticism to be aligned with Jewish (Nazarene) Christianity. Then she says that it not only became respectable to think of the Nazarenes as Gnostics, but even consider them the *source* of Gnosticism. But not so, she finally concludes. It seems closer to the truth to say that Nazarene Christianity was not at first Gnostic but that it may have become Gnostic later on.

When weighed against our own findings, Pétrement's observations and final conclusion slip into place with a precision seldom found when dealing with obscure periods of ancient history.

Jesus' brother James, *not* Peter, was the leader of the Nazarene Christians in Jerusalem. Gnosticism sprang from ancient Nasara (Nazarene) doctrine, but it was Paul, not James, who developed this doctrinal anomaly, and it was James the *orthodox* Nazarene-cum-Essene who rejected it. So in effect Pétrement and the scholars she quotes are each correct in their own way. Yes, Gnosticism did spring from Nazarene beliefs (the heterodox branch which saw Issa as divine), but the Nazarenes of Jesus' time were of the orthodox branch, and it was Paul (at the direct instigation of Jesus) who introduced and developed the alternative strand of Nazarene doctrine in alignment with Samaritan-cum-Israelite beliefs of similar, if not identical, origin. And yes, the Nazarene community of James did eventually succumb, in part, to Gnostic teachings, so confusing the issue, but at the same time showing that Nazarene thinking had always flirted with doctrinal disaster – hence Paul's attempt to get the Nazarenes on side. Later, Pétrement asks where we should look to find pre-Christian Jewish Gnosticism, for among scholars, she says, it is always presupposed but never demonstrated. Perhaps the publishers of Kamal Salibi's book *Conspiracy in Jerusalem* ought to post out a few copies to help settle this question once and for all.

It is thought probable that the Nag Hammadi library was buried in a jar to save it from the searching fingers of Christian heresy-hunters from Rome. Orthodox Christians would not have done this: they would more likely have burned these codices. Burial in a jar was the method used for preservation; burning was the method of elimination. The burning of the great library at Alexandria by fanatical Christians at the end of the fourth century marks orthodoxy out as not only narrow-minded but downright dangerous. When Christianity became the officially approved religion of the fourth century, the tables were turned and the victims of Roman persecution became the persecutors. Dr Pagels records that 'Christian bishops, previously victimized by the police, now commanded them.'[29] To own a book denounced as heretical was to be classified as a criminal. Books considered heretical were burned and destroyed, their owners arrested and punished. In the fifth century, the Abbot of the White Monastery at Panopolis in Egypt threatened the heretics thus: 'I shall make you acknowledge . . . the Archbishop Cyril, or else the sword will wipe out most of you.'[30] And for what this white-hot

anger, this seething hatred? Principally because the Gn
claimed to have discovered a self greater than the conscious
self within the self which when known automatically dismantled
religious parochialism. The Gnostic teacher Monoimos admirably
summed up this realization when he said:

> Abandon the search for God and the creation and other matters of a
> similar sort. Look for him by taking yourself as the starting point.
> Learn who it is within you who makes everything his own and says,
> 'My God, my mind, my thought, my soul, my body.' Learn the
> sources of sorrow, joy, love, hate . . . If you carefully investigate these
> matters you will find him in yourself.[31]

To Gnostic Christians, the idea that salvation could only be found
within the confines of Church orthodoxy was an utter nonsense.
Deep within itself, the human spirit was free; a politico-religious
institution enamoured of power could not reveal that. And
neither could it *sense* it. Its senses were all taken up with
superfluous intellectual notions allied to its unconscious desire for
power, wealth and status. Specific issues such as the organization
of authority and the role of women in the Church revealed
that the Gnostic Christians 'shared a fundamental religious
perspective that remained antithetical to the claims of the
institutional church'.[32] This fundamental religious perspective
held that everything needed for salvation could be found within
the human psyche – the psyche was the 'gateway' to sacred truth.
Ritual instruction was available to initiates, and such initiations
were part of a system or discipline which enabled individuals of
both sexes to confront, and be confronted by, the deeper aspects
of their own natures. Coded systems of expression were in use to
designate what might be expected at the different internal levels,
and powerful chanting techniques involving strangely articulated
vowel sounds were used to still the chatter of the conscious mind
and direct the flow of conscious energy. Hippolytus reports that
Simon Magus claimed that an infinite power resided as a latent
condition in all human beings, and that this power was the root of
the universe.[33] And there was much talk of 'silence' and 'depth'
and 'energy', and of 'holy powers' that could be communicated
with during out-of-the-body experiences. There were even
'mighty energies' which had to be handled with great care and
respect. And finally there was some kind of mysterious break-
through into a new kind of consciousness where a greater self

took over from the lesser self. Orthodoxy, on the other hand, offered the Creed, the confession of simple beliefs about Jesus, baptism and the Eucharist. Widespread although Gnostic Christianity was, attractive as it certainly was to many, it was orthodoxy that won the day – the mass of the people simply found it easier to follow a clearly defined belief system than to take up the disturbing task of facing their own natures.

GOD AS ALIEN OTHER

A N Wilson says that for Paul, Jesus was a 'new being' who heralded the existence of a 'new type of humanity'.[34] For Gnostic Christians, this 'new type of humanity' could only arise when individuals interacted with the mystic Christ at the appropriate levels of consciousness. To believe in the Christ was not enough; one had to 'experience' the Christ at the archetypal level. Even an experience of the mystic Christ because of intense belief was not enough – such an experience was merely emotional, of the mind and not of the heart, of being. Emotional attachment to Jesus might afford great satisfaction, even change the whole tenor of the surface life, but it did not afford Knowledge, Wisdom or Revelation, and it did not constitute real transcendence.

As a regulatory force on human behaviour, the Creed was useful, the discipline of the Church of social benefit, but it had to be followed up with in-depth teaching which allowed each and every Christian the opportunity to become 'whole' within themselves, not merely 'good'. The emphasis had to be taken away from sin and guilt and redirected towards the enlightenment of the mind through the penetration of illusion. *Gnosis* was 'insight', not the acceptance of dogma. The self was something to be known, understood and appreciated, not something that had to be squashed out of existence because it was intrinsically evil. Evil and good were related; they were not separate. At the level of physical existence, evil and good formed a dualism, but at the level of the Godhead, which was *outside of time* and *beyond cause and effect*, they were one and the same. The God worshipped by orthodox Christians and Jews was a creation of the mind, a projection, an illusion, an objectivized intuition. The God of the Gnostics was the God which truly existed by *not existing at such a banal level*.

Orthodoxy had great difficulty with such ideas. Thoroughly institutionalized, it required an objectively existing God with whom it could interact as an 'object out there somewhere'. Yet its own higher theology contradicted such a view – the existence of God being denied phenomenal objectivity for obvious reasons. In Clement's theological vision, God the Father was 'infinite' and 'inexpressible', apprehensible only through 'grace' and 'revelation'. And as Clement was well aware, First Causes were difficult to discover and hard to describe. He points to the central issue by saying: 'For how can that be spoken of which is not genus, differentia, species, individual, number, accident, subject of accident?'[35] God could not even be described as the 'Whole', for that implied spatial extension and God was the creator of the whole universe. God was therefore without dimension or limit, without form and necessarily nameless, beyond such concepts as 'Good', 'Mind', 'Existence', or any other name we might append for the sake of communication. For descriptions derived from qualities that could not be applied to God – He was *beyond* 'quality', and as such beyond all objective knowledge. And then comes Clement's integrated Gnosticism: 'But the Son is Wisdom and Knowledge and Truth and all that is akin to these, and he admits of demonstration and explanation.'[36] Faith in the Cosmic Logos is vital, but faith *without* knowledge is an incomplete state. God the Father brings us *from* faith *to* knowledge by means of the Son (the Cosmic Logos as a divinely expressed archetype), and knowledge of the Son and the Father which follows the Gnostic Rule – the rule of genuine *gnosis* – is an intuition and apprehension of truth through 'the Truth'.

There was in fact not much wrong with the Gnostic conception of God, or with its idea of the Son as a divinely expressed archetype; it resonated perfectly well with the deepest of Jewish and Christian attempts to express the inexpressible. Where the difficulty lay was in the Gnostics' baffling claim that the 'objectivized' God of the Christians and the Jews was a blind and insensitive creative demiurge which had no knowledge of a Higher Power. Orthodoxy could not get at what that meant with its then available theological tools, and ultimately this was the rock on which Christian Gnosticism perished. The reason for this is now blatantly obvious, but it is still not properly evaluated by present-day Christian thinkers: the Gnostics had simply discovered the vital link between religious expression and psychological comprehension – a link which Carl Jung would resuscitate and delicately express, much to the annoyance of the Jewish philosopher Martin Buber.

The Gnostic demiurge was the creator of evil (the world) because it constituted that element in human perception which caused 'differentiation' to arise – in other words, the unruly and untamed ego complex was compelled, as the book of Genesis describes, to 'name the beasts'. From a compulsion towards language and ever greater objectivization, there arose the recognition (creation) of the world and the separation of consciousness from what is termed the paradisaical or unconscious state. In control of the senses, of the mind, this ever strengthening central factor in consciousness eventually projected its own image onto the cosmos, imbued that image with human emotions, needs and desires, and the whole religious bandwagon of authority-bound beliefs about this God was set loose to bedevil humanity. This was the essence of all religious conflict, the hidden cause of human despair and brutality, the shadow across the face of God which would not go away. And yet at every stage of religious and social development, the intuition of something greater, something more profound, something majestic, universal and ungraspable accompanied each parochial religious outburst – there was *another* God, but this God was far too alien and unknowable, far too frightening to approach. Acutely aware of the God reasoned into existence by the ego, William Blake would centuries later pen his rejection of this baleful figure:

> Lo, a shadow of horror is risen
> In Eternity! Unknown, unprolific,
> Self-clos'd, all-repelling: what Demon
> Hath form'd this abominable void,
> This soul-shudd'ring vacuum? Some said
> 'It is Urizen.'[37]

FIFTEEN

THE SPIRIT OF TRUTH

*The Resurrection as a dynamic metaphor for waking up to the
nature of reality, the Holy Spirit as a 'presence' allied to that reality,
and the realization that fixed patterns of belief stifle our ability to
respond to our creative depths.*

The Gnostics knew that Jesus had eventually died an old man,
and this raw historical fact cancelled out the notion of
his resurrection having ever been a special event. He had quite
simply survived with a little help from his friends and gone on to
discover and communicate important things about God. The
Gnostic Christians possessed information on Jesus suppressed by
their orthodox counterparts, and their codices reflect this
information in bits and pieces of actual history and snippets of
conversation between Jesus and his disciples which reveal an
enlarged version of Jesus from that of the four gospels. Turning
the Resurrection into the dynamic metaphor that to be 'raised
from the dead' meant simply that one was 'awake in a new way',
they released its powerful existential meaning, spiritualized the
whole event through elaborate scriptural exegesis, brought it into
line with Jesus' private teachings, and simultaneously undermined
the notion of Apostolic Succession claimed by the orthodox
Church. All in all a clever series of moves which attempted to set
the record straight.

Dr Pagels tells us that what interested these Gnostics 'far more
than past events attributed to the "historical Jesus", was the
possibility of encountering the risen Christ in the present.'[1] To
orthodoxy, Jesus had physically resurrected and disappeared into
heaven; for the Gnostic disciples of Jesus in the Nag Hammadi
texts he was available through 'visions' *on a regular basis*. In the
Gospel of Mary, Peter is suspicious of those who claim to see the
Lord in visions, and that in spite of the fact that along with Paul
he claims the same gift. To Peter's disgust, Mary as Gnostic

initiate claims not only visions but the Lord's *continuing presence*. In this codex, as one would expect, Peter represents the conservative camp.

What is of interest here is that this 'continuing presence' is involved in teaching. Dr Pagels picks up on the fact that the Gnostics' claim to see the Lord through inner visions has political implications, but it may also be that the term 'visions' was sometimes a cover for Jesus' actually being physically present. Why should the earliest of these Gnostic gospels be viewed differently from their orthodox equivalents or from the Acts, in which the term 'vision' is used to describe highly utilitarian meetings with Jesus? It is likely, however, that a proportion of these vision stories were actually visions, for as Dr Pagels has shown, there is a possibility of Eastern influence in some of the texts[2] (or a parallel religious development), and this might account for the multiple guru-type appearance-transmissions in the minds of Jesus' followers. (I have met highly intelligent Buddhists who claim to have had such transmissions from their living teachers.) But there is also the fact that the later Gnostic writings were probably inaccurate representations of early texts, not true facsimiles. Professor Morton Smith surmises that Jesus may have hypnotised his disciples during their baptismal initiations, but I think this unlikely – at least, I do not think such a scheme could explain everything that happened after the Resurrection. Paul was not a disciple, and it is Paul who is recorded as having been most frequently visited by Jesus.

Standing up to Peter's accusations of falsity, Mary triumphs and vindicates the Gnostic challenge to the Church's now established triple order of bishops, priests and deacons. It is interesting to note at this point the similarity between Mary's response to Roman Catholic orthodoxy, and Paul's earlier response to Nazarene orthodoxy – they both claim not just equal authority but an authority which *surpasses* that of the original disciples due to *immediacy of contact*. This was probably because Jesus, as the elder brother, and therefore the legitimate heir to the Davidic throne, carried more authority than James in spite of his probable role as Teacher of Righteousness and *second* Messiah. And the reason for this extended authority is that the Gnostic Christians, like Paul, are in possession of an authority given directly to them by Jesus prior to his death. As we have shown fairly conclusively that Paul was himself a leader of definite

Gnostic sympathy, this should come as no surprise. And neither should it come as a surprise that after Jesus' death, James is known to have considered himself to be a 'messiah' – a rather strange notion if the consensus line is taken, but not at all strange if James is viewed as the priestly Messiah over against Jesus as the regal messiah.

Playing with the theme of resurrection, one Gnostic teacher tells his student (Rheginios) not to suppose that the Resurrection is an apparition or fantasy – it is the world that is the apparition, not the Resurrection. Remarking on this incident from the *Treatise on Resurrection* found at Nag Hammadi, Dr Pagels writes: 'Like a Buddhist master, Rheginios' teacher . . . goes on to explain that ordinary human existence is spiritual death. But the resurrection is the moment of enlightenment.' She then quotes this extraordinary teacher's evaluation of resurrection, and we learn that coming back from the dead means 'the revealing of what truly exists . . . and a migration into newness'. To understand this, we are told, is to be spiritually alive; it is to be resurrected from the dead *right now*. And then comes the key statement: 'Why do you not examine your own self, and see that you have arisen?' And again, those Christians who say they will die first and then rise have, according to this unnamed teacher, got it completely wrong. What they must do is 'receive the resurrection while they live'. So runs the *Gospel of Philip*, and the text finishes off with a flourish: 'it is necessary to rise "in the flesh", since everything exists in it.'[3] I am indebted to Dr Pagels for this list of statements.

How strange that Christian orthodoxy has never really fathomed or satisfactorily explained what such sentences mean. They have almost always been interpreted as bizarre prattlings and pushed aside as irrelevant. But they are not irrelevant. There is a hidden meaning in such statements, and it carries exact information not only on how it is possible to perceive the world differently, but on how to immediately bring about this change in perception. And as stated elsewhere, not just in terms of existentially seeing through the rather obvious inadequacies of society, or of being thrust unasked into a basically brutal universe (many Christians of the early second century found this fact disturbing), but in terms of a change in perception so dramatic that it is eventually life-transforming. These Gnostic Christians were in possession of a teaching which cut a swathe through orthodoxy's theological blunderings, and that teaching was the root of all advanced Gnostic schools of transcendence. In her fascinating and extensive book *A History of God*, Karen Armstrong puts the Gnostic vision into a sensible context:

> Eventually this type of Christianity would be suppressed but we shall see that centuries later Jews, Christians and Muslims would return to this type of mythology, finding that it expressed their experience of God more accurately than orthodox theology . . . These myths were never intended as literal accounts of creation and salvation; they were symbolic expressions of an inner truth.[4]

More accurate indeed.

Paul's concept of the Grand Design was in esoteric alignment with Gnostic explorations. To Paul, Jesus was not God, he was God's 'first creation', the revealed archetype of his intentions – this was also James' belief. Paul's ideas were grounded in Jewish-Arabian teachings and in the mystical speculations of the Essean-Essene. To Paul, Jesus was important because at his baptism he had received the 'gifts of the Spirit' promised to the Messiah.[5] As Messiah, Jesus is the second Adam, the *Adam Kadmon*, the great archetype expressing God's purpose. And so Luke's genealogy of Jesus travels right back to Adam, who is 'the son of God'.[6] And Paul is fully schooled in the esotericism of his time and people, in the language and symbols of the Jewish mystery schools and of the great Gnostic teachers. He speaks of 'angels' and of 'powers'; he claims to have known someone (probably himself) who reached the 'third heaven'; and he believes implicitly that each Christian must depend on the Holy Spirit to guide them into *all* truth.

The Jesus of Roman orthodoxy was quite different. Reduced to a singularized pagan version of the Jewish conception of a 'nation' influencing God's attitude because of its holiness, Jesus is theologically manipulated into being a heretical literalism, a straitjacketed representative of ideas disconnected from the main body of developed Jewish-Gnostic teachings. Mightily stepped down from being a reflection of God as Shekinah, the idea of the Light Adam as Jewish Messiah slowly emerged, developed, and became transformed through Jewish-Christian *gnosis* into the psyche's archetypal zero meridian point. From there it was brutally literalized by Roman orthodoxy into a pagan mystic Christ and theologically turned into the heresy of God incarnate in human flesh. Quite a jump; quite a journey; quite an exercise in human ingenuity.

But should Roman orthodoxy be so sorely castigated for rein-
venting the Jewish Messiah as Supreme Being? The Church may
have turned into an authority-bound institution which eventually
lost sight of its basic premise, indeed of its very foundation, but
without it, surely, the correcting force of Christianity would not
have survived – Gnostic Christianity, whatever its merits, simply
lacked organizational capacity. And with the demise of Christianity, Rome would never have been conquered spiritually, or
barbaric customs regulated, or social fear alleviated, or systems of
humane judgement invented. Knowledge of the world and control
of the world would have been set back by centuries. If Gnosticism
had won the day, if everyone had been finally directed 'inward'
instead of 'outward', if sin and guilt had been swept under the
psychic carpet and the great surge of learning swapped for
the tomfoolery of meaningless vowels endlessly intoned, then the
result would have been an arresting of the whole intellectual life
of the West.

True? Untrue? Half-true?

Carl Jung was of the opinion that the Unconscious – the dark,
fertile root of the psyche of which we are *consciously unconscious*
most of the time – must eventually be recognized as existing, and
carefully approached if 'wholeness' is our goal. This dark root of
the psyche is conceived of as a territory, a vast territory within
which it is possible to get lost. It would seem that the Gnostics
learned how to gain entrance to this territory, and with all the
skill of intelligent explorers methodically mapped each step they
took. But there are of course two territories. Above this dark,
subterranean land lies the Realm of Light – what Blake called *The
Land of Ulro*, and Czeslaw Milosz has defined as 'that realm of
spiritual pain such as is borne and must be borne by the crippled
man'.[7] Lord of this realm is the human ego, central and aloof and
certain and often absolute in its opinions. 'I am God', says Urizen.
'What I loose on earth, will be loosed in heaven.' This latter
remark, culled from what is quite obviously an additionized text
in the gospel of Matthew, and prefaced (by myself) with Blake's
intuitive vision of the ego playing God, amply shows that
Christian orthodoxy has a great deal to answer for – the many
benefits of Western civilization have not necessarily come to us
because of Christian orthodoxy but, more often than not, *in spite*
of Christian orthodoxy. But Czeslaw Milosz's statement does
temper this somewhat: it is perhaps *necessary* that the crippled

man bear the pain of the *Land of Ulro*. What am I saying? I am trying to say that if there is an ontological base to reality, then whatever the shape of that reality, we have to bear it to become whole. But what a pity that so many human beings have had to suffer so much, for so long, for all the wrong reasons.

SOPHIA IMPRISONED

Karen Armstrong asserts that after the destruction of the Temple the Rabbis began to talk of the Holy Spirit (interchangeable with 'Shekinah'), of a 'presence' capable of making itself known in a rushing wind, a blazing fire, the clanging of a bell, or even in a sharp knocking sound.[8] Literal as these descriptions seem to be, they are obviously coded terms for depth-experiences of a mystical or psychic nature, and reflect New Testament terminology. The Rabbis were also of the opinion that when God descended on Mount Sinai each Israelite had experienced God differently – that is, subjectively. Armstrong comments on this fact thus: 'God had, as it were, adapted himself to each person "according to the comprehension of each".'[9] She then quotes an important Rabbinic insight: 'God does not come to man oppressively but commensurately with a man's power of receiving him,'[10] and tells us that God 'could not be described in a formula as though he were the same for everybody'.[11] This, in a nutshell, was what the Gnostic Christians believed. Everybody experienced God differently, within the limits of their own capacities, their own gifts, and this meant that the presence of God could not be standardized. Change God into a doctrinal formula suitable for mass consumption and you effectively closed the door on Christianity's inner archetypal resonance.

Similarly with the gift of the Holy Spirit. The gospel of John, usurped for purposes orthodox *and* Gnostic, tells us that Jesus breathed on his disciples to endow them with his authority. 'Receive ye the Holy Ghost. Whose soever sins ye remit, they are remitted; and whose soever sins yet retain, they are retained'.[12] This reflects Matthew's gospel, in which Peter is singled out and given special authority by Jesus. Both passages reveal orthodoxy consolidating its power with a little bit of not-so-subtle interpolation. But the stakes in Matthew are much higher; it is no longer 'sins' we're dealing with, it is now 'prohibitions' and 'permissions'. The injunction now reads: '. . . whatsoever thou shalt bind on earth shall be bound in heaven: and whatsoever thou shalt loose on earth shall be loosed in heaven.'[13] The reason we know for sure that these texts have been interpolated is that they make Christian orthodoxy all-powerful – the Holy Spirit is changed into a commodity and allied to episcopal authority. Those who receive the Holy Spirit are *in charge*. Oddly enough, it is over the gift of the Holy Spirit that Peter savagely denounces Simon Magus. Or is it Paul he savages? And is it perhaps the other way around?

From being a gift which *all* Christians were supposed to receive to properly kick-start their spiritual life, the Holy Spirit was eventually siphoned off and changed into that which passed mysteriously and invisibly from bishop to bishop, and ultimately from Pope to bishop to divinely signify apostolic appointments. Reduced to the rather vague term of 'comforter' (*parakletos*) for the masses – a term borrowed directly from the lost Arabian gospel of the Nazarenes – the Holy Spirit became the guiding force behind Church doctrine; that is, it became the conduit through which doctrinal change or modification was made. *Guided* by the Holy Spirit, the Holy Father was able to make decisions and press into service doctrinal formulations believed to be sanctioned by God's direct inspiration. All in all, a neat little situation with which no one could argue – particularly when the idea of 'infallibility' began to float around vaguely in the background to double-anchor such propositions in eternity. 'I am God', says Urizen. 'What I loose in . . .' But all quite differently expressed in Christian Gnosticism where the Holy Spirit was symbolized by *Sophia* (wisdom), given feminine characteristics (creative power), and made more to resemble the 'still small voice' of Elijah's desert experience.

Known also as 'the Spirit of Truth', this presence within not only strengthened the individual, it also taught and clarified spiritual truth for the individual.[14] In John's indisputably gnostic gospel Christians are informed that the Holy Spirit as 'comforter' will guide them into *all* truth, and that the many things Jesus hasn't got time to say right at that moment will be later communicated to them through this interior presence.[15] No mention here of bishops or deacons or any other intermediary, just a promise of direct communication with the Father through the Holy Spirit. Picking up on this important point, Michael Grant writes:

The earliest attestation to an expected Second Coming of Jesus is in a letter of Paul. But even thereafter it did not take root everywhere, since the author of John's gospel, at a considerably later date, is still able to write as if he who will come at the end of the world will not be Jesus at all but another figure altogether whom he describes as the Counsellor (Paraclete) or the Spirit. And similar indications that the visitant may not be Jesus have survived in the other gospels as well.[16]

In Christian thought these figures have been collapsed into one another – Jesus *is* the 'comforter' or 'counsellor' that will attend upon the individual Christian. But as Michael Grant has shown, there is every reason to believe that Jesus was talking about a phenomenon *other than himself*, a phenomenon certainly related to himself as Shekinah (a 'reflection' of God on earth in the form of Messiah), but ultimately separate from himself because he was not literally God. This is where all the problems arise: Christian thinkers lost sight of what Jesus represented in strict Jewish/ sectarian terms. And the reason that this interior 'counsellor' (Spirit of Truth) will teach the disciples what Jesus himself had not had time to teach them is because he himself possessed the *same* internal source of truth, not because he was teaching them on some other level of being. Ideas of a subtle and delicate nature have been sandwiched together and made a nonsense of by a later orthodoxy intent on establishing their now paganized version of Jesus as indisputable ruler of the whole universe.

But there is a problem here in relation to the Qumran Essenes. J H Charlesworth reveals that the idea of the Holy Spirit at Qumran went beyond that of a visitor from within. He has this startling fact to pass on:

At Qumran 'the Holy Spirit' is angelic and a separate being (hypostasis); it is not the holy spirit of God but 'the Holy Spirit' from God. As F F Bruce perceived, it 'is remarkable' that a phrase or term so seldom found in the Old Testament and apocryphal writings should appear so frequently and importantly 'in the New Testament and other Christian literature, and also in the Qumran texts'.[17]

Remarkable indeed. For if the term 'Holy Spirit' is not used technically in the Old Testament as in the New, is seldom found in apocryphal literature, and the only other source for it is in the documents of Qumran, then that rather suggests that that is where this literal conception of the Holy Spirit came from in the first place. This rather places Christian scholars in a double-bind, for there, tantalizingly within reach, is a form of proof for a belief other than the one I'm proposing, but it cannot be touched. And because a quite literal Holy Spirit at Qumran is proposed by Barbara Thiering – that is, a human being carrying the 'title' of Holy Spirit – the plot thickens further still. Charlesworth adds that the Qumran Essenes 'developed the concept of "the Holy Spirit" to substantiate their claims against the Temple priests and their choice to live in the desert'.[18]

As Gnostic Christians eventually claimed, and Jesus confirms in the gospels, there would come a Spirit of Truth which would assist Christians in their spiritual researches. But because Jesus was not literally this Spirit of Truth, did not ascend into the sky, dematerialize, and then turn up again as this Spirit, it can be said that 'visions' of him after the crucifixion probably refer to a physical and not a phantom Jesus being present. And when we read in the Gnostic gospels that Mary and many another spoke with Jesus after the crucifixion, we can take at least some of these incidents at face value, not just write them off as spurious inventions. The confusion over these issues was brought about by orthodoxy's attempt to smooth Jesus' post-crucifixion presence out of existence. Hence his immediate elevation into heaven. It was necessary to get him out of the way so that a double problem could be solved – the problem of the Kingdom's not having arrived, and of Jesus' eventual physical death. With a Grand Return at some distant date, the inauguration of the Kingdom of God on earth could be indefinitely postponed. And what better way to control the disparate elements of the Church than to amalgamate Jesus with the promised Spirit of Truth and make him not only an upholder of the status quo but the orthodox arbiter of all levels of Christian spirituality. And so necessary a move, for the Pauline camp to which Jesus had without doubt belonged was infused with the most potent of Gnostic ideas concerning individual freedom: the Holy Spirit was available to *all* Christians. It was not just a 'power' for the legitimizing of orthodoxy's new dynasty of Roman emperors in embryo, it was a disruptive power within the individual which released the energy of change.

MORE ABOUT THE KINGDOM OF GOD

In the Old Testament, legitimate prophets of God were recognized as having the Holy Spirit within them: they spoke the 'truth' because of this indwelling Spirit. In the eyes of the sectarians John the Baptist had revived the antique age of the prophets, and as John's replacement, Jesus himself was referred to as a 'prophet' on many occasions. The whole point of being a prophet was that such figures saw God active not only in the past but in the present and in the future. For the Jews, history had not stopped with Moses, as it had done for the Samaritans. In historical terms God's kingdom was yet to come. And with the coming of this kingdom would come the blessing of Israel, and the other nations. This blessing was, according to Jesus, two-fold: the blessings associated with intuiting the Kingdom's presence before it actually appeared, and the reality of the Kingdom physically present at a later date.

But the New Testament seems to give three senses, or levels, in which the Kingdom could appear:

(1) in the midst of the group;
(2) within the individual; and
(3) as a physical phenomenon.

In Matthew's gospel Jesus bewilders the Pharisees by saying that his casting out of devils means that the Kingdom of God has drawn near to them;[19] and in Luke's gospel he tells them that the Kingdom of God does not come through 'observation', but that it is within them.[20] In other texts he talks of the Kingdom's imminence, of its being in the near future, and of it already beginning to materialize because of his mission. Of course, after Jesus' actual death at an advanced age, the idea of the Kingdom's arriving on earth physically was abandoned as an expectation, and the rather grandiose notion of Jesus' making a dazzling physical Return out of the woodwork as triumphant Messiah died with him. Way back in 1870, a worried theologian put it this way: 'Christ either deceived mankind by conscious fraud; or he was himself deluded; or he was divine. There is no getting out of this trilemma.'[21] Because it is fairly certain that Jesus had no intention of deceiving anyone, and that he was not divine, it can be said with confidence that his expectation of the Kingdom of God's arriving on earth physically was an understandable

delusion allied to Jewish tradition and sectarian hopes. Sim[
put, he was not perfect.

Michael Grant is of the opinion that the term 'within' ought
be translated as 'among', so giving us the idea that the Kingdom is
in the process of arriving. And he tells us quite clearly that the
'within' school of thought so favoured by Tolstoy 'belongs to a
realm of ideas subsequent and alien to Jesus'.[22] This would be
tenable if orthodox beliefs had constituted what the early
Christians held to be true, but as we have seen on a number of
levels, orthodoxy only partially reflected, and more often than not
distorted, what Jesus actually stood for. On one level the idea of
the Kingdom's being 'within' was not subsequent and alien to
Jesus: it was basic to his teachings as his mission to the Gentiles
through Paul's elaborate Gnostic Christology attests. So it can be
said that the Gnostic gospels reflect not some hairbrained
theological scheme developed after Jesus had departed for heaven,
but a psychologically difficult-to-interpret scheme of thought
based on the Kingdom within as an experience. The physical
Kingdom of God never materialized as Jesus hoped it might, but
in the end the interior Kingdom proved much more efficacious.
Yes, there was a subsequent development of the idea of the
Kingdom, and it did take place after Jesus was really dead and
gone. But this idea was not a fabrication foisted on him by people
alien in thought and deed; it was a teaching intrinsically related to
the many lost or muddled aspects of his own spiritual discoveries.

Dr Pagels clears up the whole problem when she writes that the
Gospel of Thomas 'ridiculed those who thought of the "Kingdom
of God" in literal terms, as if it were a specific place'.[23] The
Kingdom was 'inside' *and* 'outside'. It was in fact 'spread out
upon the earth', but only those who had had their eyes opened
could see it. The 'sons of interior knowledge' who had gained the
power to 'speak their own names' (who were aware of their own
intrinsic identity) were aware of the Kingdom within and without.
As noted earlier, Dr Pagels equates the Kingdom with a
'transformed consciousness', and this seems to describe advanced
Gnostic experience – the Kingdom was in a sense a mode of
perception, a *state of being* which allowed creation to reveal its
invisible presence, and the self to reveal its stable centre. The
Kingdom was already there, here, in fact everywhere; it just could
not be detected when the limited self was in full control of the
senses. Governed by the demiurge (the differentiating ego), an

individual might speak of God's Kingdom, of God's truth, of God's majesty, but what that individual's ego conceptually intuited as God was quite likely to be an inflated version of itself projected onto the archetypal horizon of consciousness. One break of the ego's hold on perception, and there immediately appeared a rudimentary awakening of the senses which, if developed and sustained, eventually afforded a spiritual awakening of a permanent nature.

THE HERCULES MYTH

In his wonderful and sometimes frightening book *The Dream and the Underworld*, the psychologist James Hillman reminds us that Hercules 'had to go mad, literally, in order to understand the underside of things'. He adds, interestingly, 'maybe because his journey to Hades was a mess'.[24] So what went wrong for Hercules? Hillman describes the problem succinctly: he simply did not know how to behave in the underworld. He arrives full of aggression, draws his sword, fires an arrow into Hades' shoulder, slaughters the underworld cattle, wrestles the herdsman, chokes Hades' dog Cerberus, and claims to have overcome death. The enemy of death, Hercules stands heroically at the entrance to the underworld and defies what he does not understand. For he is not fully divine; he is only half-and-half. And when the human half attacks the divine half, the human half automatically assumes the role of the divine portion – in its own estimation the Herculean ego is then in control *as a god*. Isolated from its psychic background, or 'underworld', from its depth, from its dark interior silence, the Herculean ego becomes psychopathic, and even when involved in good works and charity and apparent love of neighbour cannot but end up 'warlike' and 'controlling' because of its missing half. Hillman says that the question in mythology is whether Hercules was ever initiated into the Greater Eleusinian mysteries. If not, then he missed out in that change of consciousness which effectively carries the ego from dayworld life to nightworld death.[25]

This 'change of consciousness' is identical to that other change of consciousness described by Dr Pagels in relation to the advanced Christian Gnostics. Such Christians came to know themselves at the deepest levels and discovered that their own mind was the 'father of truth'.[26] But this 'mind' was not the conscious mind, the ego-driven mind or the Herculean mind: it was mind functioning in the grip of deep meditative silence. Such silence released the knowledge that one was not needful of dogma· or doctrines or another's authority – the mind could be *disciple to itself*.[27] The author of the *Gospel of Philip* tells us that truth must be clothed in symbols, that it did not come 'into the world naked, but . . . in types and images',[28] and James Hillman tells us that the heroic ego literalizes the imagined because it lacks metaphorical understanding. Through ignorance of the imagined and the imaginative the heroic ego effectively shuts down creative communication between psychic levels and reduces itself to an automaton – it sees without seeing, hears without hearing, knows without knowing.

The knowledge gained through communing with oneself in silence and in depth was not of a hit-and-miss variety. These Christian Gnostics knew exactly what they were doing, and why. There were meditational programs, levels of initiation, techniques of spiritual discipline. They knew that nothing could be accomplished without stilling the mind, without reducing the chaos of thoughts and emotions coursing through the human biosystem. And it wasn't just a matter of a few pictures in the mind's eye followed by the claim of personal revelation, as some of the Church Fathers seem to suggest. It was more often than not many years before the disciple broke through and experienced the divine presence in image and symbol. There was often psychic turmoil, even terror, and the disciple's progress was continually monitored by an experienced teacher. The policy of such teachers was that disciples must advance step by step through nine specific levels of instruction, and at each level find the answers they sought within themselves. At the advanced levels of internal activity, 'holy powers' offered specific instructions, and with the assistance of dramatized initiations the disciple as student was trained to fully open up to God. Dr Pagels remarks that historians, because they are generally intellectuals, tend to 'interpret the controversy between orthodox and Gnostic Christians in terms of the "history of ideas", as if ideas, themselves assumed to be the essential mainspring of human action, battled (presumably in some disembodied state) for supremacy'.[29]

This captures the exact nature of the problem the early Church Fathers had with their Gnostic Christians – they considered their teachings mere variations of orthodox doctrine, and did not realize that such symbols and images reflected the spiritual baseline out of which the rudiments of ancient Nasara Christianity had first appeared. Christian Gnostics were not simply batting 'ideas' backwards and forwards; they were deeply involved in an experiment ancient in origin. The images and symbols they recorded from their own minds were not cerebrally generated or imaginatively fabricated in the ordinary sense: they were 'rescued' from the depths of the psyche, compared and interpreted, and used as signposts for those who came after.

It is extremely difficult for some people to understand what this means. Amputated from their inner life, from the subtle movement of images and symbols within their consciousness while asleep, or in reverie, they consider real only those things which their senses objectively validate. Emotion is relegated to the level of the irrational, its refined expression as *evaluative feeling* virtually ignored. And yet great poetry, or music, or mathematics may move us deeply, elicit a sophisticated response from us that could not exist without emotion's play within the biosystem. For emotion, unruly as it is, dangerous as it often is, can sometimes be brought to a pitch of sensitivity so great that for a moment it transforms our consciousness. To cultivate this potentially sophisticated baseline of awareness is to open a door within the psyche which affords glimpses of the self far beyond its surface limitations.

Trying to communicate something of what this might mean on the creative level (I'm working from memory here), D W Harding writes of 'flotillas of meaning coming across the horizon of consciousness which should not be intercepted too soon'.[30] We have to slow down: we have to learn to wait on the threshold and allow creative awareness to form within us as delicate sensations. We have to learn not to 'intercept too soon' what might arise unexpectedly from our own inner depth – that is, pull too quickly out into the light of conscious scrutiny some half-formed realization. It's a waiting game. It's a play of forces within the psyche. It's the beginning of communication with a self other than the one we consciously equate with our personality. In *Descartes' Error*, Antonio Damasio is quite certain that we need the help of emotion to function properly. He tells us that the 'fragile instruments of rationality need special assistance'. But there is of course the danger of being influenced adversely by 'biological drives such as obedience, conformity, the desire to preserve self-esteem, which are often manifest as emotions and feelings'.[31] But basically emotion is the key element in learning and decision-making.

As C G Jung so accurately states: 'Self-recollection . . . gathers together what is scattered and multifarious'.[32] James Hillman speaks of this kind of inner work as 'cooking'. This 'cooking of the psyche' through paying conscious attention to it produces, as one would expect, new concoctions. These concoctions rise as symbols, and these symbols are experienced as 'densities of feeling' long before they begin to appear as images. Hillman teases us towards a comprehension of what all of this might mean when he says:

> Emotions are crafted into distinct materialised shapes. Their language . . . specifies what's the matter in the emotion. The fingers of the complexes may tear one to shreds in the night, for sleepers are workers; but as they tear, they shape each emotion into its form.[33]

We are each 'baked' or 'cooked' in a different way during sleep, and often awaken to ourselves full of silent wonder. But to consciously approach one's inner domain is to take this natural process one step further; it is to wait, alert and uninterfering, for what psyche has to offer, to avoid erecting predetermined conceptual filters at the threshold and end up erroneously interpreting everything offered in either a psychologically trivial or a religiously dogmatic fashion.

BORN OF THE SPIRIT

John's gospel contains a powerful passage which fundamentalists and evangelicals love to quote:

> That which is born of the flesh is flesh; and that which is born of the Spirit is spirit. Marvel not that I said unto thee, Ye must be born again. The wind bloweth where it listeth, and thou hearest the sound thereof, but canst not tell whence it cometh and whither it goeth: so is every one that is born of the Spirit.[34]

This verse, innocent as it may look, is in fact highly subversive in terms of orthodox Christian beliefs. Christians of a more literal persuasion contend that it points to what separates the 'saved' Christian from the 'churchgoer'. They mean by this that the

saved Christian has taken Jesus into his or her heart as an
experience, and by doing so gone through the process of 'rebirth'
mentioned by Jesus to Nicodemus. This is however to
dramatically misunderstand what John is trying to say – and that
in spite of verses seemingly advocating something of this nature.
The problem is that Jesus had a new script written for him, a
script which makes him quite literally the Son of God, and by
inference God incarnate. And because of a lack of comprehension
concerning Jewish mystical teaching and sectarian speculation,
the writer-editors of the gospels bent everything about Jesus in the
general direction of their pet pagan notions. This absurd idea
eventually took root to such an extent that its underlying meaning
in relation to the Messiah (Christ) as Archetypal Man or Light
Adam was lost or only dimly perceived, and the result was an
enforced literalism which grew steadily and eventually hardened
into the dogma of the Creed.

   Christians whose spiritual life seems to rest wholly on the
assumption that Jesus was somehow God will buck at such a
suggestion, but they will just have to buck and settle down and
start thinking if they are really serious about the Christian
experience. To ignore what has been going on in the New
Testament since the first century is not only to ignore history, it is
to ignore the struggle for power in which all groups with a strong
'message' engage. After the destruction of the Jerusalem Temple
Roman Christianity went through many persecutions, some of a
horrendous nature, survived to tell the tale, and eventually
overcame Rome's pagan hierarchy and transmuted it into
a Christian theocracy. No mean feat! Gibbon believed that
Christianity was directly responsible for Rome's decline, that it
subversively undermined the Roman system of government and
caused it to collapse from within. Whatever the mechanics of the
situation, the result of Christianity's presence in Rome was an
eventual switchover from pagan beliefs to a state-controlled
religion holding up Jesus the failed Jewish Messiah as its central
focus – an amazing cheek, when one thinks about it!

   From being a criminal crucified by Rome, Jesus by proxy ended
up on the throne of the Caesars! But what a Jesus. Not the Jesus
we know from the New Testament. Not the Jesus meek and
mild who loved little children. Not the Jesus who wept over
Jerusalem's rejection of his messianic message. And certainly not
the Jesus who speaks so eloquently to Nicodemus in John's

gospel. No, another Jesus displaced the Caesars: the Jesus of orthodoxy's hungry imagination – the Jesus who had devolved from archetypal expression of God to that of literal Lord of the Universe. The demiurge had incarnated and was on the loose, and God help you if you didn't bend the knee. From being the persecuted, Christians became the persecutors, their ego-inflated Jesus lording it over the hearts of men and women *from within*! No escape from this Jesus – *this* Jesus fully backed orthodoxy's claim to power.

The Jesus who said to Nicodemus that those who were born of the Spirit were like the wind, that the Spirit was in principle 'unpredictable', was not the Jesus who ended up in Rome. And neither is he the Jesus who rules the imagination of today's Christian literalist. This Jesus understood that to be intercepted by the Spirit of Truth is to be confronted not with a fixed pattern of belief but by a subtle intuition of truth from deep within which constantly challenges too precise an interpretation of the spiritual life. The spiritual life is not a 'belief', and neither is it experiences allied to beliefs: it is an opening up of the psyche, an introduction of the mind to its own extraordinary dimensions, a bringing into dialogue of the so-called conscious mind and the so-called unconscious mind. This is not to demote the spiritual life to the level of the psychological, to rob it of its transcendent dimension: it is to enlarge the narrow religious definition of the spiritual and recognize that ultimately there is no real point of differentiation between the two when one confronts one's own depths in silence, when the 'noise of belief' has stilled and the still small voice of a more sensible self has the chance to be heard. There is a voice, but it does not shout slogans or quote biblical texts: it subsumes everything conscious by its density, by its intense and sometimes electric presence. And it is not evoked by wailing prayers or rote prayers or haranguings of the heavens; it is evoked by shutting up, by recollecting (gathering together) the self in silence until all that is scattered and multifarious and disparate and daft comes together into a new and illuminating pattern.

This was how it was for the advanced Christian Gnostics, their more magically-minded brethren being as deluded by the novel and the purely psychic as any indiscriminating New Ager of today. The Roman pagans, slaves to the unseen world, were into birds' livers, the stars, monsters, poltergeists and demons, and the low-grade Gnostics were right on their heels with just as many wonders. But as with 'prophecy', and the many other gifts of the Spirit extant in the early Pauline Church prior to the Roman invasion of Judea, Roman orthodoxy would have trouble accommodating such untoward and unpredictable elements. It would reinterpret the 'freedoms' talked of by Paul, and like the Nazarene orthodoxy from which it sprang place anything which contradicted Church doctrine on the heresy hit list. The Spirit could no longer 'blow where it listeth'; it had to knuckle down and obey along with everyone else what had been loosed on earth by Christ's apostolic representative – the Bishop of Rome was flexing his pontifical muscles.

THE CREATIVE FEMININE

The Unconscious does not actually exist – there is no such realm. The Conscious does exist, but we are mostly 'unconscious' of its existence, and as such doubly unconscious of what lies above, below, or beyond our normally limited conscious state. This is the nature of our spiritual dilemma. Spiritual? The 'spiritual' is, as we have seen, allied to the Spirit of Truth; the Spirit of Truth is allied to the Archetypal Man; and the Archetypal Man, being without fixed gender in spite of ancient chauvinism, is allied to the Light Adam within which male and female coexist – 'androgyny' is the name of the game. Paul the astute theologian agrees: 'in Christ there is neither male nor female'. Simple when you have the key; utterly obscure when you don't. Capable of unravelling all sorts of complexities when the archetypal theme is understood; subject to profound intellectual error when the archetypal key is either ignored or lost. Paul's 'Christ' is *not* God: he is the archetypal key by which the many different aspects of psyche can be accessed if Christianity happens to be your religious paradigm.

Gnostic Christians battled with the idea of androgyny because they knew from experience that powerful energies (Powers) were operative within the psyche. Opposites balanced one another. Male and female principles joined and separated within consciousness and produced very different conceptions of spiritual truth. Goodness jostled evil, and evil good. The divine source was seen as a bisexual Power which produced male-female beings within which the feminine resided as ground of being. In the

Genesis myth, Adam was described as two beings in one – he bore
the female within him.[35] In the opening book of the Bible it did
not say that God made man in *his* image, and leave it at that; it
said something quite different. 'And God said, Let us make man
in our image, after our likeness.'[36] Us? Our? Dr Pagels reports
that to the Gnostics creation was androgynous, and God dyadic[37]
– *he* was not one, but two, just as the Genesis narrative suggests:
the other half of the 'us' was *she*. Is this then the same God who
later declares that he is a jealous God, and that beside him there is
no other? In the Gnostic texts this God is seen not only as
arrogant, but as having forgotten that he too issued from the
feminine. It is said that his 'mother' scolds him for believing that
he is alone, and calls him a 'liar'. Because this God is none other
than the differentiating demiurge who perceptually creates the
world, and the demiurge is the human ego utterly ignorant of its
feminine baseline, it can be seen plainly that what the Gnostic
Christians were talking about was not some external set of
affairs, some grandiose drama played out in the heavens, but deep
and subtle movements within the psyche dressed up in the coded
language of mythology. They had simply understood what made
them tick as human beings, and were fascinated. Any wonder that
there was such an explosion of symbols and images?

What a contrast to the orthodox Christian Church which had
narrowed everything down to a grocery list of beliefs *about* Jesus.
If you believed this story as opposed to that story you were either
out, or in, or highly suspect, depending on who was running the
theological show. Dr Pagels notes that everything belonging to
the Gnostic Christians – secret gospels, revelations, mystical
teachings, etc – were kept out of the New Testament canon and
branded as heretical. And then she identifies the central issue: 'By
the time the process of sorting the various writings ended –
probably as late as the year 200 – virtually all the feminine
imagery for God had disappeared from orthodox Christian
traditions.'[38]

Advanced Gnostic experience had revealed what the conscious
mind, the ego mind, the Herculean mind did not wish to know:
everything created by the heroic ego was founded on feminine
energies, on dark, fertile proddings from deep within the psyche.
There was an obscure realm of inner activity which the ego-
personality nucleus of consciousness could not fathom, feared to
enter, yet was ever fascinated by. For like the Sirens who tempted

Odysseus and his crew to abandon the safety of their ship, the boundary of being similarly suggested a relaxing of conscious controls. Here, then, was the basic reason for Gnosticism's exclusion by orthodoxy – it equated Gnostic creativity with the dark and mysterious creative power of the feminine, saw *any* acceptance of this 'power' as a giving way to pagan cultic practice, and drew back in fear.

How paradoxical.

According to the Gnostics, the male creator god's mother (*Sophia* – Wisdom) was no longer acknowledged by her son (the isolated ego-personality) as the 'matrix' within which ideas and symbols and images formed as if by magic – in fact the son no longer knew that the 'mother' existed. Alone and apparently in control, the son lorded it over the creation and demanded worship. Genuinely frightened of such notions, orthodoxy fashioned fail-safe mechanisms for its fast-growing membership and created theological filters in the form of prayers and hymns and gospels to stop heterodox notions coming through the mind's subjective screen. For once allow entrance to such subversive energies, and the whole fabric of sensible, coherent religion would crumble into dust. After a faltering start, Christianity had finally come of age, dismissed its irrational attachment to unconditional freedom of the spirit, and inaugurated a whole new spiritual direction for humanity based on a set of potent ideas stripped of their sectarian background.

The story of the 'son' and the 'mother' succinctly captures the relationship between the ego and the matrix of consciousness within which it resides. The symbolism is exact: the ego is unconscious of its place in the scheme of things, whereas the creative matrix is discreetly conscious of everything going on. And this applies to both men and women. Both are governed by the ego complex. Both are capable of limited evaluations of their own natures. Both are blind to the fact that they function in an unconscious or unaware manner most of the time. And both think that their particular natures constitute the better approach to life and living. But in fact *both* are quite wrong. The ego-personality, whether male or female, is always limited and blind and silly and irrational and daft and didactic when amputated from its dynamic psychic base. And yet it isn't really amputated from that base at all – just blind to the fact that such a base exists. The mother is always there, patiently there, lovingly there, and every-so-often terrifyingly there. She waits mostly in the wings, but sometimes one can feel her breath on the back of one's neck. And it is her drawing close which constitutes discovery and the surprise of creative insight, the alighting suddenly and unexpectedly on some idea or image or symbol which delicately and subtly expresses some unforeseen truth. However, due to a pathological closing of doors between psychic levels, the ego, left to its own devices, produces out of itself sharp-edged, hard, conflicting ideas which bedevil the world in spite of their often highly polished and 'reflective' exteriors. And yet even this description is inadequate, for the creative matrix of consciousness is *always* involved – it is just that its offerings are more often than not amalgamated with the ego-personality's limited schemes and values. A revolution needs to take place in consciousness before such stutterings of perception and conception can be transformed into a living dialogue within psyche.

In his monumental study of creativity, *The Act of Creation*, Arthur Koestler accuses the mathematician Henri Poincaré of being unable to shake off the rationalist hubris of the nineteenth century. We are told that Poincaré worked by intuition, but that he could not allow intuition to be anything other than a mechanical process governed by conscious aesthetic ability. Yes, there was another realm, but it was really just a sorting office. Calling this other realm the 'subliminal self', Poincaré sings its praises but admits to being unable to accept that it might actually be superior to the conscious self. This is to say that the unconscious – or to be more precise, that of which the conscious mind is mostly unconscious – is capable of doing what the conscious mind cannot do. Koestler says that Poincaré relegates this apparently superior self to the role of 'an automatic mixing machine in the basement'.[39] According to the Gnostics this 'mixing machine in the basement' was in fact another self, a Self with a capital S with which it was possible to set up a living dialogue. But there are dangers in trying to set up such a dialogue, and these dangers – perceived but only dimly appreciated by the rationalist Church Fathers – were beaten up into an attitude of terror and rejection because no one seems to have understood the difference between 'underground' and 'underworld'.

James Hillman draws our attention to the fact that there are two Greek words, not one, to denote things to do with the Great

Mother of analytical psychology. These words are *gē* and *chthōn*.[40] The first is of the earth and in it; the second is below the earth and beyond it. Hillman ably tackles the complexities of these two terms and introduces a third, *Demeter*, to describe 'growth', so giving us *a Demeter-Gē-chthōn* complex. The real question, says Hillman, 'turns on how one regards earth'.[41] I agree: *that* is the pivotal question. We are then told that 'nature' and 'earth' have psychic functions as well as terrestrial functions.[42] And there are correspondences: darkness of soul and blackness of soil; psychical depths and concrete depths; initiation mystery and fertility rite. Everything is interconnected; the polytheistic mind did not always separate the three levels. In relation to late first- and early second-century Christianity, this is an important observation. On the level of literal-mindedness, this tendency to merge Demeter and *gē* and *chthōn* was, I think, the established Church's basic mistake when interpreting Old Testament descriptions of the varying Goddess cults, the 'high', as opposed to the 'low', mystery initiations of the Greeks, and the vibrantly alive ideas put out by their Gnostically-inclined fellow Christians at their best: they simply saw no difference between fertility rite and initiation mystery, between underground and underworld, between depth experiences of psyche and limited cultural expressions of death and resurrection allied to nature. And more importantly, they saw no difference between Shekinah and Jesus. Blind to the different levels, they formulated a belief system out of dynamic archetypal materials, but denied those who accepted this belief system the right to pursue these living symbols to source. Those who did so were immediately in trouble.

But all of this only happened later. The infant Church did not have these particular problems. The feminine was not feared either by the early Christians or by Jesus himself. In fact the reconciliation between male and female talked of by Paul was both social *and* spiritual; as with the Gentile position in relation to the Jews, and slaves in relation to freemen, so too with the rights of women in relation to men. Here, in a sense, was the Kingdom of God becoming visible. But things were still moving slowly. Paul would have to advise slaves to obey their masters.[43] And as Dr Barbara Thiering points out in her book *Created Second*, Luke's gospel reveals that 'Physically and genetically different people – the blind, the lame, and the deformed – are all welcome at the heavenly banquet.'[44] The many levels of exclusion believed to be right and proper by the Jews and the Essenes had been annulled by Jesus, and underlay in part the split from Qumran Essenism and John's old-fashioned sectarianism. This was why he had had such a high profile, why he was listened to so eagerly by the masses – he had turned religious custom and prejudice on its head.

The Church that Paul founded at Jesus' instigation fully implemented the new freedoms for women which so separated it from Jewish, Nazarene and general Essean-Essene orthodoxies. It was not an easy thing to do. He bucked the system where he could and suffered at the hands of the Nazarenes because of it. Women were not debarred from holding ecclesiastical posts, or from the exercising of spiritual gifts – in fact the very opposite was true. Dr Thiering writes: 'The gift of preaching and teaching was not denied to women in the apostolic Church, as the case of Priscilla and the existence of an order of prophetesses shows.'[45] So those verses suggesting that Paul was in favour of women's remaining silent, etc, are textual tamperings flatly contradicted by other verses of an earlier period. To deny that this is the case is to be in the grip not just of bad scholarship but of an irrational fear of the feminine.

The freedoms initiated in the Pauline Churches must have been on everyone's lips. Rabbinical law stated clearly that women should sit apart from men in the synagogue to ensure that 'uncleanness' was not at any level communicated. Paul drove a proverbial truck through this law by stating that such uncleanness had been 'nailed to the cross'.[46] Women, along with slaves, the deformed and the foolish, were to have a new life, a new status, a recognition of their intrinsic value never before experienced. And Jesus had inaugurated the basics of this attitude towards women himself. He conversed with women about things that mattered; he shocked his disciples by talking to a Samaritan woman about his Messiahship; he had women as part of his entourage; he depended on these selfsame women for financial support; he did not decline being touched by women; and if the Gnostic gospels have anything going for them historically, he taught and initiated them into the deeper aspects of his teachings as the Bethany incident seems to suggest.[47] To ignore such an obvious revolution in attitude to women in the New Testament is not just to be out of step with the facts, it is to be utterly insensitive to psychological reality – behaviour backed by the Spirit of Truth (the psyche in creative dialogue with itself) does not veer wildly from age to age: it reveals underlying consistencies and coherences.

But there is one other issue to address before bringing this chapter to a close – the issue of supposed differences between male and female consciousness. Dr Thiering captures the essence of this problem by reminding us that the move towards reconciliation between male and female clearly spells out the early Christian ideal of men and women being recognized for what they are at base: human beings. She puts it like this: 'most of the time, I am just being human, and so is he.' She adds, 'It is an error of classification to say that there is a "male" or a "female" personality, the error of confusing the part with the whole . . . There is a primary unity between us, and it is this that the Christian ideal underlies.'[48] This 'primary unity' is to be seen in the many shared gifts men and women possess, in the 'qualities' they express. The Christian ideal is not doctrinal precision, it is 'personhood', not priesthood. Emancipation from sexism is not women acting like men, or men acting like women: it is men and women discovering their mutual strengths and gifts in *androgyny*. Androgyny is the baseline of being, the mysterious boundary where men and women melt into one another without trace.

SIXTEEN

THE JOURNEY TO HELL

The Church's masterstroke in defining the human psyche as the underworld, the making of our creative depths into Satan's dark domain, and the demonizing of that domain as an alternative to the Christian path.

In the introduction to his study of Carl Jung's *Seven Sermons to the Dead*, Stephan Koeller records an interesting conversation between two Hungarian refugees in the American Information Service reading room in Innsbruck. The year is 1949. It is bitterly cold, and snow is heaped up outside. One of the refugees is of impressive appearance and intellect, an ageing ex-member of the Jesuit Order and the youngest professor ever to hold a seat at a Hungarian university. The other is a young and precocious student of philosophy with a desire to become a priest. As it turns out, Stephan Koeller is himself the second person in this duo, the older man's interest in him stemming from his fascination with the Gnostics. Professor 'J', as Koeller calls him, is about to come into possession of a strange book called *The Seven Sermons to the Dead* written by Carl Jung in 1916. This treatise, offered as if from the hand of the Gnostic teacher Basilides, is concerned with the deeper aspects of Christian Gnosticism. Talking about Jung prior to the arrival of a certain Father 'Z' with the book in question, Professor 'J' refers to Jung as *Hexenmeister*. Translated into English, this rather odd word turns into 'warlock', and 'warlock' of course refers to a male witch, or *wizard*.[1]

Many Churchmen still perceive Jung in this role, and it is interesting to note that the term *Hexenmeister*, used initially as a form of compliment, as pointing to Jung's extraordinary ability to delve deeply into the mystery of conscious and unconscious processes, has now changed into an attitude of smug rejection among rationalists. Merlin, it could be said, has been encased in ice for a second time. James Hillman says, 'Gnostic writings . . . describe a snow-and-ice region of the underworld.'[2] Jung and Merlin and lots of others are held captive in such a realm in the Christian imagination. To Dante, this iced ninth circle of the Inferno was the archetypal hell inhabited by Lucifer the Light-bringer.

THE UNDERNEATH OF THINGS

To Plato, 'archetypal ideas' were the fundamentals of existence; or, as he put it in the *Laws*: 'Everything is full of gods'. In his excellent intellectual history of the West, *The Passion of the Western Mind*, Richard Tarnas explores the pivotal ideas which the great minds of Western civilization have produced, and draws our attention to the fact that for Plato the archetypes constituted 'the intangible substrate of all that is tangible'.[3] In the context of this book, however, what is of prime interest is the question that Tarnas asks of himself, the question whether in fact Plato believed that gods or mythic beings were intrinsically related to the intangible substrate of reality, and to the archetypes as ruling principles. Or was it just a way of talking? Tarnas states that Plato at times favoured a more abstract approach, but that he again and again returns to a 'distinctly Homeric tone'[4] and treats serious philosophical and historical matters in 'the form of mythological figures and narratives'.[5] And then with a flourish he shows just how intertwined in Plato's thinking the idea of gods and mythic beings and archetypes and substrates of reality really were: 'Depending on a specific dialogue's context,' he explains, aiming at a valuable insight, 'Zeus, Apollo, Hera, Ares, Aphrodite, and the rest could signify actual deities, allegorical figures, character types, psychological attitudes, modes of experience, philosophic principles, transcendent essences, sources of poetic inspiration or divine communication, objects of conventional piety, unknowable entities, imperishable artefacts of the supreme creator, heavenly bodies, foundations of the universal order, or rulers and teachers of mankind.'[6] And the point aimed at? Simply that Plato's gods defy too precise a definition, and that he infused his most philosophically earnest moments with such figures when language threatened to destroy 'the numinous essence of things'.[7] No fool, Mr Plato – and, as we shall see, fully aware of the nature of the problem facing all human beings in relation to their encounter with reality.

Plato knew what Carl Jung would find out, Western intellectuals would forget or try to ignore, and orthodox Churchmen
would ignore and attempt to suppress – that the non-spatial
universe of our psychic nature conceals 'an untold abundance of
images which have accumulated over millions of years of living
development and become fixed in the organism'.[8] Referring to
what Poincaré called the 'subliminal self', Jung uses the term
'psychic non-ego', and talks of this ego filling the non-spatial
space of consciousness with images of such potency and power
that all we can do at our best is misunderstand them. What we
cannot do is deny their existence. Throughout our lives we each
experience such images in dream or in reverie, and on occasions
are psychically overpowered by their extraordinary presence
within us. Jung tells us that it is a mistake to treat an archetype 'as
if it were a mere name, word or concept'. It is actually 'a piece of
life, an image connected with the living individual by the bridge
of emotion'.[9] This again raises the issue of emotion's role in
psyche – a subject of great importance. Tarnas points out that
Plato may on occasions use mythical beings as pure allegory and
nothing else, but his archetypes are multidimensional and move
fluidly between one level and another, Eros at one moment
standing for the sexual instinct, at the next as a metaphor for the
'philosopher's passion for intellectual beauty and wisdom'.[10]
This capacity to work on multiple levels of meaning and
expression in relation to myth and archetype is then defined as a
'unique confluence of the emerging rationalism of Hellenic
philosophy with the prolific mythological imagination of the
ancient Greek psyche'.[11]

The psychologist James Hillman suggests that our inability to
properly relate to our 'complexes' is because we have robbed
them of 'image' and 'voice'. In our attempt to rationally
understand our deepest psychic levels, we have left ourselves
stranded with mute abstractions subject to the whims of
intellectual interpretation. Plato was not merely emerging from a
stage in Greek intellectual development, he was immersed in
a creative archetypal stream which afforded him insights and
ideas and a grasp of reality so profound that many present-day
philosophers are still writing footnotes on other philosophers'
footnotes about him. To imagine for one minute that Plato was
somehow less than he could have been because of his use of
mythical beings and archetypes is erroneous. Without those

'images' and 'voices' and 'emotional stirrings' his creative imagination would not have penetrated to the depth that it did. And into the depths he did go, hook, line and sinker. And from up out of those depths he returned with an enriched appreciation of the geometry of form and a subtle and telling sense of how consciousness worked in conjunction with reality.

One reason for so much about the world coming up out of the psyche is the fact that the psyche is dynamically linked to the world. Karl Kerenyi was of the opinion that in 'symbols' the world itself is *speaking*. Jung agreed. To him 'psyche' stretched all the way down into the darkness of physical matter. At these deep levels of autonomous functioning psyche was extinguished in the body's materiality, and at base this meant that psyche *was* world.[12] Another level described by Erich Neumann was that psyche projected archetypal images into the cultural canon, caused changes in the real world as a result, and was itself changed by the world in relation to reactions in the collective unconscious experienced as sociological upheavals.[13] This is an important observation, but what Jung and Kerenyi were pointing at is even more important – at least, it is in relation to this chapter. Their thesis was that psyche and matter were intrinsically related. The problem for psyche was that at the higher levels of conscious functioning, at the level of differentiation and abstraction, it automatically lost sight of its deep relationship to body and world and fell into inadequate rationalistic explanations for just about everything.[14] Jung sums up this situation with characteristic force:

> In reality we can never legitimately cut loose from our archetypal foundations unless we are prepared to pay the price of a neurosis, any more than we can rid ourselves of our body and its organs without committing suicide.[15]

The physicist Paul Davies continues to pose the question of whether mathematics resides only in the heads of mathematicians, or if it is in fact intrinsic to the physical world. This is to ask, in another way, whether reality is purposive or whether it is without intrinsic meaning. And it is also to suggest that 'intelligence' has somehow formed out of the stuff of the material universe and that this universe is now scrutinizing itself. Davies puts it this way:

> Through my scientific work I have come to believe more and more strongly that the physical universe is put together with an ingenuity so

astonishing that I cannot accept it merely as a brute fact. There must, it seems to me, be a deeper level of explanation . . . Furthermore, I have come to the point of view that mind – i.e. conscious awareness of the world – is not a meaningless and incidental quirk of nature but an absolutely fundamental facet of reality.[16]

Jung too was of this opinion. In fact, he seems to have believed that consciousness might perhaps be the prime ingredient in the formulation of a general theory of everything. Wolfgang Pauli agreed. Jung and Kerenyi's idea of psyche *as world* seems to resonate with Davies' perception of things reasonably well, and it may be that we are about to rediscover Jung and Kerenyi and many other frontier thinkers.

THE LAZARUS PARADIGM

In his study of pagans and Christians in the Mediterranean world from the second century CE to the conversion of Constantine, Robin Lane Fox cites the question put by Alexandra, priestess of Demeter, to the god Apollo concerning the frequent appearance of the gods to girls and women, to men and children of the city of Miletus: 'What does such a thing mean? Is it the sign of something good?' This question, cut in stone, reveals her seriousness. Fox adds: 'In the old civilised Miletus, the squares and colonnaded streets were stalked by the gods, bringing close encounters into the life of every man, woman and child.'[17] He then equates what was happening in Miletus with Homer's epic poem where the gods mixed freely with human beings, and identifies this question and its answer with 'religious crisis', 'breathtaking anxiety' and 'anxiety and exaltation'.[18] He asks: 'Is it, then, the missing proof of deep unease, the mood of a pagan city while Christians were putting down their roots?'[19]

What should not be assumed is that this kind of intercourse with the gods was everywhere the same in the pagan world. It was not. The Greeks and their neighbours were every bit as blasé about the gods as many Christians are about their own capital-G God. There were levels to the mysteries, and the public version, although ritualized, afforded little more than entertainment and the pleasure of being with friends. No, when the gods really did visit, the pagan mind quaked with fear. There was a distinct difference between going to the gods in the social context, and the gods coming to you in the context of *psyche*. When psyche erupted, everyone held their breath.

In its early years, Pauline Christianity helped produce such eruptions, but with the formation of Catholic orthodoxy such visitations from within diminished until all that was left were desiccated symbols 'stiffened by dogma',[20] to use Jung's description. Any attempt to 'make the journey' to the gods was frowned upon. The underworld was anathema. Why? Because what came up out of the underworld threatened just about everything the Church stood for. The underworld was 'unpredictable', 'contradictory' and 'ambiguous'. Everything in it was 'upside-down' or 'back-to-front'; there was nothing straightforward in it. Once allow Christians to make contact with the inner world of psyche, and they were never quite the same again – they returned from the experience believing themselves to be acquainted with Powers not recognized by the Church Fathers as spiritually legitimate. Such Christians became unmanageable, believed themselves to have the right to assembly without a bishop, spoke gibberish about God, and considered themselves free and beyond the Church's credal rulings. Didn't they realize that Christ had annulled the underworld and the gods by returning from the dead? By his doing so 'all Christians were forever exempted from the descent'.[21]

In *Death and the Underworld*, James Hillman castigates the orthodox Church for having made Lazarus the paradigm for all humanity – eternal life is no longer to be found in the underworld, only in its destruction.[22] The Halls of Hades have to be demolished, the eruptions of psyche stilled like the Sea of Galilee under the Saviour's outstretched hand. Like Hercules, Christ had overcome Hades; 'death' was now 'sin' and defined as 'the last enemy'.[23] The underworld of the psyche was now 'hell', not the realm of the psyche's creative forces. As the domain of evil and the devil, the underworld would be changed into a place of horror, a place of terror, a place to be avoided at all costs. Hillman captures the transition exactly when he says, 'Christianism, in a two-sided masterstroke, both did away with the underworld and horrified it as the perpetual alternative to the Christian path. Christianism or underworld: one had to choose, and who would choose the horror?'[24] The taboos against 'psyche' were in place, and they would be endlessly refined until eventually even the slightest indication of 'underworld' experience would

be interpreted as evidence of 'Satanic' activity. Faust was crying in
his crib.

PSYCHE AND SOUL

Living symbols which rise up from within a human being reveal
dogma to be a lie. Religious formulas for everything pertaining to
psyche kill off living symbols. Symbols which have become overly
familiar are meaningless because they are most probably dead. A
life totally governed by dogma may flow along easily for years,
but when it comes apart, it comes apart like no other. Profound
experience is feared by orthodox Christianity because it favours
the surfacing of what is within psyche. The surfacing of what is
within psyche does not automatically point to psychosis, but to a
'journey' *under*taken – sometimes this journey is *under*taken by
a psyche in *deep* trouble. This journey is Faustian by implication,
but in reverse; it is an 'ensouling' act and it requires a *deep*
relationship with psyche. Psyche *is* soul. To ignore psyche is to
deprive soul of nourishment. Faust is not someone who sells his
soul to gain knowledge; he is someone whose fixation with
knowledge results in a loss of soul – the deterioration of spiritual
capacity in relation to psyche. His damnation is not because he
has sold his soul to the devil but because he never properly
developed a soul in the first place. In Iranian tradition, he who
betrays the pact with life witnesses himself at the end of life as an
atrocious figure. Mutilated, virtually exterminated, and to all
intents and purposes aborted as a human being carrying the
highest potential, the 'betrayer' confronts his own shadow, his
Ahrimanian darkness instead of his celestial mirror of light.

Johann Wolfgang von Goethe, the greatest exponent of the
Faust legend, fully understood the nature of the archetypal level
and did not at any time advocate a superstitious surrender to
forces natural or supernatural. Subhuman abdication of moral
responsibility was anathema to this great mind – hence his
rejection of Romanticism. Tracing Faust's progress back into the
past, he wends his way through the eighteenth and sixteenth
centuries, the Middle Ages and classical antiquity, penetrates
back to the origins of life itself, and comes out into the arms of
what he terms 'the Mothers', the timeless source of all forms
of being – the *feminine matrix*. He was conscious of religion as

'archetypal': that is, he saw all religion as expressing the same ground of being, and was truly Gnostic in his unwillingness to destroy their individual strengths. Truth lay in the embracing of 'opposites', he believed. This was his creative fountain. It was also Carl Jung's.

Although criticized for his rejection of 'analysis', Goethe was in fact fully in favour of analysis, but consciously balanced each act of analysis with an act of *synthesis*. One of his favourite maxims was that analysis and synthesis 'must alternate as naturally as breathing in and breathing out'.[25] This was no Faust; this was an elegant psyche in balance with itself, a psyche which in every expression of art undertaken sought the taming of the Dionysian by the Apollonian – but never in the sense of replacing the psyche's unitive powers with lustreless fabrications of the intellect. He knew that a balance must exist, and in his myth of Faust reveals the soul of Western man at war with itself. In awe of the mystery of the universe as any intelligent human being must be, he was 'as impatient of the sterilities of logic chopping as of the inflations of metaphysics'.[26] So great was Goethe's archetypal presence that on meeting and talking with him in Erfurt Napoleon exclaimed, '*Voilà un homme!*'

Darkness and light. Negative and positive. Good and evil. Faith and dogma. Faith? Isn't 'faith' about believing what the Church teaches? Not at all. Having faith in what the Church teaches is merely 'belief' by another name. Faith proper has nothing whatsoever to do with belief – it has to do with *trust* in the face of cosmic ambiguity and uncertainty, as Dr Peter Cameron attests. Faith throws a new complexion onto the face of matter, or, if you prefer, gives what matters a new quality. Certainty and clarity and belief are not Christian virtues; they are false securities. Radically disturb certainty or clarity and the whole edifice of religious belief shakes. There are too many things not within our capacity to grasp for certainty or clarity to ever take permanent root in psyche. This is to say that beliefs which breed and under-score literal-minded interpretations of archetypal events are acts of spiritual sabotage. Consciously manipulate others through the auspices of such beliefs, and you stand guilty of assisting in the suicide of souls in the making.

But if psyche is soul, how then can we have a rudimentary soul? Simply because it is the dynamic interaction between conscious and unconscious elements of psyche which forms soul. We lose our souls by gaining the whole world and paying no attention to the fact that in the process we have ceased intrinsically to exist as a presence to ourselves. We are not there, or here, or in fact anywhere, most of the time – we evaporate into *process of mind*. When we relate to another, we mostly relate out of an empty base camp, and only occasionally are brought into self-focus by trauma. It takes death and pain and horror to momentarily re-congregate our scattered pieces of psyche and re-integrate them into the semblance of a person. In Basilides' system of *gnosis*, the 'Saviour' was the perfected spiritual man *within* psyche – Jesus perceived as archetypal process and wholeness. On reaching 'perfection' (the subtle balance of conscious and unconscious forces), the self became *real*; that is, it was clothed with a proper (immortal) soul, one that would not revert to its previous lopsided condition.[27] This is to say that immortality is not ours for the rather cheap price of believing in the Jesus story as the Church teaches it – that is to make a nonsense of everything spiritual. Jesus is not a 'something' to be believed in; he is an expression of something innate, something generic, something that already belongs to consciousness as *possibility*. He is the archetype of our growing up, of our maturity, of our coming of age, of our *seeing through* things. He is a metaphor for our coming back to our senses from out of a comatose state. What he is *not* is a once and for all time human sacrifice that we can rely upon to shield us from our own stupidity.

James Hillman says that Christianity and the 'underworld' fell into opposition on the material, functional, and logical levels. He is also of the opinion that we have been 'left in a condition where Christian consciousness and psychological soul-making . . . have been forced into contradiction'.[28] Hillman was my second source for the notion of soul-making. (I will get to my primary source on this fascinating aspect of spiritual growth and comprehension later.) And he tells us that Jung's problem with the 'Christ' figure of Christianity was that it wasn't dark enough to be psychologically stable – opposition to the underworld in Christian teaching had inadvertently *lightened* the figure too much. As an archetype allied to upperworld consciousness only, Christ is made to destroy the underworld, and in doing so becomes the reverse of what he actually stood for as Jesus the Nazarene. Soul-making is a process towards death (Thanatos/ Hades) because it prepares the ego for dismantling and reassembly through a process of *deepening*. To deny the ego the chance to enter into this transformative relationship with psyche is to deny it life, for such a relationship is the equivalent of a resurrection from the dead. Hillman battles against the Christian idea of 'resurrection' because it smacks of a fantasy to sidestep the process of deepening, the difficult and dangerous process of ego dismantling and reassembly. And in line with this he also frowns on the fantasy of 'rebirth' in psychology, and on dream interpretations which pull images up out of the depths like fish and leave them to die stranded and gasping in a foreign environment. I sympathize. But in this instance the resurrection image comes from Gnostic Christianity, and as such is perhaps more properly integrated with psychological reality.

Christianity's long-term historical and theological defence against making 'soul' is not just a problem, it is a literal nightmare which has to be faced if Western consciousness is ever to mature and stabilize. Continue to ignore the root cause of this nightmare, and the daylight psychosis of a civilization in deep crisis will intensify. During the 1930s and 1940s we saw what the disabled collective ego could accomplish, but the chaos of the next conflagration will make that episode in human history look like a mere squabble. We are heading inexorably towards global disaster on more than one front (ecological as well as psychological), and the whole spiritual climate of the Christian West is abetting instead of stemming the coming breakdown. And as I said in the Prologue, this is not scaremongering. Breakdown is virtually inevitable as we progressively harm the planet and lose our nerve in the face of literalist and anarchic forces bred out of our own ineptitude, out of our stubborn unwillingness to appreciate the symbolic images delivered to us from psyche with the respect and attention they deserve. We will not admit to being empty. We will not admit to being at a total loss. We will not admit to being secretly scared to death. The psychosis of alienation, separation, loneliness and rational breakdown is all around us and *in* us, but we continue to mouth either Christian or secular platitudes as a response to our deepest needs. Jung sums up the Church's dilemma thus:

> The advocates of Christianity squander their energies in the mere preservation of what has come down to them, with no thought of building on to the house and making it roomier. Stagnation in these matters is threatened in the long run with a lethal end.[29]

On the level of the everyday, this 'lethal end' is an inability to accommodate any other level of being beyond that of the religiously sentimental: I go to Church because it makes me feel good. I like the singing. It is the only time I feel at peace with myself. It sets me up for the week. Reduced to the level of a rather dry and brittle sponge, the religiously naive individual un-questioningly absorbs and accepts and follows Christian doctrine on most matters. Some have a little more say, but they too are hedged around by a barrage of beliefs which leave them either guilty and at a loss, or smugly self-satisfied. God is in his heaven in spite of the frightful mess of the planet, and the contradiction of his backing the status quo is hardly noticed. The whole spiritual machine has ground to a halt; it is static and stationary and still and stagnant. Locked into a spiral of destructive behaviours which cannot be stopped without stripping our economies, we wake and sleep, sleep and wake, and quite mindlessly go about our business hoping that it will all somehow sort itself out. And all the while we are being nudged from within, sometimes gently, sometimes not so gently, sometimes with the force of a hurricane. Who am I? What am I? Why am I? Where am I? Am I? The Church's answer, as usual, is profound: *Jesus loves me this I know, for the Bible tells me so.*

Jesus was more specific: he gave the world a single sign – the sign of Jonas.[30] Jonas, better known as Jonah, was said to have been swallowed by a whale and to have spent three days and three nights in the whale's belly. Likening himself to Jonah, Jesus pointed to the coming 'ritual' of his crucifixion and burial, and intimated that he too would be incarcerated in darkness for three days and three nights. As he was in fact in the tomb for no more than a day and a half, his reference to Jonah cannot be taken in a literal vein – the story was a metaphor for something. Might it be that that 'something' was a ritualistic journey into the underworld of his own psyche? A journey made through the auspices of a final act of will which completed a spiritual journey and transformed him into another kind of human being? His reference to being 'in the heart of the earth'[31] could signify a process of initiation (in conjunction with crucifixion) which completed a long worked for transformation. If this was the case, and I think there is every reason to believe that something of this nature was going on, then redemption through suffering was not some gratuitous gift dumped on beleaguered human beings of all ages, it was a

condition of psyche finally reached by Jesus himself, a transcendent state available to anyone who chose the path of conscious
suffering. What I mean by this will be explained in detail later.
Suffice to say that some of the disciples took to worshipping him
afterwards. Emerging from the tomb victorious, his presence – as
the New Testament attests – was utterly unnerving.

As with some of the other ideas in this book, Christians will
find this a difficult suggestion even to consider. But as will be seen
later, alternative interpretations concerning Jesus' motives and
aspirations can be forwarded in the face of entrenched dogma,
and these alternatives resonate not with loopy New Age thinking
but with advanced discovery at both the psychological and
philosophical levels. Yes, Jesus had Israel and the Kingdom of
God in mind at the same time, but as the Messiah, as the chosen
Archetypal Man of Israel, he was engaged in something more
than a magical conjuring act; the Kingdom spelt out a 'new
humanity' *on earth*, and he was among its first-fruits.

Yet he still somehow believed in a literal transformation of the
Earth as a result of his efforts. The Kingdom of God was at hand.
It was imminent. It was just around the corner. A man grounded
in his time and culture, even he expected the impossible: the direct
intervention of God in human affairs. The Zealots were
unnecessary. The Romans (the Nazarenes believed) would be
overcome, but not by physical force – the heathen should be left
to God's vengeance rather than opposed by force. The
surrounding nations would realize their mistake and willingly join
Israel in praise of the one true God. But it didn't happen that way.
The Romans blitzed Judea, and Israel was instead dispersed
among the nations. When this outcome became obvious, Jesus
must have done some straight thinking, and a deal of praying.

The 'lethal end' promised by Jung for those who prefer
doctrinal stagnation to that of creative exploration, is a bad
death. It is a psychological fact that if you dam yourself up, you
end up damned. The journey that has to be made by each and
every one of us is not at all easy – in fact, it is very, very difficult.
But it has to be made – consciously made. We either wake up and
get on with it, or stay asleep and 'dream' our lives away. Jesus
stopped dreaming; he woke up. The responsibility of the Catholic
Church today, in conjunction with her Protestant neighbours, is
to assist people to wake up to the 'depths' of their own quite
extraordinary natures, for in the depths their natures conceal

things majestic and unexpected. But before this can be done, our religious institutions have some straight thinking and a deal of praying to do. And it is time they started talking to one another, seriously, before it is too late, before some psychic epidemic wipes us all out and reduces our beautiful planet to ashes. The Christ image, prefabricated and delivered in all its tinsel glory, is again showing its other face, preparing to shock us out of our lethargy with a surprise turn of events – the Kingdom of God is simply too difficult for the collective ego to deliver; hell on earth is a much easier alternative. As Jung points out, the Nazis made a lot of capital out of the idea that Hitler 'was continuing and completing the work of the Reformation'.[32] The imagination of the ego amputated from psyche through systems of distorted belief is truly frightening.

THE NEW HUMAN BEING

The sign of Jonas as profound experience of psyche signals the appearance of the 'new man', the new human being whose physical gender is of no consequence. Jung calls this new man the 'more comprehensive Man, that indescribable whole consisting of the sum of conscious and unconscious processes'.[33] This new human being, this 'whole', is, as Jung carefully points out, the 'antithesis of the subjective ego-psyche'.[34] This Self is not super-human; it is not super-Man released from the pages of a comic book; and neither is it the ego inflated and let loose like a balloon driven by its own meagre system of propulsion. It is the *Anthropos*, the Ideal (in Platonic terms), the Perfect archetypal human being (in Judeo-Christian *and* Iranian terms) residing potentially within each and every one of us. Such a human being is neither male nor female – polarity is swallowed up in full consciousness. In this context 'repentance' has nothing whatsoever to do with 'sin' or 'guilt', it has to do with *awakening*. Once again Jung comes to our assistance: 'The sin to be repented, of course, is unconsciousness.'[35] And as God, in Gnostic terms, is (on one level) the ego-psyche projected onto cosmos, then this God too must wake up to its own limited nature.

This is not as strange an idea as some Christians might think, for has not the fulminating God of the Old Testament been replaced by that of the New? But before there can be conjunction between conscious and unconscious processes, there must necessarily be transition, collision and confusion between such processes,[36] a kind of war in heaven, if you like. The early Church Fathers were truly bewildered by the welter of images and symbols produced by their Gnostic brothers; they considered such productions unseemly. But if one considers that Gnostic Christians were seriously *at work* within themselves, it is not at all surprising that they produced ever new and original expressions of the truth they experienced within psyche. The 'truth', they discovered, was not credal, something to be 'believed' by the conscious mind. It was rather an on-going 'depth' experience which could never be repeated in exactly the same way twice. Yes, there were touchstones, symbols of such complexity and profundity that they did not have to be replaced, but the more basic experiences belonged to individuals, and individuals are what they are by way of difference. Beneath the seeming confusion lay an extraordinary coherence, an exact expression of psyche which the early Church Fathers were quite incapable of handling. As representatives of an orthodoxy whose grocery list of fixed truths could not be tampered with, these upright custodians of the Faith had no option but to condemn their Gnostic brothers and sisters for the sin of *originality*.

Consciousness did not come out of nowhere: it formed within what is termed the unconscious as a 'potentiality', and subsequently became conscious. So it can be said that the ego-psyche (the differentiating principle, or demiurge) *is* the *Anthropos* (the potentially 'whole' human being as Archetypal Man) at root base. The problem is that this potentiality towards consciousness eventually got locked in matter; or, as the Gnostics put it, was 'caught in the embrace of Physis'. This is the key statement, the key concept which, if explored carries us beyond the literalism of some kind of spirit-entity descending from above (from God) into a human body, and reveals instead a dynamic movement within psyche in much the same terms as the philosopher Joseph von Schelling would describe centuries later. Herein lies the terrible secret of the Gnostics, and the exact nature of our human predicament. We are perceptually caught or locked in matter. But as stated, not in the way literalists believe – we are not spirits *imprisoned* in bodies; we are, rather, conscious human beings locked into a process of perception which bedevils our potential humanity, a process of perception from which escape is very, very difficult.

This process of perception is allied to unconsciousness, but it is an unconsciousness belonging to the conscious mind, not to the backgrounding matrix of psyche. What has to be grasped is the fact of our being mostly held in a state of relative unconsciousness during what we term normal daily conscious activity – a hard fact to detect for the simple reason that we are unconscious of being unconscious at the time! But how can such a thing be? How can we be unconscious while conscious? Surely that is a contradiction in terms? *That* was what the Church Fathers did not understand either. Struggling with Gnostic Christian symbolism and terminology, they could not detect the nature of the problem identified by their Gnostic brethren for the simple reason that consciousness, by its very nature, has a blind spot – its own almost permanent unconsciousness of that which is supposedly conscious: the self. The ego spends its time dividing and segmenting the world, both inner and outer, and believes itself to be fully sentient. But it isn't. Its perceptual sentience is incomplete. No more than an automaton most of the time, a bundle of reflexes and stimulus-response mechanisms as any behaviourist will attest, the ego remains oblivious to the existence of the 'self' and drives on relentlessly into whatever has usurped its attention. This means, in essence, that we do not properly exist in such moments because we seldom make any conscious effort to bring our existence into conscious focus. We take our existence for granted. We assume that we are still functioning as a conscious human being, but have in fact ceased to consciously exist and have become a system of habit reflexes. To say, in such a moment, that we are 'conscious', is only to say that we are forever conscious *of*, but hardly ever conscious *as*, ourselves. Like Blake's Urizen, we are far too busy dividing the ninefold darkness to realize that something greater is at our elbow, nudging us, trying to attract our attention. Caught second by second in the embrace of *Physis* (in our constant identification with matter, or with what we consciously 'think' *matters*), we progressively de-soul ourselves and arrive at our death empty-handed.

The words of Monoimos are again applicable at this point:

Seek him from out thyself, and learn who it is that taketh possession of everything in thee, saying *my* god, *my* spirit, *my* understanding, *my* soul, *my* body; and learn whence is sorrow and joy, and love and hate, and waking though one would not, and sleeping though one would not, and getting angry though one would not, and falling in love though one would not. And if thou shouldest closely investigate these things, thou wilt find Him in thyself.[37]

I have used Jung's version of this quote, along with his emphasis on the 'my', because it pinpoints what I wish to draw attention to. But I have to admit (with trepidation) that I think Jung wanders from the point somewhat when analysing this statement of Monoimos. He gets into Indian lore and draws a comparison with the *Kena Upanishad*, wends his way back to the text and notes that even in the second century 'the ego was considered the exponent of an all-embracing totality, the self'.[38] Fine. But I think Monoimos 'the Arab' was asking his readers to detect not just the fact that the ego was very much in control, but that over and against this ego was a 'self' that we must get to know if we want to educate the self that generally runs the perceptual show.

This other self, the 'Him in thyself' referred to by Moniomos, is only brought into focus when the behaviour of the little self, the ego, is tabulated and understood. There are two 'hims' in the text, but only one is capitalized. The first 'him' is the one we must seek, not because it is the best but because we have to understand *how* it works. It makes everything into a personal belonging: everything is *my* this and *my* that. The second 'him' is *Him*, that which backgrounds and, in a curious split kind of way, allows us to observe the oddity of the lesser self's activities. Basically, Monoimos is telling us that we are out of control, that we cannot *do* because we are continually being *done*, that we are in constant opposition to ourselves. But if we properly investigate this fact, if we observe what it is 'that takes possession of everything' in us, then we will discover another self, a self which does not claim things as its own, a self which does not *identify* with the world. To find this other self we too must learn how to restrain the lesser self, the ego complex, from continually flexing its muscles and identifying with the world as image, idea or event. For as we saw earlier, the ego-psyche or demiurge or differentiating principle *is* the *Anthropos* or archetypal being *in potentia* – which is to say that we are, deep within, already free.

Jung tells us that the Gnostics were psychologists, and in quoting Hippolytus, shows them to have been engaged in a very serious bit of psychological/religious research – to be exact, the meaning of the soul in relation to the 'whole man'.[39] For the Gnostics the knowledge of man was conceived of as the beginning of a process of wholeness, and the knowledge of God as the knowledge of perfect wholeness. Even Clement of Alexandria agreed: 'It is the greatest of all disciplines to know oneself; for when a man knows himself, he knows God.'[40] And how was all of this arrived at? Jung spells it out: 'Gnosis is undoubtedly a psychological knowledge whose contents derive from the unconscious. It reached its insights by concentrating on the "subjective factor"'.[41] Subjective, introspective behaviour is not held in any great regard today – it is known to produce all kinds of aberrations. But as the Gnostics discovered, a subjective probing of psyche can produce startling results if it is done in a disciplined context. Such a context already existed with the ancient Schools of the Prophets, the followers of the Way of the desert, the advanced Greek mysteries, and in systems of exercise and breathing and mental discipline from the East. The tools for a systematic exploration of psyche and the religious impulse were available, and the Gnostic Christians, following the clear ground plan given to Paul by Jesus, took up the task.

KNOW THYSELF

Richard Tarnas writes that in Socrates' view 'any attempt to foster true success and excellence in human life had to take account of the innermost reality of a human being, his soul or psyche.'[42] Tarnas adds that Socrates brought a new awareness of the soul/psyche to the Greek mind, and that he established the soul as 'the seat of the individual waking consciousness'.[43] We are then told that he affirmed the Delphic motto 'Know thyself', and that he believed genuine happiness could be found only through self-knowledge and an understanding of the psyche.

But perhaps the most telling observation made of Socrates by Tarnas is that he 'gave the impression of a man unusually at one with himself'.[44] Like the Gnostics, Socrates detested secondhand truth; it was better to self-destruct in dialectical argument, he believed, than to accept someone else's truth as your own. Considered by some dangerous to the stability of the society because of his scepticism about just about everything, he eventually fell foul of a political plot against the Sophists, was classed among them, and met death rather than exile due to his stubborn unwillingness to compromise his philosophical principles. Profound self-knowledge rooted in the depths of psyche made Socrates the kind of man he was, and the man he was expressed 'a truth that was in some sense universal, grounded in divine truth itself'.[45] If something was 'good' or 'true' or 'beautiful' then it was related, so Socrates believed, to an archetypal equivalent beyond time, a level of absolute, perfect existence with which only pure intellect could make contact. Pure intellect? For Socrates, intellect was more than a mere 'tool of the mind', it was 'the divine faculty by which the human soul could discover both its own essence and the world's meaning'.[46]

Tarnas's contribution to an understanding of Greek philosophy in relation to Socrates is of paramount importance because it carefully separates what he terms the 'naturalism of the Ionian physicists and the rationalism of the Eleatics' from the archaic period (Homer), but draws our attention back to the relationship between the empirical and the archetypal as developed by Socrates, and on Socrates' behalf by Plato. An intellectual journey away from such a conception had been going on for some time, and between them, Socrates and Plato reversed the trend and again established the link with the world's 'archetypal' foundation. Tarnas says:

> Divine absolutes once again ruled the cosmos and provided a foundation for human conduct. Existence was again endowed with transcendent purpose. Intellectual rigour and Olympian inspiration no longer stood opposed. Human values were again rooted in nature's order, both of which were informed by divine intelligence.[47]

Tarnas's description of Socrates as 'a man unusually at one with himself' could just as easily be applied to Jesus who, like Socrates, ended up as an archetype in his own right – albeit one fabricated into existence and disastrously skewed from the base archetype of Universal Man which he represented in Jewish religious tradition. Socrates truly represented the Universal Man, the ideal, the archetypal man of Greek tradition who aspired to know himself through a deep knowledge of soul as psyche. Jesus, on the other hand, was hijacked and forced to represent Christian orthodoxy's ridiculously literal idea of a sexual and ethical paragon utterly removed from the real world *and* the deep-structure archetypal world of psyche – perfection at the archetypal level had been changed into a vision of human perfection wrought within mind and body by the ego as demiurge. In ancient Iranian exegesis it was possible for a human being to reach the summit of spiritual achievement and become what was known as a 'non-specific individual, of archetypal individuality'.[48] So writes Henry Corbin in *The Man of Light in Iranian Sufism*. This is to describe spiritual vocation as a relationship with the archetype of 'completeness', something of which Jesus must have been fully aware in his own fashion. Having completed himself through meditation and initiation and reached the level of Perfect Nature, he would then have become, in his own eyes, and in the eyes of others, a living archetype representing the species at its highest level of spiritual evolution. And so he could say that he was not only the Way, but that he was also the Truth, and more importantly for our purposes here, that he was the *Light*. The 'Sons of Light' (the Essenes) would not agree, but only because he no longer shared in the group's warlike aspirations.

The Gnostic Christians, imbued with the same spirit of inquiry as Socrates concerning reality and the place of human beings in it, would harass the Church not so much by what they said and wrote but by the very fact of their existence – they were a constant reminder that something other than an epistemological truth both existed and mattered. But we have a fairytale image of the Church's growth over the first two centuries – a tale mostly told by Churchmen long after the event, and viewed through a theological prism which deflects rather than reflects. Dr Schonfield prises open the situation and reveals a Christianity at odds with Judaism and the Nazarene mother-church at Jerusalem, a Christianity at pains to sidestep identification with the Jesus of Jewish history and concentrate on a paganized version of Paul's Gnostic Christ. The End of Time and the inauguration of the Kingdom of God had not taken place as earlier expected, so the only thing left to do was smooth out of textual existence any embarrassing allusion to Christianity as it had first developed, consolidate the Church's power base, and rein in those elements which tried to keep the earlier idealism intact. Smudging the timing of the Christ's Grand Return by making Jesus say that only the Father knew the exact hour, the Kingdom's supposedly imminent appearance was neatly shelved and changed into a threat which could be used to whip the faithful who were unfaithful back into line. For things were already getting out of control as the epistles and Revelation suggest. Gentile Christians were falling by the wayside in droves. Permissive behaviour was rife – particularly on the eastern fringe of the Roman Empire – and there was a refusal by many Christian communities to recognize episcopal authority.

The threats were many, the sins listed just as many. A clean-up was just around the corner.[49] In the same manner as history had been made to neatly conform to Church needs and aspirations, the moral and theological clean-up operation engaged in by the Catholic Church proved to be at the expense of soul and psyche. History had been revised to make the Jews into a scapegoat nation, to make the Nazarenes all but disappear, and theology would now be revised and tightened up to exclude those who believed, along with Socrates, that every human being had access to archetypal truth. The Delphic motto read 'Know thyself', and this *knowing* would be transmuted into *believing* in *the self of another* – the advent of the personality cult had arrived.

SEVENTEEN

A PRESENCE OF SELF

The discovery of an entirely new faculty of attention, the ongoing problem of a Christianity unconscious of its own unconscious state, and the lost art of conscious suffering.

In language which is accessible, the philosopher Jacob Needleman tackles the central issue facing all of us in his thought-provoking book *Lost Christianity*: the issue of the self. Needleman is Professor of Philosophy at San Francisco University, and supposes there to have been a 'hidden tradition' of Christianity lost to us, a tradition which approached the self in a manner quite different from Christianity today.

I stumbled on Needleman's book quite by accident, opened it at random, read a few paragraphs and realized immediately that I had found a configuration of ideas and experiences and opinions closely related to my own general thesis. According to Needleman, the human body had a spiritual role to play, and this role involved forces of being little understood by Christian thinkers. Faith had turned into 'belief', and on the heels of belief had come violence and self-deception and manoeuvres of the mind governed by fear. Strong stuff – and that was only the tip of the iceberg. Homing in on the distinction between consciousness of self and the 'unconscious reactions of both thought and emotion',[1] Needleman arrived at the fact that 'all the right thinking in the world will not change my essential nature, my intimate self, my very being',[2] and quickly reached the conclusion that we each have to fully comprehend the 'seductive property of the thinking function'.[3]

According to this highly unusual philosopher, the central issue facing all of us is 'the activation within the being of man of an entirely new faculty of attention'.[4] I did a double-take on those words. Self-observation had nothing whatsoever to do with thoughts and emotional reactions about oneself;[5] it had to do with looking without association and being vulnerable;[6] and it also had to do with 'double attention'. Needleman's description of 'double attention' caught my own attempt to describe the act of seeing that belongs to the larger self – the self which looms into view as a presence when the constantly fussing little self is made to shut up and observe. Needleman recognized that such a condition of psyche could not be brought about through rote prayers or single-direction meditations or motivationally suspect attempts of the little self (the ego) to burst out of its limited sphere of action. It could only be enticed to appear when the system of attention was simultaneously directed towards the inner and the outer, so forming a balancing *tension* in psyche. This answers of course to the lost methodology of the early Christians lampooned as 'Gnostic' – and if Jung's assessment of these Gnostics has any validity at all, what they discovered is about as powerful a spiritual technique as it is possible to identify in any religious discipline. But not so for Roman Catholic Cardinal Jean Daniélou, Professor of Primitive Christianity at the Institut Catholique, in Paris. In this man's opinion, 'the saved are those who believe, regardless of their level of interior life'.[7] I am indebted to Professor Needleman for this quote.

Other philosophers have written cogently of the incomplete self and its problems, but Needleman pushes further and identifies this incomplete self as 'the enemy of man'.[8] He means by this that the tendency of human beings is to 'give trust to what is only a part of the mind or self, to take the part for the whole, to take a subsidiary element of human nature as the bringer of unity or wholeness of being'.[9] Advocating a 'spiritual psychology' in place of an unbending and limited theology of belief like that of Cardinal Daniélou's, Needleman then asks: 'What kind of help does man need? And what must he – what can he – contribute from himself?'[10]

The answer given is complex, for how can an incomplete self contribute anything of worth – and is this not exactly what the Church has been stating for centuries? So are we intrinsically poisoned by 'sin' and incapable of making a move without the Church's help? Or are we capable of linking up with our larger, subjective self and causing a revolution in psyche? The Church's assessment is the former. Needleman's assessment is the latter. Yes, we are caught in the psychological dilemma of not knowing how to unharness ourselves from debilitating mental and emotional processes, from a part of ourselves ruling as if it were the whole, but that does not mean that such an unharnessing either cannot take place, or can only take place as a result of conditional beliefs, sublimation or repression – nothing could be further from the truth. As it turns out, we each and every one of us do have the capacity to 'wake up out of the dream of *Physis*'; it's just a matter of catching on to what that means in experiential terms. And as Church leaders are themselves predominantly caught in the psychical dream associated with embodiment, with the senses functioning in only one direction, then no matter how hard they try, the impetus towards real freedom of psyche (soul) cannot properly surface. This is the bottom line, and it seems that we have to literally trip over it before it makes any sense.

THE DILEMMA OF MODERN CHRISTIANITY

There is a statement in the very first chapter of Needleman's book which fully captures my own unease when I hear Christians talk about the efficacy of other religious forms, and of past Christian forms once thought heretical. When I first came across this phenomenon, I was delighted, indeed grateful, that the barriers of prejudice were finally beginning to crumble. But after listening intently to many such statements, I began to doubt the motives of those so inclined. Similarly uneasy, Professor Needleman describes his reaction thus:

> Why was I so troubled by the nun who spent hours each morning reading the sermons of the great Meister Eckhart and who told me she was experiencing all the things he had written about? Why my gnawing irritation at an organisation of Protestant ministers who were collectively practicing Tibetan prostrations in order to bring back the 'sacralization of the human body,' which, they claimed, was the original teaching of Christ? Why my sense of frustration after a long conversation with a Jesuit living in the Far East who, after many years of association with Taoists and Ch'an Buddhists, tells me that 'we can use Buddhism to approach God, but only Christianity can take us inside God'?[11]

Interesting comments. So why so distrustful?

Christians all over the Western world are now practising Eastern meditation in a Christian context. Using ancient techniques, such Christians approach their God anew and find that he exists in a manner never before suspected. Undergoing all kinds of inner experiences, these broad-minded Christians seem to get the best of both worlds and return from their experiences changed and even more certain that God's incarnational plan really was enacted 2,000 years ago. What has been missing from the Christian life, so it seems, has been direct experience of God – utilitarian prayers and haranguings of the heavens are emotionally satisfying, but not exactly practical, or even ethical, when examined in the light of modern theology or viewed with a modicum of common sense. How could we have viewed God in such a fashion for such a long time? How could we have believed that mouthing words to the ceiling, or into the hard, brown wood of a pew could influence the Creator of the Universe? What did we think was going on up there, or out there, or wherever? And more to the point, what was going on inside of us? What were we seeing, or sensing, or thinking at the back of our minds as we prayed in such a fashion? Did we really think we were on some kind of cosmic telephone? Or did we just not think about what we were doing at all?

The question is, what is actually going on when a Christian uses Zen meditation, or Tibetan or Hindu techniques to approach the God of their spiritual imaginations? And what on earth is going on when that God actually turns up as a *presence* to bless their attempts? Needleman puts his finger on the sore spot when he says 'It is not the experience of God that is drawing Christians to contemplative practices, but the experience of existing as such.'[12] Could this be true? And if true, then surely just as efficacious with God as without God? In fact, more so if God's presence is experienced.

The answer, I'm afraid, is not at all. For if the experience of the greater self, of the subjective self, of the *real* self is *interpreted* as that of an object other than the self, then the prayer or meditation has failed. Why? Because the primary purpose of meditation is not the realization of God's presence, or of Jesus' presence, or the production of images or sensations allied to such beings – it is the cancellation of all such imaginings in the direct apperception of 'being'. All the rest is hallucination. This is not psychology run amuck, and neither is it religion denied – it is simply the 'mystery' of being human allowed to fully arise. Without this *sustained* basic experience, and the accumulation of energy or 'psychic force' that accompanies it, all else is fantasy – even when what appears seems relevant. Needleman writes: 'I see that everything else, no matter what grandiose or pious names we use . . . has been and is a substitute for my existence and therefore conceals the fact that *I am* not.' He then completes this extraordinary observation by telling Christians that unless they become intrinsically real to themselves then they are involved in 'unconscious Christianity' – that is, a Christian experience within which the Christian as 'living being' is *missing*. Quoting from the journal of a certain Father Sylvan, a mysterious character on whom the whole text of *Lost Christianity* hinges, he calls this stage of non-being 'Christianity without Christians'.[13]

Here then is the difference between the religion *about* Jesus, and the religion *of* Jesus. And here also lies the problem of 'metaphysical idolatry' as described by Henry Corbin in his study of Iranian Sufism, the problem of the spiritual imagination out of control, the problem of how to teach the lower ego 'to deny and reject *all* pretensions to divine prerogatives, *all* claims inspired in the soul by the instincts of possessiveness and domination.'[14]

BRASS TACKS SPIRITUALITY

The Catholic mystic Thomas Merton was of the opinion that there was something deep within us which had to be awakened before what Christ taught could become part of us. This is an interesting concept. Having earlier postulated the existence of a 'primal consciousness' or 'inner self', he later came to directly equate this hidden inner self with God[15] – a heretical idea worthy of the ancient Christian Gnostics, and of Clement of Alexandria. Realizing that it was the surface consciousness and not the inner consciousness that had to wake up, Merton began to develop a more accurate assessment of psyche and its spiritual dimension. Needleman acknowledges Merton's insights as belonging to an inner struggle rather than to academic speculation, and in turn draws our attention to the Russian thinker G I Gurdjieff's emphasis on 'consciousness of self' as the key to all sacred traditions. For at base this seems to be what all sacred traditions are trying to point to – some more accurately than others, some in such a roundabout fashion that one begins to suspect corrupted texts. So scrambled have some of the sacred traditions become that 'awareness' and 'presence' and 'consciousness of self' have

ceased to carry their original message or meaning and become no
more than an exhortation to 'try hard'.

The above observation is important not just by way of spotting
texts that have lost their edge: it is also important on the level of
Christian aims and sensibilities. For if the heart of Christianity
has been lost, or obscured, or grossly misinterpreted, then the
whole edifice is trundling towards destruction, and the civilization
attached to it is going in the same direction. Needleman puts it
this way:

> The outcome of this search for what has been lost will determine the
> future of the whole Christian tradition. And we who are looking in
> from the outside, trying to understand the need they feel, may be
> shocked to realise that upon this issue may depend our own future as
> well, and indeed the very life of man on this planet.[16]

So the key issue is that of clearly defining what is meant by
'awareness' and 'presence' in many of the ancient, and not so
ancient, Christian texts, and in attempting to go beyond the
accepted or circumscribed levels of interpretation given to them.
For might there not be hidden there, or perhaps even be blatantly
available although not recognized, vital information capable of
carrying us toward our own proper awakening?

If the worlds of 'attention' and 'prayer' are finally identified as
one and the same world, then the human soul may very well be an
accumulation of energies in psyche which have to be brought into
existence moment by moment. Gurdjieff was certainly of this
opinion, and there is a growing realization in transpersonal
psychology that the human soul, or psyche, is not a spiritual
configuration of a forever fixed dimension, or character, but
rather a living substance wrestled moment by moment into
dynamic existence and expression through the medium of a
continually deepening appreciation of *being* in the world. Strip
psyche of being, hold being in unconscious suspension as a result
of constant mental distraction, and the result is a biologically
driven automaton liable to stamp a soulless vision on everything
around it.

Thomas Merton's suggestion that Christ's teachings could not
truly become part of us if we were not consciously awake to our
own existence, to our tendency of *being* consciously submerged in
thought most of the time, is theologically important. As a
statement it resonates with those of some of the Church's most

powerful thinkers from the past, and is at the cutting edge of present-day philosophical enquiries. But it is so extremely difficult to get the point of this argument across to those who presume themselves to be consciously awake without impediment, that it takes all one has to just keep the point in view and not succumb to verbal contortions. Ultimately, no verbal proof can be advanced – only the theoretical directive to pursue the issue into psyche until the rather unnerving facts of the situation become experientially clear.

Even Merton did not fully grasp the seriousness of the situation to start with, inadequately interpreting the advances of Zen Buddhist meditation in relation to 'mind' as of the 'natural order', and therefore not actually spiritual in essence, just useful, as a spade is useful. Only later would he realize that 'mindfulness' was not just a mere technique which Christians could borrow and use to deepen and sharpen their concentration when attempting to approach their God, but a fundamentally necessary condition of psyche without which a Christian spiritual life, or any kind of spiritual life, or for that matter a properly human life, was an impossibility. To be consistently empty of intrinsic attention, of the fact of one's moment-by-moment existence as a living being, was not merely to be deficient, or inefficient, or not properly 'tooled-up' for the job: it was to be so far below the standard required for an authentic interaction with self and world that one could only be classified as sub-human.

CHRIST CONSCIOUSNESS

Quoting Dom Aelred, prior of a Benedictine monastery in England and leading Catholic thinker who advocated that Christianity absorb Eastern meditational techniques, Needleman closes in on the central issue of 'Christ consciousness', and through Aelred's comments reminds us that in Mahayana Buddhism 'the faithful are encouraged to believe that the Buddha's luminous state of consciousness – what is held to be his supreme degree of wisdom and compassion – is open to everyone.'[17] In relation to the Buddha this is obvious to most people – but it is not at all obvious in relation to Christ. In Christianity 'Christ consciousness' has turned into a hybrid theological point which makes the historical Jesus as the Christ a consciousness which must be *put on* by Christians like a well-fitting jacket. It is not a matter of discovering that you too have a consciousness which can be transformed as Jesus' consciousness was transformed. It is a matter of mysteriously *superimposing* Christ's actual consciousness on one's own. By doing so, one becomes a Christian – or, to be more exact, a *possessed* human being. By some curious means one is now not only wearing the Christ jacket, one is also in Christ's pocket, so to speak!

The same quality of difference in interpretation exists here as in the case of whether Jesus was actually raised from the dead by God, or whether he managed to somehow *escape* death in spite of the odds against him. Christian thinkers will argue that it is the spiritual fact of 'Christ consciousness' that ultimately different-iates Christianity from the other major religions: sharing in Christ's consciousness is more than elevating oneself through mental discipline to an advanced level of conscious control. I agree: that is the major difference. But I would argue that this is to entirely miss the point of early Christian teaching – indeed, it is to take Paul's often literal-sounding language and use it without discrimination on the symbolic level.

Awareness of the calibre of one's awareness is not just a psychological state, a kind of psychic playground within which the ego secretly preens itself: it is the first rudimentary step in a progression of steps necessary even for Christians. Christ consciousness is not Christ's actual consciousness literally superimposed on the Christian psyche, it is the 'waking up' to the *boundary of being as an experience*. The religious thinking built around this question has bred conflict down through the ages, and will continue to breed conflict into the future unless it is finally recognized for the theological nonsense it is. In alignment with ancient Jewish traditions, with the actual traditions and insights and esoteric practices and sectarian speculations backgrounding the consciousness of Jesus as self-proclaimed Jewish Messiah, he was the archetype of the Perfect Man (humanity), and should not be literalized into a pagan evocation of a god. *That* is the Church's greatest theological *faux pas*, and it has become so ingrained in Christian thinking that to remove it will probably take a second Reformation.

Christ's consciousness is Jesus' God-centred consciousness perceived in his words, deeds and presence. Christ conscious-ness was the consciousness of an ordinary man intensified to that of a fully awake man who consciously took on the role of the 'Christ' or last Messiah of Israel. That's all. And that's why he was the *last* Messiah. The archetypal configuration is believed to have completed itself in him – that is, he reached the level of Complete Man, and managed to sustain the condition. To make Jesus into God is to miss the whole point of his physical and spiritual existence – the point which allows *all* human beings access to transcendence. This is where the whole idea of Jesus' saving power comes from, an idea reduced to the level of the absurd by those who prefer emotional entanglement with a phantom, to that of a sustainable freedom from limited emotional reactions. It is the fact of Jesus' humanity that is of prime importance in the story of his life, and that is why I have laboured throughout this book to draw attention to the flesh and blood man.

From being an ordinary human being he found the will to break out of the cage of his shared sub-human consciousness into that of the properly human. So great was that basic move, that transition from sleep to wakefulness, from submerged conscious awareness to full conscious awareness aligned with thought and deed, that humanity has not stopped talking about it since. For far, far too long, ordinary human beings have been denied access to Christ's higher consciousness by a Christianity bound to the notion of a Christ so unimaginably elevated that he must forever remain out of reach. Why? Because Christianity early on lost the key to what such a phenomenon might mean, or be, and is only now beginning to wake up to the fact that that might be the case. Here then is the religion *of* Jesus, the religion *of* primary Christianity which was categorically not just a religion *about* Jesus. The difference between those two terms is enormous, and should be explored by all Christians seriously concerned with the shape of the Church to come.

But concomitant with such a view is the realization that New Age techniques geared to the production of less fearful, more confident, and more centred human beings, is at best a well-intentioned exercise in futility unless the same principle of sustained attention is applied at both the conceptual and practical levels. New Agers are as prone to conscious sleep as any clergyman, and like clergymen, are constantly in danger of reducing the knowledge they possess to the level of the banal. 'Awareness' and 'attention' and 'really being there' are buzz terms often used by

New Age practitioners, but such terminology is meaningless unless attention is paid to what 'attention' signifies at the deepest levels of being, and what 'awareness' signifies in relation to attention functioning at an optimum level. Awareness and attention are not one and the same thing: they are contingent upon each other's simultaneous existence.

Optimum attention is a directed energy of perception held in close association with awareness as a perceptual field. In relation to objects *in* the world, or to the world *as object*, attention is a narrowing down or focusing. With regards to the self as observer, awareness is that which allows me to exist to myself *alongside the object of attention* without displacement occurring. Through 'intentionality' awareness can be made to regularly include the self as *presence* in its general field, but this is a matter of training, and is generally experienced not by intention but by accident. Some therapists cultivate self-presence, but alas it is seldom practised beyond the therapy room. This is the Berlin Wall of psyche, the dividing line between *being* asleep, and *being* awake.

Biological 'life' holds the key to comprehending both the nature of our natures, and the fact that our natures are utterly out of sync with our better intentions and our spiritual ambitions. In a lengthy extract from the journal of Father Sylvan (a Christian monk from an unspecified monastery in the Middle East), Jacob Needleman presents to us an unusual series of ideas culminating in some very interesting statements about mind and body. Talking of human emotions, Father Sylvan casually suggests that modern attempts at self-development are not 'results' in the proper sense, but merely 'rearrangements of psychic material'.[18] We are 'under the thrall of influences which pervade the earth and for which human emotional forces are nothing more than fuel'.[19] Meaning what? Meaning that what were once thought of as 'demons' functioning in the world of matter, is actually *mind descending, or dividing, into form and substance*.[20] Psychic energy, transmitted from mind to body captures this interaction, and is of an instinctual *and* an emotional nature.

In the animal kingdom instinctual energy has perfected itself and is virtually fixed. In humans, according to Father Sylvan's biological scheme, emotional energies are highly developed and offset the power of purely instinctive reactions. This is termed 'protopathic'. Father Sylvan points out that along with human beings the higher animals are also emotionally governed, but it is in the human that we see emotion overpowering instinct and the mechanical giving way to consciousness. Although emotion can be pernicious, it is emotion-cum-feeling that the neurologist Antonio Damasio identifies not only as holding in place the larger goals of human behaviour, but as instrumental in the creation of self-consciousness. Father Sylvan is on the same track, linking into our general thesis with the observation that 'life is to a great extent created and maintained through the expression of emotional energy.'[21] This suggests that we have swapped instinct for emotion and landed ourselves in a different kind of prison – a psychic prison where everything is governed by emotional reactions and habit patterns and occasional instinctual nudgings. Emotionally manipulated by our own passing thoughts, or by the emotionally-driven behaviours of others, we succumb constantly to, and are habitually controlled by, a crossfire of suggestions. Here then is the nature of our dilemma, and it is in response to this dilemma that religion and philosophy and psychology have arisen.

Cutting to the heart of the issue, Father Sylvan tells us that 'modern man's prayers have no effect; they do not reach God . . . People's prayers have no resonance, no power.'[22] Recognizing Socrates and Plato as teachers, Father Sylvan presents us with a curious directive from what he terms the 'ancient sceptics'. He tells us to 'separate our sense of self from all thoughts and logical reasonings in order to reach the relative void from which the certainty-that-has-no-name may speak'.[23] The what? If we want to love our neighbour, then what we need is power and energy, not a life *absorbed by our emotional reactions to others*.[24] Our high ideals, 'let loose in the world like packs of marauding dogs'[25] disguise the fact that our natures are unchanged, that we are merely acting as if we have attained freedom. And then he names the name of the game. Why are our lives so difficult? 'Because the experiencer is absent and needs to be born and grow within us.'[26]

In the parable of the Prodigal Son, the returning profligate is described as having 'wasted his substance'. Father Sylvan defines this as referring to his 'inner attention', and links this loss of inner attention to being wrapped up in sensations and thoughts to such an extent that the soul could be described as 'being in exile'.[27] In a different context he also speaks of 'the accumulation of the force of inner attention'.[28] And if we bring these two statements together, then the word 'substance' may itself be more substantial than generally thought.

Alluding to this accumulation of psychic energy, Needleman links it to 'deep self-questioning', and describes the result of such accumulation thus: 'The soul comes into existence and begins to gather itself into an independent entity.'[29] Father Sylvan refers to such accumulations of 'substance' as the *esotericism of energy*, a phrase which carries us just about as far away from 'beliefs about' as it is possible to get, and introduces us to the hidden mechanics of attention both as an experience and as a hidden generator of an *extended self*. Here, then, is the centre of the cyclone, the heart of the issue in relation to Being. The 'hidden teaching' is therefore not some hidden set of directions *about* something or other that has to be 'believed'; it is quite simply what is hidden inside each and everyone of us *in potentia*.

But it should be said that the idea of an 'extended self' is not foreign to Christian thinking: it is part of Paul's misunderstood doctrine concerning resurrection. With reference to the physical body after death, Paul declares that it will be 'raised a spiritual body'. Alluding to this statement in *The Illusion of Immortality*, Corliss Lamont quotes Canon B H Streeter:

> We may suppose that during our life on earth we are, although we know it not, building up an unseen celestial body which is a sort of counterpart of our earthly body but more exactly adapted to the expression of the character which our thoughts and conduct are all the while developing.[30]

This is an interesting statement, not because it seems to support our thesis but because it is yet again an ancient truth reduced to the level of the banal. It places the emphasis of the Christian life exactly where one would expect it to be: in ethics and morality. It is being 'good' that gets you this special soul-body; it is has nothing to do with being awake and aware and properly conscious. All you have to do is believe in Jesus, live a good 'Christian' life (whatever that might be), and everything is on course.

But what if the creation of this spiritual soul-body is not dependent on our being good, or nice, or temperate, or modest, or whatever, but on our being properly conscious, properly awake and aware, properly available to ourselves, to others, and to the world? Indeed, properly human? What if goodness, governed as it often is by subjective personality factors, isn't enough? What will happen then? Will we enter eternity with only a bit of a soul-body? Will we, perhaps, have a soul-body so weak in construction that it eventually blinks out? Could the promised destruction of hell be no more than incomplete souls self-destructing because the fuel of attention has been missing throughout earthly life? A personal ethic and a strong sense of morality are obviously necessary, but they must surely be of secondary importance to that of the quality of awareness backing them.

Introducing us to the fourth-century spiritual master Evagrius Ponticus, Needleman notes that he was officially condemned as a heretic because of his view of Christ's nature, and adds that he was as misunderstood 'as the term "gnosticism"'.[31] Strangely enough, Evagrius was a pupil of Clement of Alexandria, and of Origen. Origen was eventually classified as doctrinally untrustworthy, and Needleman thinks this may have been due to the influence of one Ammonius Saccas, a thinker of extraordinary power and depth who introduced Hermeticism to Western and Eastern Europe. What is of interest here is the term *apatheia* as coined by Evagrius, a term translated as 'apathy', but in his definition of things meaning not 'apathy' but 'without emotions', or more accurately still, 'freedom from emotions'.[32] As mentioned earlier, 'life is to a great extent created and maintained through the expression of emotional energy',[33] and it is our inability to control such emotions that leads us into many a confrontation with others, or causes us to react violently within ourselves in spite of showing little on the surface. Happy or sad, depressed or elated, or just plain numb from the emotional battering we sometimes take, we get through our daily existences and drop off the end into the oblivion of sleep often thankful to be out of it all. Sandwiched between the dream of being awake, and aware, and in control when most of the time we aren't, and drained by the huge expenditure of emotional energy each day demands, we enter the darkness of psyche and are confronted by yet another kind of dream, the dream of a soul trying to form, the dream of a psyche hell-bent on making us aware of the soul's precarious *formings* and *unformings*.

Enter Father Sylvan with the observation that the Church 'long ago mis-identified the locus of human freedom. Because of this error, the whole of Western civilization is crashing against a brick wall.'[34] Oddly enough, I referred earlier to the dividing line between *being* asleep and *being* wake as the 'Berlin Wall', and this neatly extends my metaphor. So what was going on in the early Church that is not going on in the present one? There was much talk in the old Church of 'inner warfare' and 'struggle' and 'beating off the Devil', and it has been assumed that such terms referred to no more than Christians' doing their best to be Christians. But such statements might in fact point not to the human spirit bravely battling with evil in ordinary terms, indeed *our* terms, but of human beings in possession of 'exact knowledge' waging war on their emotions as a skilled military tactician wages war on an enemy. And yet even then the Church was so intent on building a long-term edifice against the onslaught of *visible* evil in the world, that this kind of knowledge and practice was lost and remembered only as a series of dry injunctions or 'thou shalt nots'. Those who persisted in drawing attention to the *real* questions, to the *real* doctrinal problems, to the *real* nature of the Christ and the *real* purpose of the Church were labelled 'heretic' and excommunicated or destroyed. And so Father Sylvan's accusation against his own Church, the accusation that Western civilization is crashing against an *emotional* brick wall because the evolving second-century Church swapped its spiritual responsibilities for political power, is, as we have seen in chapter after chapter, a cold-blooded fact.

In their meditations, the Christian Gnostics discovered that the silent contemplation of God afforded 'knowledge' of soul-processes – but orthodoxy refused to listen. Already blind, or at best unsympathetic to such practices, and more interested in spreading the faith *about* Jesus than in the faith *of* Jesus, the Church banned any such attempt at inner exploration outside of sanctioned monastic practices of a limited nature. Labelling the followers of *gnosis* in her midst as 'Gnostics', perfectly sincere individuals were branded heretic and made to carry the stigma of Gnosticism in much the same way as Jews would later carry the yellow star of Israel. And so a term of abuse became a name, and the name came to signify Christian deviants who found fixed Church doctrine unacceptable and unnecessary. But as Dr Pagels attests in her thorough and illuminating study of Gnostic ideas and practices, Christian Gnostics arrived at such a stance not out of spurious spiritual procedures but as a result of arduous spiritual training. Yes, there were those who lost their bearings and caused all sorts of problems for the fledgling Church, but the Church's real *gnosis* was founded not on deviance and reprobate action, on egomania masquerading as sacred truth, but on precise and legitimate contemplative techniques of which we are only now becoming aware. In her delicately constructed study of Gnostic teachings and origins, Simone Pétrement describes Gnostic intentions as 'a feeling of transcendence pushed to its limit'.[35] Orthodoxy then and orthodoxy now hates any allusion to *gnosis* or things 'secret' or 'hidden', and pretends that the Christian revelation is complete and simple and available to all through the action of *belief* in Jesus as the Christ. But nothing could be further from the truth. Christianity is *not* complete, it is anything but simple, and the belief that 'belief' is enough is without doubt its least worthy or attractive feature.

THE MYSTERIOUS MR GURDJIEFF

In his biography of George Ivanovitch Gurdjieff, James Moore pens an interesting portrait, a portrait full of contradictions and anomalies and tantalizing glimpses of a very powerful man apparently trying to communicate a rather odd philosophy of consciousness. On the level of being contradictory, it is thought by some that he was an out-and-out charlatan. On the level of anomalous mental and physical behaviour, his approach to important philosophical questions was seen as 'irregular'. And on the level of being tantalizing, he did seem to possess a radical kind of knowledge that turned everything thought about human consciousness on its . . . head? Born in the Greek quarter of Alexandropol, in Russian Armenia, sometime around 1866, this walking enigma eventually ended up in France with a coterie of highly intelligent people hanging on his every word. Claiming somewhere in the east to have studied and practised techniques specifically designed to rouse people out of conscious trance, Gurdjieff introduced his pupils to what he termed 'conscious suffering', and after months and years of 'work' on themselves, these pupils came to agree that what he taught was truly transformative.

What is remarkable about the journal bequeathed to Professor Needleman by Father Sylvan is that it not only refers to Gurdjieff directly but that it also speaks of this strange man's thinking on the subject of 'being' as 'the sacred language of Mr Gurdjieff'. Sacred? Gurdjieff was well known for linguistic irreverence, so was there perhaps a little bit more to this Greco-Armenian than his detractors would like to think? Yet how curious, for James Moore records that on one occasion Gurdjieff remarked to an overconfident priest 'that collar you wear is like a carnation a prostitute wears when she menstruates.'[36] So why Father Sylvan's interest in Gurdjieff? And why the notion that Mr Gurdjieff's language was 'sacred'?

The more one reads Father Sylvan's journal extracts, the more one begins to suspect that this monk's unnamed monastery in the Middle East was engaged in practices closely aligned not only with Gurdjieff's expositions but with a lively and perhaps highly idiosyncratic monastic tradition connected directly to first-century Christianity. There are far too many correspondences in Father Sylvan's terminology with Gurdjieff's terminology and the ancient teachings of the Christian Gnostics not to suspect a link. And Father Sylvan's statement that it is through the medium of total self-inquiry 'that the forces of good and evil can meet and be reconciled within us' firmly cements that impression in place.[37] So the question arises: where did Gurdjieff get his ideas from? Where in the historical hinterland of his life did he stumble upon the dynamics of 'conscious attention'?

That Gurdjieff was himself trained and highly skilled in the dynamics of conscious attention was accepted without question by those who knew and worked with him. It was not just a matter of esoteric head-knowledge sold to a few innocents; it was a matter of an exact teaching communicated through novel procedures and often exasperating tactics, a teaching communicated to Gurdjieff by a series of high-order teachers probably of Sufi orientation. A graduate of what he called 'the chief Sarmoung Monastery', Gurdjieff claimed to have arrived there blindfolded, and to have sworn a vow of eternal secrecy as to its whereabouts. This, in essence, was the only proof offered for a training presumed successful, and Moore records that some allegorists 'construe Gurdjieff's entire monastery story symbolically'.[38] But it could not be denied, there was something powerful going on in this man – something which virtually forced those in his company to be aware of themselves – and it was in some curious fashion intrinsically related to Christianity. Gurdjieff, in spite of much non-Christian behaviour (in the eyes of some), was nonetheless involved in a process which Father Sylvan believed to be more authentically Christian than what was generally accepted as such. For Gurdjieff criticized those who believed that the Church's injunction to 'Love thy neighbour' was a reasonable demand – how could anyone love anyone to order, he asked? It was impossible. You might as well ask them to hate on order. And so in Gurdjieffian terms one was presented with a conundrum, the conundrum of a command to love everyone without the opening up of those capacities within oneself which made it possible. This was the lost element in Christianity, the lost heart of Christ's teachings so carefully teased out into the open by Professor Needleman.

TWO KINDS OF SUFFERING

In Gurdjieff's scheme of things there were two kinds of suffering: the emotional suffering we inflict upon ourselves due to our intolerably low conscious state; and a suffering which can be intentionally brought to bear on the self as a result of heightened awareness. This second suffering, in spite of how it may sound, is not in the least masochistic: it is simply the result of gaining conscious control of our wayward emotions. For that is the crux of the matter – our wayward emotions, our inability to stop reacting – and it is all related to our being constantly taken by surprise. Surprised by a remark, we flare up. Surprised by an unwanted visitor, we show annoyance. Surprised by something not going quite our way, we feel a surge of negative energy. Ever surprised by events and happenings because we live submerged conscious lives and hardly ever surface, we bump and buffet our way through hours and days and months with only the most rudimentary awakenings of the self to our credit. Consciously cocooned and caught up within ourselves, we surface only sufficiently to stop other human beings from recognizing that we too are in the same psychic state as they. The blind lead the blind. The deaf lead the deaf. The insensitive demand sensitivity from the insensate.

Gurdjieff's point was that if one was going to suffer, then why not get something out of it? Rather than just be overpowered by one's emotions, beaten to the punch by them on every occasion, why not suffer in a different and more positive fashion? Rather than be taken constantly by surprise, rather than find oneself thrust willy-nilly into either this or that emotion, why not learn to observe such happenings within oneself, and then learn how to short-circuit emotional chain-reactions before they happened, or at least gain the wit to pounce on them as they occur? To wake up to what was going on meant of course that we had to wake up to what was going on on another level altogether – the level of our being so consciously involved in things (even God) that we did not properly see, or hear, or feel the flow of life. So there were in effect two awakenings necessary: awakening to the existence of the self through the arousal of self-presence over against the world; and awakening to how the self behaved in relation to the world when it was consciously asleep.

This second awakening meant the awakening of the newly awake self to the real nature of the human dilemma – namely, the double dilemma of emotion masquerading as feeling, and the compulsive associative apparatus of mind masquerading as thought – and this in turn meant *suffering in a new way*. Or as Father Sylvan put it: 'It is not demanded of us that we always be in the state of the heart which grants us visions and self-mastery. It is only demanded of us that we know the state we are in.'[39] To know the state that we are in is to suffer not because of our lack of awareness (our normal condition) but for the very reason that we are aware of how unaware we are.

Here then is the brick wall that the Church (and Western civilization) keeps bashing against in spite of having so much to say about emotions and their effect on the human mind. Father Sylvan's directive to 'know our state' is exactly Gurdjieff's point about 'attention' being the foundation of *all* spiritual life, for without such a base the attempt to love or understand or truly appreciate anyone or anything is no more than a dream, our self-inflicted suffering an exercise in futility related to compulsive reactions on the emotional and thinking levels. To wake up is to suffer. Why? Because to wake up and *stay awake* is to consciously displace reactions and replace them with decisions – acts of *will* rather than acts perpetrated in an awake dream. The more extensively this dream is shattered, the greater the conscious suffering. For to be conscious is to be fully present, and to be fully present as we think and feel and act and communicate our way through an hour or a day, is to realize that we are predominantly at the mercy of thoughts and emotions in the service of a dreaming self. As Jesus said on the cross, 'Father, forgive them; for they know not what they do.'[40]

In the so-called 'apocryphal' *Acts of John*, the writer reveals the double-level context of suffering as cited by Father Sylvan and his spiritual mentor Gurdjieff. The text has Jesus say:

> For thou couldest not at all have understood what thou sufferest if I had not been sent unto thee, as the word of the Father . . . If thou hadst known how to suffer, thou wouldest have been able not to suffer. Learn thou how to suffer, and thou shalt be able not to suffer.[41]

As can be seen from this text, the Gnostic Jesus' conception of suffering was not at all the same as that of his disciples – one had to *learn* how to suffer, not just have suffering thrust upon one through the vicissitudes of life. It is clear from this text, and from many other so-called apocryphal texts of early origin, that the Jesus of the gospels understood the meaning of conscious suffering in relation to sustained awareness of self and world. What we find in these *gnosis*-oriented texts is that Jesus taught his disciples a deal more than the mere fact of his Messiahship; there is real teaching going on behind the scenes, a teaching which only barely makes its way into the synoptic gospels. And this teaching is about 'awareness' and 'presence' and 'conscious suffering' and 'levels of consciousness' in relation to 'thought' and 'emotion'. Everywhere one looks, this is what one finds. And even when a text is scrambled beyond recognition, or is simply a compilation of ideas and images quite obviously not properly understood by the compiler, the same profound themes can be detected. And in the writings of the early Church Fathers the same themes are present, but in a manner quite obviously divorced from the ancient tradition of *gnosis* directly communicated from teacher to pupil as in the case of Clement, and then Origen.

Centuries later, H P Lidden and Bishop Gore would argue about whether Jesus actually suffered on the cross, or whether by some curious fluke of consciousness he suffered *without* suffering (*apathos apathen*), and in that moment the ancient underlying theme of the Gospel story would again resonate its way to the surface. For ultimately the question of his suffering or not suffering on the cross had nothing whatsoever to do with that dread happening: the question had arisen in the quite different context of how to handle ordinary everyday events. Aware of what it really meant to be a conscious human being, Jesus had revealed to his disciples that human suffering was the result of unconscious reactions, and that real suffering, transformative suffering, was directly related to knowing and understanding this fact. Out of such knowing came comprehension of self and love of neighbour.

As reflected in the sixth-century Codex Cantabrigiensis (see Chapter Nine), Jesus' injunction to the man working on the Sabbath has to do with his level of awareness, with his capacity to be present to himself. He says to this breaker of the Sabbath, 'O man, if thou knowest what thou doest, thou art blessed, but if thou knowest not, thou art accursed and a transgressor of the Law.' Nothing could be plainer than what the Jesus of this text is getting at: he is telling this man that if he doesn't have the requisite level of conscious awareness then he is bound by the Law, but if he is awake and aware and properly conscious then instead of being bound he is free – not to break the Law whenever he feels like it, but to be able to make *real* decisions. This Jesus is not advocating some form of early socialism; he is alerting the man to the core problem facing all human beings – submerged awareness of self.

It is, I think, from a teaching of this nature that improperly informed Christians later fabricated doctrines allowing themselves inordinate freedoms, and it was against such abuses that the Church reacted, not realizing that they were dealing with a distorted truth of immense power. And the very fact that such a powerful statement has been attributed to Jesus suggests a real, and not a spurious, connection with gospels other than the synoptics – for what he has to say in the so-called apocryphal gospels about suffering and awareness and consciousness resonates not only with reality, with what is now beginning to be understood about the human psyche, but also with the canonical gospels.

The so often quoted command of Jesus to love thine enemy, in this context, takes on a whole new meaning. And his many other statements of a similar vein speak not of a dry morality but of a teaching which constitutes 'living water'. Robert Graves and Joshua Podro suggest that Jesus 'insisted on the need for gratitude to one's enemies when their hostility pointed to faults in oneself'.[42] They add:

> All these sayings present an ethical ideal that makes no concession to human frailty . . . Thus in Matthew 5:38–48 the ideal of human goodness is carried to a point where all personal pride must be

surrendered: 'If your enemy sues you for your shirt, let him have your coat as well rather than prolong a quarrel in which you are as likely to be wrong as he is. Never resist a personal attack: if your enemy strikes you on the right cheek, show your peaceful intentions by also turning the left. But on God's behalf, or in defence of an ill-treated innocent, be unexceptionally firm and bold.[43]

Such a counsel of perfection makes no sense except in a teaching situation. But this should not be construed as Jesus' teaching no more than the ethical principles of Judaism; it should rather be seen as a teacher's pertinent way of instructing his close disciples in a life-transforming process. Yes of course it is better for us and the world if we stop reacting in an off-the-cuff manner, but that is not the point. The point is to emotionally digest and consciously appreciate the abrasive power of holding one's anger and resentment at bay. And this is not just to boil inside, to bottle everything up and pay the price of repression later; it is to feel the pain of such anger and resentment but not to allow it to take over, not to allow emotion to run your movements, your thoughts and your replies. *That* is where the transformative energy comes from. *That* is morality in the service of intelligence, attention, awareness and change. And it has nothing whatsoever to do with Stoic indifference or a self-congratulatory perfection; it has to do with undergoing real suffering in the depths of being just as Jesus underwent real suffering in Gethsemane and on the Cross. And it also has to do with the accumulation of transformative energy in the biosystem, the *substance* of the spiritual life. *That* is the lost dimension of Christianity, the lost dimension of Judaism, the lost dimension of Islam, and the lost dimension of Greek philosophy as expounded by Socrates. To know the self is not just to know *about* the self: it is to be engaged in the painful process of bare-bones self-realization at the emotional level. Is it any wonder that the bulk of people preferred a grocery list of beliefs?

THE FINAL STATEMENT

The word 'Gnosticism' eventually turned into a term of abuse, a description of just about anything that did not exactly align itself with the rapidly growing consensus theology of the second-, third- and fourth-century Church. Yet there was, as mentioned earlier, the *gnosis* of Paul and the early first-century Church – a profound inner teaching which would later deteriorate into sometimes crazy reflections of itself lacking intrinsic meaning. But this does not mean that this inner teaching ceased to exist. Lost to both the ruling orthodoxy and to many *gnosis*-inclined experimenters it certainly became, but continue it did in spite of such obstacles.

Ever careful not to ruffle apostolic feathers, Father Sylvan sets the picture straight and makes a point of saying that what he is talking about is *not* Gnosticism. But what he means by this is at first vague, for he goes on to show that the principal Gnostic forms were not only valid but constituted advanced forms of religious thinking and experience far outstripping Christianity's present grasp of Jesus' teachings. And then all is clear, for he tells us that strictly speaking, 'Gnosticism is not a heresy of the Church, but a heresy of *gnosis*.'[44] Here, then, is the lost perspective as well as the lost language with which to discuss and explore this issue – later Gnosticism (third/fourth-century) was not a distortion of credal notions: it was a tantalizingly close approximation of early Christian *gnosis* isolated from its living root. Once again Simone Pétrement comes to our aid. Splitting the Gnostic texts into early and late, she shows quite conclusively that the early Gnostic materials were quite intelligible, the later texts not only complicated and obscure but riddled with pagan ideas borrowed from before and after the appearance of primary Christianity.[45] In the later texts, earlier experiences of a psycho-spiritual nature are literalized; in the early texts, these same experiences are much more accessible.

The result of such findings is to realize that the Gnostic demiurge was not a corrupt theological concept created by deranged minds; it was a psychologically exact perspective revealing that concepts belonging to the unreal 'I' of the incomplete self can get 'between the soul and the direct experience of its supreme possibility'.[46] And in relation to the Gnostic 'God that is beyond God', Father Sylvan, like the medieval Dominican Meister Eckhart, tells us that the God beyond God belongs to the self in its completeness, just as the God of popular imagination belongs to the incomplete self.[47] The inner *gnosis* of Christianity, we are told, is composed of symbols which have been misunderstood and misinterpreted and rejected because the key to their comprehension has been lost – there are different levels of being, and *gnosis* 'shows us our failure to respond'.[48]

This fully encapsulates what every serious researcher has been looking for – the start of a new language which will allow for sensible debate and discussion of Christian origins and the meaning of morality. And by way of a final statement, I can think of no better than this from Father Sylvan's remarkable journal:

Ego is the systematic affirmation of emotional reaction. This system is fuelled by the energy of attention. Therefore as long as a man has no control over his attention his possibilities remain imprisoned in the ego no matter what ideals he espouses and no matter what efforts he expends.[49]

Muslim mystical writers refer to Jesus as *Isa bin Yusuf* (Jesus son of Joseph) and think of him as Prophet, Teacher and Messenger. Rafael Lefort informs us so in his book *The Teachers of Gurdjieff*, and adds for good measure that he is given the rank of *Insan Kamil* – 'Complete Man'. When tracking down Gurdjieff's teachers on a journey through the Middle East which took him as far as Baghdad, Damascus, Jerusalem and Cairo, Lefort met disparate types of men all with one thing in common: they were part of a 'school of learning' which for centuries had taught the inner working of Islamic spirituality. And perhaps long before Islam itself appeared on the scene, for as any Muslim knows, Muhammad did not create a new religion, he simply reconnected the Arab mind to an ancient stream of lost spiritual knowledge. Near the end of his search for those who had schooled Gurdjieff, Lefort meets with a certain Sheikh Daud Yusuf, and is sent to Jerusalem with the directive to *think about the traditions of Isa bin Yusuf*.

How strange that Islam should recognize Jesus as Prophet and Teacher and Messenger and Complete Man, and that Judaism should reject him and name him apostate Messiah. Why should this be, I wonder? What was it about Jesus the Jew that made Muhammad accept him as an equal? For Jesus is named 'Prophet' by Muhammad, and recognized by Islam as one of a line of Prophets ending with Muhammad himself. So was it just a ploy to annoy the Christians and upset the Jews? Or was there perhaps more to Jesus the Nazarene than meets the eye?

This question carries us back to Professor Kamal Salibi's contention that the Jesus of the gospels came originally from Arabia, that he was an Arabian Jew of royal descent, and that the Nazarenes were directly related to the ancient Arabian Nasara who had followed a Messiah-figure called 'Jesus' (*Isa/Issa*) in 400 BCE. This Jesus, whose followers had split into two streams – one orthodox, the other at loggerheads with the by then well-established Judaism of Ezra – was the Jesus of the Koran, an almost mythical Jesus whose exploits exactly reflected those of the miraculous, phantom-like Jesus of the synoptic gospels.

In the eyes of the sectaries this earlier Jesus was a legitimate contender for the throne of Israel in spite of his being a descendant of Aaron. The Jews accepted only a scion of the house of David as Israel's legitimate Messiah, whereas the sectaries as advocates of the old Israelite monotheism of their forefathers, held what Salibi calls 'the special notion of a Messianic pair: a priestly Messiah of the house of Aaron, and a regal Messiah of the house of David'.[1] This idea of a 'double Messiah' was held by the Qumran Essenes, and reflected the beliefs of the ancient Arabian Nasara whose offshoot, the Nazarenes, was led by Jesus and subsequently by members of his family, as history so clearly attests. So there was probably more to Jesus' rejection by the Jews than the fact that he came from Galilee and spoke with a roughish, country accent. It may well have been the fact that he was an Arabian Jew of sectarian persuasion with not quite as direct a link to the house of David as his double genealogy in the New Testament so clumsily attempts to prove. As Maurice Bucaille observes in *The Bible, the Qur'an and Science*, 'The genealogies of Jesus as they appear in the gospels may perhaps be the subject that has led Christian commentators to perform their most characteristic feats of dialectic acrobatics, on a par indeed with Luke's and Matthew's imagination.'[2]

Without going into the intricacies of what Bucaille means by that, suffice to say that Jesus' family tree as it appears in the gospels is highly suspect. Robert Graves and Joshua Podro draw attention to the fact that 'Matthew's genealogy consists of two unrelated lines tacked together: the first Davidic, the second Aaronic.' And they think it strange, indeed remarkable, 'that no genealogy corresponding with Luke's record from Nathan to Jesus can be found anywhere in Hebrew literature'.[3] So in Matthew we have the rather odd inclusion of an Aaronic line (the same priestly line as *Issa*), and in Luke we have a genealogy that runs 'modestly through Nathan, a son of David who never came to the throne'.[4]

What concerns us here, however, is not the accuracy or inaccuracy of the New Testament genealogies, but the fact that Jesus is given a human genealogy and made part of the normal chain of being. The gospels make it plain that Jesus was the son of Joseph and Mary by physical means. Statements to this effect are everywhere to be found in the New Testament: 'Is not this the son of Joseph?' (Luke 4:22); 'Is not this Jesus the son of Joseph whose father and mother we know?' (John 6:42); 'Joseph the husband of Mary, of whom was born Jesus, the Christ' (Matthew 1:16); and 'Son, thy father and I have sought thee sorrowing' (Luke 2:48). In Acts 2:30, Peter tells us that Jesus was 'of the fruit of David's loins according to the flesh'; and Irenaeus records that the Ebionites considered Joseph to be Jesus' father.

Jesus did not appear from nowhere and in relation to nothing, and neither did Muhammad. Both had a distinct background, and some kind of revelation. Both were Prophets. And it is quite possible that Jesus, like Muhammad, came from the Hijaz area of western Arabia, or was brought up as a Nazarene (Essean-Essene) because members of the family had migrated from the 'Nazareth' in that area. Nazarene beliefs as developed by Jesus were just as much at odds with Judaism as those of the ancient Nasara had ever been, and as Salibi shows, the Christianity which developed with Paul as an offshoot of Nazarene doctrine, was not a branch of Judaism as Christian scholars have come to believe, but a parallel, sister-religion stemming from the ancient Israelite mono-theism so well preserved and developed at Qumran. The Essenes are without doubt the connecting factor. And as Ahmed Osman reveals in his illuminating and provocative book *The House of the Messiah*, Jesus' connection with the Essenes is now pretty certain, but in a manner complicated by ancient history.

THE EXISTENTIAL VACUUM

Osman utterly reverses Dr Barbara Thiering's thesis of Jesus as the Wicked Priest of Essene writings brought forward to the time of the gospels. He has it that the Jesus of the gospels actually existed no fewer than 14 centuries earlier, as *Joshua*. The name 'Joshua' (*Ye-ho-shua* in Hebrew) has the same meaning as 'Jesus' (*Ye-shua*), and the King James Bible makes the names 'Joshua' and 'Jesus' interchangeable. It appears, strange as it may seem, that many of the early Church Fathers believed these two figures to be one and the same. Origen clearly thought this to be the case. 'Up to this point,' says Clement's brilliant pupil, speaking of Joshua, 'nowhere has there occurred a mention of the blessed man Jesus. Here first the brilliance of this name shone forth.'[5]

As with Burton L Mack's findings in relation to a Jesus whose disembodied 'sayings' and 'doings' were elaborately embroidered and made into a 'life' that had no actual material existence in New Testament terms, Osman rejects the gospel Jesus and pushes him back to the time of Moses. He advances quite fascinating reasons for doing so, and it may well be that he has identified a historical Jesus over and above that of Professor Salibi's other Jesus (*Isa/Issa*) who appeared around 400 BCE. But unlike Salibi he adopts Burton L Mack's approach and drops the gospel Jesus into an existential vacuum, introduces a quite astonishing range of research linking Jesus and the Jews to Egyptian history, and creates a picture within which the early gospel Christians, due to 'ancient teachings', were 'forced . . . to come out of hiding in their closed communities and to tell their story, adapting it to the new age'. So says the book's cover blurb. This leaves us, however, with New Testament Christians but no actual Christ.

There is a certain similarity between Osman's and Salibi's texts, but the overall thrust of each is in a different direction in spite of overlaps, and this probably explains Osman's silence on Salibi's prior publications *Conspiracy in Jerusalem* and *The Bible Came From Arabia*. What concerns us here is not the change in direction, but the overlaps in text where already familiar terms like 'Nazarene' or 'Issa' take on further significance. Salibi postulates a historical background for the Nazarenes which places them in Arabia around 400 BCE. Called at this time Nasara, these early followers of Issa (rendered in Greek *Iēsous*, 'Jesus') split into two groups, one orthodox, one heterodox, and it was the teachings of these groups that Paul is said to have retrieved from Arabia during his curious three-year stay in that country. Unlike Salibi, however, Osman's scenario does not develop a gospel Jesus aligned with Isa/Issa, but he does have other things to say about Isa/Issa and the Nazarenes which throw further light on New Testament relationships.

ESSA AND THE ESSA-ENES

For instance, he tells us that the Nazarenes were a 'Gnostic sect' like the Essenes, and that the Koran not only accepts Jesus as the actual Messiah of Israel (Christ), but gives the name Nasara (Nazarenes) to his followers. And then comes a real eye-opener.

With regard to the name 'Isa/Issa' as found in the Koran, Osman
writes it as *Essa* (as it is actually pronounced in Arabic), and links
it directly to the Greek variation of the name 'Essenes' – *Essaioi*.
Writing of this sect in 30 CE, Philo Judaeus refers to the Essenes as
Essaeans, and makes it clear that it was not originally a Greek
word. In that *Essa* was the term used in the Coptic Egyptian
language for 'Jesus' in the first century CE,[6] and the selfsame name
is, as we have seen, the Arabic name *chosen* for 'Jesus' in
the Koran, the long-dreaded connection between Jesus and the
Essenes seems to have been made. *Essaioi*, or 'follower of Essa',
would therefore make the Essenes *followers of Jesus!* And as the
Essean-Essene splinter group led by Jesus, and some other
factions of the Nazarenes in Arabia contacted by Paul were most
probably Gnostic in orientation, and historically related to the
similarly-oriented Samaritans with whom history stopped at
Moses, then the identification of Joshua as a curious forerunner
of Jesus 1,400 years before the accepted date is perhaps not as
silly as it may sound. Something is going on here, and it is more
than phonetics.

In the story of the Transfiguration, one of the two prophets to
turn up is Moses. Osman points out that when Moses was trans-
figured due to having been in the presence of the Lord on Mount
Sinai, the only person to have accompanied him was Joshua –
Jesus. We have of course the option to discount such a passage as
no more than the writer/editors of the gospels playing word-
games – that is, reversing an Old Testament text and using it to
make a point about Jesus' authority and status. But what if this
way of interpreting things is just the modern mind tripping over
its own linear feet? What if this story has actual historical
significance in relation to the Jesus of the gospels? What if this
story is in the New Testament not by way of typification but to
make us aware of a teaching (sectarian) running all the way from
Joshua (Jesus) to Essa (Jesus) to Jesus the Nazarene? Osman
draws our attention to Paul's statement in the Epistle to the
Hebrews where, in relation to Moses, he says: 'For unto us was
the gospel preached, as well as unto them: but the word preached
did not profit them, not being mixed with faith in them that heard
it.'[7] What a strange verse. The *same* gospel preached to the Jews
of the New Testament *and* to the children of Israel *at the time of
Moses*? Preposterous, surely? Not really – not when the context is
understood; not if a special teaching was being passed on century

by century. Paul consolidates his message about the distant past, the role of a Christ (Messiah) at that time, and the *type* of gospel delivered when he says: 'for they [the Israelites] drank of that spiritual Rock that followed them: and that Rock was Christ'.[8]

But isn't this just theology? Isn't it just Paul clutching at imaginative straws? Perhaps not. Perhaps he is reiterating what he found out, or was *taught* in Arabia about Jesus, indeed about *two* forerunners of the Jesus with whom he himself had so mysteriously interacted. Osman's *other* Jesus is Joshua, Moses' successor; Salibi's *other* Jesus is Isa/Issa/Essa, founder of a sect in or around 400 BCE called the Nasara (from Nasirah/Nazareth in the Hijaz, not Palestine) which will emerge in New Testament times as the Nazarenes in close affiliation with the Essenes, or Essa-enes – followers of a *pre-existent* 'Jesus' as their name now suggests. This makes the Jesus of the New Testament a Jesus who stems from both the war leader Joshua and the religious leader Essa, and as a reflection of the Samaritan belief that God manifested himself to Moses as a physical incarnation, is capable of carrying a divine implication in his nature. Here, then, is the double-barrelled Messiah-figure of sectarian expectations, the leader-cum-conscious archetype who, on this occasion, will reject violence and choose the Way of peace. And here also, behind the psychic scene, as it were, are the strange, disembodied and immaterial Jesuses of the Gnostic Christian imagination, a double-exposure Jesus as phantom superimposed on the real Jesus by Paul in his elaborate theology of the mystic Christ. Ignorant of what lay behind Paul's highly complex ideas, the Roman Church will be left with a walking theological contradiction, a Jesus who confounds both Jew and Christian as he is edited into the multifaceted Jesus of the gospel story and carried into the future.

In the gospels, Jesus is directly linked with the Nazarenes. According to Salibi, the Nazarenes were 'followers of a post-exilic Israelite prophet called Issa whose teachings were in conflict with those of Ezra, the founder of post-exilic Judaism'.[9] Tellingly, Jesus is mistaken for a Samaritan in John's gospel, and the Samaritans too were an Israelite sect which rejected Ezra's religious authority. The question is, why? The answer to this question lies hidden in Jewish history, but like Christian history at the time of Constantine, Jewish history has been tidied up and made uniform in relation to religious ideas generated during and after the Babylonian exile. Skilful hands have been at work in a process of editing which has collapsed events into one another, rearranged orders of information, and in general either obscured or utterly eradicated events considered historically embarrassing. This is not at all surprising, considering the human desire for continuity and coherence, but it does make life difficult for anyone who attempts to unravel the story of Israel and her neighbours. Suffice to say that Isa/Issa/Essa preached a monotheism much at variance with that of Ezra's Judaism, and that Jesus took the same route, advocating a much more relaxed and individually centred experience of both God and Law in alignment with Samaritan spiritual development. Was this then similar in vein to the gospel preached by Joshua in the role of Messiah cited by Paul? We will probably never know, but if Paul's statement about this Messiah is anything to go by, then a message contiguous with that of Essa and Jesus was delivered to and rejected (not understood?) by the ancient Israelites.

A MONSTER OF THE EMOTIONS

This brings us back to Robert Eisenman's theory that Jesus' brother James was the Essene Teacher of Righteousness. Eisenman, like Burton L Mack, virtually discounts Jesus' actual existence and makes him into what N S Silberman calls an 'abstract theme'. Why? Because in a Dead Sea Scroll wisdom text carrying the title 'The Children of Salvation and the Mystery of Existence', two Hebrew words *Yesha* and *Yeshuato* suggest an understanding of 'salvation' allied to what is perhaps a double variation on the name of Jesus (*Yeshua*). This apparently led Eisenman to think that Jesus may never have existed in real terms, but that he was a religious abstraction carrying the idea of salvation and no more. Interesting. But when we consider this text in the light of Salibi's Isa/Issa, and Osman's Essa, we arrive not so much at an abstraction but at yet another definite proof of a 'phantom Jesus' from the past who most probably relates to the leader of the ancient Nasara. Carrying a 'redemptive quality' for reasons which are obscure, and perhaps worrying, the mantle of this ancient Jesus will be donned by the Jesus of the New Testament and made to live again – or, conversely, die again as part of some obscure rite. Here, then, is the probable blueprint for Jesus' every move, and statement. And if this theme of a dying saviour allied to Isa/Issa/Essa was part and parcel of Qumran Essene doctrinal thinking, then just maybe the whole extraordinary story of Jesus' arrest, trial, crucifixion and resurrection were all part of a complex ritual which we may never fully fathom.

Eisenman is of the opinion that some of the Dead Sea Scrolls belong to the first century CE, and not to the second century BCE as generally supposed – there is growing evidence for this opinion. And in this he is in agreement with Barbara Thiering and a few others. If this proves to be the case, Jesus is going to have to be evaluated anew. And if it is not the case, he is still going to have to be re-evaluated on the basis of what is to all intents and purposes his name turning up within the name chosen by the Qumran community to describe itself. This simply cannot be avoided. The genie is out of the lamp and will not go back in again.

As can be seen from the way all of this comes together, the Thiering scenario of Jesus as a renegade leader who split the Essenes doctrinally into two groups is in no way impossible in spite of Ahmed Osman, Burton L Mack and Robert Eisenman. In fact, everything hangs together reasonably well on the historical level, and is certainly more faithful to the facts than the Church's historians are seemingly willing to admit. For Christian scholars, although obviously aware of Nazarene importance and their role as direct and lasting antagonists of Paul, have chosen down the centuries to emphasize the secondary phase of the early Church's existence, and either ignored, or with dexterity camouflaged, the fact that the Nazarene Jewish Christian Church as primary phase was not really a Christian Church at all. And to top it all off, the fact of Paul's mystic Christ of distinct Gnostic orientation being hijacked and turned into a pagan literalization due to writer/editor misunderstandings has been sublimated and made to stand as a hybrid historical truth. It can of course be argued quite legitimately that Jesus was God, in the mystical sense, but such a statement cannot in all honesty be turned the other way around – it is simply not a reversible proposition at any level of argument. Carrying 2,000 years of doctrinal mismanagement on his shoulders, Jesus the Nazarene is daily crucified anew and made as nothing by those who claim to love him. But it is Father Sylvan who again puts it best.

The myths and symbols of the past only evoke our emotions. And not until you reach the heart should you permit yourself to speak the ancient language. Until then, even Christ must be chased out of your mind. You have made Him into a monster through your emotions and conditioning.[10]

Strong stuff. Enough to get you kicked out of just about any Christian establishment for heresy. And that carries me back to some very revealing statements made to Professor Needleman by a certain Father Vincent who became bothered by 'the vanishing of identity',[11] and who ended up realizing that his 'identity did not even exist during . . . religious experiences'.[12] More and more disgusted with his psychic condition, with his mental disappearing act during 'every petty annoyance or emotional outburst', he came eventually to realize that there was a great need for 'some new rule of living, that could guide modern people towards the awakening of presence'.[13] It strikes me that people like Father Vincent and Father Sylvan and the unclassifiable Mr Gurdjieff had, as Professor Needleman states, 'discovered the same missing link'.[14]

'Missing' and 'lost' amount to the same thing, and this missing perspective involving presence of self intercepted through a possible but seldom activated double attention (self and other) appears to be the basis of a lost system of knowledge known to, and practised by, the so disparaged early Gnostic Christians – a group of people safeguarding an ancient teaching which became garbled but which at no time actually died out, as the existence of Gurdjieff's mysterious teachers prove. Gnosticism is *not gnosis*, as Father Sylvan rightly warns, but it is overly didactic to dismiss the beating heart of Gnostic Christianity and lump it indiscriminately with any old madcap idea lying around. In fact it is a crime against the truth to do so.

RADICAL DEVIATION

Like Father Sylvan, Dr Schonfield was never shy in saying what was on his mind, and at the end of *Those Incredible Christians* he states: 'Catholic Christianity is based on a radical deviation, which progressively by dubious ways and means was converted into an orthodoxy.'[15] Circumstances favoured the growth of a predominantly Hellenistic viewpoint within the late first-century and early second-century Church, and this viewpoint eventually overcame the old Nazarene vision of Jesus as Jewish Messiah through an astute use of Paul's Christological vision. Now the idea of Paul's vision being usurped and made bend to orthodoxy's utilitarian purposes will not be accepted by Christian apologists – in fact it will be cried down as a rank misinterpretation of those events which led to the formation of the Catholic Church. But in conjunction with the virtually ignored role of the Nazarenes in Jesus' life, the uncomfortable fact of Paul's profound Christology's being woven into a tapestry of belief subservient to a surface creed of political hue is the principal fact that has at worst been consciously denied, or at best overlooked. With the benefit of a false continuity set up between Nazarene, Petrine and Pauline viewpoints, the Catholic Church has been able to legitimize all of its historical moves since roughly the end of the first century. Now an unwillingness to face the historical facts is understandable – there is a lot at stake for the Catholics and the Anglicans and the many other Protestant denominations who proffer their versions of ultimate truth – but in this day and age such historical fudging can no longer be accepted or condoned: it is simply time to lay the historical cards out face-up so that everyone can read them in the cold, hard light of the present day.

What these cards tell us is that Jesus was the son of man, and the son of woman, and as such was not literally God in any shape or form. He was flesh and blood and bone and culture; he was taste and touch and emotion and feeling; he was hope and ambition and success and failure; and he was, above all, courage and faith and transformation. We are told that he survived his crucifixion and appeared to many; I believe that he did just that. But I do not believe that the up-there-somewhere God of Christian orthodoxy or fundamentalist imagination somehow broke the rules of creation and literally raised him from the dead. Such a God does not exist; there is no such being. The God of Jesus was not the Christian God of today, and neither was he Israel's wilderness God re-imagined. He was neither. He was the God beyond such Gods, the God who feeds ravens, and human beings, from within.

REFERENCES

PROLOGUE

1 Martin Ralph, *A Crisis of Truth* (1982), p 103
2 Blamires, Harry, *The Secularist Heresy* (1981), Intro, p 1
3 *Ibid*, Intro, p 3
4 Martin, Ralph, *A Crisis of Truth* (1982), p 77
5 Blamires, Harry, *The Secularist Heresy* (1981), p 40
6 Martin, Ralph, *A Crisis of Truth* (1982), p 76
7 Blamires, Harry, *The Secularist Heresy* (1981), p 40
8 *Ibid*, Intro, p 3
9 Wright, N T, *Who was Jesus?* (1994), p 80
10 Graves, Robert and Podro, Joshua, *The Nazarene Gospel Restored*, (1953), Foreword, p xxii
11 Jung, C G, *Aion* (1979), p 109
12 Luke 24:39
13 Mack, Burton L, *The Lost Gospel: The Book of Q and Christian Origins* (1993), p 207
14 *Ibid*, p 256
15 Cameron, Peter, *Heretic* (1994), p 10
16 *Ibid*, p 14
17 *Ibid*, p 2
18 Needleman, Jacob, *Real Philosophy* (1990), Intro, p 15
19 Cameron, Peter, *Heretic* (1994), p 211

1 DR JEKYLL & MR HYDE

1 Schonfield, H, *The Essene Odyssey* (1984), p 12
2 Schonfield, H, *The Passover Plot* (1967), p 2
3 Schonfield, H, *Those Incredible Christians* (1969), Intro, p xiii
4 Young, Frances, *The Myth of God Incarnate*, essays edited by John Hick (1977), p 25
5 Schonfield, H, *Those Incredible Christians* (1969), Intro, p xii
6 Cupitt, Don, *The Myth of God Incarnate*, essays edited by John Hick (1977), p 145
7 Schonfield, H, *Those Incredible Christians* (1969), Intro, p xii

[8] *The Mercury* (Hobart, Australia), Tuesday 24 Jan 1995

[9] Schonfield, H, *Those Incredible Christians* (1969), Intro, p xv

[10] Schonfield, H, *The Passover Plot* (1967), p 4

[11] Cupitt, Don, *The Myth of God Incarnate*, essays edited by John Hick (1977), p 145

[12] *Ibid*, p 143

[13] Mack, Burton L, *The Lost Gospel: The Book of Q and Christian Origins* (1993), p 251

[14] Schonfield, H, *Those Incredible Christians* (1969) p xiii

[15] Augstein, Rudolf, *Jesus, Son of Man* (1977), p 9

[16] Baigent, Leigh and Lincoln, *The Messianic Legacy* (1986), p 9

[17] *Ibid*

[18] Spong, John Shelby, *Resurrection: Myth or Reality?* (1994), p 12

[19] Cameron, Peter, *Heretic* (1994), p 8

[20] Bultmann, Rudolf, *Jesus*, p 11

[21] Craveri, Marcello, *The Life of Christ* (1970), p 167

[22] Cupitt, Don, *The Myth of God Incarnate*, essays edited by John Hick (1977), p 135

[23] *Ibid*, p 134

[24] *Ibid*, p 135

[25] *Ibid*, p 134

[26] *Ibid*, p 135

[27] Young, Frances, *The Myth of God Incarnate*, essays edited by John Hick (1977), p 27

[28] *Encyclopedia Britannica* (1968), vol 10, p 583

[29] Cupitt, Don, *The Myth of God Incarnate*, essays edited by John Hick (1977), p 137

[30] *Ibid*, p 139

[31] Klauser, Theodore, *A Short History of the Western Liturgy* (1969), pp 32–7

[32] Goulder, Michael, *The Myth of God Incarnate*, essays edited by John Hick (1977), p 64

[33] Schonfield, H, *The Passover Plot* (1967) Intro, pp 3–4

[34] Young, Frances, *The Myth of God Incarnate*, essays edited by John Hick (1977), p 31

2 THE PAGANIZING OF CHRISTIANITY

[1] Augstein, Rudolf, *Jesus, Son of Man* (1977) p 25

[2] *Ibid*, p 46

[3] Charlesworth, J H, (ed.) *Jesus and the Dead Sea Scrolls* (1993), p 14

[4] John 11:50–52

[5] Augstein, Rudolf, *Jesus, Son of Man* (1977), pp 46–7

[6] Gal 2:4

[7] Augstein, Rudolf, *Jesus, Son of Man* (1977), p 25

[8] Cupitt, Don, *The Myth of God Incarnate*, essays edited by John Hick (1977), p 142

[9] Wilson, Ian, *Jesus, The Evidence*, p 30

[10] *Ibid*, p 35

[11] *Ibid*

[12] Mack, Burton L, *The Lost Gospel: The Book of Q and Christian Origins* (1993), p 239

[13] *Ibid*, p 5

[14] Augstein, Rudolf, *Jesus, Son of Man* (1977), p 23

[15] Wilson, A. N., *Jesus* (1992), p 89

[16] Craveri, Marcello, *The Life of Jesus* (1970), p 230

[17] *Ibid*, p 56

[18] Cupitt, Don, *The Myth of God Incarnate*, essays edited by John Hick (1977), pp 141–5

[19] Baigent, Leigh and Lincoln, *The Holy Blood and The Holy Grail* (1982) p 287

[20] Wright, N T, *Who was Jesus?* (1994), p 57

[21] Cupitt, Don, *The Myth of God Incarnate*, essays edited by John Hick (1977), pp 3–4

[22] Craveri, Marcello, *The Life of Jesus* (1970), p 322

[23] *Ibid*, pp 136–7

[24] Houlden, Leslie, *The Myth of God Incarnate*, essays edited by John Hick (1977), pp 127–8

[25] Cupitt, Don, *The Myth of God Incarnate*, essays edited by John Hick (1977), p 137

[26] Charlesworth, J H (ed.), *Jesus and the Dead Sea Scrolls* (1993), p 160

3   THE ESSENE CONTRIBUTION

[1] Charlesworth, J H (ed.), *Jesus and the Dead Sea Scrolls* (1993), p 11

[2] Craveri, Marcello, *The Life of Jesus* (1970), p 75

[3] Charlesworth, J H, (ed.) *Jesus and the Dead Sea Scrolls* (1993), p 39

[4] Otto Betz, *Jesus and the Dead Sea Scrolls* (1993), edited by J H Charlesworth, p 97

[5] *Ibid*, p 98

[6] Charlesworth, J H (ed.), *Jesus and the Dead Sea Scrolls* (1993), p 11

[7] *Ibid*, p 14

[8] Craveri, Marcello, *The Life of Jesus* (1970) pp 70–1

[9] Schonfield, H, *The Essene Odyssey* (1984), p 1

[10] Charlesworth, J H (ed.), *Jesus and Dead Sea Scrolls*, (1993), p 19

[11] Sacchi, Paolo, *Jesus and the Dead Sea Scrolls* (1993), edited by J H Charlesworth, p 124

[12] Charlesworth, J H (ed.), *Jesus and the Dead Sea Scrolls* (1993) pp 26–7

[13] Schonfield, H, *The Essene Odyssey* (1984), p 1

[14] *Ibid*, p 5

[15] Jeremiah 33:17–22

[16] Schonfield, H, *The Essene Odyssey* (1984), p 5

[17] Thiering, Barbara, *Jesus the Man* (1992), p 6

[18] Leigh, Baigent and Lincoln, *The Messianic Legacy* (1986), p 54

[19] *Ibid*, p 54–6

[20] Charlesworth, J H (ed.), *Jesus and the Dead Sea Scrolls* (1993), Foreword, p xxxv

[21] Leigh, Baigent and Lincoln, *The Messianic Legacy* (1986), pp 55–6

[22] *Ibid*, p 58

[23] *Ibid*, pp 58–61

[24] Schonfield, H, *The Passover Plot* (1965), p 30

[25] *Ibid*

[26] *Ibid*, p 31

[27] *Ibid*, p 99

[28] Vermes, Geza, *Jesus the Jew* (1973), p 44

[29] *Ibid*, p 46

[30] *Ibid*, p 46

[31] *Ibid*, p 48

[32] Baigent, Leigh and Lincoln, *The Holy Blood and The Holy Grail* (1982), p 286

[33] Schonfield, H, *Those Incredible Christians* (1968), p 41

[34] Schonfield, H, *The Passover Plot* (1965), p 155

4   THE NAZARENE PARTY

[1] Pétrement, Simone, *A Separate God: The Origins and Teachings of Gnosticism* (1995), pp 229–30

[2] Schonfield, H, *The Passover Plot* (1965), p 200

[3] *Ibid*, p 201

[4] *Ibid*

[5] *Ibid*, p 203

[6] Baigent, Leigh and Lincoln, *The Messianic Legacy* (1986), p 70

[7] Craveri, Marcello, *The Life of Jesus* (1967), p 323

[8] Baigent, Leigh and Lincoln, *The Messianic Legacy* (1986), p 70

[9] Frazer, J G, *The Golden Bough* (1922), vol 1, pp 1–5

[10] *Ibid*, vol 1, p 17

[11] *Ibid*, vol 1, p 18

[12] *Ibid*, vol 1, p 19

[13] Salibi, Kamal, *The Bible Came from Arabia* (1985), p 147
[14] Frazer, J G, *The Golden Bough*, (1922), vol 1, pp 24–5
[15] Schonfield, H, *The Passover Plot* (1967), p 16
[16] *Ibid*, p 26
[17] *Ibid*, p 27
[18] Baigent, Leigh and Lincoln, *The Messianic Legacy* (1986), p 47
[19] Craveri, Marcello, *The Life of Jesus* (1967), p 80
[20] Thiering, Barbara, *Jesus the Man* (1993), p 26

5   PAUL'S TWIST OF PERCEPTION

[1] Schonfield, H, *Those Incredible Christians* (1969), p 47
[2] *Ibid*, p 48
[3] Schonfield, H, *The Passover Plot* (1967), p 207
[4] *Ibid*, p 210
[5] *Ibid*, p 213
[6] Vermes, Geza, *Jesus The Jew* (1981), p 168
[7] Schonfield, H, *The Passover Plot* (1967), p 218
[8] *Ibid*, p 219
[9] Craveri, Marcello, *The Life of Christ* (1970), p 155
[10] Epiphanius, *Adv. haer.* xxx, 16:25
[11] Craveri, Marcello, *The Life of Christ* (1970), p 155
[12] Graves, Robert and Podro, Joshua, *The Nazarene Gospel Restored* (1953), p 17
[13] Acts 9:27
[14] Graves, Robert and Podro, Joshua, *The Nazarene Gospel Restored* (1953), p 804
[15] Epiphanius, *Heresies* xxx, 16
[16] Romans 9:1–2
[17] 2 Cor 9:8–20
[18] 1 Cor 9:20–22
[19] Luke 24:44
[20] Luke 24:39
[21] Rev 3:20
[22] Mark 6:48: Matt 14:22–34
[23] Luke 24:27
[24] John 21:25
[25] 1 Cor 15:14
[26] Matt 28:17–20
[27] Klausner, Joseph, *Jesus of Nazareth* (1926), p 358
[28] 1 Cor 15:5–8
[29] Acts 26:1–32
[30] Acts 19:40

[31] Acts 24:14
[32] Acts 22:14
[33] Acts 9:10
[34] Acts 10:11–17
[35] Acts 26:26
[36] Acts 25:18–19

6 THE ARABIAN CONUNDRUM

[1] Schonfield, H, *The Passover Plot* (1967), p 218
[2] Gal 1:17–18
[3] Gal 1:20
[4] Salibi, Kamal, *Conspiracy in Jerusalem* (1988), p 27
[5] Acts 9:26–27
[6] Gal 1:7–8
[7] Gal 1:18–19
[8] Gal 2:6
[9] Acts 8:1
[10] Acts 13:9
[11] Salibi, Kamal, *Conspiracy in Jerusalem* (1988), p 16
[12] 1 Cor 2:7
[13] 1 Cor 3:2
[14] Klausner, Joseph, *Jesus of Nazareth* (1926), p 130
[15] Matt 10:5–6
[16] Mark 7:25–29
[17] Matt 15:24
[18] Mark 7:28
[19] Matt 11:1–4; Luke 14:16–24
[20] Klausner, Joseph, *Jesus of Nazareth* (1926), p 295
[21] *Ibid*
[22] Gal 2:4, 11–14
[23] Klausner, Joseph, *Jesus of Nazareth* (1926), p 384
[24] Acts 4:13
[25] Gal 2:14
[26] Augstein, Rudolf, *Jesus, Son of Man* (1977), p 97
[27] *Ibid*, p 98
[28] 1 Cor 3:2
[29] Matt 28:18
[30] Klausner, Joseph, *Jesus of Nazareth* (1926), p 41
[31] Acts 21:18–26
[32] Gal 2:12
[33] Klausner, Joseph, *Jesus of Nazareth* (1926), p 41
[34] *Ibid*, p 234

[35] Schonfield, H, *Those Incredible Christians* (1969), p 111
[36] Salibi, Kamal, *Conspiracy in Jerusalem* (1988), p 138
[37] Schonfield, H, *Those Incredible Christians* (1969), p 123
[38] Leigh, Baigent and Lincoln, *The Messianic Legacy* (1986), pp 64–5
[39] Schonfield, H, *Those Incredible Christians* (1969), p 123
[40] *Ibid*
[41] Luke 2:7
[42] Rom 8:29
[43] Baigent, Leigh and Lincoln, *The Messianic Legacy* (1986), p 89
[44] Eusebius, *History* 1:7
[45] *Ibid*, 3:19–20
[46] 1 Tim 1:4; Titus 3:9
[47] Matt 16:13–19
[48] Salibi, Kamal, *Conspiracy in Jerusalem* (1988), p 138
[49] Schonfield, H, *Those Incredible Christians* (1969), p 125
[50] *Ibid*, p 127
[51] Goulder, Michael, *The Myth of God Incarnate* (1977), essays edited by John Hick, pp 64–84
[52] *Ibid*, pp 68–9
[53] Pétrement, Simone, *A Separate God: The Origins and Teachings of Gnosticism* (1995), p 231

7   PRIMORDIAL CHRISTIANITY

[1] Salibi, Kamal, *Conspiracy in Jerusalem* (1988), p 58
[2] *Ibid*, p 47
[3] *Ibid*, p 46
[4] Eisenman, Robert and Wise, Michael, *The Dead Sea Scrolls Uncovered* (1992), p 181
[5] Salibi, Kamal, *Conspiracy in Jerusalem* (1988), p 47
[6] *Ibid*, pp 4–5
[7] *Ibid*, p 52
[8] *Ibid*, p 59
[9] *Ibid*, pp 58–9
[10] Schonfield, H, *The Passover Plot* (1967), p 205
[11] *Ibid*, p 216
[12] *Ibid*, p 218
[13] Salibi, Kamal, *Conspiracy in Jerusalem* (1988), p 50 (see Koran, Sura 19:30)
[14] Schonfield, H, *The Passover Plot* (1967), p 238
[15] Pétrement, Simone, *A Separate God: The Origins and Teachings of Gnosticism* (1995), p 471

[16] Graves, Robert and Podro, Joshua, *The Nazarene Gospel Restored* (1953), Foreword, p xvi

[17] Schonfield, H, *Conspiracy in Jerusalem* (1988), p 231

[18] Schonfield, H, *The Essene Odyssey* (1984), p 144

[19] *Ibid*, p 147

[20] *Ibid*, p 145

[21] *Ibid*, p 147

[22] Schonfield, H, *The Passover Plot* (1967), p 36

[23] *Ibid*, p 59

[24] Isaiah 9:1–2

[25] Psalm 78:2

[26] Schonfield, H, *The Passover Plot* (1967), p 84

[27] Mark 14:43

[28] *Ibid*

[29] Mark 14:54

[30] Mark 14:30

[31] Schonfield, H, *The Passover Plot* (1967), p 138

[32] Craveri, Marcello, *The Life of Jesus* (1970), p 392

[33] *Ibid* p 392

[34] Doane, T D, *Bible Myths* (1971), p 132

[35] *Ibid*

[36] *Ibid*

[37] Schonfield, H, *Those Incredible Christians* (1969), p 249

[38] Doane, T D, *Bible Myths* (1971), p 382

8   THE NEW TESTAMENT REVISITED

[1] Thiering, Barbara, *The Gospels and Qumran* (1981), p 15

[2] Wright, N T, *Who was Jesus?* (1994), p 31

[3] Charlesworth, J H (ed.), *Jesus and the Dead Sea Scrolls* (1993), p 4

[4] Silberman, N A, *The Hidden Scrolls* (1995), pp 177–192

[5] Thiering, Barbara, *Jesus the Man* (1992), p 4

[6] *Ibid*, p 377

[7] *Ibid*, p 21

[8] Salibi, Kamal, *Conspiracy in Jerusalem* (1988), pp 52–3

[9] Thiering, Barbara, *Jesus the Man* (1992), p 28

[10] Schonfield, H, *The Passover Plot* (1967), p 201

[11] Matt 11:12

[12] Schonfield, H, *Those Incredible Christians* (1969), p 123

[13] *Ibid*, p 158

[14] Schonfield, H, *The Passover Plot* (1967), p 205

[15] Thiering, Barbara, *Jesus the Man* (1992), p 34

[16] Ezra 7:1–5

[17] Thiering, Barbara, *Jesus the Man* (1992), p 28
[18] Salibi, Kamal, *Conspiracy in Jerusalem* (1988), p 107
[19] *Ibid*, p 64
[20] Luke 1:5
[21] Thiering, Barbara, *Jesus the Man* (1992), p 24
[22] Gal 4:4
[23] Graves, Robert and Podro, Joshua, *The Nazarene Gospel Restored* (1953), Foreword, p xi
[24] Salibi, Kamal, *Conspiracy in Jerusalem* (1988), p 47
[25] Baigent, Leigh and Lincoln, *The Messianic Legacy* (1986), p 27
[26] Grant, Michael, *Jesus* (1978), p 96
[27] Salibi, Kamal, *Conspiracy in Jerusalem* (1988), p 83
[28] Thiering, Barbara, *The Qumran Origins of the Christian Church* (1983), p 59
[29] *Ibid*
[30] Salibi, Kamal, *Conspiracy in Jerusalem* (1988), p 49
[31] *Ibid*, p 47
[32] Meizer, Fritz, 'Transformation of Man in Mystical Islam', essay in Eranos, *Man & Transformation*, Bollingen Series, xxx 5 (1964), p 48

9   THE JEWISH-ESSENE BACKGROUND

[1] Graves, Robert and Podro, Joshua, *The Nazarene Gospel Restored* (1953), Intro 1, p 9
[2] Klausner, Joseph, *Jesus of Nazareth* (1926), p 9
[3] *Ibid*
[4] Goulder, Michael, 'The Myth of God Incarnate', essays edited by John Hick (1977), p 84
[5] Charlesworth, J H (ed.), *Jesus and the Dead Sea Scrolls* (1993), p 3
[6] *Ibid*, p 20
[7] *Ibid*, p 14
[8] *Ibid*, p 25
[9] *Ibid*, p 26
[10] *Ibid*, p 76
[11] Sacchi, Paolo, *Jesus and the Dead Sea Scrolls* (1993), edited by J H Charlesworth, p 135
[12] Mack, Burton L, *The Lost Gospel: The Book of Q and Christian Origins* (1993), p 251
[13] Sutherland, Stuart, *Irrationality: The Enemy Within* (1992), p 45
[14] Silberman, N A, *The Hidden Scrolls* (1995), p 178
[15] Klausner, Joseph, *Jesus of Nazareth* (1926), p 19
[16] *Ibid*, p 20

[17] Sacchi, Paolo, *Jesus and the Dead Sea Scrolls* (1993), edited by J H Charlesworth, p 124

[18] Klausner, Joseph, *Jesus of Nazareth* (1926), p 35

[19] *Ibid*, p 36

[20] *Ibid*, pp 28–39

[21] Salibi, Kamal, *Conspiracy in Jerusalem* (1988), p 42

[22] Klausner, Joseph, *Jesus of Nazareth* (1926), p 210

[23] *The Dead Sea Scrolls*, Compass, ABC Television Australia (1995), presented and produced by Michael Waterhouse for Roger Bolton Productions and BBC North, in association with the Israeli Broadcasting Authority (1994)

[24] Klausner, Joseph, *Jesus of Nazareth* (1926), p 211

[25] Koran 3:52; 5:111–2; 61:14

[26] Klausner, Joseph, *Jesus of Nazareth* (1926), p 109

[27] *Ibid*, p 111

[28] *Ibid*, p 211

[29] Goulder, Michael, *The Myth of God Incarnate*, essays edited by John Hick (1977), p 69

[30] Klausner, Joseph, *Jesus of Nazareth* (1926), p 198

[31] *Ibid*

[32] *Ibid*

[33] Craveri, Marcello, *The Life of Jesus* (1970), p 71

[34] Klausner, Joseph, *Jesus of Nazareth* (1926), p 201

[35] *Ibid*, p 202

[36] *Ibid*, p 213

[37] Klausner, Joseph, *Jesus of Nazareth* (1926), p 69

[38] Luke 6:1–5

[39] Eisenman, Robert and Michael Wise, *The Dead Sea Scrolls Uncovered* (1992), p 222

[40] Young, Frances, *The Myth of God Incarnate*, essays edited by John Hick (1977), p 21

[41] *Ibid*

[42] *Ibid*, p 22

[43] *Ibid*

[44] *Ibid*, p 23

[45] *Ibid*, p 29

[46] *Ibid*, p 23

[47] *Ibid*, p 29

[48] *Ibid*

[49] *Ibid*

[50] *Ibid*, 32

[51] *Ibid*

10   THE HUMAN DILEMMA

[1] Niebuhr, Reinhold, *The Meaning of Life*, essays edited by E D Klemke (1981), p 45

[2] Cupitt, Don, *The Myth of God Incarnate*, essays edited by John Hick (1977), pp 142–3

[3] *Ibid*, p 138

[4] *Ibid*

[5] Schonfield, H, *The Passover Plot* (1967), p 4

[6] Schonfield, H, *Those Incredible Christians* (1969), p 18

[7] Wiles, Maurice, *The Myth of God Incarnate*, essays edited by John Hick (1977), p 152

[8] *Ibid*, p 153

[9] *Ibid*, p 154

[10] *Ibid*

[11] *Ibid*, p 155

[12] *Ibid*, p 159

[13] *Ibid*, p 161

[14] *Ibid*

[15] Quoted from an article (*Be In It to Win It*) by Frank Divine in *The Australian Magazine*, 5–6 Aug 1995

[16] Mack, Burton L, *The Lost Gospel: The Book of Q and Christian Origins* (1993), p 251

[17] Spong, John Shelby, *Resurrection: Myth or Reality?* (1994), p 13

[18] *Ibid*, p 19

[19] Niebuhr, Reinhold, *The Meaning of Life*, essays edited by E D Klemke (1981), p 52

[20] Pagels, Elaine, *Adam, Eve, and the Serpent* (1988), p 125

[21] Clark, Mary T, *Augustine, Philosopher of Freedom* (1958), p 49

[22] Williams, Norman, *The Idea of the Fall and of Original Sin*, Bampton Lectures/1924 (1927), p 170

[23] *Ibid*, p 189

[24] *Ibid*

[25] *Ibid*, p 195

[26] *Ibid*, p 182

[27] Mack, Burton L, *The Lost Gospel: The Book of Q and Christian Origins* (1993), p 250

[28] *Ibid*, p 237

[29] Graves, Robert and Podro, Joshua, *The Nazarene Gospel Restored* (1953), p 789

[30] 2 Thess 3:10–12

[31] Thiering, Barbara, *Jesus the Man* (1992), p 160

[32] Graves, Robert and Podro, Joshua, *The Nazarene Gospel Restored* (1953), p 807

11   THE GNOSTIC LEGACY

[1] Corbin, Henry, *The Man of Light in Iranian Sufism* (1978), p 13
[2] Schonfield, H, *The Passover Plot* (1965), p 200
[3] Acts 8:9–10
[4] Goulder, Michael, *The Myth of God Incarnate*, essays edited by John Hick (1977), p 65
[5] 2 Kings 17:23
[6] Goulder, Michael, *The Myth of God Incarnate*, essays edited by John Hick (1977), p 68
[7] *Ibid*, p 69
[8] *Ibid*
[9] Macdonald, J, *The Theology of the Samaritans* (1964), p 106, as quoted by Michael Goulder in *The Myth of God Incarnate*, essays edited by John Hick (1977), p 69
[10] *Ibid*, p 72
[11] *Ibid*, p 74
[12] Acts 1:8
[13] 1 Cor 1:17–18
[14] Goulder, Michael, *The Myth of God Incarnate*, essays edited by John Hick (1977), p 76
[15] Eph 1:8–9
[16] 1 Cor 1:19
[17] Eph 3:3
[18] Goulder, Michael, *The Myth of God Incarnate*, essays edited by John Hick (1977), p 80
[19] Phil 4:5
[20] Goulder, Michael, *The Myth of God Incarnate*, essays edited by John Hick (1977), pp 82–3
[21] 1 Cor 15:13–17
[22] 1 Cor 15:50–54
[23] Schonfield, H, *The Passover Plot* (1967), p 34
[24] *Ibid*, p 267
[25] *Ibid*, p 199
[26] *Ibid*, p 202
[27] Graves, Robert and Podro, Joshua, *The Nazarene Gospel Restored* (1953), p 33
[28] Thiering, Barbara, *Jesus the Man* (1992), p 106
[29] Armstrong, Karen, *A History of God* (1994), p 113
[30] Pagels, Elaine, *The Gnostic Gospels* (1981), p 5
[31] Goulder, Michael, *The Myth of God Incarnate*, essays edited by John Hick (1977), p 67
[32] Pagels, Elaine, *The Gnostic Gospels* (1981), p 53
[33] *Ibid*, p 126

[34] *Ibid*, p 126
[35] *Ibid*, Intro, p xvii
[36] *Ibid*, Intro, p xv
[37] Churton, Tobias, *The Gnostics* (1987), p 30
[38] *Ibid*
[39] *Ibid*, pp 48–9
[40] *Ibid*, p 50
[41] 1 Cor 2:9–16
[42] Pagels, Elaine, *The Gnostic Gospels* (1981), p 32
[43] *Ibid*, p 15
[44] Pétrement, Simone, *A Separate God: The Origins and Teachings of Gnosticism* (1990), p 3
[45] *Ibid*, p 4
[46] *Ibid*, p 12
[47] Mead, G R S, *Fragments of a Faith Forgotten* (1960), pp 146–7
[48] *Ibid*, p 148
[49] *Ibid*, p 159
[50] *Ibid*
[51] *Ibid*, p 162
[52] *Ibid*, p 123
[53] *Ibid*, p 175
[54] *Ibid*, p 176
[55] Pagels, Elaine, *The Gnostic Gospels* (1981), p 57
[56] Craveri, Marcello, *The Life of Jesus* (1970), p 209
[57] *Ibid*, p 210
[58] *Ibid*, p 211
[59] *Ibid*
[60] Hoeller, Stephan A, *The Gnostic Jung* (1985), p 83

12   A TERRIBLE SECRET

[1] Churton, Tobias, *The Gnostics* (1987), p 61
[2] *Ibid*, p 24
[3] Pétrement, Simone, *A Separate God: The Origins and Teachings of Gnosticism* (1990), p 22
[4] Hoeller, Stephan A, *The Gnostic Jung* (1985), p 38
[5] Jung, C G, *Memories, Dreams, Reflections* (1963), p 181
[6] Mead, G R S, *Fragments of a Faith Forgotten* (1960), p 148
[7] Bettenson, Henry, *The Early Church Fathers* (1991), p 17
[8] *Ibid*
[9] Hoeller, Stephan A, *The Gnostic Jung* (1985), p 66
[10] Bettenson, Henry, *The Early Church Fathers* (1991), p 17
[11] Pagels, Elaine, *The Gnostic Gospels* (1981), p 81

[12] Hoeller, Stephan A, *The Gnostic Jung* (1985), p 19
[13] Pagels, Elaine, *The Gnostic Gospels* (1981), Intro, p xxii
[14] *Ibid*, Intro, p xix
[15] *Ibid*, p 123
[16] *Ibid*, p 125
[17] Hoeller, Stephan A, *The Gnostic Jung* (1985), p 20
[18] *Ibid*
[19] Pagels, Elaine, *The Gnostic Gospels* (1981), p 162
[20] Churton, Tobias, *The Gnostics* (1987), p 18
[21] Mead, G R S, *Fragments of a Faith Forgotten* (1960), p 19
[22] *Ibid*, p 136
[23] Hoeller, Stephan A, *The Gnostic Jung*, (1985), p 19
[24] Pagels, Elaine, *The Gnostic Gospels* (1981), p 126
[25] *Ibid*, pp 71–2
[26] *Ibid*, p 72
[27] *Ibid*, p 73
[28] *Ibid*
[29] Rom 16:7
[30] Goulder, Michael, *The Myth of God Incarnate* (1977), essays edited by John Hick, p 67
[31] Keck, Leander E, 'The Second Coming of the Liberal Jesus?' Review in *Christian Century*, 24–31 Aug 1994, p 784
[32] Grant, Michael, *Jesus* (1978), p 110
[33] *Ibid*
[34] *Ibid*, p 112
[35] Pagels, Elaine, *The Gnostic Gospels* (1981), p 77

13   MULTIPLE REVERSALS

[1] Charlesworth, J H (ed.), *Jesus and the Dead Sea Scrolls* (1993), p 8
[2] Matt 16:23
[3] Matt 4:1–11
[4] John 1:36
[5] John 1:41
[6] Charlesworth, J H (ed.), *Jesus and the Dead Sea Scrolls* (1993), p 151
[7] John 1:32
[8] John 1:34
[9] Matt 11:2
[10] Wilson, A N, *Jesus* (1992), p 113
[11] *Ibid*
[12] *Ibid*, p 114
[13] Matt 11:12
[14] Charlesworth, J H (ed.), *Jesus and the Dead Sea Scrolls* (1993), p 152

[15] Luke 24:11
[16] Schonfield, H, *Those Incredible Christians* (1969), p 245
[17] *Ibid*, p 171
[18] Eusebius, *Eccl. Hist.* 111, xxxii
[19] Pétrement, Simone, *A Separate God: The Origins and Teachings of Gnosticism* (1990), p 14
[20] Schonfield, H, *Those Incredible Christians* (1969), p 124
[21] *Ibid*, p 171
[22] *Ibid*, p 128
[23] Phil 1:16
[24] Schonfield, H, *Those Incredible Christians* (1969), p 127
[25] 2 Tim 4:16
[26] Schonfield, H, *The Passover Plot* (1965), p 243
[27] *Ibid*, p 242
[28] *Ibid*, pp 244–6
[29] *Ibid*, pp 246–250
[30] Graves, Robert and Podro, Joshua, *The Nazarene Gospel Restored* (1953), p 817, quoting Irenaeus *Heresies* 111.1.1, and Eusebius *Ecc. Hist.* 3, xxxi, 2
[31] *Ibid*, quoting Eusebius *Ecc. Hist.* 3, v, 3
[32] Schonfield, H, *Those Incredible Christians* (1969), p 129
[33] *Ibid*, p 159
[34] Acts 10:40–41
[35] Pagels, Elaine, *The Gnostic Gospels* (1981), p 31
[36] *Ibid*
[37] Wilson, A N, *Jesus* (1992), pp 6–7
[38] *Ibid*, p 42
[39] *Ibid*, p 20
[40] 1 Cor 11:23
[41] Wilson, A N, *Jesus* (1992), p 21
[42] *Ibid*, p 27
[43] 1 Cor 11:23–27
[44] Acts 18:9–10

14   THE EYE OF THE STORM

[1] Kuhn, A B, *Shadow of the Third Century* (1949), p 50
[2] *Ibid*, p 44
[3] *Ibid*, p 42
[4] *Ibid*, p 213
[5] Pagels, Elaine, *The Gnostic Gospels* (1981), p 126
[6] *Gospel of Philip* 64:23–24, in *NHL* 139, as quoted by Elaine Pagels in *The Gnostic Gospels* (1981), p 125

[7] Pagels, Elaine, *The Gnostic Gospels* (1981), p 124

[8] Kuhn, A B, *Shadow of the Third Century* (1949), p 213

[9] *Ibid*

[10] Kahl, J, *The Misery of Christianity* (1971), p 63

[11] Pagels, Elaine, *The Gnostic Gospels* (1981), p 153

[12] *Ibid*, p 155

[13] *Ibid*, p 152

[14] Mead, G R S, *Fragments of a Faith Forgotten* (1960), p 280

[15] *Ibid*, p 147

[16] Smith, Morton, *Jesus the Magician* (1978), p 290

[17] Pagels, Elaine, *The Gnostic Gospels* (1981), Intro, p xxii

[18] *Ibid*, Intro, pp xxii–xxiii

[19] Graves, Robert and Podro, Joshua, *The Nazarene Gospel Restored* (1953) p 365

[20] Pagels, Elaine, *The Gnostic Gospels* (1981), Intro, p xxxi

[21] *Ibid*, Intro, p xxxiii

[22] *Ibid*, Intro, p xxxv

[23] *Ibid*

[24] *The Nag Hammadi Library* (1988), edited by James M Robinson, Intro, pp 3–4

[25] *Ibid*, Intro, p 6

[26] *Ibid*, Intro, p 7

[27] *Ibid*

[28] Pétrement, Simone, *A Separate God: The Origins and Teachings of Gnosticism* (1990), p 468

[29] Pagels, Elaine, *The Gnostic Gospels* (1981), Intro, p xviii

[30] *The Nag Hammadi Library* (1988), Intro, p 20

[31] Hippolytus, *REF* 8, 15, 1–2, as quoted by Elaine Pagels in *The Gnostic Gospels* (1981), Intro, p xix

[32] Pagels, Elaine, *The Gnostic Gospels* (1981), p 146

[33] *Ibid*, p 162

[34] Wilson, A N, *Jesus* (1992), p 42

[35] Bettenson, Henry, *The Early Church Fathers* (1991), p 169

[36] *Ibid*, p 170

[37] Blake, William, *The First Book of Urizen*, Plate 3, chap 1, 1–6

15   THE SPIRIT OF TRUTH

[1] Pagels, Elaine, *The Gnostic Gospels* (1981), p 14

[2] *Ibid*, Intro, pp xx–xxi

[3] *Ibid*, p 14

[4] Armstrong, Karen, *The History of God* (1994), p 114

[5] Isaiah 11:2–3

[6] Luke 3:38

[7] Milosz, Czeslaw, *The Land of Ulro* (1984), flyleaf

[8] Armstrong, Karen, *The History of God* (1994), p 89

[9] *Ibid*

[10] *Ibid*

[11] *Ibid*

[12] John 20:22–3

[13] Matt 18:18

[14] John 14:26

[15] John 16:12–13

[16] Grant, Michael, *Jesus* (1978), p 34

[17] Charlesworth, J H (ed.), *Jesus and the Dead Sea Scrolls* (1993), p 21

[18] *Ibid*

[19] Matt 12:28

[20] Luke 17:21

[21] Grant, Michael, *Jesus* (1978), p 30

[22] *Ibid*, p 31

[23] Pagels, Elaine, *The Gnostic Gospels* (1981), p 154

[24] Hillman, James, *The Dream and the Underworld* (1979), p 110

[25] *Ibid*, pp 111–2

[26] Pagels, Elaine, *The Gnostic Gospels* (1981), p 158

[27] *Ibid*

[28] *Ibid*, p 60

[29] *Ibid*, p 171

[30] Harding, W D, *Experience into Words* (1974)

[31] Domasio, Antonio R, *Descartes' Error* (1995), p 191

[32] The Mysteries, *Papers from the Eranos Yearbooks* (1955), p 329

[33] Hillman, James, *The Dream and the Underworld* (1979), p 134

[34] John 3:6–8

[35] Pagels, Elaine, *The Gnostic Gospels* (1981), p 67

[36] Genesis 1:26

[37] Pagels, Elaine, *The Gnostic Gospels* (1981), p 67

[38] *Ibid*, p 68

[39] Koestler, Arthur, *The Act of Creation* (1964), p 165–6

[40] Hillman, James, *The Dream and the Underworld* (1979), pp 35–6

[41] *Ibid*, p 36

[42] *Ibid*, p 37

[43] Col 13:22; 1 Cor 7:21

[44] Thiering, Barbara, *Created Second* (1973), p 48

[45] *Ibid*, p 40

[46] Col 2:14

[47] Luke 10:38–42. The Mary of this passage is likely to have been Mary
Magdalene, the very Mary who claims in the uncanonical books to

have received a special revelation from Jesus. As the first person to see his empty tomb, and the first to see Jesus when he was resurrected, Mary has for many attained a status greater than Jesus' mother. Many Church Fathers refused to identify Mary of Bethany with Mary Magdalene, but the idea was emphatically supported 500 years later by Pope Gregory I

[48] Thiering, Barbara, *Created Second* (1973), pp 50–51

16 THE JOURNEY TO HELL

[1] Hoeller, Stephan A, *The Gnostic Jung* (1985), Intro, p xiii
[2] Hillman, James, *The Dream and the Underworld* (1979), p 168
[3] Tarnas, Richard, *The Passion of the Western Mind* (1991), p 12
[4] *Ibid*, p 13
[5] *Ibid*
[6] *Ibid*
[7] *Ibid*
[8] Jung, C G, *Psychological Reflections* (1974), p 42
[9] *Ibid*, p 43
[10] Tarnas, Richard, *The Passion of the Western Mind* (1991), p 14
[11] *Ibid*
[12] Jung, C G, *Psychological Reflections* (1974), p 45
[13] Neumann, Erich, *The Origins and History of Consciousness* (1973), p 390
[14] Jung, C G, *Psychological Reflections* (1974), p 45
[15] *Ibid*, p 46
[16] Davies, Paul, *The Mind of God* (1992), p 16
[17] Fox, Robin Lane, *Pagans and Christians* (1986), p 102
[18] *Ibid*, p 103
[19] *Ibid*
[20] Jung, C G, *Psychological Reflections* (1974), p 48
[21] Hillman, James, *The Dream and the Underworld* (1979), p 85
[22] *Ibid*
[23] 1 Cor 15:26
[24] Hillman, James, *The Dream and the Underworld* (1979), p 88
[25] *Encyclopedia Britannica*, vol 10 (1965), p 528
[26] *Ibid*, p 529
[27] Mead, G R S, *Fragments of a Faith Forgotten* (1960), p 272
[28] Hillman, James, *The Dream and the Underworld* (1979), p 89
[29] Jung, C G, *Aion* (1979), p 109
[30] Matt 12:39
[31] Matt 12:40
[32] Jung, C G, *Aion* (1979), p 102

[33] *Ibid*, p 189
[34] *Ibid*
[35] *Ibid*, p 192
[36] *Ibid*, p 194
[37] *Ibid*, p 222
[38] *Ibid*, p 223
[39] *Ibid*, p 222
[40] *Ibid*
[41] *Ibid*, p 223
[42] Tarnas, Richard, *The Passion of the Western Mind* (1991), p 33
[43] *Ibid*
[44] *Ibid*, p 32
[45] *Ibid*, p 36
[46] *Ibid*, p 38
[47] *Ibid*
[48] Corbin, Henry, *The Man of Light in Iranian Sufism* (1978), p 97
[49] Schonfield, Hugh, *Those Incredible Christians* (1968), pp 211–217

17   A PRESENCE OF SELF

[1] Needleman, J, *Lost Christianity* (1990), p 38
[2] *Ibid*
[3] *Ibid* p 39
[4] *Ibid* p 42
[5] *Ibid*
[6] *Ibid*, p 33
[7] *Ibid*, p 51
[8] *Ibid*, p 40
[9] *Ibid*
[10] *Ibid*, p 65
[11] *Ibid*, Intro, p 4
[12] *Ibid*, p 117
[13] *Ibid*, p 152
[14] Corbin, Henry, *The Man of Light in Iranian Sufism* (1978), p 74
[15] Needleman, J, *Lost Christianity* (1990), p 121
[16] *Ibid*, p 124
[17] *Ibid*, p 110
[18] *Ibid*, p 92
[19] *Ibid*
[20] *Ibid*
[21] *Ibid*, p 93
[22] *Ibid*, p 95
[23] *Ibid*

[24] *Ibid*, p 96
[25] *Ibid*
[26] *Ibid*, p 101
[27] *Ibid*, p 171
[28] *Ibid*, p 119
[29] *Ibid*, p 168
[30] Lamont, Corliss, *The Illusion of Immortality* (1959), pp 53–4
[31] Needleman, J, *Lost Christianity* (1990), p 136
[32] *Ibid*, p 137
[33] *Ibid*, p 93
[34] *Ibid*, p 139
[35] Pétrement, Simone, *A Separate God: The Origins and Teachings of Gnosticism* (1995), p 25
[36] Moore, James, *Gurdjieff* (1991), p 302
[37] Needleman, J, *Lost Christianity* (1990), p 174
[38] Moore, James, *Gurdjieff* (1991), p 31
[39] Needleman, J, *Lost Christianity* (1990), p 83
[40] Luke 23:34
[41] Lefort, Rafael, *The Teachers of Gurdjieff* (1984), p 46
[42] Graves, Robert and Podro, Joshua, *The Nazarene Gospel Restored* (1953), p 6
[43] *Ibid*, p 7
[44] Needleman, J, *Lost Christianity* (1990), p 195
[45] Pétrement, Simone, *A Separate God: The Origins and Teachings of Gnosticism* (1990), p 17
[46] Needleman, J, *Lost Christianity* (1990), p 197
[47] *Ibid*
[48] *Ibid*, p 204
[49] *Ibid*, p 191

EPILOGUE

[1] Salibi, Kamal, *Conspiracy in Jerusalem* (1988), p 64
[2] Bucaille, Maurice, *The Bible. The Qur'an and Science*, p 102
[3] Graves, Robert and Podro, Joshua, *The Nazarene Gospel Restored* (1953), p 66
[4] *Ibid*, p 65
[5] Osman, Ahmed, *The House of the Messiah* (1992), p 56
[6] *Ibid*, p 38
[7] Heb 4:2
[8] 1 Cor 10:1–4
[9] Salibi, Kamal, *Conspiracy in Jerusalem* (1988), p 100
[10] Needleman, J, *Lost Christianity* (1990), p 212

[11] *Ibid*, p 76
[12] *Ibid*, p 77
[13] *Ibid*
[14] *Ibid*, p 78
[15] Schonfield, H, *Those Incredible Christians* (1969), p 170

BIBLIOGRAPHY

Armstrong, Karen, *A History of God*, Mandarin, London, 1994
  The First Christian: St Paul's Impact on Christianity, Pan, London, 1983
Augstein, Rudolf, *Jesus the Man*, Urizen Books, New York 1977
Baigent, M, Leigh, R, Lincoln, H, *The Holy Blood and the Holy Grail*, Jonathan Cape, London, 1982
  The Messianic Legacy, Jonathan Cape, London, 1986
  The Dead Sea Scrolls Deception, Jonathan Cape, London, 1991
Ballou, Robert O, *The Other Jesus*, Doubleday, New York, 1972
Barzun, Jacques, *The House of Intellect*, Mercury Books, London, 1959
Bennett, J G, *Intimations/Talks with J G Bennett at Beshara*, Samuel Weiser Inc, New York, 1975
  Deeper Man, Turnstone Books, London, 1978
  Transformations, Claymont Communications, West Virginia, 1978
  Is There "Life" on Earth?, Bennett Books, Santa Fe, New Mexico, 1989
Bermant, Chaim, *The Jews*, Sphere Books Ltd, London, 1979
Bettenson, Henry, *The Early Church Fathers*, Oxford University Press, New York, 1991
Birney, Robert C and Teevan, Richard C, *Instinct*, D Van Nostrand Company Inc, An Insight Book, Princeton, New Jersey, 1961
Blamires, Harry, *The Secularist Heresy: The Erosion of the Gospel in the Twentieth Century*, SPCK, London, 1981
Bowman, Archibald Allan, *A Sacramental Universe*, Princeton University Press, New Jersey, 1939
Buber, Martin, *The Way of Man According to the Teachings of Hasidim*, Routledge & Kegan Paul, London, 1950
Burrows, Millar, *The Dead Sea Scrolls*, Secker & Warburg, London, 1956
Bucaille, Maurice, *The Bible, The Qur'an and Science*, The Socialist People's Libyan Arab Jamahiriyah, Tripoli (no date)
Cameron, Peter, *Heretic*, Doubleday, Sydney, Australia, 1994
  Fundamentalism and Freedom, Doubleday, Australia, 1995
  Necessary Heresies, New South Wales University Press, Sydney, Australia, 1993
Charlesworth, J H, *Jesus and the Dead Sea Scrolls*, Doubleday, New York, 1993

Churton, T, *The Gnostics*, Weidenfeld and Nicholson, London, 1987

Clark, Mary T, *Augustine*, Desclée Company, New York, 1958

Collins, Paul, *Mixed Blessings: John-Paul II and the Church of the Eighties*, Penguin Books, Victoria, Australia, 1986

Corbin, Henry, *The Man of Light in Iranian Sufism*, Shambala, Boulder, 1978

Craveri, Marcello, *The Life of Jesus*, Grove Press Inc, New York, 1970

Crossan, John Dominic, *Who Killed Jesus?*, Harper, San Francisco, 1995
Jesus: A Revolutionary Biography, Harper, San Francisco, 1994
The Essential Jesus, Harper, San Francisco, 1994

Damasio, Antonio R, *Descartes' Error*, Picador, London, 1995

Davies, Paul, *The Mind of God*, Simon & Schuster, London, 1992

Doane, T W, *Bible Myths*, University Books, New York, 1871

Doresse, Jean, *The Secret Books of the Egyptian Gnostics: An Introduction to the Gnostic Coptic Manuscripts Discovered at Chenoboskion*, Hollis & Carter, London, 1960

Dray, William H (ed.), *Philosophical Analysis and History*, University of Toronto, 1966

Dulles, A S J, *The Survival of Dogma/Faith. Authority, and Dogma in a Changing World*, Doubleday, New York, 1973.

Eisenman, Robert and Wise, Michael, *The Dead Sea Scrolls Uncovered*, Element, Shaftesbury, Dorset, 1992
The Dead Sea Scrolls and the First Christians, Element, Shaftesbury, Dorset, 1996

Filoramo, Giovanni, *A History of Gnosticism*, Blackwell Publishers, Massachusetts, 1992

Fox, Robin Lane, *Pagans and Christians*, London, 1986
The Unauthorized Version, Penguin Books, London, 1991

Frankl, Victor E, *Man's Search for Meaning*, Hodder & Stoughton, London, 1964

Frazer, Sir James George, *The Golden Bough: Studies in the History of Oriental Religion, Adonis, Attis and Osiris*, Vol II, Macmillan & Co Ltd, London, 1922

Friedman, Maurice, *Martin Buber: The Knowledge of Man*, Harper Torch Books, New York, 1965

Gartner, Bertil, *The Theology of the Gospel of Thomas*, Collins, London, 1961

Gaster, H Theodor, *The Scriptures of the Dead Sea Sect*, Secker & Warburg, London, 1957

Grant, Michael, *Jesus*, Sphere Books, London, 1978

Grant, Robert M, *Gnosticism: An Anthology*, Collins, London, 1961

Graves, Robert and Podro, Joshua, *The Nazarene Gospel Restored*, London, 1953 (publisher not known)

Graves, Robert and Patai, Raphael, *Hebrew Myths*, Cassels, London, 1964

Grisel, Dr Ronald, *Sufism*, Ross Books, Berkeley, California, 1983

Harding, W D, *Experience into Words*, Penguin Books, Middlesex, England, 1963

Hick, John H, *Philosophy of Religion*, Prentice Hall, Inc, University of Birmingham, England, 1973

Hillman, James, *The Dream and the Underworld*, Harper & Row, New York, 1979

Insearch. Psychology and Religion, Spring Publications Inc, Dallas, Texas, 1984

Hoeller, Stephan A, *The Gnostic Jung and the Seven Sermons to the Dead*, The Theosophical Publishing House, Wheaton, Illinois, 1985

Holl, Adolf, *Jesus in Bad Company*, Collins, London, 1972

James, William, *The Varieties of Religious Experience*, Collins, Fount Paperback, London, 1981

Jaspers, Karl, *Man in the Modern Age*, Doubleday Anchor Books, New York, 1957

Reason Revisited, Gill and Macmillan, London, 1971

Johnson, Paul, *A History of the Jews*, Phoenix, London, 1994

Jonas, Hans, *The Gnostic Religion: The Message of the Alien God and the Beginnings of Christianity*, Beacon Press, Boston, 1963

Joyce, Donovan, *The Jesus Scroll*, Ferret Books, Melbourne, Australia, 1972

Jung, C G, *Memories, Dreams and Reflections*, Collins and Routledge & Kegan Paul, London, 1963

Psychological Reflections, Routledge & Kegan Paul, London, 1974

C J Jung Speaking: Interviews and Encounters, Thames & Hudson, London, 1978

Aion, Researches into the Phenomenology of the Self, translated by R F C Hull, Bollingen Series XX, Princeton University Press, New York, 1979

Kahl, Joachim, *The Misery of Christianity: A Plea for Humanity Without God*, Pelican Books, Middlesex, England, 1971

Kazantzakis, Nikos, *The Saviour of God: Spiritual Exercises*, translated by Kimon Friar, Simon & Schuster, New York, 1960

Kepel, Gilles, *The Revenge of God*, Polity Press, Oxford, 1994

Kersten, H and Gruber E R, *The Jesus Conspiracy*, Element, Shaftesbury, Dorset, 1994

Kingsland, William, *The Gnosis or Ancient Wisdom in the Christian Scriptures*, George Allen & Unwin, London, 1954

Klausner, Joseph, *Jesus of Nazareth*, The Macmillan Company, New York, 1925

Klemke, E E (ed.), *The Meaning of Life*, Oxford, 1981 (publisher not known)

Koestler, Arthur, *The Act of Creation*, Hutchinson, London, 1964

Konner, Melvin, *The Tangled Wing: Biological Constraints on the Human Spirit*, Penguin Books, Middlesex, England, 1984

Kuhn, Alvin Boyd, *Shadow of the Third Century: A Revaluation of Christianity*, The Theosophical Publishing House, Wheaton, Illinois, 1949

Lamont, Corliss, *The Illusion of Immortality*, Wisdom Library, a Division of Philosophical Library, New York, 1959

Laski, Margharita, *Ecstasy In Secular and Religious Experience*, Cresset Press, London, 1961

Ling, Trevor, *A History of Religion East and West*, The Macmillan Press Ltd, London, 1982

Mack, Burton L, *The Lost Gospel, The Book of Q and Christian Origins*, Harper, San Francisco, 1993

Martin, Ralph, *A Crisis of Truth*, Servant Books, Michigan, 1982

Mead, G R S, *Fragments of a Faith Forgotten*, University Books, New York, 1960

Moore, James, *Gurdjieff*, Element, Shaftesbury, Dorset, England, 1991

Moule, C F D, *The Birth of the New Testament*, Adam & Charles Black, London, 1962

Murphy, John L, *The General Councils of the Church*, The Bruce Publishing Company, Milwaukee, 1960

Needleman, Jacob, *The Indestructable Question*, Arkana/Penguin Books, London, 1994
Lost Christianity, Element, Shaftesbury, Dorset, 1990
A Sense of the Cosmos, Arkana, London, 1988

Neumann, Erich, *The Origins and History of Consciousness*, Routledge & Kegan Paul, Bollingen Series XLII, New York, 1973

Nott, C S, *Teachings of Gurdjieff*, Routledge & Kegan Paul, London, 1974

Osman, Ahmed, *The House of the Messiah*, Harper Collins, London, 1992

Pagels, Elaine, *The Gnostic Gospels*, Vintage Books, New York, 1981
Adam, Eve, and the Serpent, Random House, New York, 1988

Paglia, Camille, *Sexual Personae*, Penguin Books, Middlesex, England, 1991

Pauwels, Louis, *Gurdjieff*, Times Press Ltd/Douglas, 1964

Pelletier, Kenneth R, *Towards a Science of Consciousness*, A Delta Book, New York, 1978

Perowne, Stewart, *Caesars and Saints, The Evolution of the Christian State, 180–313 AD*, Hodder & Stoughton, London, 1962

Kaufmann, Walter, *Martin Buber, I and Thou*, Charles Scribner's Sons, New York, 1970

Pétrement, Simone, *A Separate God: The Origins and Teachings of Gnosticism*, Harper, San Francisco, 1995

Pike, Nelson, *God and Evil, Contemporary Perspectives in Philosophy Series*, Prentice Hall Inc, New Jersey, 1964

Quick, Oliver C, *Doctrines of the Creed*, The Fontana Library, London, 1971

Quispel, Gilles and Scholem, Gershom, *Jewish and Gnostic Man*, Eranos Lectures 3, Spring Publications Inc, Texas, 1987

Read, Herbert, *The Origins of Form in Art*, Thames & Hudson, London, 1965

Robinson, M James (ed.), *The Nag Hammadi Library*, Harper & Row, San Francisco, 1988

Rops, H Daniel, *The Church of Apostles and Martyrs*, J M Dent & Sons, London, 1948
The Church in the Dark Ages, J M Dent & Sons, London, 1959
The Catholic Reformation, J M Dent & Sons, London, 1962
Jesus in His Time, Eyre & Spottiswood, London, 1961

Ryle, Gilbert, *The Concept of Mind*, Penguin Books, Middlesex, England, 1976

Salibi, Kamal, *Conspiracy in Jerusalem: The Hidden Origins of Jesus*, I B Tauris & Co Ltd, London, 1988
The Bible Came From Arabia: A Radical Reinterpretation of Old Testament Geography, Pan Books, London, 1985

Schonfield, Hugh, *The Passover Plot*, Element, Shaftesbury, Dorset, 1993
Those Incredible Christians, Element, Shaftesbury, Dorset, 1985
The Essene Odyssey, Element, Shaftesbury, Dorset, 1984
The Authentic New Testament, Dennis Dobson, London, 1956
Jesus: A Biography, Banner Books, London, 1948

Schuon, Frithjof, *Christianity/Islam*, World Wisdom Books, Indiana, 1985

Selby, Peter, *Belonging: Challenge to a Tribal Church*, SPCK, London, 1991

Shanks, Hershel, *Understanding the Dead Sea Scrolls*, Vintage Books/Random House, New York, 1993

Silberman, Neil Asher, *The Hidden Scrolls*, BCA in arrangement with William Heinemann Ltd, London, 1995

Spong, John Shelby, *Resurrection: Myth or Reality?*, Harper, San Francisco, New York, 1994
Born of Woman: A Bishop Rethinks the Birth of Jesus, Harper, San Francisco, 1971

Star, Leonie, *The Dead Sea Scrolls: The Riddle Debated*, ABC Book, Sydney, Australia, 1991

Stein, Murray, *Jung's Treatment of Christianity: The Psychotherapy of a Religious Tradition*, Chiron Publications, Illinois, 1986

Suhr, Elmer G, *The Ancient Mind and its Heritage: Exploring the Hebrew, Hindu, Greek and Chinese Cultures*, Exposition Press, New York, 1960

Szekely, Edmond Bordeaux, *From Enoch to the Dead Sea Scrolls*, Academy Books, San Diego, California, 1975

Sutherland, Stuart, *Irrationality: The Enemy Within*, Penguin Books, London, 1994

Talbot, Michael, *The Holographic Universe*, Grafton Books/Harper Collins, London, 1991

Tarnas, Richard, *The Passion of the Western Mind*, Ballantine Books, New York, 1993

Thiering, B E, *Created Second: Aspects of Women's Liberation in Australia*, Family Life Movement of Australia, Sydney, Australia, 1973
Redating the Teacher of Righteousness, Theological Explorations, Box 2197, Sydney, Australia, 1979
The Gospel of Qumran, (as above), Sydney, Australia, 1981
The Qumran Origins of the Christian Church, (as above), Sydney, Australia, 1983
Jesus the Man, Doubleday, Sydney, Australia, 1992

Vermaseren, M J, *Mithra, the Secret God*, Chatto & Windus, London, 1963

Vermes, Geza, *Jesus the Jew: A Historian's Reading of the Gospels*, Fontana/Collins, London, 1981

Walsh, R and Vaughan, F (eds.), *Paths Beyond Ego: The Transpersonal Vision*, Jeremy P Tarcher/Perigee, Los Angeles, 1993

Weiss, Johannes, *Earliest Christianity: A History of the Period AD 30–150*, Vol II, Harper Touchbooks, New York, 1965

Weizsacker, Carl Fredrich von, *The Ambivalence of Progress: An Essay on Historical Anthropology*, Paragon House, New York, 1988

Wilber, Ken, *The Atman Project, A Transpersonal View of Human Development*, The Theosophical Publishing House, Wheaton, Illinois, 1989

Wilber, Ken, Engler, Jack and Brown, Daniel P, *Transformations of Consciousness*, Schambala, Massachusetts, 1986

Williams, John Alden, *Islam*, George Braziller, New York, 1962

Williams, N P, *The Ideas of the Fall and of Original Sin*, Bampton Lectures, 1924, Longman Green & Co Ltd, London, 1927

Wilson, A N, *Jesus*, Flamingo/Harper Collins, London, 1992

Wilson, Bryan, *Religion in Sociological Perspective*, Oxford University Press, New York, 1983

Wilson, Edmund, *The Dead Sea Scrolls 1947–1969*

Wilson, Ian, *Jesus, the Evidence*, Book Club Associates, London, 1984.
  Holy Faces, Secret Places, Doubleday, Ontario, Canada, 1988
Wright, N T, *Who Was Jesus?* SPCK, London, 1994

INDEX